Microsoft Power BI Data Analyst Exam Guide

A practical guide to becoming a Power BI professional

Peter ter Braake

bpb

www.bpbonline.com

First Edition 2026

Copyright © BPB Publications, India

ISBN: 978-93-65894-325

LIMITS OF LIABILITY AND DISCLAIMER OF WARRANTY

To View Complete
BPB Publications Catalogue
Scan the QR Code:

www.bpbonline.com

Dedicated to

My family

About the Author

Peter ter Braake is currently working as an independent Microsoft data platform professional. He studied physics at the University of Utrecht, the Netherlands, in the late 1980s and early 1990s. Quickly after graduating, he went into IT and found his passion to be data. He became a **Microsoft Certified Teacher** (**MCT**) in 2002. This was also the time that he became Microsoft Certified. His first certification was Microsoft Certified Database Administrator: Microsoft SQL Server 2000. He has kept his Microsoft certifications up to date ever since. He was a Microsoft **Most Valued Professional** (**MVP**) for a couple of years.

Currently, Peter works a lot with Microsoft Fabric as a data engineer, Power BI as a data analyst, and Azure Machine Learning as a data scientist.

As an MCT, he teaches a lot of courses at various training providers and on-site for his customers. These courses can be official Microsoft courses or customized courses that target specific goals for their customers.

As a consultant, Peter helps his customers with advice on various data-related issues. These are often design or performance issues.

About the Reviewer

Riccardo Perico began his career in IT back in 2010. After a brief stint as an ERP consultant, he transitioned into the data realm.

Over the years, he explored the world of data from multiple angles, working as both a database administrator and a BI architect. His expertise spans across databases, BI, and cloud technologies, and he is a Microsoft Certified Professional in several areas, including databases, BI, and Azure.

A four-time Microsoft MVP in the data platform category and a recognized Microsoft Fabric Super User, Riccardo is a well-known figure in the data community. He is one of the leaders of the Power BI User Group Italy and has spoken at major events such as the Power Platform World Tour and Global Power Platform Bootcamp in Italy.

His speaking engagements extend across Europe, with appearances at Azure Saturday, SQL Saturday, Data Saturday, and various other community-driven events.

In addition to speaking, Riccardo has contributed to the data community as a technical reviewer for several notable publications.

Last but not least, he is a hard rock and heavy metal enthusiast.

Acknowledgement

I would like to acknowledge the valuable contributions of my colleagues and co-workers during the many years working in the tech industry who have taught me so much and inspired me to look beyond my daily work routine. Moreover, I would like to specially thank Karthikeyan Sabesan for taking an active interest in contributing to the book's contents.

I am thankful to my family for their patience, motivation and encouragement at every juncture and for constantly pushing me to pursue my ambitions and goals. We appreciate each other as a team, to have kept up the resolve to take this book to completion and inspiring each other.

I am grateful to BPB Publications for their guidance and expertise in bringing this book to fruition. It was a long journey of revising this book, with valuable participation and collaboration of technical reviewers, and editors.

Most of all, I would like to thank all the readers who have taken an interest in this book and for their support in making it a reality. Your encouragement has been invaluable.

Preface

Working with data, or better phrased, understanding your world by the use of data, is core to almost every successful business nowadays. Power BI is a powerful tool to help you with that. This book aims to help you get the most out of Power BI and, with that, out of the opportunities that lie ahead of you. It also aims to guide you in passing Microsoft's official Power BI exam: Microsoft Certified: Power BI Data Analyst Associate.

Comprising 16 insightful chapters, this book covers all topics essential for working with Power BI and passing the exam successfully. The book starts with some necessary background on why data is important and why data modeling is even more important.

Chapters 3 and 5 focus on preparing data using Power Query. Chapter 3 starts with applying basic data transformations. Chapter 5 focuses on automating solutions or being prepared to get new data in the future.

Chapter 4 and 6 focus on visualizing the data, where Chapter 4 starts with basic theory on what an effective report is. Not all visuals are insightful, so careful consideration on how to setup your report is essential in creating effective reports. Chapter 6 focuses on more advanced concepts and especially on creating compelling interactive reports.

Chapters 7 through 10 focus on creating a semantic model. Chapter 7 explains the basics of semantic models and especially the relationships between tables,which are an important aspect of the model. Chapters 8 and 9 focus on **Data Analysis Expression (DAX)**. DAX is the language behind the semantic model that allows us to enrich our data analysis capabilities. Chapter 10 introduces concepts and best practices to make Power BI scalable and allow for greater datasets.

Chapters 11 through 13 describe the Power BI portal and collaborating with the reports that have been created. Chapter 11 focuses on security, a topic with ever-increasing significance. Chapter 12 provides a tour of the portal, and Chapter 13 focuses on the actual endresult: creating a Power BI app.

To finish the book,Chapter 14 discusses the monitoring of the entire Power BI system. Chapter 15 introduces **artificial intelligence (AI)** capabilities in Power BI.

This book is designed to cater to all professionals who want to start working with Power BI and/or want to pass the exam PL-300 Microsoft Certified: Power BI Data Analyst Associate. There are no prerequisites for reading the book. However, affinity with data is a must, and some affinity with the use of code is a prerequisite.

Through practical examples, comprehensive explanations, and a structured approach, this book aims to equip readers with a solid understanding of Power BI. Whether you are a novice or an experienced learner, I hope this book will serve as a valuable resource in your journey of exploring Power BI.

Chapter 1: Introduction to Data and Power BI- **Business intelligence** (BI) is a process to prepare and use data to gain a competitive advantage. Lessons learned over the last decades have made people understand that data needs to be combined, prepared, and modeled before it can be used. Those lessons learned can be found in the setup of Power BI. Understanding the evolution of business intelligence is understanding the components of Power BI. The first chapter explains the components found in the tool Power BI from a historical perspective.

Chapter 2: Dimensional Modeling- Power BI is a tool that allows you to create compelling visualizations of your data with just drag-and-drop. However, to make that work as easily as it sounds, the data must be modeled correctly. This chapter teaches you the basics of dimensional modeling. It is a commonly accepted best practice to model your data into a dimensional model before starting to use the data.

Chapter 3: The Basics of Power Query- This chapter introduces the basic working of Power Query. Power Query is used to transform and prepare the data. There are a lot of data transformations available in order to deal with miscellaneous data or data modeling issues. This chapter focuses on the often-used basic transformations. The chapter uses the theory of the previous chapter and transforms our sample data into facts and dimensions.

Chapter 4: The Basics of Visualizations- This chapter provides an introduction to visualizing data. There are a lot of different types of visualizations to choose from. There are a lot of questions to be asked of the data. Choosing which visualization answers the question in the most effective way is an important part of developing reports and dashboards. This chapter is about choosing the right visuals and how to actually create the visual. The chapter also describes how to change the formatting of the visual to your personal liking.

Chapter 5: Advanced Techniques of Power Query- This chapter focuses on automating Power Query solutions. Depending on the data you have and the questions you need answered using that data, Power Query can be straightforward. It can also become rather complex. You need to be prepared for complex situations, where, for instance, new data will be stored in new files. This chapter focuses on the language M of Power Query and on how to use it to automate your data loading and preparation solutions.

Chapter 6: Create Interactive Reports- This chapter explores the interactivity capabilities of Power BI reports. The chapter builds on the skills learned in *Chapter 4, The Basics of Visualizations* to make the reports more effective by allowing users to be actively involved with the data in the report. It introduces drill down and drill through, amongst other things, to allow users to really get insights into their business processes.

Chapter 7: The Basics of Semantic Models- You cannot create reports in Power BI without a semantic model. The semantic model is basically the part that makes drag-and-drop reporting possible. The reports created so far in the book are based on a default semantic model that is automatically created when data is imported into Power BI. This chapter explores the semantic model. It explains the various types of relationships between tables of data and when to use which relationship. It also explains a lot of other settings that make the result of drag-and-drop reporting better.

Chapter 8: DAX- This chapter introduces DAX. DAX is the programming language behind the semantic model. It can be used to enrich the data model. With DAX, we can create calculations, calculated columns, and calculated measures. Sooner or later, you will have to use DAX to answer the questions that live within an organization. This chapter uses a lot of practical examples but focuses mainly on understanding the concept behind DAX. It explains the concept of context and shows how to play with context to make reports even more informative.

Chapter 9: Advanced DAX Concepts- This chapter goes one step further than the previous one. 80% of what you need to do using DAX can be simply done by using all the DAX functions that are readily available. Some of the real added benefits will take a little more effort. You need to understand iterators and context switches. This chapter teaches the slightly more difficult techniques of DAX.

Chapter 10: Scalable Power BI Solutions- This chapter focuses on larger datasets. Larger can be defined here as the scenario when you have issues within Power BI with everything taught so far in the book, because of the amount of data you have. This chapter teaches you concepts and tricks to use when you have large datasets. You will learn about different storage modes, aggregations, incremental refresh, and more.

Chapter 11: Security- This chapter focuses on securing Power BI. Security can be found at different levels throughout Power BI. The chapter teaches how to configure **row level security (RLS)** within a report. It also describes object level security and how to secure semantic models, reports, and dashboards once they are published to the Power BI service.

Chapter 12: Working with the Power BI Service- The Power BI service is the cloud portal where semantic models and reports are published to, once we need to collaborate on them with multiple people. It is also the place where we can create Power BI dashboards. This chapter focuses on functionality and settings found in the service. It describes workspaces, domains, folders, and a whole lot of settings that you can adjust to customize your Power BI environment.

Chapter 13: Create App- After the previous chapter, you will realize that the Power BI portal can be a daunting environment for users who just need to use the reports. For these users, we can create Power BI apps. This chapter describes what Power BI apps are for, how you can create and customize them for different audiences, and how to share them with the intended users.

Chapter 14: Monitor Power BI and Fabric- This chapter focuses on keeping an eye on the system. Our reports are made available to users, and you need to keep track of their usage. Some reports might not be used at all or not anymore over time. Some reports might grow, either in how often they are used, by how many different users they are used by, or in the amount of data behind the report. Knowing how the system is used helps in keeping the system healthy. It also helps in knowing whether you are using the right license. This chapter describes the tools available for administrators to monitor Power BI and its usage.

Chapter 15: Copilot in Power BI- This chapter introduces AI in Power BI. Copilot, Microsoft's AI assistant, is integrated into Power BI in multiple ways. This chapter describes where and how you can use Copilot throughout Power BI.

Chapter 16: Practice Exam- Since this book helps you prepare for the official Microsoft exam PL-300 Microsoft Certified: Power BI Data Analyst Associate, it helps to know what sort of questions you can expect on the exam. This chapter provides some example questions that help you prepare for the exam even better.

Code Bundle and Coloured Images

Please follow the link to download the
Code Bundle and the *Coloured Images* of the book:

https://rebrand.ly/d952da

The code bundle for the book is also hosted on GitHub at
https://github.com/bpbpublications/Microsoft-Power-BI-Data-Analyst-Exam-Guide.
In case there's an update to the code, it will be updated on the existing GitHub repository.

We have code bundles from our rich catalogue of books and videos available at
https://github.com/bpbpublications. Check them out!

Errata

We take immense pride in our work at BPB Publications and follow best practices to ensure the accuracy of our content to provide an indulging reading experience to our subscribers. Our readers are our mirrors, and we use their inputs to reflect and improve upon human errors, if any, that may have occurred during the publishing processes involved. To let us maintain the quality and help us reach out to any readers who might be having difficulties due to any unforeseen errors, please write to us at: errata@bpbonline.com

Your support, suggestions and feedback are highly appreciated by the BPB Publications' Family.

Piracy

If you come across any illegal copies of our works in any form on the internet, we would be grateful if you would provide us with the location address or website name. Please contact us at business@bpbonline.com with a link to the material.

If you are interested in becoming an author

If there is a topic that you have expertise in, and you are interested in either writing or contributing to a book, please visit www.bpbonline.com. We have worked with thousands of developers and tech professionals, just like you, to help them share their insights with the global tech community. You can make a general application, apply for a specific hot topic that we are recruiting an author for, or submit your own idea.

Reviews

Please leave a review. Once you have read and used this book, why not leave a review on the site that you purchased it from? Potential readers can then see and use your unbiased opinion to make purchase decisions. We at BPB can understand what you think about our products, and our authors can see your feedback on their book. Thank you!

For more information about BPB, please visit www.bpbonline.com.

Join our Discord space

Join our Discord workspace for latest updates, offers, tech happenings around the world, new releases, and sessions with the authors:

https://discord.bpbonline.com

Table of Contents

CHAPTER 1

Introduction to Data and Power BI

Introduction

This chapter introduces you to the concept of data analysis and analytics. It describes the context in which a data analyst performs his or her role. It also provides a historical overview of data warehousing. Data analysis is not new. Organizations have been using data for years already. By now, we have a good idea of what works and what pitfalls to watch out for. Lessons learned in the past in **business intelligence** (**BI**) in general, and data warehousing specifically, are used today in Power BI development. So, it is worth your time to learn about those experiences from the past.

Power BI uses what we learned about successful data warehousing, which is why Power BI is a lot more than a visualization tool. It comprises a lot of components. This chapter introduces you to all Power BI components. It also outlines Power BI licensing.

Structure

This chapter covers the following topics:

- Introduction to business intelligence
- Historical overview
- Introducing Power BI

- Power BI use case
- Power BI Desktop and the Power BI service
- Power BI licensing

Objectives

By the end of this chapter, readers will know what BI is. You will also know and understand typical data warehousing terms like **online analytical processing (OLAP)**, **extract, transform, and load (ETL)**, and cubes. You will understand data quality issues and the need to prepare data before use.

Besides more theoretical terms, you will learn about Power BI Desktop and the Power BI service and understand the difference between them. You will also understand Power BI licensing.

Introduction to business intelligence

Data has become increasingly important to businesses and is generated with everything you do. Using all the generated data to gain insight is paramount to every business. The Japanese scientist, *Shinya Yamanaka,* once stated that the main business model for companies in the future would revolve around data; by that, he meant that a bakery would not earn money by selling bread but by collecting, using, and potentially selling data. More recently, it is people like *Mark Zuckerberg* and *Jeff Bezos* who declare similar things. *Facebook (Meta)* did not become rich from the license money people pay to use Facebook. It is free. That is to say, Facebook is gathering data, your data, and making money with that data.

Of course, most companies are not Facebook or Amazon, but small local companies also gather data. Each company and individual works with data. This may be customer-related data, patient data when in health care, product or service-related data, sales data, measurements, or event data from **Internet of Things (IoT)** sensors, and so on. The list is endless. Gathering this data and then not using it would be plain silly. We can analyze the data, learn from the data, and turn that knowledge into good use. Turning data into information, insight, and action is what we call BI, or to put it in other words:

BI is providing the right people with the right information in the right format at the right time in order to make the right decision.

This definition is straightforward. The challenges come from the word right that is used five times in the definition. In real life, you need to pay close attention to each occurrence of the word right. Let us analyze this definition.

The most important word here is decision. It is all about decision-making. Learning something and doing nothing with it can be ok in fundamental science (and it sometimes seems to be ok in politics as well), but generally speaking, we want to do something with the knowledge we gained. Gaining a competitive edge is what is said oftentimes about BI, but that means that you change things because you have new or more insights into processes, customer behavior, the market in general, etc. and by applying changes, you hope to, for instance, increase sales, reduces costs, increase productivity, decrease sick leave, etc.

The definition speaks about the right decision. However, the data analyst may not be responsible for decision-making; however, a manager is, but if the data analyst provides the manager with data to support the decision-making, the data analyst is responsible for the correct interpretation of the data. Proper visualizations are a part of making sure the audience understands the data. Good visualizations can turn data into information. So, we make the right visualization, so decision-makers have the right information to make the right decisions.

If we go back to our definition of BI, we get to the part where it says the right information. We need proper data for that, and very often (more often than not), we do not get proper data. Consider, for instance, a list of patients in a hospital with around 30% of duplicate rows in that table. The first step in being a data analyst is to analyze the raw data. This is where you first see that you might have a problem with duplicates (we will discuss more potential issues later in this chapter). This step is called **exploratory data analysis (EDA)**.

EDA is your first look at raw data. You spot potential issues like duplicate rows. You do a first check on what values are in your data, like calculating statistics like average, min, and max values of different columns. It is where you get to know your data.

The second step, after having done the initial EDA, is solving any issues you found, like in this case, de-duplicating the dataset. The third step is then to perform the actual data analysis to see what we can learn from the data. In our example, with patient data, we want to learn about our patients from this dataset. The main point here is that raw data is seldom good enough to use directly. It needs preparation before we can use it and make it into the right information.

We have now explained two occurrences of the word right in our definition. The other occurrences are slightly more straightforward. The person who has to make a decision is the right person to receive the information, and they need it at the time the decisions need to be made (or preferably before that). Delivering it in time, in some cases, proves to be a challenge, but the need for timely information is clear.

The last right of the definition is about the right format. Data can be visualized in a lot of different ways. Different formatting, like showing data in a 3D pie chart vs. showing the same data in a bar chart, might lead to completely different interpretations of the data, which can be something that you specifically were looking for, or it might lead to unintentional misinterpretation of the data. When visualizing data, you need to be aware of what message you want to tell what target audience. It will further be discussed in *Chapter 4, The Basics of Visualizations*.

To recap, we live in a world of data. Data plays an important role in our everyday lives. Being able to use all that data to your advantage is an important skill nowadays. Doing so will not always be easy, but at the end of this book, you will have a good head start to become a proficient data analyst using Power BI. First, let us have a closer look at the data within organizations.

Data in organizations

Data-driven working seems to be the holy grail for a lot of companies, which leads to situations where management at some point decides they want the company to work data-driven. More often than not, it starts a data warehouse project or, more recently, a data lake implementation within the IT department. On other occasions, BI software like Power BI is purchased so people can create reports and analyze data. However, data-driven work is a lot more than building a data warehouse or purchasing visualization software. People within the organization need to change how they perform their daily tasks, and the organization as a whole needs to be organized and managed differently.

Data-driven work is more a management style, a way to organize a company, than anything else. To be successful, we have to realize that. Maybe change management is more important than starting an IT project. Data-driven work is anything but an IT project or, even more generally, a project. It is a way of working.

Before you start any BI initiative, it can be useful to perform a maturity scan of the organization. Maturity models have been developed to get an idea on where a company stands in regard to using data.

Figure 1.1 shows a simplified maturity model. All the way to the left, you will see maturity Level 1: Unaware. Even in companies that should be classified as being in this stage, people work with data, and Power BI can be a very useful tool for those people. There are probably no formal requirements for these reports.

As can be seen in the following figure, there is no formal decision-making process. Maybe data plays a role in decision-making, maybe not. The data we use and how it is prepared is not formally described:

Level 1: Unaware	Level 2: Opportunistic	Level 3: Standardize	Level 4: Company wide	Level 5: Transformative
No formal decision making Process Ad-hoc reports	Limited number of users Spreadmarts Shadow systems Data inconsistencies	Executive sponsor Central data marts Central direction, both technical and in business definitions	Business Intelligence Competence Center Corporate datawarehouse	Agile Innovative

Figure 1.1: Maturity model

When a company states the ambition to become data-driven, it should first determine its current situation in regard to the maturity model. Then, they should decide on what their ambition is. With the current situation and the ambition stated clearly, a path towards that ambition should be determined. You cannot be on level 1 today and expect to be on level 5 tomorrow. That will take time, and more importantly, you will have to go through all the stages to successfully get to the desired level.

This book is not about how organizations can become data-driven and what they have to do to reach their ambitions, but it is important to have some understanding of the different maturity levels because Power BI can play an important role in all levels. Power BI may be used differently, though. Before we take a look at different Power BI use cases, let us first look at how BI has evolved over the years. Power BI takes advantage of lessons learned in the past, and we as Power BI developers can take advantage of those lessons learned in all the different scenarios Power BI supports.

Historical overview

In the 1980s, relational databases were introduced. If you take a look at the marketing from that time, you will read texts like information at your fingertips or be able to always make informed decisions. We came from the mainframe era, where there was limited data and information available, and it was hard to get, but the promise of the relational database was that everyone could send queries to the database and get answers immediately. Systems like **customer relationship management (CRM)** were built, and it was said we could use all the data generated by those applications in real-time. The ambitions back then were no different than our current ones.

In the real world, it turned out not to be as easy as marketing promised. A couple of problems were encountered when trying to do more complex reporting or analysis on these operational systems. Microsoft nowadays makes the same promise, that you can connect Power BI to basically any operational system that generates data, start analyzing the data and use it for reporting straight away. This approach did not work previously, and we now have to make sure we do not make the same mistakes today with Power BI. Let us see what we can learn from the past.

The most important problems that we encountered were as follows:

- Data complexity
- Impact on source systems
- Data quality
- Lack of a consistent 360-degree view
- Lack of historical data

Data complexity

Databases that support operational applications like **human resources (HR)** applications, CRM applications, **enterprise resource planning (ERP)**, **electronic patient dossiers (EPD)**, to name just a few, are most of the time databases that use a normalized data model. An example of how that may look can be seen in *Figure 1.2*.

The goal of *Figure 1.2* is not for you to understand this data structure at this point. It is just an illustration to show that normalized database structures can become really complex.

Figure 1.2 is a subset of a simple example database:

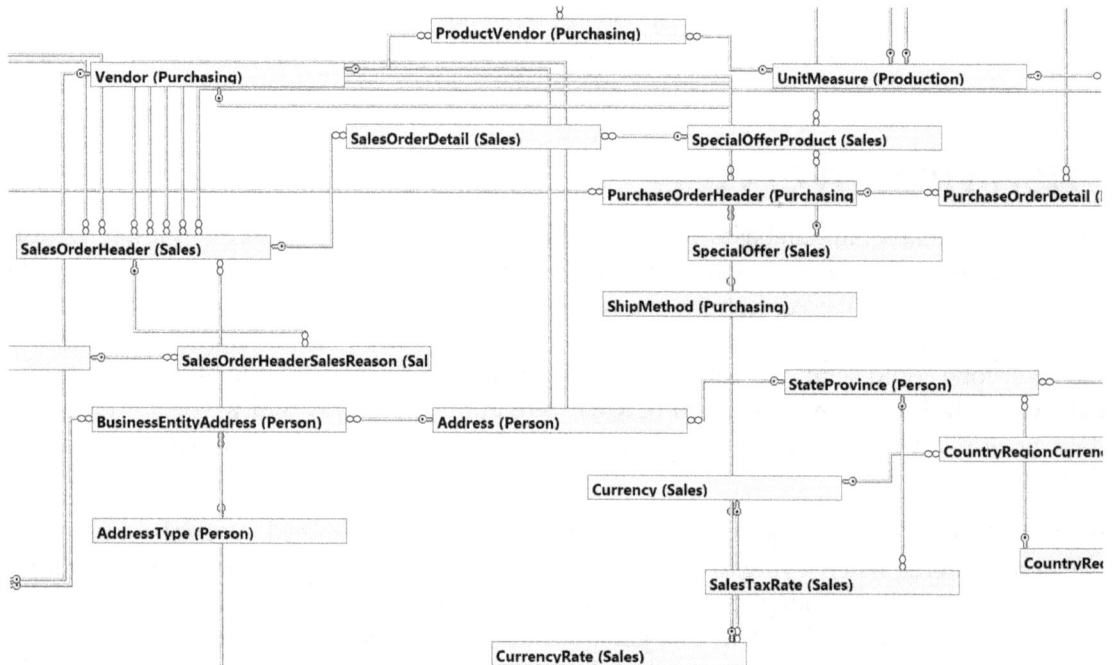

Figure 1.2: *Normalized data model*

The database, as shown in *Figure 1.2*, is an example of the adventure works database, which is a fairly simple example database that Microsoft uses a lot. Real world database can become a lot more complex, and some databases have over 100.000 tables. Complexity by itself is not necessarily bad. It however, leads to two negative effects as follows:

- Error-prone

- Productivity

The more the complexity increases, the bigger the chances of errors. Queries to get the data out of the database correctly become complex as well. People make more errors when writing complex code as opposed to simple code. You can import a table schema, as shown, into Power BI and create reports based on these tables. Within Power BI, you will at some point need to write **Data Analysis Expressions** (**DAX**). These DAX expressions can become incomprehensibly complex when using normalized databases, as shown in *Figure 1.2*. You want to stay away from that, especially when accountability becomes important. You will learn about dimensional modeling in *Chapter 2, Dimensional Modeling* where you create easy-to-use data models.

Another issue might be the productivity of report builders. When the complexity of the data, and especially the complexity of the data model, increases, so does the time it takes to develop good, effective reports. With HR being a big part of operational costs for a lot of companies, having people work more efficiently is important. Ideally, we want to enable data analysts and report builders alike to focus on content and not on complexity. By simplifying the data model, we simplify data analysis and report creation, making better use of the expensive resource that is human capital.

Impact on source systems

Data analysis or extensive use of reports puts an extra strain on the database being used. This may impact the database and, with that, the application that the database is supporting negatively. The application can very well be one of the primary processes of the company. Although effectively working with data is important, the primary processes are even more important.

With the compute power available today and the optimized database engines we have, this argument is not nearly as important as it was thirty years ago. We can develop Power BI reports in such a way that we minimize the impact the report has on the source it uses, but even so, a lot of database administrators do not want us to query their database directly.

Data quality

Companies nowadays have a lot of data, but more often than not, that data has issues that prevent companies from using the data as-is. The quality of the data is bad. There are always issues with data in operational sources. In our definition of BI at the start of this chapter, we used the word right a lot. The definition of BI states that we need the right information, and we need proper data to get the right information. More likely than not, you do not get proper data. Issues that you may encounter may be as follows:

- Duplicate rows
- Missing data
- Incorrect data
- Inconsistent data
- Homonyms and synonyms
- Other issues

Let us start at the top of the list. Consider a **Patient** table in a hospital. It would not be surprising that the table contains up to (or even more) than 30% of duplicate patients. *General Data Protection Regulation (GDPR)* may forbid you to use anything like a citizen service number, so you cannot be sure. However, looking at first name, last name, birth date, and address may give you the impression that many duplicates exist in your dataset. With all those duplicates, a lot of patient analysis that can potentially be done would be meaningless. You will need to deduplicate the data before starting any analysis. Doing so on the original table is probably out of the question. You need to extract the data first, prepare the copy, and do the analysis on the copy.

Missing data is a very common issue as well. Consider a web shop where you have to create an account before you can order anything. Some of the information you have to enter is obligatory, like your last name and email address, but the date of birth might, for instance, not be mandatory. A lot of people will leave it empty. That leaves you with a lot of missing values in the dataset.

Continuing on the date of birth example, suppose the date of birth was mandatory. Some people will enter their real birth date. Others will just type in a fake birth date. January 1st of 2000 is an often-seen birth date in customers' data of online shops. Other values, like January 1st of 1970, may show up more than statistically expected. It is the data represented by zero in Unix-based systems. Instead of missing data, we are now faced with incorrect data. There are a lot of examples of incorrect data. You have to figure out what this means for the data you are going to work with, especially when you pretend to present the right information.

Data can be correct but inconsistent at the same time. Suppose, for instance, you have a customer who lives in the city of *Seattle, Washington*. Most people working with Microsoft are familiar with this city. Now, suppose that the same customer lives in *Australia*. The value of Australia in itself can be correct, just as Seattle can be. However, the combination of both is not correct. They are inconsistent with each other. This does have an impact when analyzing where your customers are located.

As a last example, let us look at homonyms. Suppose we again analyze customer data, especially in which city our customers live. For this example, we focus on our *Belgium* customers solely. In Belgium, part of the people speak French, and the other part speaks Dutch. The first group calls their capital *Bruxelles*, the Dutch-speaking people call it *Brussel,* and English-speaking people call it *Brussels*. Using the data as-is, with different values for the same city, will not lead to correct results when used in drag-and-drop reporting like in Power BI. In terms of data, you have three entirely different cities. In the real world, it is of course one and the same city. You may also have other variations in the database where people made typos when entering the city name. Again, if you do not prepare your data before doing any sort of analysis on the data, you run the risk of getting incorrect results. Even a simple analysis of counts per city may be more complex than it seems at first glance.

Lack of a consistent 360-degree view

Companies never have just a single database or a single source of data. They have multiple sources. Those sources are partly complementary and partly overlapping. Companies can, for instance, connect to an order entry system and, by combining all orders of a single month, calculate their monthly sales, or they connect to their invoicing or bank system and derive monthly sales from there. More often than not, you will get two different answers.

Your first step when creating a Power BI report is to choose the data to use. You will have to decide which source to use for the report you are going to make. You may have to analyze first whether or not you get the same answers from both systems. When the numbers are different, the choice becomes more difficult but also a lot more important. These are difficult decisions to make. Sometimes there may be obvious reasons for the differences. The order entry system may have used the order date to calculate sales, where the other system used an invoice date. In this case, you simply choose the definition of sales you need for the report.

Another example might be when you need to combine information about sales people from the CRM system with identities coming from Microsoft Entra. There should be a match in Entra for every sales person, but in real life, it could be difficult to match the entries from both systems. Missing data, typos in email addresses, old email addresses from before Entra was introduced, or from before the merger with another company can all be reasons for this.

Lack of historical data

The last potential issue when working with data from operational systems is the potential lack of historical data. One issue may be that, for instance, six months ago, the company migrated to a new CRM system. Comparing today's business with last year is all of a sudden complex because you need to combine the data of the old system with the data of the new system, and even though it is the data about the same process, there is likely not a one to one match between how the data is stored.

More importantly, it is the lack of historical data of what we call the dimensions. Suppose you want to analyze what products are popular in what parts of a country. You do have all historical sales transactions available, so you know exactly who bought what, but also suppose that every time a customer moves to a new address, the old address is overwritten with the new address. This is what happens in a lot of operational applications.

In this scenario, you will match a historical sales transaction to a current address. So, products sold to a student living on a university campus may now very well be linked to an urban area where a lot of families with young children live. The sold products get linked to the wrong part of town.

As with issues described earlier, a fairly straightforward analysis becomes difficult or even impossible to do.

When marketing promised us all those years ago how easy it was to connect to the database and get information out of it to support decision-making, they overlooked these issues.

Today, with Power BI, the promise is the same as it was back then. It is easy to connect to almost any source. Once connected, you start building reports immediately using simple drag-and-drop, but all the issues described here are applicable to today's data sources. You have to be aware of the problems your data poses to you, and you have to find and implement fixes before you can do meaningful analysis on your data.

Instead of focusing on issues, let us focus on possible solutions. In the 90s, data warehousing became popular to overcome the issues mentioned in the section. So, let us have a look at data warehousing.

Data warehouse

In the 90s, companies started creating data warehouses to overcome the issues as discussed.

Figure 1.3 shows a simplified data warehouse architecture:

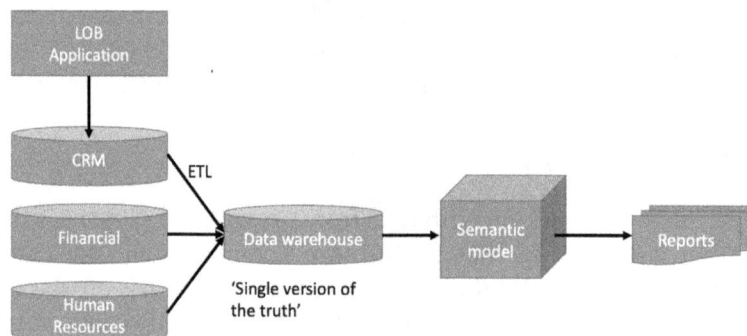

Figure 1.3: *Simple data warehouse architecture*

In *Figure 1.3*, there are three different databases supporting **line of business** (**LOB**) applications. This means there are three data sources available to use for reporting and analysis. With data warehousing, a BI team extracts the relevant data from the source systems to load the data into a new database, that is, the data warehouse. By doing so, it gives them the opportunity to transform the data while doing so. Probably, the most valuable part of data warehousing is the ETL process. Nowadays, people creating data warehouses and implementing ETL processes are called **data engineers**.

The transform part of the ETL process allows data engineers to first and foremost use a different table structure to store the data. The first issue described is the complexity of the normalized operational databases. Data engineers have the opportunity to make it simpler.

There are multiple architectures and data modeling techniques that can be used. This book is not about data warehouse architectures. Although the lessons learned in the past with data warehousing, and especially the data modeling techniques applied in data warehousing, are relevant. The data modeling technique preferred for Power BI is **dimensional modeling**. The result of a dimensional model database is what is called a **star schema**.

Figure 1.4 is an example of a simple star schema: the star in *Figure 1.4* emphasizes the design with a central table surrounded by other tables, together creating the form of a star:

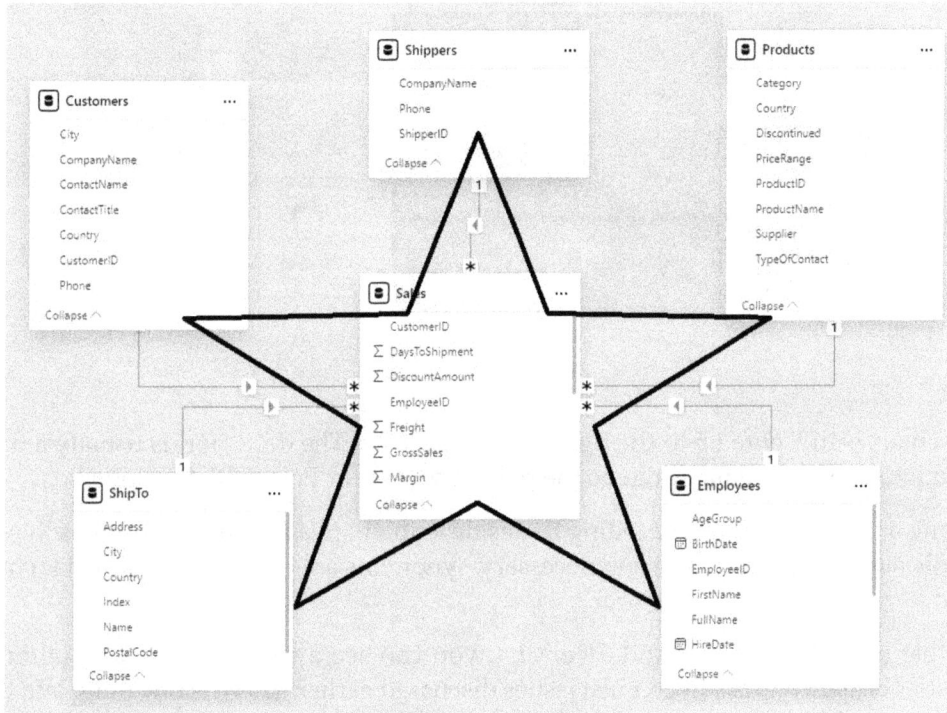

Figure 1.4: *Star schema*

Refer to *Figure 1.2* and compare it to *Figure 1.4*. A lot of people will agree it looks a lot simpler. It is a Power BI best practice to base all your work on data modeled into a star schema. It will improve your Power BI report dramatically. Easier report development leads to higher quality reports, less performance issues, and with current Fabric licensing, it will be cheaper too.

Take notice of the text 'Single version of the truth' under the data warehouse in *Figure 1.3*. One of the issues described previously is the lack of consistency between different source systems and the lack of a consistent 360-degree view of an organization because of it. With all the relevant data placed into a single data warehouse, which is now used as the source for reporting and analysis, the lack of consistency is solved. When you always go to the same place with questions, you always get the same answer. The underlying integration problem has been solved in the ETL process. A more modern line than 'Single version of the truth' is 'single version of the facts', referring to the fact that different people may still interpret data differently, even though they get the same data.

A more modern architecture involves the use of data lakes instead of data warehouses. It is just a modern version of old-fashioned data warehousing, more geared towards big data and the cloud. There is not much difference from a Power BI development perspective.

Figure 1.5 shows a data lake architecture:

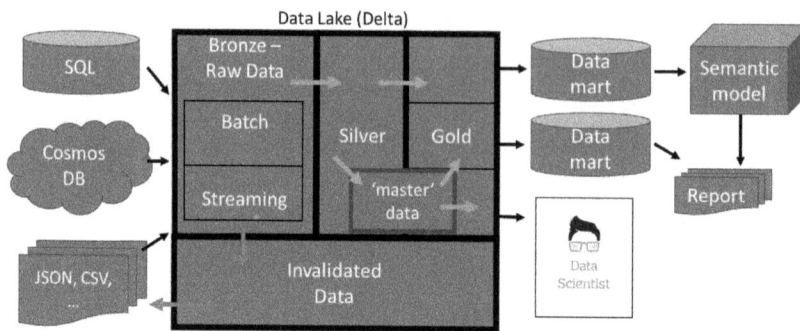

Figure 1.5: data lake

The data mart is in *Figure 1.5* to the right of the data lake. The data mart is usually a database modeled into a start schema. It can be the perfect source for Power BI developers.

In creating a star schema, all preceding issues described are as good as possible solved. Data is deduplicated when applicable and necessary, synonyms are resolved, etc. The data has been cleansed.

Notice that in both *Figure 1.3* and *Figure 1.4,* you can see a semantic model. Building data warehouses or data marts solved most issues discussed earlier. There is one thing left, though, we want to enable as many people as possible to create reports, and we want them to be as productive as possible as well. That means that it should be really straightforward and simple to create reports. We try to reach that ambition by making drag-and-drop reporting tools like Power BI. However, there is a cap between how well drag-and-drop works and the functionality provided by databases. In the 90s, we started creating OLAP cubes to bridge the gap between technical-oriented databases and drag-and-drop tools. Today, we call that extra layer a semantic model.

All the preceding is about lessons learned in the past. Applying these lessons learned increases the quality of any BI platform. It is, therefore, essential to take these lessons forward and take advantage of them when working with Power BI.

Introducing Power BI

Up to the zeroes of this century, you would use Microsoft SQL Server when implementing BI solutions. Data warehouse developers would create data warehouses in SQL Server using **SQL Server Integration Services (SSIS)** as an ETL tool. They would then implement an OLAP cube (semantic model) using **SQL Server Analysis Services (SSAS)**. The reports and data analysis would then be done using either **SQL Server Reporting Services (SSRS)** or Excel. To enable more people to create compelling reports faster, Microsoft introduced some add-ins in Excel. Power Pivot, Power Query, and Power View. A bit later, these three add-ins were combined to create a new product, that is, Power BI.

Today, Power BI still has three main components. Power Query is still called **Power Query**. It is a visual low-code/no-code ETL tool. Power Pivot has evolved into what we now call a Power BI semantic model, and Power View does not exist anymore as a name, but it is what we know Power BI best for: the visualizations that make up our reports.

The three Power BI components, combined with the lessons learned from data warehousing, are shown in *Figure 1.6*:

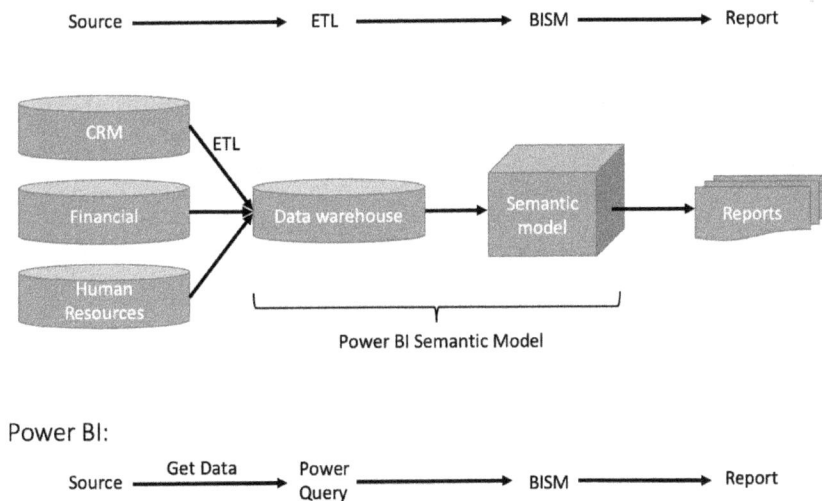

Figure 1.6: Power BI compared to data warehousing

When comparing *Figure 1.6* to *Figure 1.3*, we see that Power BI took the lessons learned from the past and basically allows the Power BI developer to create a data warehouse and semantic model. It uses an ETL tool to read data from various sources and allows transformations before loading the data into its own semantic model. Once the data is modeled, it can be visualized.

Power BI does not have a separate data warehouse and semantic model. However, you will learn that you load data into tables within your Power BI solution (you will learn about this later in the book). You can then set all sorts of settings that are typical for a semantic model, as shown in *Chapter 7, The Basics of Semantic Model*. On top of that, you will enrich the data by adding calculated measures using the semantic model language DAX, as can be read in *Chapter 8, DAX*.

Power BI ideal sources

Power BI supports over 140 different data sources that you can connect to, and the first step in developing a Power BI report is always to get data. The first and sometimes difficult decision to make is where to get the data from.

Refer to *Figure 1.7*:

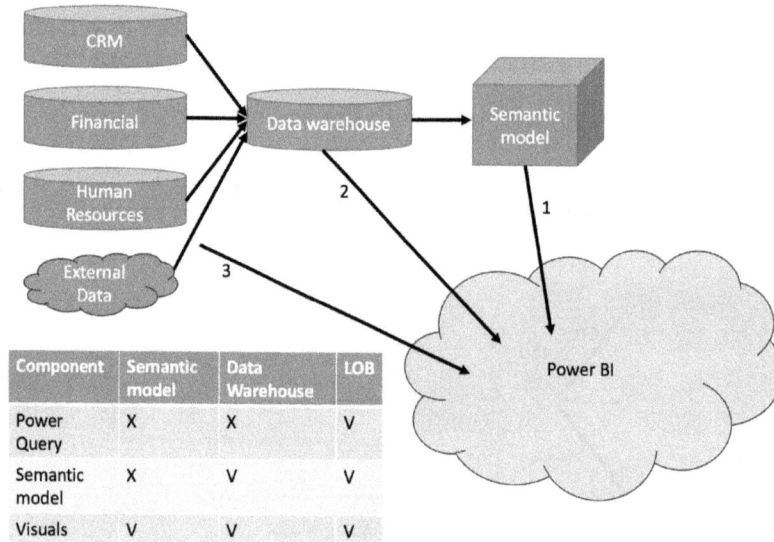

Component	Semantic model	Data Warehouse	LOB
Power Query	X	X	V
Semantic model	X	V	V
Visuals	V	V	V

Figure 1.7: Power BI possible sources

In the preceding figure you see the data warehouse architecture for the third time, but it now includes Power BI. Notice the numbers next to the arrows pointing to Power BI, and also notice the table in the bottom left corner.

The arrow with *number 1* shows the ideal scenario. You have to create a report, and there happens to be a semantic model, either in Power BI (Fabric) itself or one created in Azure Analysis Services, and this model also happens to be exactly what you need for your report. You then connect to the semantic model from Power BI, and you can start making visuals immediately. You do not have to bother with ETL and data modeling because that has been done already, as denoted by the X in the table. All you have to focus on is creating visuals.

Very often, a semantic model will not be available, or the ones that are available do not suit your needs. The next best option is then to connect to a star schema modeled data warehouse/ data mart. Extra ETL functionality needed will be minimal to none, but you do have to create a semantic model before you can create visuals.

If both a semantic model and a data mart are unavailable, it is not a concern. You have all the tools to create them yourself inside your Power BI solution. You simply connect to any data you can find and take it from there. In this situation, you may need to spend a lot of time preparing your data, and once that is done, you have to turn it into a proper semantic model. After all that work, you will be ready to create nice visuals.

So, whatever the situation is, Power BI is a tool that can make you succeed in most data endeavors. The amount of work it takes can vary a lot, depending on the situation you find yourself in.

Now that you have an understanding of the different components inside Power BI and why they are there, it is time to return to BI maturity models and different Power BI use cases.

Power BI use case

To get an understanding of different Power BI use cases and how Power BI can be used, let us start by stating just two opposite use cases, as follows:

- Corporate reporting
- Ad-hoc analysis

Corporate reporting

With corporate reporting, report developers create reports for decision-makers. The creator of the report is someone other than the user of the report. Oftentimes, the reports are used over a longer period of time, maybe even for years. Decision-makers can be everyone in an organization, including C-level managers. The higher in the hierarchy the decision-maker is, the more important it becomes that the information on the reports is correct. Important decisions are based on the report. Accountability and lineage become important. Consistency with other reports may be crucial. Extra requirements next to just what the report should show become increasingly important.

To make sure you can meet the extra requirements, you will have to put more effort in the Power BI solution you develop. Refer to *Figure 1.7*, ideal sources for Power BI. With corporate reporting connecting to either a data warehouse or even an existing semantic model may be crucial. In both cases, the ETL process and the resulting data store are centrally developed and, hopefully, documented. Centrally defined business rules are applied, and everything is thoroughly tested. The data in the data warehouse is probably the best data you have in terms of consistency and quality. Both resolved and remaining data quality issues are known in the datawarehouse and can be made visible by creating reports on data validations and data corrections done during the ETL process.

For this all to be true, an organization must probably be in level three of the maturity model, as shown in *Figure 1.1*, or in a higher level of the maturity matrix.

Ad-hoc analysis

A true data analyst will often think outside the box. Maybe he or she gets some external data and starts investigating the impact on the business. You can, for instance, download weather data to analyze whether sales in your company are influenced by the weather. If this is done ad-hoc or for the first time, it is almost certain the data needed is not already present in a well-formatted data mart, let alone a semantic model. All the data preparation needed will have to be done for this project.

Sometimes, analyses like those described previously are merely playing around with data without knowing whether there will be a valuable outcome. In such a scenario, you do not want to spend days or weeks on data preparation just to find out that there is nothing to find out. Applying best practices, documenting all your decisions and code, and checking all formulas against established business rules simply takes too much time. Connect to your data and visualize it as soon as possible, and go from there.

This ad-hoc scenario can be valuable in all levels of the maturity model of *Figure 1.1*. Organizations in level one do not have a data warehouse in place to use. They often also do not have central business rules defined, let alone anything like data governance in place. Any report, no matter how it was developed, has added value.

In level five of the maturity model, employees are encouraged to be innovative and work data-driven. When decisions are made during departmental meetings or board meetings, reports must adhere to predefined standards, which is our first use case, but individuals may improve their personal performance by using data. Personally, in this case, the word improve is imperative, and how that goal is reached is of less importance, but if, let us say, a sales person spends 90% of his time creating personal dashboards instead of selling stuff, the manager will most likely not be too happy. Best practices may not be as important as quick gains.

Other use cases

The two described use cases are the two extremes when it comes to all use cases. A team report may be more important than a personal report and is likely not as important as a report meant for C-level management. For each report you are going to develop, it makes sense to think about the use case that determines how you want to proceed, which best practices to adhere to, and what prerequisites the report should meet.

Now that you understand that Power BI can be used in a lot of different scenarios and that what is expected of the report may vary, it is time to see what components Power BI is made of.

Power BI Desktop and the Power BI service

Power BI is made out of two main components as follows:

- Power BI Desktop

- Power BI service

Power BI Desktop

Power BI Desktop is the Power BI development tool. This is where you create new reports. In Power BI Desktop, you will find all the functionality we discussed so far. You will find the Power Query Editor inside Power BI Desktop to do all necessary data preparation. You can also create the semantic model in Power BI Desktop, and last but not least, you can create the reports using Power BI Desktop.

Power BI Desktop is a free application. Either go to **https://www.microsoft.com/en-us/download/details.aspx?id=58494**, and download it, or find Power BI Desktop in the *Microsoft Store* app on your work station. The installation is straightforward; you can just follow the instructions of the installer. Everybody can download and use it. The only limitation is that it is a Windows App; you cannot install it on a MacBook, for instance.

Once you open Power BI Desktop, it works much the same as Office applications. Like you create **.xlsx** file when working with Excel, you create a **.pbix** file when working with Power BI Desktop. As long as your report is a work in progress, you store the **.pbix** file somewhere locally, on a file share, or perhaps in OneDrive. When you double-click on a **.pbix** file, Power BI Desktop will start, allowing you to work with the report. Like with any file, you can share the file with co-workers who can open it in Power BI Desktop as well.

Even though you can share file **.pbix** file with others, this is not the way to share a report with others. Collaborating with the reports is done using the Power BI service.

Power BI service

Power BI service is a cloud portal where you upload reports for usage and sharing. You can browse to **https://app.powerbi.com/** on any browser to login into the service. You do need a Power BI login to be able to get into the portal. Power BI is part of the bigger Microsoft 365 ecosystem. This means that you usually login with your email address. When set up correctly, you will probably be logged in automatically.

Once a report is uploaded from Power BI Desktop to the service, it is split into the report itself and the underlying semantic model. So, a single Power BI Desktop file results in a semantic model and a report. With proper permissions, other users can base their reports on the now available semantic model.

With a semantic model being available in the service, new reports can be created directly in the portal. You cannot create semantic models in the service, but you can create reports and edit existing reports directly in the portal. However, what you can and cannot do in the portal also depends on the permissions you have. You will learn about the service, sharing of content, and permissions in *Chapter 12, Working with the Power BI Service*.

A prerequisite of sharing reports is a proper license. Let us have a look at the licensing options available.

Power BI licensing

Licensing may change; please refer to **https://www.microsoft.com/en-us/power-platform/ products/power-bi/pricing** for up-to-date information. You can also download a licensing guide from this site to get more extensive information on the license that suits your company the best.

Roughly, you can distinguish six types of licenses, as follows:

- Free
- Power BI Pro
- Power BI **Premium Per User** (**PPU**)
- Power BI Embedded
- Fabric capacity reservation
- Fabric capacity pay-as-you-go

Free

Power BI free is exactly what it says, it is for free. This, of course, means it is a limited version. The most limiting restriction is probably that you cannot share reports with others. It is basically a single-user environment. Another restriction is that Microsoft does not allow a private email address for Power BI accounts. So, you cannot create a free account to try out Power BI using an outlook.com or Gmail account.

Apart from these restrictions, there are other technical limitations.

Check the following site for details:

https://www.microsoft.com/en-us/power-platform/products/power-bi/pricing

When we want to share content, both the person sharing a report as well as the person that the report is shared with need a paid license (with embedded as the exception).

Power BI Pro

Power BI Pro costs (at the time of writing) 10 US dollars per user per month. This license is a good fit for small companies, both in terms of the number of users as well as the size of the datasets they intend to work with. Pro is included in Microsoft 365 E5 and Office 365 E5 licenses.

Some limitations include a semantic model size limit of a maximum 1 GB per semantic model. On top of that, there is a maximum storage limit of 10 GB per license. It allows for a maximum of 8 data refreshes per 24 hours.

Power BI Premium Per User

Power BI Premium is twice as expensive as Pro. You may pay 20 US dollars per person per month. Premium runs on dedicated capacity, making the performance, that you may expect, more stable. It is also less restrictive. You have a maximum of 100 GB per semantic model and 100 TB of total storage with up to 48 refreshes per 24 hours.

Not only is Power BI Premium less restrictive on sizing, but it also comes with more functionality. It, for instance, allows connections using **XML for Analysis (XMLA)** endpoint, which can be really convenient for developing larger semantic models. Refer to *Chapter 10, Scalable Power BI Solutions*.

Power BI Embedded

The Microsoft site does not list a fixed price for Power BI Embedded. You have to contact sales to get a quote. This license is meant for companies that want to use Power BI visuals inside their own website (so outside of the Power BI service) to be used by anyone who can access that site. You normally need a paid license to view Power BI content that is shared with you, but companies cannot ask the visitors of their site or portal to have a Power BI license. With embedded, you pay for the users of your site.

Fabric capacity reservation

Power BI is part of the larger Fabric ecosystem. Fabric is a suite of functionality allowing organizations to implement cloud data lake implementations, creating lakehouses, data warehouses, and SQL databases. It also comes with a couple of ETL options, allowing for large-scale ETL. It comprises data science, real-time data, and other functionality as well, and of course, data visualization using Power BI.

There are multiple Fabric licenses starting with the smallest (F2) and going all the way up to a F2024 license. The price you pay for Fabric depends on the geographic region you are in. With Fabric capacity reservation, you pay a fixed amount no matter how intensively you use Fabric. This is different for Fabric capacity pay-as-you-go.

Fabric capacity pay-as-you-go

With Fabric capacity pay-as-you-go, you pay for what you use. When you are not doing anything in Fabric, you do not pay anything. You just pay for what you use. Reserved capacity is roughly 40% cheaper, but you can earn that back when you have longer periods of inactivity.

Sharing Power BI reports requires additional Power BI Pro or Power BI PPU licenses unless you have a Fabric license F64 or above.

Conclusion

Working with data is an important aspect of everyday life within organizations. There is more data available than there used to be, and using it becomes more important. Having a proper tool to work with data and knowing how to use that tool under which circumstances is important. Knowing how well an organization already is at working with data may be important to provide the proper context of working with data.

Power BI is Microsoft's data visualization tool. However, we saw that it is a lot more than just that. Data needs to be prepared and modeled correctly to be able to analyze it and find meaningful insights from it, and also to create reports from it. Power BI can connect to all sorts of data sources. This includes a well-structured source with nicely prepared data, like data warehouses or raw data stored in semi-structured or unstructured files. No matter what the situation, you can build solutions on top of that data using Power BI.

Before we dive into Power BI report development, we will first discuss star schema data models, or in other words, dimensional modeling in *Chapter 2, Dimensional Modeling*. A star schema is a specific table structure. Setting up a proper star schema is really important in creating efficient and effective Power BI reports.

Multiple choice questions

1. **What is the most ideal source to base Power BI reports on?**
   a. Data warehouse
   b. ERP systems
   c. PDF files
   d. Semantic model

2. **You work at a startup with 10 employees. All datasets used are small. What license is probably a best fit?**
   a. Free
   b. Pro
   c. PPU
   d. Fabric pay-as-you-go

3. **What is the ideal data model to perform data analysis?**

    a. A dimensionally modeled data model

    b. A normalized data model

    c. A pivot table

    d. A single flat table

Answers

1	a
2	b
3	a

Join our Discord space

Join our Discord workspace for latest updates, offers, tech happenings around the world, new releases, and sessions with the authors:

https://discord.bpbonline.com

CHAPTER 2
Dimensional Modeling

Introduction

Dimensional modeling and star schemas were introduced in the first chapter; however, we will tap into the concepts in a detailed manner in this lesson. Power BI works best when data is modeled following the rules of dimensional modeling. It is commonly agreed that using a star schema, which is the result of dimensional modeling, is the best practice in Power BI development.

Dimensional modeling was first introduced by *Ralph Kimball* as a design method for data warehousing. Although the theory of dimensional modeling is quite old, it is still a widely used technique in the world of reporting and data analysis. Performance and ease of use are at the core of dimensional modeling as they are crucial to Power BI development. Thus, this chapter will become a foundation to learn all about Power BI and creating star schemas.

If you are new to working with data and have never touched on data modeling at all, you may find this chapter a bit challenging; however, you will understand it once you get familiar with the concepts.

Structure

This chapter covers the following topics:

- Dimensional modeling
- Steps to design a star schema
- Design a fact table
- Design dimension tables

Objectives

Upon reading and understanding this chapter, you will be able to create a star schema data model. You will know how to analyze raw data used for reporting and transform it into a star schema. Along with that, you will be able to design and distinguish between facts and dimensions, thereby understanding their relationship.

Most importantly, you will be skilled to model any data into facts and dimensions.

Dimensional modeling

There are three main theories that describe how to model data that needs to be stored in a relational database. Each theory leads to a different table structure. Relational databases and normalized databases are often seen as one and the same, although that is not theoretically true. A relational database is a database that stores data in tables, but it does not prescribe a certain table structure. A relational database simply means the usage of tables to store data.

Tables are predefined structures representing entities in our world. Entities can be people, things, or events. In a sales scenario, we may want to store customers' data (people in a *business-to-consumer* scenario, businesses in a *business-to-business* scenario). We also store data describing the products we sell. Products are things or objects that we store data of. Lastly, we store the data describing the purchase orders. This is data describing events.

Predefined structures mean that we store attributes about the entities, which translate to columns in the table. A customer table, for instance, might have columns for first name, last name, email address, address, and so on.

Power BI internally uses what is called a **tabular model**. It means that you start by designing your own database, called the data model or the semantic model. You must design this database. This means that you have to decide which tables you want to use. Often, the desired tables will not be a one to one match with the data you are going to use. Thus, you need to transform the raw data into a suitable data model.

Database design is about which tables to use. You must understand how to divide all the data you need to store over tables and whether you are going to use a single table, a few tables, or many tables. There are three ways to design your database, and they are as follows:

- Normalizing
- Data Vault
- Dimensional modeling

Normalizing data

A normalized database is a database optimized for what is called an **online transactional processing (OLTP)** workload. This workload is common for **line of business (LOB)** applications. Consider a web shop selling products to consumers. A potential customer visits the web page and searches for a specific product. They get all the information about that single product on the screen. Another example can be of a doctor seeing a patient. The doctor now needs all the information about this single patient. We read a lot of columns from a single (or maybe a few) rows in both scenarios.

OLTP systems are also the systems where data comes into existence, which means that we write to the database a lot. The customer of the web shop creates an account and then places an order. The doctor may write a prescription. In both cases, new rows are added to tables.

An OLTP system should be optimized for writing to the database and for working with a small number of rows but with a lot of columns. Normalized databases are optimized for this kind of workload. To state it roughly, normalized databases are optimized for writes.

Normalizing data minimizes redundancy. In short, it minimizes storing the same data values multiple times. It does that by dividing the data over a lot of tables. Depending on how far a database designer takes the normalizations process, it can lead to thousands of tables or worse. Refer to *Figure 1.2* to see an image of a normalized database.

The key point here is that a normalized database is not optimized for analysis. You will very often connect Power BI to LOB applications, meaning to normalized databases. The table structure of the database you are going to use to create Power BI reports is not ideal for Power BI report development and data analysis in general. It is recommended to transform your data before using it.

Data Vault

A Data Vault structure is a database design strategy that optimizes the database for just storing the data. It is a database design optimizing a database for flexible storing of large amounts of historical data. A Data Vault structure is, however, even more complex than the structure of normalized databases. That makes it worse than normalized databases from a Power BI perspective.

A Data Vault is not optimized for a specific use case (or it must be for nightly **extract, transform, and load** (ETL) processes. When companies do large-scale data warehousing, the first task is to store all relevant data from different source systems into a single data warehouse, as we studied in *Chapter 1, Introduction to Data and Power BI*. The data warehouse should be generic. Whenever there is a (Power BI) use case, the data needed for that particular use case should be modeled for that use case specifically.

Dimensional modeling

The third way to design a database is to use the technique known as **dimensional modeling**. The result of dimensional modeling is called a **star schema**, as shown in the following figure:

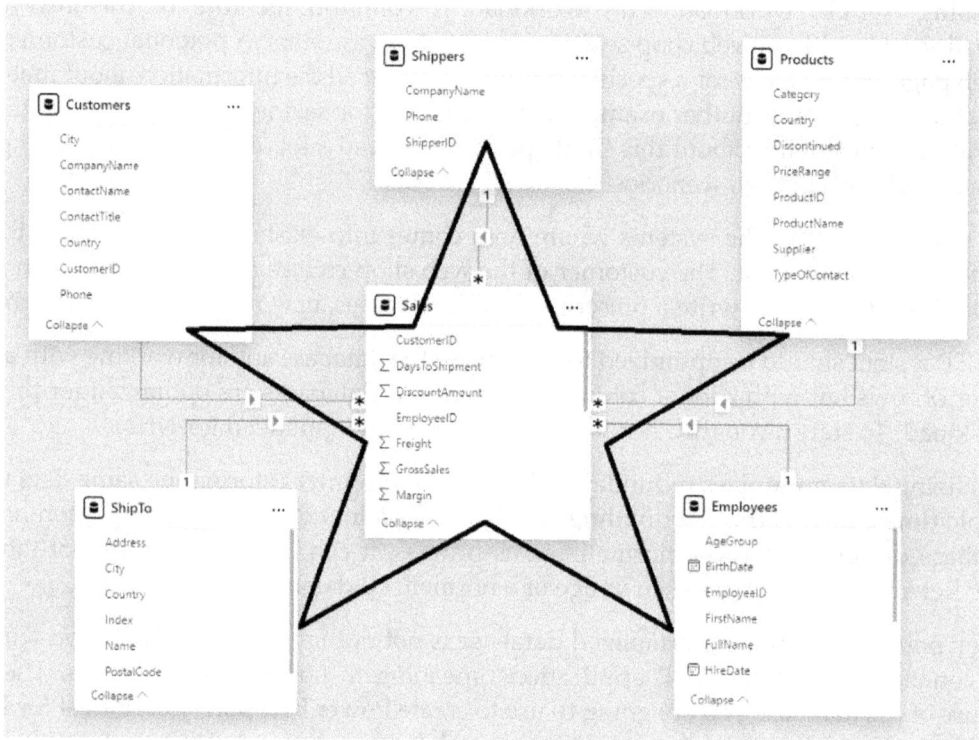

Figure 2.1: Star schema

In the preceding chapter, we discussed possible issues when working with operational (read LOB) applications, and one of them was the complexity of normalized databases.

Star schemas aim to be intuitive and good for performance. It should be intuitive to a business user, not a technical person. Performance should be optimized for an OLAP workload.

For instance, you create a report for C-level management of a grocery store. They might be interested in the revenue per store. They also want to see the trend of said revenue over the last 24 months for comparison. Looking at this request, you need only three columns: revenue, store, and month. However, you do need two years of sales transactions to create the report.

Normalized databases are optimized to work with many columns from a few rows at a time. Dimensionally modeled databases are optimized to work with just a few columns from many rows. This is what you typically need for Power BI visualizations and data analysis in general. Consider a pivot table, a visualization often-used. A pivot table has rows, columns, and cells. You put one of your columns on the rows of the pivot table. You put another column on the columns of the pivot table. You add a third column to the pivot table to be used to populate the cells of the pivot table. In this example, you use just three of your data columns.

> *The golden rule of data modeling is always the same: always use star schemas.*[1]

> *-Alberto Ferrari* and *Marco Russo*

Tabular lets a developer deviate from the regular star schema architecture. Although it is seldom a good idea.

Steps to design a star schema

According to *Ralph Kimball,* there are four steps to designing a star schema that are as follows:

- Choose process
- Determine grain
- Define facts
- Define dimensions

Choose process

This is often an obvious step in Power BI report development. For instance, when the sales manager of a company asks for sales reports/dashboards, you will work on the sales process of the company. Another example could be that you need to create a report to gain insight into sick leave in the company. In this example, you are working on the **human resource (HR)** process. The current request you work on determines the business process that you will be required to model.

It is important to know that in dimensional modeling, you model the process rather than the data itself. Normalizing data is modeling the data and its dependencies, but to optimize your model for the current use case, which needs to create insights in a certain process, you take the process as a starting point, not the data itself.

---

[1] **https://www.sqlbi.com/**

Determine grain

Determining the grain, you are going to use is a vital step. The grain is the level of detail at which you store the data. The more detailed your data is, the more insights you can derive from it. However, the drawback is that the dataset will be significantly larger when you store the data in more detail.

Let us assume that we work for a grocery store. This grocery store has about 200 branches throughout the country, and every time a single product is scanned at a store cash register, a new line is entered into its **point of sale** (**POS**) system. Try to imagine how many rows are entered into the system daily for a single store and multiply that by 200.

Try to visualize a five year sales trend and multiply the number of rows you estimated by five and then by 365. The answer will be the number of rows that you are dealing with. When you need more years of history or when there are significantly more than 200 stores, your dataset will increase significantly as well.

You can answer almost any question with the help of the rows described here. For example:

- Do we sell more bread in the morning or in the afternoon?

- What is the average time of day that we are out of milk?

- Is the ratio between what we earn by selling food and other items different during the weekend compared to weekdays?

- How often are soda drinks and chips bought together, and so on....

However, you could have been tasked with developing a report for the C-level management. They are interested in seeing the breakdown of the sales in each individual store to understand the trends and fluctuations over the last five years. If you aggregate the raw data from the POS system to one row per store per day, it will be merely 5 times 365 times 200 rows, which is almost nothing to Power BI. Your report will be way cheaper and faster with this aggregated small dataset. Of course, the insights that you can derive from this will be drastically reduced.

You have skimmed through a brief overview of Power BI licenses. A semantic model can only be 1 GB in size with a Pro license. The size increases with more expensive licenses. It also means that you may be able to use cheaper licenses when you work with smaller datasets. Choosing the level of detail of the data that you will use to create your Power BI reports is a balancing act between more data and more insights that you can derive from the data, versus better-performing and potentially cheaper solutions. Therefore, try to investigate what the lowest level of detail needed for a report is and pre-aggregate your data to that level. We will discuss the more advanced option of Power BI aggregation tables in *Chapter 10, Scalable Power BI Solutions*.

The result of this step of dimensional modeling should be a grain statement. A grain statement says something like *we store revenue by day, by customer, by product*.

Note: **With this grain statement, you store one row in your Power BI model even when the same customer buys a product in the morning and then comes back in the afternoon of the same day to buy the same product a second time.**

You could change the grain statement into something like *we store revenue by day and time, by customer, by product*.

The grain statement already tells you something about the dimensions you will use (day, customer, product). We will discuss the dimensions in a later section in this chapter. But let us first look at an example.

Northwind database example

We will use the Northwind database to create reports throughout this book. Northwind is a very old example database that Microsoft used before 2005. Though old, it is still nice data to play with and to learn Power BI with. Northwind is a database storing sales orders. Northwind buys delicacy products from all around the world from its suppliers. These products fall into eight categories. The **Products** are sold by **Employees** to **Customers**. Each sales transaction is stored as an **Orders** with accompanying **Order_Details**. *Figure 2.2* shows the Northwind database. The words in bold are the tables in this database:

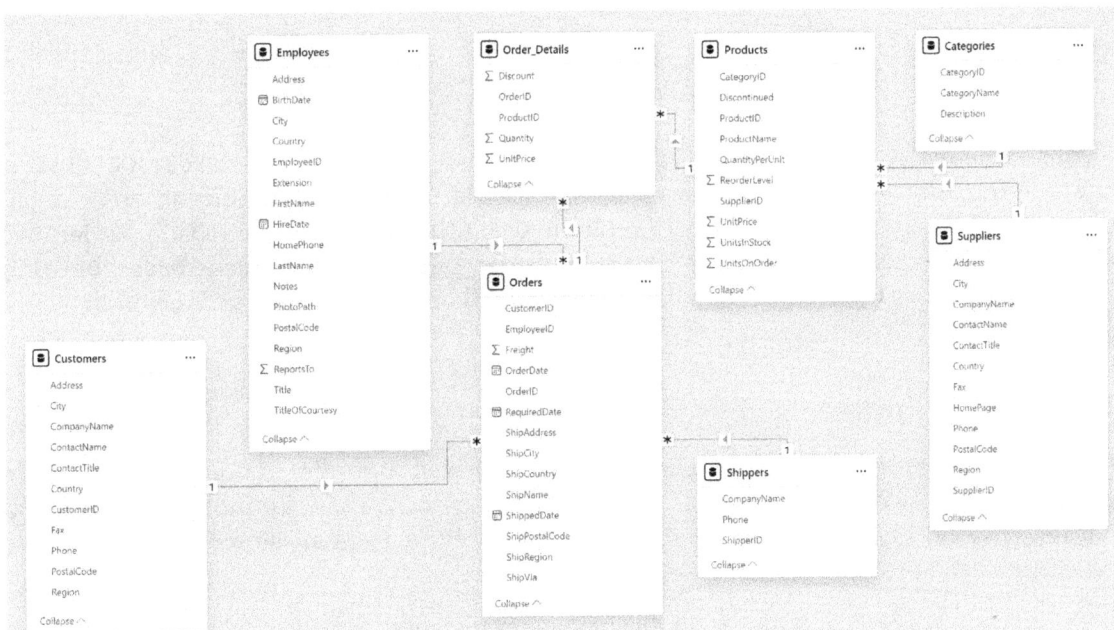

Figure 2.2: *Northwind OLTP*

Figure 2.2 shows the database schema or **entity relationship diagram (ERD)** of Northwind. It is an example of a simple and normalized database. For this book, we want to work with the most detailed level data available for us. In other words, we want to work with the lowest granularity possible. Therefore, we must analyze the Northwind database to see what data we have in the database. To help you understand the Northwind database, *Figure 2.3* and *Figure 2.4* provide a preview of the data stored in the **Orders** table and the **Order_Details** table:

OrderID ▾	CustomerID ▾	EmployeeID ▾	OrderDate ▾	RequiredDate ▾	ShippedDate ▾	Sł
10249	TOMSP	6	5-7-1996 00:00:00	16-8-1996 00:00:00	10-7-1996 00:00:00	
10260	OTTIK	4	19-7-1996 00:00:00	16-8-1996 00:00:00	29-7-1996 00:00:00	
10267	FRANK	4	29-7-1996 00:00:00	26-8-1996 00:00:00	6-8-1996 00:00:00	
10273	QUICK	3	5-8-1996 00:00:00	2-9-1996 00:00:00	12-8-1996 00:00:00	
10277	MORGK	2	9-8-1996 00:00:00	6-9-1996 00:00:00	13-8-1996 00:00:00	
10279	LEHMS	8	13-8-1996 00:00:00	10-9-1996 00:00:00	16-8-1996 00:00:00	

Figure 2.3: Preview of Orders table

OrderID ▾	ProductID ▾	UnitPrice ▾	Quantity ▾	Discount ▾
10260	62	€ 39,4	15	0,25
10260	70	€ 12	21	0,25
10263	16	€ 13,9	60	0,25
10263	30	€ 20,7	60	0,25
10263	74	€ 8	36	0,25

Figure 2.4: Preview of Order_Details table

Figure 2.2 shows that the **Orders** table has a relationship with the table **Order_Details**. It is a one to many relationship. Each order has several **Order_Details**, but an order detail (order line) belongs to a single order. The column **OrderID** defines this relationship. **OrderID** is unique within the **Orders** table, it is not within **Order_Details**. As the name **Order_Details** already suggests, it stores more detailed information than the **Orders** table. We will therefore use **Order_Details** as the granularity of our reports.

Defining facts

Facts make processes measurable. Facts tell you how well a process is doing. They provide insight into a process and allow for objective comparisons. They are mostly numerical in nature. They can be aggregated to higher aggregation levels. Facts are stored in a central table called the **fact table**.

Let us take an example to understand this better. For instance, you ask a sales manager how it is going, and he says that it is going well. You query him about the reason behind his response. Possible answers might be: *sales are up, our market share has increased, we have better margins than before*. This means that this manager measures the sales process using sales, market share, and margin. These are all examples of facts, and they should be stored in the same table, the fact table.

You may have heard of **key performance indicators (KPIs)**. A KPI is a management instrument that usually provides insight with respect to the current status or progress of a business process.

A KPI consists of four components:

- Actual
- Target
- Status
- Trend

The actual component of a KPI is always a fact. A KPI, for instance, can be defined as a minimum margin that must be made on sales transactions to be profitable as a company. The actual margin is compared with a preset target.

The target is also a fact. This fact, however, is stored in a separate table from the facts that make up the actuals of your KPI's. This is necessary because you may define the targets for a year at the end of the previous year. This means that you have targets without actuals.

Additionally, the third component of a KPI is the status. The status is a business rule that defines when you are happy and when you are not. For example, if the margin is higher than the preset target, you are happy. This is often shown graphically.

Let us take an example of a traffic light. Green means the actual is better than the target. You have to define up front what you mean by better. For sales, better will probably mean more sales than the target amount. For sick leave, however, better is more likely when you have fewer sick leaves than the preset target.

A KPI may also have a trend. The trend shows whether the status, good or bad, is better or worse than in the previous period. Therefore, it adds a time component to the KPI.

All KPIs that are defined for a process are facts in your dimensional model. However, you may have more facts than KPI's since not every fact measures something critical.

Let us assume that we have to create Power BI reports for sales. Our first step is to create a table called the fact table that has a column for every fact. So, if the facts are sales, margin, quantity sold, and discount provided, you may create a table as shown in *Figure 2.5*:

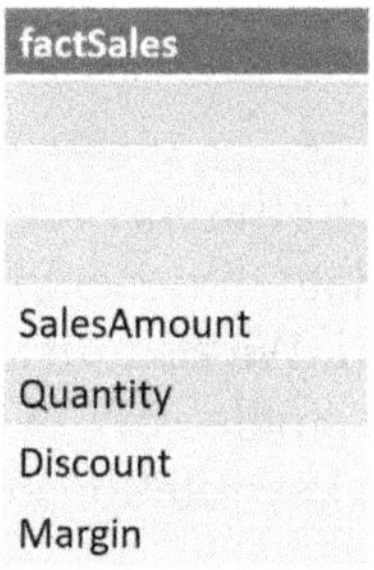

factSales

SalesAmount
Quantity
Discount
Margin

Figure 2.5: Fact table

The number of rows stored in the fact table depends on the grain you chose in the previous step. In this case, let us continue with the grain statement, *we store revenue by day, by customer, by product*. This means that you will have a row for each day that a customer bought a product. If the customer buys five different products on the same day, you will have five rows. If the customer buys the same product twice on the same day, it will be stored as a single row.

Let us have a look at the dimensions before we discuss facts in more detail.

Defining dimensions

Now that we have facts in a fact table, it is time to think about dimensions. Facts are just numbers. However, only having a number is not very informative. We can say: *a million*, and you would have no clue what it means. *One million in revenue* would be slightly better. However, saying that, *we have one million in revenue per month* is far more informative. Each figure needs context to derive meaning from. With the addition of per month, you get an idea if it is a small, mid-sized, or large company. It turned the number one million into information.

The context needed to give meaning to the facts is what we call dimensions. Dimensions are separate tables in our star schema. So, to continue with our example of wanting sales by month, we now need a column for month in a dimension table. *Figure 2.6* shows how the dimension is added to the fact table:

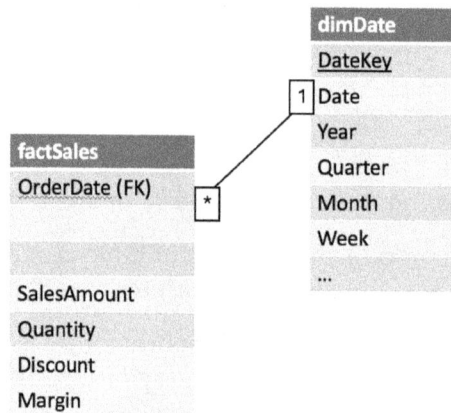

Figure 2.6: Fact table with date dimension

We added a column called **OrderDate** to the fact table. This column serves as the so-called foreign key to the added date table or date dimension. For every sales transaction, the date at which the transaction occurred is stored. We add this date as a column to the fact table. Each row in the fact table now references a single row in the date table by using the **OrderDate** column. This is a primary key—foreign key relationship or simply a relationship between the two tables.

The date table stores a single row for each day on the calendar. A row is added to the date table even if you do not have a sale on a specific day. In *Chapter 8, DAX*, you will learn about Power BI time intelligence functions that do require you to have a table like this. If you do not have one, it is easy to generate it in Power BI, as you will learn later.

Notice the different columns in the date table. In Power BI, you create reports by dragging columns from tables onto your report canvas, as will be explained in *Chapter 4, The Basics of Visualizations*. The consequence of this is that if you need to create a sales by month report, you need to have columns for sales and month.

With the date table as shown in *Figure 2.6*, you can do sales by month as well as by year, by quarter, by week, and by day. The three dots denote that you may add columns as needed to support working with other periods.

In addition to that, you must understand the difference between the usage of the columns in the different tables. When describing most visuals in a report in English, you will get a sentence like *sales by month* or *margin by product*. Whatever is before the word *by* is a fact and should come from the central fact table. Whatever is after the word *by* is a dimension attribute and should come from a separate table than the one in which the fact is stored in. It should come from a dimension table.

We can say the same, but then from the perspective of a visual. Whatever you use on the axis of a visualization is a dimension attribute and should be stored in a dimension table. Whatever is used as a value is a fact and can be found in the fact table. Whenever you are unsure whether a column is a fact or a dimension, think about how you will use it.

Circling back to our grain statement *by day, by customer, by product*, we still have some work to do. We add dimension tables for customers and products in the same way we added a date table before. The resulting database schema now looks like *Figure 2.7*:

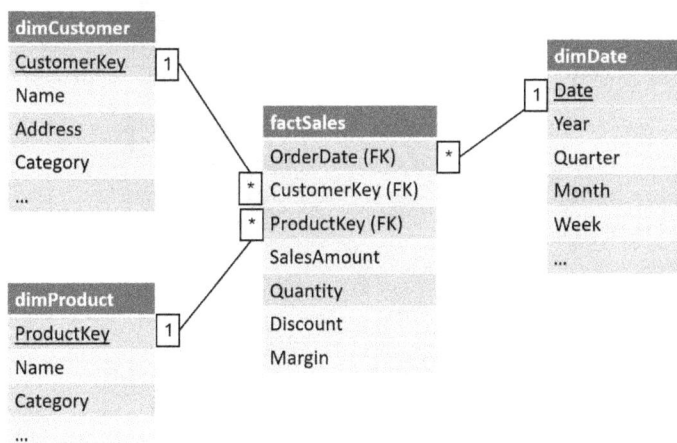

Figure 2.7: Fact table plus dimensions

When we added the date table, we also added the column **OrderDate** to the table **factSales**. Now that we have added the tables **dimCustomer** and **dimProduct**, we have added the columns **CustomerKey** and **ProductKey** to the fact table. This ensures that every row in the fact table uniquely references a single row in the dimension tables. We now have our one row per day, per customer, per product as declared in the grain statement. We can now do sales by product, sales by category, sales by customer name, and so on.

Once you have added all the dimensions that were mentioned in the grain statement, you may be ready, but there could be more dimensions. In this case, there may be, for instance, special promotions. You may have to analyze the impact of the promotion on your sales. You can add a table with a row for each promotion that we have had. Your model now looks as shown in *Figure 2.8*:

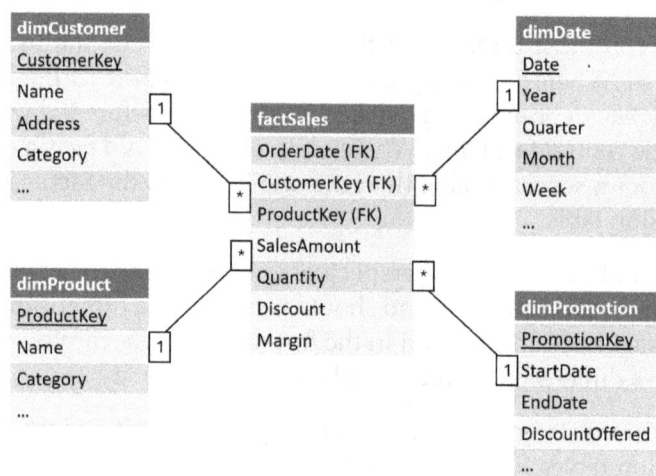

Figure 2.8: With dimPromotion

Dimensional modeling is an iterative process. It makes you go back and forth between the steps.

When you get data to use for a Power BI report, it may very well not be organized into facts and dimensions. You will analyze the raw data, decide on how you will use the data, and then turn it into facts and dimensions.

Now that you know the steps to a star schema, let us take a closer look at both facts and dimensions.

Designing a fact table

In modeling, we speak about facts. Power BI uses measures. Often, the words, facts, and measures are used as synonyms, which is acceptable most of the time. However, there is a distinction that we can make.

Power BI will automatically aggregate numerical data when you drag a numeric column onto your report design canvas. The column that you drag onto the canvas is a fact. The resulting value that is displayed in the report is the measure. That value, in most cases, is an aggregation of the values stored in the fact column in the fact table.

Suppose you have a completely blank report, and now you drag the column **SalesAmount** from the fact table as shown in *Figure 2.5* onto your report canvas. Even though you may have thousands of rows (or many more) in your fact table, Power BI will show a single value on your report. Unless you configure it differently, it will use the **SUM** function to combine all the values in the different rows into a single value. So, the values as they are stored in individual rows are facts, the aggregated values as shown in the report are the measures. Measures get calculated from facts.

When you think about Power BI, summing your facts by default, you may conclude that summing values is not always what you need. There are three different types of facts:

- Additive facts
- Non-additive facts
- Semi-additive facts

Additive facts

Additive facts are facts that are correctly aggregated using a **SUM** function.

For instance, you have $200.000 in sales from selling bicycles and $100.000 from selling bike-clothing. Your overall sales are now $300.000. Having $200.000 in sales in country A and $100.000 in country B also adds up to an overall sale of $300.000.

Furthermore, $200.000 sales in January and $100.000 in February also make $300.000 in total sales. This means whether you do sales by product category, or by country, or by month, you can always add up the numbers to get the overall sales.

Sales here is an example of an additive fact. Using the **SUM** function will correctly aggregate the facts to less detailed information. The default aggregation function Power BI uses is the **SUM** function.

Non-additive facts

The simplest way to explain non-additive facts is with the help of the following example:

You have a margin of 6% when selling bicycles. The margin is 5% when you sell bike-clothing. If we do nothing and let Power BI do its default behavior, Power BI will tell us the overall margin is 11%. It simply adds the numbers 5 and 6 together, like it did for sales amounts in the previous example. Percentages in general cannot be added together. The **SUM** function results in wrong data.

Semi-additive facts

Apart from additive and non-additive facts, you also have semi-additive facts. Suppose you have bank accounts with a balance for each account. Also, suppose you had €300 in your account in January and €400 in February, which amounts to €700 in total.

Another example that you may consider here is that you have €200 and your friend has €300, which amounts to €500 in total. This means that adding balances over the customer dimension is fine, but doing the same over the time dimension leads to wrong results. You can use the **SUM** function only sometimes. Hence the term, semi-additive. Most of the time, it is the date dimension that cannot be aggregated using the **SUM** function.

Have a look at the fact table of *Figure 2.5*. There is a fact called **Margin** in the fact table. Suppose for a specific row the margin is 5%. There are three ways to store this:

- 5

- 0.05

- $ 25,00 (when $ 25,00 amounts to 5%)

Power BI automatically uses the **SUM** function unless you specify otherwise. **Margin** stored as an amount is an additive fact. Summing it will result in the correct values. When you need to show a margin as a percentage on your report, you will have to calculate the correct percentage yourself. However, when you store it as a percentage (or as a whole number), you will still have to calculate it yourself because automatic behavior will never result in correct values.

Storing the margin as an amount makes your report less prone to error and may lead to fewer calculations needed when showing a report. The last makes the report cheaper and may lead to being able to use smaller fabric licenses. So, try to create additive facts whenever possible.

Designing facts

The facts used in the examples so far are obvious. However, with a little creative thinking, there might be more facts available to you. A still rather simple example is calculating the number of days between when an order was placed and when the invoice was sent. Another measure could be the days between the invoice date and the payment date. Calculating these measures can be done within a Power BI report using **Data Analysis Expressions** (**DAX**). However, doing so during the ETL phase, meaning using Power Query and adding the result as a column to your fact table, is smarter. It will make your report easier and, by that, less error-prone and cheaper because it needs less Fabric capacity units when working with Fabric licenses.

Let us look at another example where you have orders, and you keep track of orders with a total amount of more than $10.000. You can write DAX code in your Power BI report that counts the number of rows with a value of 10.000 or more. You can also add a column called **Greater10000** and store the value **1** or **0** in it, depending on is the value stored in the column

SalesAmount. With this column added to the fact table, you can now simply **SUM** this column to get the correct values. Easier functions are less error-prone and take less Fabric capacity units.

It is always a good idea to add facts to the fact table using Power Query. When that is possible, try to solve issues (complexity) by applying data modeling techniques using Power Query and only use DAX when necessary.

A fact table has two types of columns. It has a foreign key for every dimension, plus it stores the facts. The foreign keys play an important role. Almost every number that you will show on Power BI reports will use a fact combined with a dimension attribute. Power BI joins the fact table and the dimension table to present the desired result. As a result, having efficient keys is important. Inefficient keys may slow down report rendering and need more Fabric capacity units to process report rendering.

Efficient keys are columns with the data type whole number. Try to use numbers wherever possible to link the fact table to dimension tables.

Having seen these three tips, check out our Northwind sample database.

Northwind database example

Please refer to *Figures 2.2* to *2.4*.

Looking at *Figure 2.2*, we can see that the table **Order_Details** stores data at the most detailed level. The table **Order_Details** defines the grain of the star schema we want to create. It makes sense to look at this table for facts. At first glance, we can see three facts in this table:

- **Discount**
- **Quantity**
- **UnitPrice**

When looking at the column **Discount** in *Figure 2.4*, you see the value **0.25**. In this case, you need to know that it means a discount of 25%. Instead of using this column as-is, we will turn it into **DiscountAmount**. We will, during data loading, calculate the actual dollar amount to turn the discount into an additive fact.

Quantity is a fact without a doubt as-is.

We may need to discuss whether **UnitPrice** is a fact or not. If we want to analyze the average unit price over time by product category, **UnitPrice** is what is being analyzed using the dimensions date and category to provide context. This makes it a fact.

There are more facts that we can derive from this data, such as:

- Gross sales
- Net sales

The three basic facts mentioned do not tell you how many dollars you earned, but that can be computed using those three basic facts. For this, we define gross sales as the dollar amount before subtracting discounts and net sales is the actual dollar amount received. You can refer to *Table 2.1* to see the formulas used.

In the table **Orders**, there is a column called **Freight**. This column stores the cost Northwind made to ship the products to its customers. This is by itself a fact, but can also be used to calculate margin. There is, however, an issue. We know sales at the level of the **Order_Details** table. Freight is only tracked at the order level. That means the grain is different, and we cannot add freight to our fact table that has the detail as its grain.

There are two possible solutions. The theoretically best solution is to make two separate fact tables. One for the facts that we know at the detail level, and a separate fact table for the facts known only at the order level. Sometimes, however, you can split a fact. In this case, we will divide the cost evenly over the number of distinct products sold in an order. This means that if the freight equals 100 and there are two order details (order lines) for the order, we will add a freight of 100 / 2 in each line. Be aware that this may not be a valid solution in a lot of real-world scenarios.

The last fact we will discuss is one that we need to derive from the data. To analyze order picking efficiency, we want to know the number of days between when an order is placed and when it is shipped to our customer.

The following table shows all facts and the formulas used to calculate them:

Fact	Based on	Rule
DiscountAmount	Discount	Quantity * UnitPrice * Discount
Quantity	Quantity	
UnitPrice	UnitPrice	
GrossSales	Quantity UnitPrice	Quantity * UnitPrice
NetSales	Quantity UnitPrice Discount	Quantity * UnitPrice * (1 - Discount)
Freight	Freight	Freight / # of order lines
Margin	NetSales Freight	NetSales - Freight
DaysToShipment	OrderDate ShipDate	ShipDate - OrderDate (in days)

Table 2.1: factSales table

Design dimension tables

Dimensions provide context to numbers. This turns facts into relevant information. They are textual descriptors that help people interpret numbers correctly. Dimensions are used for two things:

- Query constraints
- Group by

Some sort of filter is applied to most reports. You may want to look at sales figures for a certain period or analyze sales in a particular country. In data analysis, we use the term: to slice and dice. It basically means that you should be able to look at a particular subset of your data.

Power BI has both slicers and filters. Users of reports can use them both interactively. Slicers and filters are based on dimension attributes because you filter the facts based on dimensions. We will learn later that Power BI automatically filters the fact table based on selections made in the dimension tables. This makes working with Power BI when your data is modeled into a star schema very intuitive.

When using dimension attributes as filters, they are used as query constraints.

We already mentioned that Power BI automatically aggregates. Aggregations are also based on the dimensions. When you want something as simple as *sales by country*, all rows pertaining to the same country are combined into a single row, and the fact is calculated using an aggregation function like **SUM**. When doing *sales by country*, the column country is said to be the group by column.

Dimensions are used to group (analyze) the data and to filter the data. This makes dimensions crucial for the analysis you can perform on the data. So, let us have a closer look at dimensions. You need to consider a couple of aspects of dimensions while designing them. More specifically, you need to consider the following:

- Attribute design
- Snowflaking
- **Slowly changing dimension (SCD)**
- Date dimension

Attribute design

When we studied fact design, we learnt that facts need to be calculated from columns. The same goes for dimension attributes. To understand this further, look at the following figure, describing the table **Employees**:

EmployeeID	LastName	FirstName	Title	TitleOfCourtesy	BirthDate	HireDate	Address
1	Davolio	Nancy	Sales Representative	Ms.	8-12-1948 00:00:00	1-5-1992 00:00:00	507 - 20th Ave. E. Apt.
2	Fuller	Andrew	Vice President, Sales	Dr.	19-2-1952 00:00:00	14-8-1992 00:00:00	908 W. Capital Way
3	Leverling	Janet	Sales Representative	Ms.	30-8-1963 00:00:00	1-4-1992 00:00:00	722 Moss Bay Blvd.
4	Peacock	Margaret	Sales Representative	Mrs.	19-9-1937 00:00:00	3-5-1993 00:00:00	4110 Old Redmond Rd
5	Buchanan	Steven	Sales Manager	Mr.	4-3-1955 00:00:00	17-10-1993 00:00:00	14 Garrett Hill
6	Suyama	Michael	Sales Representative	Mr.	2-7-1963 00:00:00	17-10-1993 00:00:00	Coventry House Miner
7	King	Robert	Sales Representative	Mr.	29-5-1960 00:00:00	2-1-1994 00:00:00	Edgeham Hollow Winc
8	Callahan	Laura	Inside Sales Coordinator	Ms.	9-1-1958 00:00:00	5-3-1994 00:00:00	4726 - 11th Ave. N.E.
9	Dodsworth	Anne	Sales Representative	Ms.	27-1-1966 00:00:00	15-11-1994 00:00:00	7 Houndstooth Rd.

Figure 2.9: Employees

These columns are used to analyze facts.

For instance, we can do sales by birth date. However, there will be some concerns related to its significance. Analyzing sales by individual birth dates is most likely not relevant. Creating a report showing sales by age, or even sales by age group, will often be more valuable. We can calculate age using **BirthDate**. We can also define and calculate age groups (for instance, below 50 and 50 or older).

Columns for age and age group may both be better for analyzing sales and customer behavior than the original column **BirthDate**. There is an issue to overcome. What you are most likely interested in is the age of a person at the time they closed a deal, not the current age. This can be done. We will discuss this in more general terms when talking about SCDs.

To analyze whether the experience of a salesperson influences their performance, you might want to calculate something like *years in service* from the column **HireDate**.

When you look at the table **Products**, you can see a column called **UnitPrice**. There is also a column called **UnitPrice** in the fact table. The column **UnitPrice** can act both as a dimension attribute as well it can act as a fact. Using it as a fact, you can do an analysis like the average price over time. As a dimension, you would use the column **UnitPrice** to analyze price elasticity.

The column **UnitPrice** can potentially hold a lot of different values. Transforming the column **UnitPrice** into a column price category can make it more valuable. This is comparable to creating age groups from birth date.

Snowflaking

A key concept of dimension tables is that they are denormalized or flattened tables. Have a look at *Figure 2.10*:

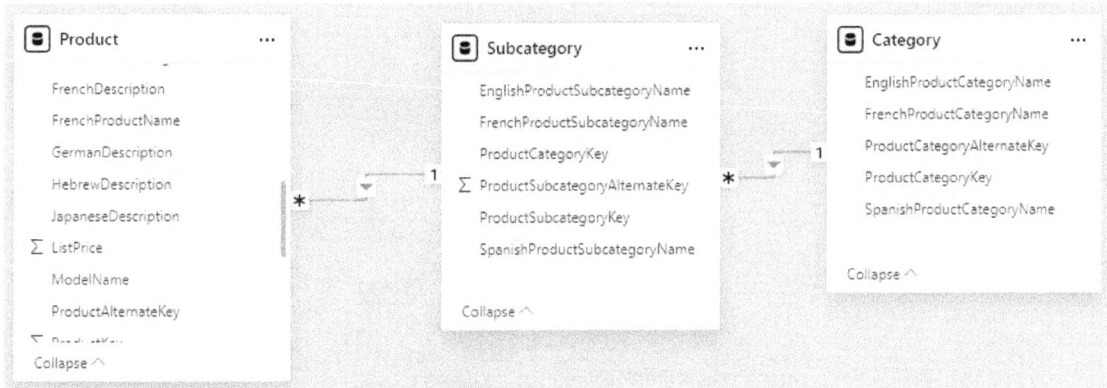

Figure 2.10: *Normalized product table*

In *Figure 2.10,* three tables are shown. The table **Product** is on the left. It stores all the products. Each **Product** is categorized into a **Subcategory**, and each **Subcategory** has multiple products in it. In a normalized database, you create a separate table to store **Subcategory** information. A **Subcategory** is, in turn, categorized into a **Category**. Categories are divided into multiple subcategories. In a normalized database, you would create a separate table to store **Category** information, as you would have the separate table for **Subcategory**. With separate tables for **Category** and **Subcategory**, you will end up with three tables in total.

In a star schema, you create a single product dimension where you combine the three tables into a single table. There are two main reasons to do so. First, you get less tables, making your design easier. Since data complexity is one of the issues described in *Chapter 1, Introduction to Data and Power BI,* a simpler model is a better model. The second reason to combine the three tables into a single dimension is performance.

For instance, you create a Power BI report showing sales by category. Using a fact table with a single product dimension, Power BI only needs to combine two tables. Keeping **Product**, **Subcategory,** and **Category** as three separate tables, Power BI will have to traverse the relationships from **Category** to **Subcategory** to **Product** to the fact table. This leads to Power BI needing more compute power to do simple things.

To recap quickly, you will combine tables that store information about the same entity. The category a product belongs to is descriptive information about the product, just as the name of the product is. Thus, they should be columns in the same table. There may be reasons, however, not to combine tables. We call that snowflaking.

To simplify, when all dimensions are flattened, the resulting data model is called a **star schema**. When one or more dimensions are normalized (like product in *Figure 2.10*), the resulting design is called a **Snowflake**.

Have a look at *Figure 2.11*:

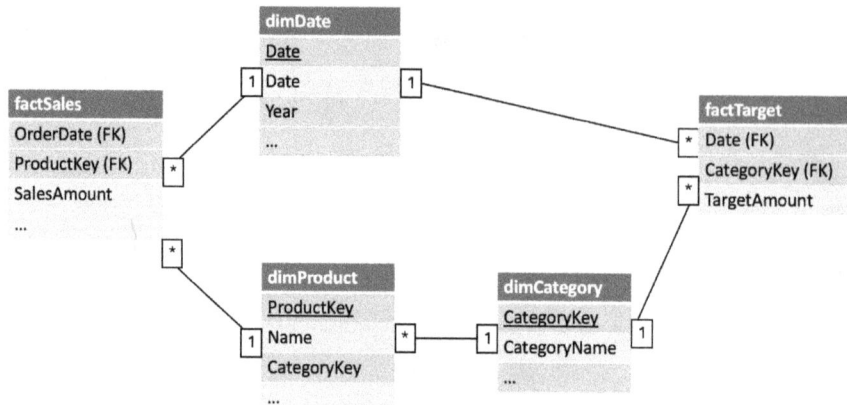

Figure 2.11: Snowflake

The table **factSales** is on the left, and all the way on the right, there is a second fact table. Sales targets are defined for each product category. For instance, the company wants to do one million dollars in sales on bikes per month. On our Power BI report, we need to compare actual sales with these preset targets. Thus, we will read both sales data and target data. For us to compare actuals from **factSales** to targets from **factTarget**, both tables need to share some dimensions. Remember, without dimensions, facts are just meaningless numbers. However, in this scenario, sales describe a product being sold on a specific day. Targets are defined as a sales amount for an entire month for a product category (not individual products). The level of detail of both fact tables is different. This is called a grain-issue. The solution is in snowflaking your data.

Notice the tables **dimProduct** and **dimCategory**. Normally, these tables would have been combined into a single dimension. By keeping them separate while having a relationship between them, we can compare sales to targets in our report. We Snowflaked (normalized) products in order to relate the table **factSales** to the table **factTarget** via the tables **dimProduct** that can be linked to **factSales** and **dimCategory** that can be linked to **factTarget**.

Slowly changing dimensions

Data may change over time, and you have to figure out how that affects your analysis. Let us go back to the example of the age category that we discussed in the section about attribute design.

As you grow up, your age category changes. Each sales transaction is linked to a customer. For example, if you keep track of the current age of a customer, you may link a sales transaction of 20 years ago to a customer who is 60 years of age currently. This customer was 40 years of age when he bought the product 20 years ago. If you try to figure out what sort of people buy your products, using the age of 40 (the age of the customer at the time the product was bought) better describes the sales transaction than using the current age of the customer. When you look at the old sales transaction, you may need to know the age of your customer at that point in time instead of their current age.

A common solution in data warehousing for this problem is called SCD type 2. Have a look at *Figure 2.12*:

Employee Key	Source Key	Name	Age	Start Date	End Date
1	S88	John	Young	1-Jan-2000	14-Apr-2020
2	S25	Jane	Young	1-Jan-2000	31-Dec-9999
3	S88	John	Old	15-Apr-2020	31-Dec-9999
...	...	...	...	...	...

Figure 2.12: SCD type 2

Look at the first and third row in the table shown in *Figure 2.12*. They both describe the same person, **John**. We know both rows describe the same person because the second column is the unique key used in the original database. The first column, **EmployeeKey**, is the key we will use in our dimension table.

When the first row was entered. In January 2000, **John** was still young. The third row tells you that from April 15th, 2020, **John** fell into the **Age** category **Old**.

All you have to do now is link each sales transaction from **John** that occurred on or before 14th of April 2020 to the first row and link the later transaction to the row with **EmployeeKey** equal to **3**.

Implementing SCD type 2 in Power BI can be tricky and often even impossible. In many scenarios, you have to figure out for yourself what has changed between the previous day and the present day. You cannot do that in Power BI. You may, however, connect to data warehouses where this is implemented. If you need SCD type 2 functionality and implement it yourself, then look at Fabric. Fabric has lots of functionality that allows you to create SCD type 2 dimension tables.

Date dimension

Almost all the analysis that people do involves analyzing data over time in some way. When you analyze a fact by something, that something is a dimension. So, we need a date/ time dimension. It is required in Power BI to have a date dimension when using DAX time intelligence functions.

In Power BI, a date dimension is a table that stores one row for each day on the calendar. It is up to you what columns you create in your date dimension. Earlier, we used the month as an example. Let us understand it further. In the following table, you see some options for a month column:

MonthNo	MonthNo2	Monthname	Monthname_short	Month_year	MonthKey	...
1	01	January	Jan	January, 2025	202501	...

Table 2.2: dimDate table

Six options are mentioned to show what a month column could look like. There are even more possible alternatives. You have to figure out which columns you want to use.

Let us start by saying you will have multiple columns for a month, more often than not. You do not choose just one, but several. You have several arguments you can use to choose which columns you need for your Power BI solution.

The first argument while deciding on the option to use is the look of the visuals in your Power BI report. When you drag a column to the axis of a bar chart, Power BI will show the values of that column as labels in the chart. You cannot change that in the reports. Values in dimension attributes become labels on your report. When you drag the column **MonthNo** from the table to your report, the numbers 1 to 12 will be on your visual axis. Using the column **Monthname**, however, will show the values **January, February**, and so on. One is not necessarily better than the other. Keep in mind, though, that you want people to interpret your chart correctly. Readable labels help people to interpret data correctly. From that perspective, the column **Monthname** might be slightly better.

Another thing to be aware of when choosing which columns to use is the default behavior of the different columns. When you create a sales by month bar chart by dragging the fact sales to your report and then adding **Monthname** to it, you will get a bar chart with 12 bars even if you have five years of sales data. Power BI will add all the Januaries together. When you add the year to the name of the month, like in the column **Month_Year**, each month's name is made unique. You will now have *5 * 12 = 60* different bars on the same bar chart.

The last thing to note here is sorting order. On a report, the order in which data is shown is important for the correct interpretation of the data. With a bar chart showing sales by month, the first bar should obviously be January. You need months to be sorted by the month number and not by the month name. The last would set April is the first month. You will learn how to do this in *Chapter 4, The Basics of Visualizations*.

As you can see, a simple column for a month can be a challenge, therefore, a week is even more important to discuss. January is the first month of the calendar year, but which week is week 1? Multiple definitions are in use. Make sure you know what definition your company is using and calculate week numbers accordingly from the date.

Another feature to note about the date dimension is the use of smart columns that may enrich your data analysis. Have a look at the following table:

FiscalYear	YearIndex	IsHoliday	...
FY 2024	-1	Yes/No	...

Table 2.3: Partial dimDate table

A lot of companies use a different calendar for bookkeeping as compared to the standard calendar. At Microsoft for instance, the years start on the first of July, thus they are half a year ahead of the normal calendar, which means that the fiscal year 2025 starts at July 1st, 2024.

During the second half of the calendar year, their fiscal year is one higher than the calendar year. With the need to report on fiscal years as well as calendar years, you need a column for both in your date table.

The second column shown in the table is interesting. It is meant to always show the difference in years between the current date and the date of the row you are looking at. In 2025, a row describing **7-Mar-2024** will have a **YearIndex** of **-1**. Using this column, some filters and calculations on your Power BI will become easier.

The last column **IsHoliday**, enriches the analytical capabilities of Power BI. You may want to analyze how holidays affect your business. When you are at a hotel whose guests are primarily business people, you may have a dip in room occupancy during the holiday season. Special promotions targeted at families during those days may increase overall occupancy. So, start analyzing your data, and after a while, see if the promotions increased occupancy during holidays.

Northwind example

Figure 2.13 shows the normalized Northwind database that you also saw in the section about star schema granularity:

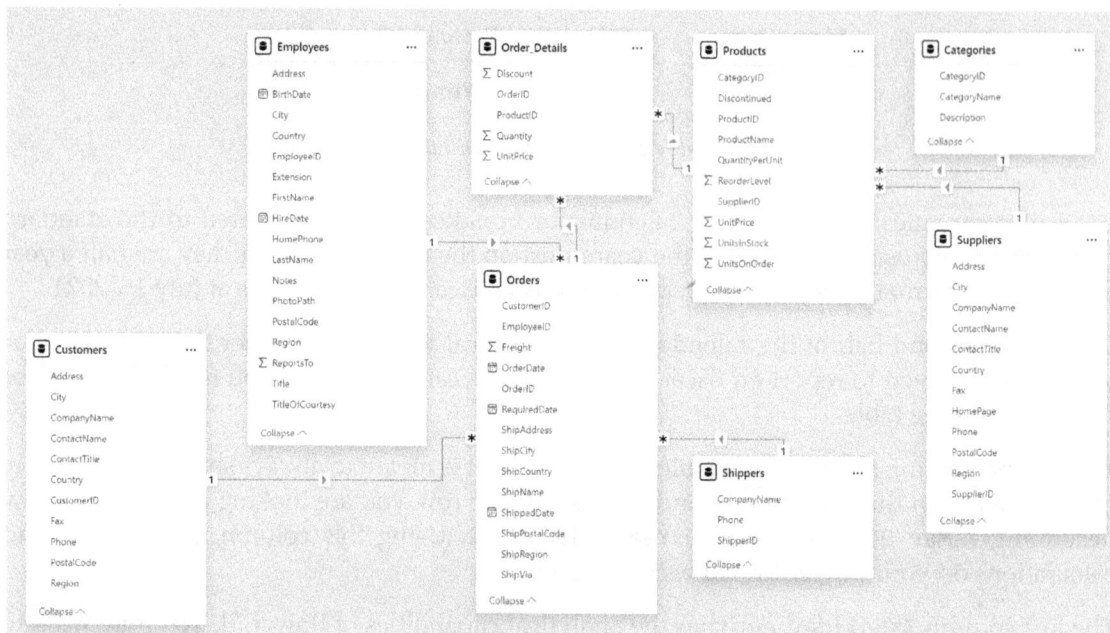

Figure 2.13: Northwind OLTP

A hopefully obvious dimension that can be derived from this database is the **Product** dimension. Using the facts that we discovered earlier, we can do something like **GrossSales** by product, and we will need a product dimension for that.

All columns in the table **Products** can serve as dimension columns except for **CategoryID** and **SupplierID**. These two columns are foreign keys to the tables **Category** and **Supplier**, respectively. Remember, though, that you may want to combine different tables into a single dimension table. Just as you know the product name of each product, you also know the category each product belongs to and the supplier we buy it from. Selecting columns based on what we will use later in the book, and after combining the table **Products** with **Categories** and **Suppliers**, the dimension table **Products** might look like the following table:

Attribute	Original table	Original column	Rule
ProductID	Products	ProductID	
ProductName	Products	ProductName	
PriceRange	Product	UnitPrice	< 20 = Cheap; < 40 = Moderate; else Expensive
Discontinued	Product	Discontinued	
Category	Categories	CategoryName	

Supplier	Suppliers	CompanyName	
TypeOfContact	Suppliers	ContactTitle	
Country	Suppliers	Country	

Table 2.3: dimProduct table

Note: **We selected just a few columns that keeps the table small. We may encounter some dataset size limitations through the Power BI license we use. Therefore, we keep the number of selected columns small, knowing we can add columns later when needed. Note further that we have one column that needs to be computed. We also renamed a couple of columns.**

The second dimension table is the customer dimension. This dimension is an almost exact copy of the table **Customers**.

The third dimension is the **ShipTo** dimension. Maybe you want to analyze the margin or shipping cost based on where orders are shipped to. You can find this data in the **Orders** table.

As a fourth dimension, we will create a **Shipper** dimension. It is again a straightforward translation from the table **Shippers**.

The last dimension is the employee dimension. It is based on the table **Employees** and will look like the following table:

Attribute	Original column	Rule
EmployeeID	EmployeeID	
LastName	LastName	
FirstName	FirstName	
TitleOfCourtesy	TitleOfCourtesy	
FullName	TitleOfCourtesy FirstName LastName	TitleOfCourtesy & FirstName & LastName
BirthDate	BirthDate	
AgeGroup	BirthDate	< 50 = Young else Old
HireDate	HireDate	
YearsInService	HireDate	Difference between today and **HireDate** in years
ReportsTo	ReportsTo	

Table 2.4: dimEmployee table

To recap, we see that we turned the normalized database that is shown in both *Figure 2.2* and *Figure 2.13* into a star schema with one fact table and five dimension tables. A date table will be added to the star schema design we create later in the book. Some columns from the original database could be used without changing, but we also created some calculated columns to enrich the data analysis capabilities of the data model. In *Chapter 3, The Basics of Power Query*, we will create the tables as described here. In *Chapter 4, The Basics of Visualizations*, we will start creating reports using the tables created in the next chapter and designed here.

Conclusion

Creating a star schema data model is key to Power BI development. Power BI itself does not have any prerequisites on how data is organized. The concept of fact tables and dimension tables exists only in our heads. Inside Power BI, a table is a table, and a column is a column. However, it is considered a best practice to transform your data into facts and dimensions before you start analyzing and visualizing the data.

An important step in defining the fact table is the grain you choose. Grain is the level of detail of your data. It directly impacts the size of your data model as well as what you can do with the data. Lower granularity (more detailed) means more rows inside your table, which means a bigger dataset. This level of detail allows you to ask much more detailed questions on your dataset.

The next chapter is about Power Query. It teaches you how to connect to different data sources. It will put the theory learned in this chapter into practice by using Power Query to transform data retrieved from a database into fact and dimension tables.

Multiple choice questions

1. **What type of columns does a fact table have?**

    a. Dimension attributes

    b. Facts

    c. Foreign key

    d. Primary key

2. **What type of columns does a dimension table have?**

    a. Dimension attributes

    b. Facts

    c. Foreign key

    d. Primary key

3. **When do you use a Snowflake model?**

    a. When you have one to many relationships between dimension attributes

    b. When you have two fact tables with different grain

    c. When you need to create a hierarchy from dimension attributes

    d. When you need to optimize the performance of your data model

Answers

1	b, c
2	a, d
3	b

Join our Discord space

Join our Discord workspace for latest updates, offers, tech happenings around the world, new releases, and sessions with the authors:

https://discord.bpbonline.com

CHAPTER 3
The Basics of Power Query

Introduction

In the previous chapter, you learnt about dimensional modeling and the difference between fact tables and dimensions. We created (in theory) a fact table and a couple of dimensions using the example database Northwind. We will connect to the Northwind database, and we will create the tables as described in *Chapter 2, Dimensional Modeling*.

Data in Power BI is read by Power Query. Power Query is an **extract, transform, and load (ETL)** tool. We need to transform the original table structure of Northwind into the desired facts and dimensions. However, Power Query is an extensive tool that uses the mashup language M. You will learn the basics of Power Query in this chapter, followed by some advanced techniques as well as the M-code in the upcoming chapters.

If you want to follow along with the examples presented in this chapter, you need Power BI Desktop to be installed on your workstation. Let us get started!

Structure

This chapter covers the following topics:

- Get data
- Select columns

- De-duplicate rows and generate keys
- Merge tables
- Custom columns
- Data types
- Aggregating tables
- Filtering rows
- Other transformations
- Challenge
- Close & Apply

Objectives

After reading this chapter, you will be able to connect to different types of data sources and read data from those sources. You will also be able to filter the data you read. You will learn how to combine tables, use tables multiple times, and create custom columns in your tables. You will see all the different data types Power BI supports and learn about their relevance. We will also have a quick look at other transformations available to you to prepare your data.

Get data

When you open the Power BI Desktop, your screen will look something like *Figure 3.1*. Power BI Desktop comes with a monthly update, meaning that screenshots in the book might be a bit outdated. The difference is not always significant.

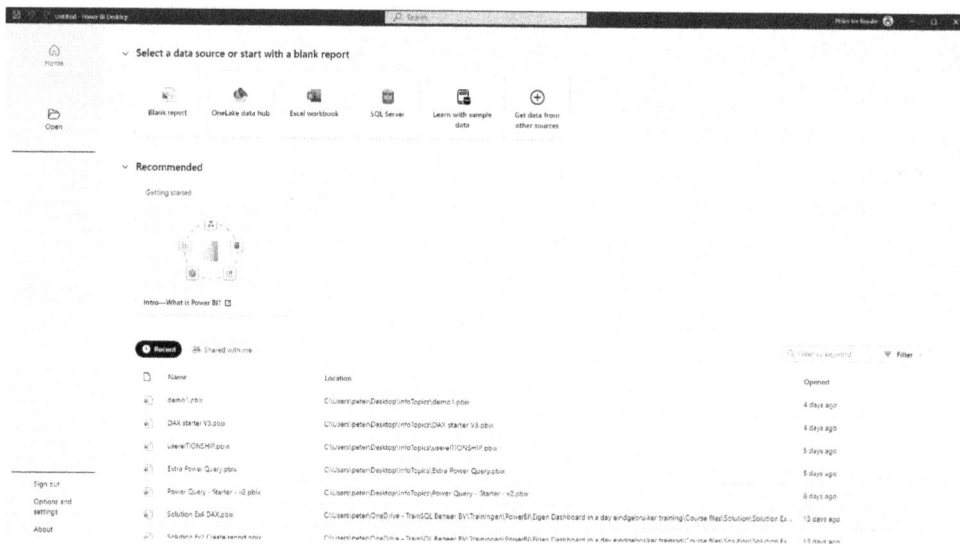

Figure 3.1: Power BI startup screen

At the bottom of the page, you will see earlier Power BI Desktop files you have been working on. Clicking on one will bring you back to that report. In the middle of the screen, you will see some tiles that present shortcuts to data sources that you may want to use. For instance, if you are going to use data stored in an SQL Server database, you can click on the tile that says SQL Server. It will immediately open a window that lets you connect to SQL Server. For now, we will start with a blank report:

1. Open Power BI Desktop, if you have not already done so.

2. Select **Blank report**. Your screen should now look similar to *Figure 3.2*:

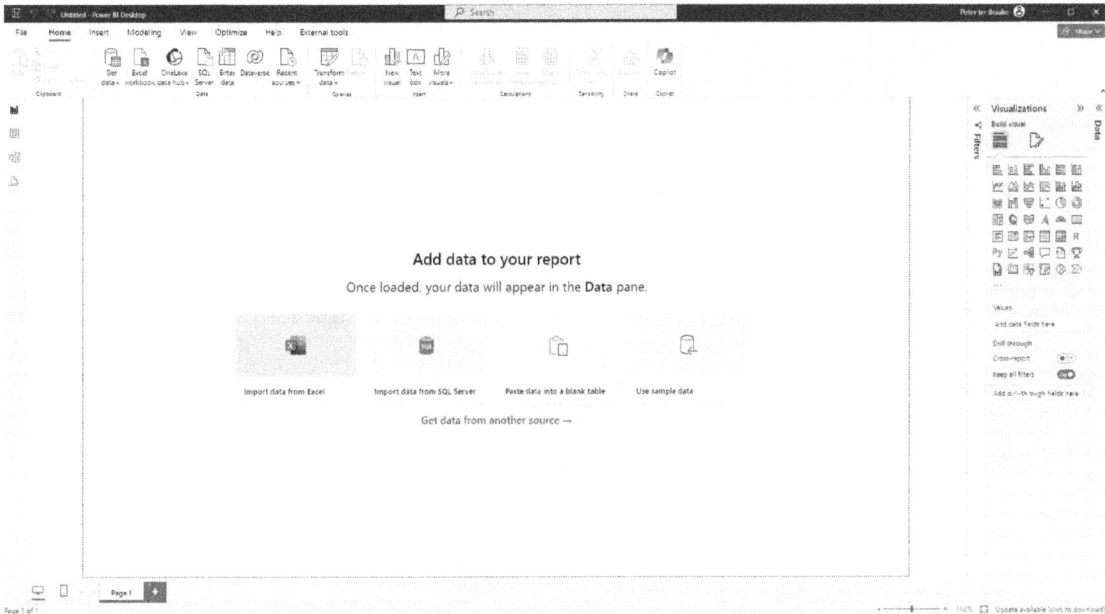

Figure 3.2: Power BI Desktop

The interface looks a bit familiar to people working with Microsoft Office applications. On top, you see the ribbons with buttons for easy access to often-used functionality. For now, notice the save icon all the way in the upper left corner, along with the menu **File** just under the save icon. You can save a Power BI Desktop file just as you can save a file in any Office application.

Depending on the regional setup of your workstation, your Power BI Desktop might be in your local language. To follow along with examples throughout the book, having all menus and buttons in English might be easier. So let us go ahead and change the language settings of Power BI Desktop.

3. Click on the menu **File**.

4. Now, click on **Options and settings** (lower, left-hand side of your screen).

5. Now, select **Options**.

   The **Options** dialog opens. Here, you can specify many settings. At this point, there is no need to go through all of them. However, the most valuable one now is on the page **Regional Settings**.

6. Click on **Regional Settings** (note that you have two pages with this name. One is located under the heading **GLOBAL**, the other one under **CURRENT FILE**. Select the global one).

7. On top of the page that opens, under **Application language**, select **English (United States)**.

8. Click on **OK** to close the dialog.

9. Restart Power BI Desktop.

   With Power BI Desktop in the language you prefer, it is time to read in data. We will go through all the items on your screen while building a Power BI report. You will be familiar with everything you see by the time you finish this book.

10. On the **Home** ribbon, click on the button **Get data**. Note that if you click in the top half of the button, the dialog for **Get Data** opens. If you click on the bottom half of the button **Get data**, a drop-down list appears showing the most common data source. It has an option **More...** that brings you to the **Get Data** dialog, as shown in the following figure:

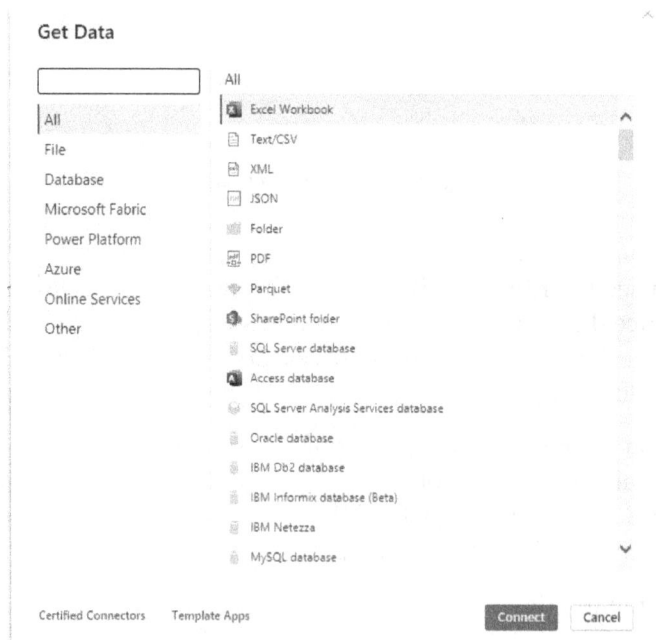

Figure 3.3: Get Data

Note: **Power BI has a long list of possible data sources that are available for use. Power Query allows for over more than 140 different data sources.**

Let us look at the most important sources:

- **SQL Server**: This is Microsoft's database management system and a much-used database at that. Both LOB systems and data warehouses can be built using SQL Server. When working with larger datasets, using SQL Server as a layer between your actual source and Power BI may be a good idea. SQL Server is available as an on-premises database, in different cloud versions, and as part of Synapse and Fabric. Chances are, you will sooner or later use SQL Server.

- **Excel**: A lot of companies today have a lot of data in Excel. If that data originates from a database, please try to connect to that database to get your data. For various reasons, like security or network connectivity, that is not always possible. Luckily, reading from Excel is easy. Some data is native Excel data. Budgets and targets are often entered in Excel.

- **Text/CSV**: You may get exports of data coming from a database that you cannot connect to directly. These exports will often come as delimited text files. **Comma separated value (CSV)** is the most common one. Power BI supports a wide range of file formats.

- **SharePoint/OneDrive**: SharePoint and OneDrive are different but based on the same underlying technology. OneDrive is where you store files in the cloud. It is part of Microsoft 365 (as Power BI is as well). Like Excel, SharePoint is used a lot and therefore stores a wealth of data. That data is accessible to you using Power BI.

- **Web**: You use Power BI's web option when you need to connect to a **software as a service (SaaS)** application. Nowadays, companies do a lot in the cloud. That means that you may need to get your data out of that cloud. Providers of SaaS applications offer **application programming interface (API)** to get your data. Using the web option, this data is available to you.

- **JSON**: More and more data comes in the form of **Java Script Object Notation (JSON)** files. It is a popular file format for data exchange over the internet or between applications. NoSQL document databases also use JSON to store data.

- **Parquet**: When working with modern data lakes, for instance, OneLake of Microsoft Fabric, files will likely be stored using the Parquet file format. Whether you know it or not, it does not matter. Power BI does and will use it just as easily as text or Excel files.

- **Fabric**: Strictly speaking, Fabric is not a data source. In the **Get Data** catalog, it is a category that encompasses multiple different sources (or technologies). Since Power BI is part of Fabric as well, it is likely you will use Fabric sources at some point.

  As already mentioned, there are a lot more potential data sources. It is not practical to go over all of them here. You will find out quickly though, that the source does not really matter. After you successfully make a connection to a source and select the data you want, data is data, and where you got it from is irrelevant.

Depending on the data source you use, you may or may not be required to enter credentials before being able to connect to your source. When working with files stored locally on your workstation, credentials are not required. However, when you connect to a database, an API, or another cloud resource, you will have to provide credentials. When everything is configured, conform best practices, you should be able to connect to most data sources without entering a username and password. The credentials you use to log into your workstation should suffice. You have to tell the data source that you want to use those credentials. You will almost always have to provide credentials, a key, or a token to connect when using APIs. In all cases, a database administrator, or in the case of an API, the supplier should provide you with the necessary information.

Let us look at three of the above-mentioned data sources in a little more detail. After we have done so, we will continue with the Northwind sample database from the previous chapter. The files used for the upcoming examples can be found in the downloads for the book. You can only follow along with the example of SQL Server when you do have an SQL Server available to you. The three data sources we will now look at are a text file, Excel workbook, and SQL Server.

Text or comma separated values

1. Make sure the **Get Data** dialog is still open.

2. Click on **Text/CSV** (there is a search box in the top left corner of the dialog for when you do not see the source you are looking for).

3. Click on **Connect**. The standard Windows File Explorer opens, allowing you to browse your hard drive and possibly file shares to find the file you want to use.

4. Select the file **Employee.csv** from the course files and click on **Open**.

   After you select a file, the data preview window opens to show the contents of the file. You use this window to check that the data looks as expected. When it does, you just click on either **Load** or **Transform Data** at the bottom of the window. If the preview does not look right, you need to look at the drop-down lists at the top of the window. You will be required to change the file origin setting when, for instance, special letters of a specific alphabet do not show correctly or when dates are wrong. Also, if you do not see the columns you expect to see, try changing the setting delimiter.

   The third drop-down list is called **Data Type Detection**. In Power BI, you create a database to use for the reports you are going to create. Data types of columns are important when creating a database. The Data Type Detection drop-down list determines whether Power BI should use all rows in your file to check whether the data is numerical, alphanumerical, or that you are dealing with dates. Power BI can use the first 200 rows only to determine data types. You can also choose not to detect data types automatically. All columns will be treated as alphanumerical. Normally, the default setting based on the first 200 rows will work just fine.

At the bottom of the window, you will see three buttons: **Load, Transform Data** and **Cancel**. Clicking on **Load** will import the data as you see it in the preview. **Transform Data** means the right data, but it needs some preparation before use. Clicking on **Transform Data** starts Power Query so that you can transform (prepare) the data. **Cancel** is self-explanatory.

5. Click on **Transform Data**.

    The **Power Query Editor** will open (see *Figure 3.4*). This is a separate window/ application from Power BI Desktop. The Power BI Desktop itself is still open in the background. We will learn the interface of the **Power Query Editor** as we go along. Notice the ribbon on top, which is similar to ribbons found in other applications, and like in Power BI Desktop. Additionally, see the query **Employee** on the left-hand side of your screen, the data preview in the middle, and **Query Settings** with **APPLIED STEPS** on the right-hand side of the screen, as shown in *Figure 3.4*:

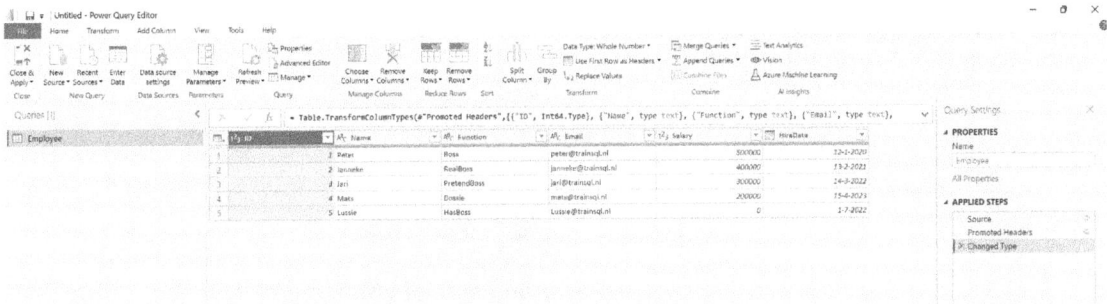

Figure 3.4: Power Query Editor

You work with queries inside the **Power Query Editor**. You read in the file **Employees.csv**, and it is now a query inside **Power Query Editor**. It is also often referred to as **table**. The preview of the data looks like (is) a table. Once you are ready with the **Power Query Editor**, the queries will be tables inside Power BI Desktop.

You may, at any point, close the **Power Query Editor** and return to it at a later point. To close it, click on **Close & Apply** on the **Home** ribbon. When back in Power BI Desktop, clicking on **Transform Data** will open **Power Query Editor** again.

We can add more data at any point in time, and it does not matter what data source we use for the additional data. You can use data coming from different sources. There may be performance implications when using data coming from different sources. There are no functional limitations when combining data from different sources.

To add more data, you can go back to the Power BI Desktop and use the option **Get Data** again. However, when you have the **Power Query Editor** still open, you can click on **New Source** in the **Home** ribbon to add new data. Let us do that and import some Excel data.

Excel

1. Click in the **Power Query Editor** on **New Source**, followed by **Excel workbook**.

2. Browse to the workbook **Import_AdventureWorks_Sales.xlsx** from the course files and select it. Click on **Open**.

    After opening an Excel file, a window called **Navigator** opens. The data preview you saw when importing **Text/CSV** data is a limited version of the **Navigator**. Excel has more to offer than a single text file, and Power BI analyzes the Excel workbook to help you. In the top left part of the window, Power Query lists all the sheets in the selected workbook. Based on formatting applied within sheets, Power Query also comes with suggested tables that can be regions of sheets or the raw data in the sheet, already prepared a little for you by Power Query. You can click on all sheets and suggested tables to get a preview of the data on those sheets or on that suggested table.

    Notice the multi-select option in the **Navigator**. You can import a single sheet or select multiple sheets at the same time.

    Also, note the **OK** and **Cancel** buttons in the bottom of the **Navigator**. When you connect to data from Power BI Desktop, you get the buttons **Load**, **Transform Data**, and **Cancel**. When you are already in **Power Query Editor**, it is just **OK** and **Cancel**.

3. Select the sheets **2024** and **2025** and click on **OK**.

    You should see three queries on the left-hand side of your screen. The query **Employee** from before and two new queries. They are called **2024** and **2025**, respectively, after the names of the sheets you imported. You can select each of the queries, and you will see the data from that query in your screen.

    An important thing to note here is that there is no difference between the query **Employee** and the two queries coming from Excel. For every data source, the first step when connecting to that source may be different. Once you are in the **Navigator** or in the **Power Query Editor**, there is no difference anymore. It does not matter where you get your data from. From this point on, data is just data, and you can use it according to your requirements. There is a nuance to this, but we will have to look at connecting to relational databases to discuss that nuance. To know further, let us discuss about importing some data from SQL Server.

SQL Server

To follow along with the steps in this section you need a SQL Server with Microsoft's AdventureWorks database in it.

1. Click in the **Power Query Editor** on **New Source**, followed by **SQL Server**.

   The dialog, as shown in *Figure 3.5*, will open:

   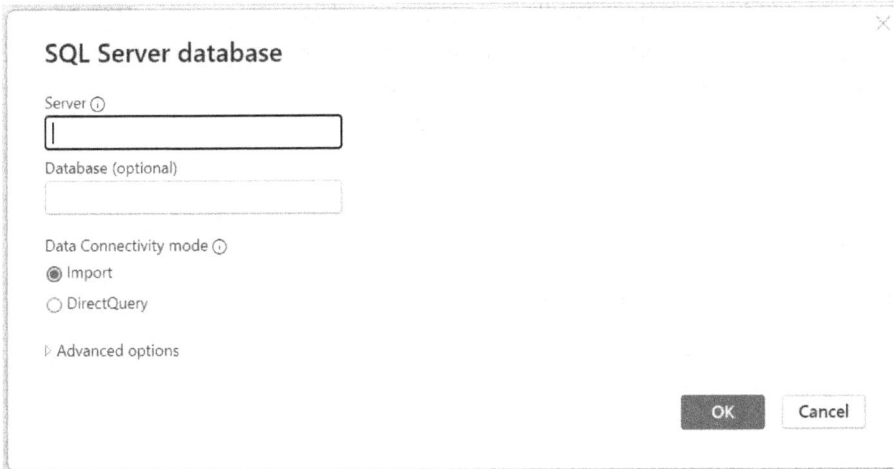

Figure 3.5: Connect to SQL Server

Connecting to SQL Server means you must provide the name of the SQL Server instance you want to connect to. A database administrator should provide you with this information. You can optionally provide the name of the database you want to connect to. With a lot of Azure SQL Database, depending on how security is setup, providing a database name is not optional at all.

The important thing to note in this dialog is the option called **Data Connectivity mode**. The default option is **Import**. It will import the data you select in the next step into Power BI. This means that Power BI has its own copy of the data. This is good for report performance, but you need to refresh your data every now and then to keep it up-to-date.

Your dataset may be too large to import. In that case, you can use the option **DirectQuery**. With this option, data is not imported, but Power BI queries the database in real-time at the time Power BI needs data. The data stays in the database and is only retrieved in bits when needed. This makes your reports slower, but data does not have to be refreshed, and there are no size restrictions to how large your dataset can be. We will talk about this in detail in *Chapter 10, Scalable Power BI Solutions*.

DirectQuery is only possible with a limited number of relational database sources. Data read from files or API's can only be imported. Another limitation of **DirectQuery** is that not all Power Query transformations are possible. Therefore, what you can do with Power Query is limited compared to what you can do with imported data.

2. Enter the name of your **Server** and **Database** and click on **OK**.

When you connect to a SQL Server for the first time, a security dialog will popup. You will have to provide proper credentials to be able to connect to your server. Proper credentials depend on how the security of the database is set up. An administrator should be able to help you connect. If you have connected to the SQL Server before, it will not ask for the credentials again. It saved your information for the first time and will reuse it to comply after that. To change the security information, go to **File** and select **Options and settings**. Choose **Data source settings** in Power BI Desktop, look for the connection to your database, and click on **Edit Permissions….**

Once you are successfully connected to the SQL Server, the **Navigator** opens. You can select tables and views from databases available.

3. If necessary, open the AdventureWorks database.

4. Select the table **Production.Product** and click on **OK**.

You will see a fourth query inside the **Power Query Editor**. You can start to transform the data as required. For the examples used in this book, we will, however work with different tables that we get from the internet. Northwind is made available as an OData feed. Before making a connection to Northwind, let us delete the queries we have created so far.

5. Right-click on the queries in the left-hand side of the screen and click on **Delete** in the popup menu. (Note that multi-select on the queries is possible.)

It is time to take it a step further and start transforming data.

Select columns

From here on, we will continue with the example we started in *Chapter 2, Dimensional Modeling*. We need to import the tables from the Northwind database.

1. Click on **Get data** button when in Power BI Desktop or on **New Source** when still in **Power Query Editor**.

2. Choose the **OData feed** option.

3. In the dialog that opens type: `http://services.odata.org/v3/northwind/northwind.svc`

4. Click on **OK**.

5. In the **Navigator**, select the following tables and click on **Transform Data** or on **OK**.
   a. `Categories`
   b. `Customers`
   c. `Orders`
   d. `Order_Details`

    e. **Products**

    f. **Shippers**

    g. **Suppliers**

6. Check that you now have seven queries with the same names as the tables you imported.

   You do not need all the columns that you find in a table. As a general best practice, delete the columns you will not use. We will start with the table **Customers**. After analyzing the data, you understand that the columns **Address**, **Region**, **PostalCode**, and **Fax** are not required. There are multiple ways to delete them.

7. Select the table **Customers** in the left-hand side of the **Power Query Editor**.

8. Select the column **Address** (click in the column header). Now either hit the *Delete* button on your keyboard or right-click in the header and select **Remove** in the popup list. You can repeat the steps for the other columns you want to delete.

   Have a look at the **Query Settings** window on the right-hand side of the **Power Query Editor** and under **APPLIED STEPS**. It shows three steps: **Source**, **Navigation**, and **Removed Columns**, as shown in the following figure:

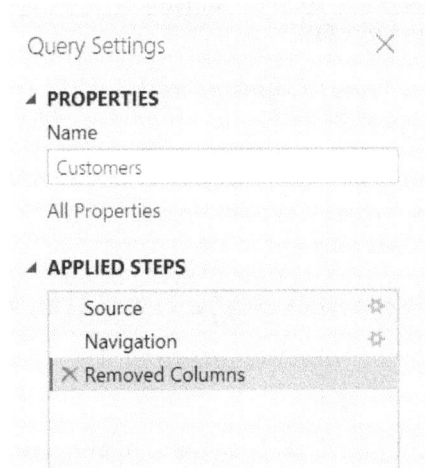

Figure 3.6: Query Settings

The **Removed Columns** step was added when you deleted the columns. When you hover your mouse over any step, a little **x**-icon is shown before the step name. Clicking on it will delete the step and, with it, undo the entire operation. Before you delete the step, notice there is no gear icon behind the name of the step **Removed Columns**.

9. Delete the step **Removed Columns** by clicking on the little delete icon in front of the name of the step.

10. Now, multi-select all the columns you want to delete and hit the *Delete* button on your keyboard. You can delete the columns one by one if you wish. The result is the same.

11. Delete the step **Removed Columns** again.

12. Now select all the columns you want to keep and right-click in the header of one of the selected columns. Note the option **Remove Other Columns** in the popup list that appears.

    The text of the option you selected is self-explanatory. You deleted the columns you did not select. However, have a look at the **APPLIED STEPS**. The third step is now called **Removed Other Columns**. More importantly, it has a little gear icon after its name. When you click on it, a dialog will appear that allows you to easily change the selection you made.

13. Click on the gear icon after the **Removed Other Columns** step.

14. Close the dialog and delete the entire step (for the last time).

15. Click on the button **Choose Columns** (upper part) in the **Home** ribbon. Note that the **Choose Columns** dialog you just saw opens, allowing you to select columns.

16. Select the columns **CustomerID**, **CompanyName**, **ContactName**, **ContactTitle**, **City**, **Country**, and **Phone**. Click on **OK**.

17. Note the step **Removed Other Columns** in the **APPLIED STEPS** and the gear icon after the name of the step.

Now that we have our first dimension table ready, let us move on to the **ShipTo** dimension. We need to do some more work to prepare that table.

De-duplicate rows and generate keys

The next table we will look at is the **ShipTo** dimension. This dimension is based on the table **Orders**.

1. Double-click on the query **Orders**. Rename it to **ShipTo**.

   The name of the query can be changed by simply double clicking the name and changing it. The name also appears in the **Query Settings** windows, in the right-hand side of the **Power Query Editor**. You can change it here as well. Right-clicking on the name of the query provides the option **Rename** in the popup menu.

2. Select the following columns for the **ShipTo** dimension (meaning remove all other columns):

   a. **ShipName**

   b. **ShipAddress**

    c. **ShipCity**

    d. **ShipPostalCode**

    e. **ShipCountry**

When you define your tables, try to have your Power BI reports that you will create using this data in mind. What will help in creating good reports is nice, understandable column names. Having all names start with *Ship* does not make sense anymore.

3. Rename all columns by removing the word *Ship* from the name. You can double click in a column header to rename it. You can also right-click in the header and select **Rename** from the popup menu.

After selecting and renaming the columns, more work might be required in preparing the data. Consider what happens when different orders are shipped to the same address. Each order is a row in the table **Orders**, and the address is entered for each order. You end up with duplicate rows. You need to de-duplicate the rows, and Power Query can help.

4. Select all the columns of the **ShipTo** query. Right-click on the header of one of the columns and select **Remove Duplicates** from the popup menu.

Note: **You go from 830 rows in the table back to just 90 rows.**

The last step in creating the **ShipTo** dimension is to define a primary **key** for this table. Power Query has the **Index Column** feature for this.

5. Click on the little arrow after the **Index Column** property on the **Add Column** ribbon. Select **From 1** in the popup.

6. Rename the column to **ShipToKey**.

7. If you prefer to have a key shown as the first column of a table, you can drag to column **ShipToKey** to the left and make it the first column.

This concludes our **ShipTo** dimension. Let us continue with the **Products** dimension.

Merge tables

In the previous chapter, we designed the **Products** dimension. Please see the table for the details:

Attribute	Original table	Original column	Rule
ProductID	Products	ProductID	
ProductName	Products	ProductName	
PriceRange	Product	UnitPrice	< 20 = Cheap; < 40 = Moderate; else Expensive
Discontinued	Product	Discontinued	
Category	Categories	CategoryName	
Supplier	Suppliers	CompanyName	
TypeOfContact	Suppliers	ContactTitle	
Country	Suppliers	Country	

Table 3.1: Product table description

The first thing to note here is that we use columns from different tables in the source database. So, we need to combine multiple tables into a single one. This is called **joining tables** in SQL and is the **Merge** functionality of Power Query:

1. Select the query **Products**.

    When you take a close look at the columns of the query **Products** you may notice the last three columns: **Category**, **Order_Details**, and **Supplier**. These columns are not really columns; they are references to other tables in the Northwind database. Power Query analyzes the source database and, knowing you may want to combine tables, tries to help you. When you ignore these columns, as done in queries **Orders** and **Customers**, they will disappear as soon as you close **Power Query Editor** to return to Power BI Desktop.

    On closer inspection, you may notice that the column **Order_Details** has a different icon than the other two and shows the text table in each cell. The text is actually a link. The table **Products** has a one to many relationship with **Order_Details**. The relationship to the other tables is reversed. They are many to one relationships.

    The next step is to combine the query **Products** with the query **Categories** using the column **Categories** we just discussed.

2. Click on the little button in the column header of the column **Categories** with an icon that shows two arrows pointing outward. It is in the right-hand side of the column header (behind the name of the column). It is called the **Expand** button.

3. In the popup that appears, remove all checkmarks except the one in front of the column **CategoryName**. Also remove the checkmark at the bottom for the option **Use original column name as prefix**. Click on **OK**.

The column **Categories** that referenced the table **Categories** is now replaced by the column you selected. In this case, that is just the column **CategoryName**. If you had kept the option, **Use original column name as prefix** selected, the name of the column would have been **Categories.CategoryName**. Without the option selected, it is simply **CategoryName**. Prefixing a column name with the table name helps to keep column names unique within the table you create. This is a requirement for each table.

As you can see in the table in the beginning of this section, we also need three columns from the table **Suppliers**. Of course, you can take the same approach as with **Categories**. However, suppose the Northwind database was not setup as nicely as it is, and Power Query would not have detected the relationship between them or consider the scenario where you need to combine queries coming from different sources. Now, Power Query will certainly not have detected possible relationships.

Instead of using the **Suppliers** column, we will join the queries by performing the necessary steps ourselves.

4. Make sure the query **Products** is still selected.

5. Click on the button **Merge Queries** almost all the way to the right in the **Home** ribbon. The **Merge** dialog appears.

6. Notice the drop-down list halfway down the **Merge** dialog. Click on it and notice it lists all queries you already have in **Power Query Editor**. Select **Suppliers**. A data preview of **Suppliers** will show.

When merging two tables, you will have to tell Power Query how that merge should be performed. Databases are setup in such a way that tables relate to each other by a common column. Normally, in one table, this column should hold unique values. This is normally the primary key. The other table has the same column (although the name may be different), but this column does not necessarily hold unique values. We speak of a primary key and foreign key relationship. You can merge two tables in a lot of ways, but most of the time, only relationships make sense.

In the example, both queries have a column named **SupplierID**. That column serves as in the query **Suppliers** and as in the query **Products**.

7. Select the column **SupplierID** in both queries in the **Merge** dialog by simply clicking in the header.

Notice the drop-down list named **Join Kind** under the second query. There are a couple of scenarios to consider while merging tables. They are as follows:

   a. **Left Outer (all from first, matching from second)**: Suppose you have products that you create yourself; these products do not have a supplier from where you purchase them or consider a product for which it is not known who the supplier is. What happens to the rows describing these products after the merge? With the left outer join, you will have the exact same rows in your table as you had before the join. You do not lose rows when there is no supplier defined for a product.

b. **Right Outer (all from second, matching from first)**: This is basically the same, but reasoned from the other table. When you have a one to many relationship, it usually makes sense to want all rows from the many side and matching rows from the one side. In our example, **Suppliers** is the one side of the relationship. This option makes no sense in our scenario because we work from the **Products** query.

c. **Full Outer (all rows from both)**: In this example, all rows from both would mean you get all suppliers, even the ones that you do not buy any products from. You will also get all products, including the ones that have no supplier. You also get all rows with a match based in **SupplierID**. This option almost never makes sense.

d. **Inner (only matching rows)**: This option returns all rows from the first table with a corresponding (matching) row in the second table. In other words, it returns all products with supplier information for products that have a matching **SupplierID**. Products that do not have a matching supplier are filtered out. The choice will often be between this option and the left outer option. No one is good or better; they are functionally slightly different, and it is up to you to decide what you need.

e. **Anti joins**: There are two anti joins that have similar behavior. Sometimes you just need the rows that have no matching rows. In a lot of cases, you can use simple filters on the table. Sometimes you merge tables to get just those rows.

Let us get back to our example. At the bottom of the **Merge** dialog, a message is displayed saying *the selection matches 77 of the 77 rows from the first table*. This means that each product has a supplier. It also means that the *left outer* and *inner join* options return the same results.

The **Merge** dialog also provides a **Fuzzy matching** option. This is a more advanced option where you try to match rows on text data where the texts may not be identical. In a normal join, the words *text* and *tekst* are different. They are not identical. With fuzzy matching, they may be similar, leading to a match.

8. Click on **OK** in the **Merge** dialog.

After the **Merge** dialog closes, a column is added to the original query with the name of the query you joined with. This new column has the **Expand** button in the header.

9. Expand the new column. Select only the columns **CompanyName**, **ContactTitle** and **Country**. Do not use column prefixes.

10. Delete all columns you do not need according to *Table 3.1* and rename the ones you keep to match the column names as depicted in *Table 3.1*. For now, just keep the column **UnitPrice** as is and do not worry about the computed column **PriceRange**. We will create that column in the next section.

You just learned two ways two merge two queries. The first was easy enough. The second is slightly more difficult. The second way gives you more options on how to join the tables. It is always possible to use this method even when Power Query cannot help you to merge queries. Therefore, it is good to have learned.

There is, however another difference between the two options. We never actually used the query **Categories** that we imported. That means that we can delete it from our list of queries.

11. Go ahead and delete the query **Categories**. However, how about **Suppliers**?

12. Select the query **Products**.

Look at the **APPLIED STEPS** in the **Query Settings** pane in the right-hand side of **Power Query Editor**. It should look like *Figure 3.7*:

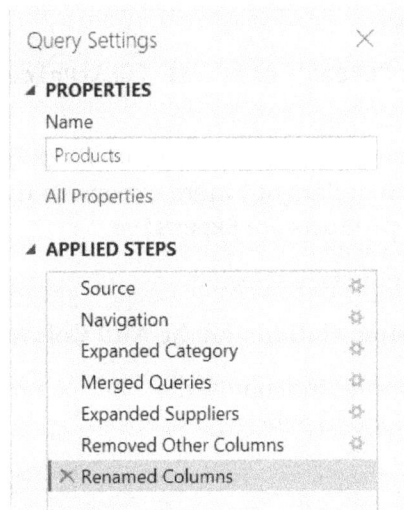

Figure 3.7: APPLIED STEPS

Note: **Every time you perform an operation in Power BI Desktop like renaming columns, removing columns, merging tables and so on, a step is added to the APPLIED STEPS list. You can select each step, and the data preview shows how your data looked after the selected step is performed. The result of all steps is the data that will get imported into Power BI. Every time the data is refreshed, all steps are performed again. The result is again imported.**

Merged Queries is a step where the **Suppliers** query gets merged with our query **Products**. If you delete the query **Suppliers** from the list of all queries, and you refresh the data, the **Merged Queries** step will fail.

Thus, we cannot delete the query **Suppliers,** but we also do not need it anymore as a separate table. All relevant columns have been added to the **Products** dimension. This is why Power Query has the option **Enable Load** that you can turn off. The query is not deleted, but the data will not be loaded into Power BI. The query will not be present as a table in Power BI Desktop.

13. Right-click on the query **Suppliers** in the list of queries and select the option **Enable Load** in the popup menu.

14. Click on **Continue** when Power Query says: **Possible Data Loss Warning**.

Notice the name of the query **Suppliers** is now shown in italic format.

Custom columns

To finish the **Products** dimension, we need to add a calculated column to the query. The formula to calculate the column is:

```
= if [UnitPrice] < 20 then "Cheap" else (if [UnitPrice] < 40 then "Moderate"
else "Expensive")
```

This formula calculates the price range a product falls in. Products cheaper than **20** dollars are **Cheap**. Products cheaper than **40** dollars but more expensive than or equal to **20** dollars are considered **Moderate**. All other products are **Expensive**.

1. Make sure the query **Products** is selected.

2. Click on the button **Custom Column** on the **Add Column** ribbon.

3. Use the preceding formula and name the new column **PriceRange**. The **Custom Column** dialog should look like the screenshot of *Figure 3.8*:

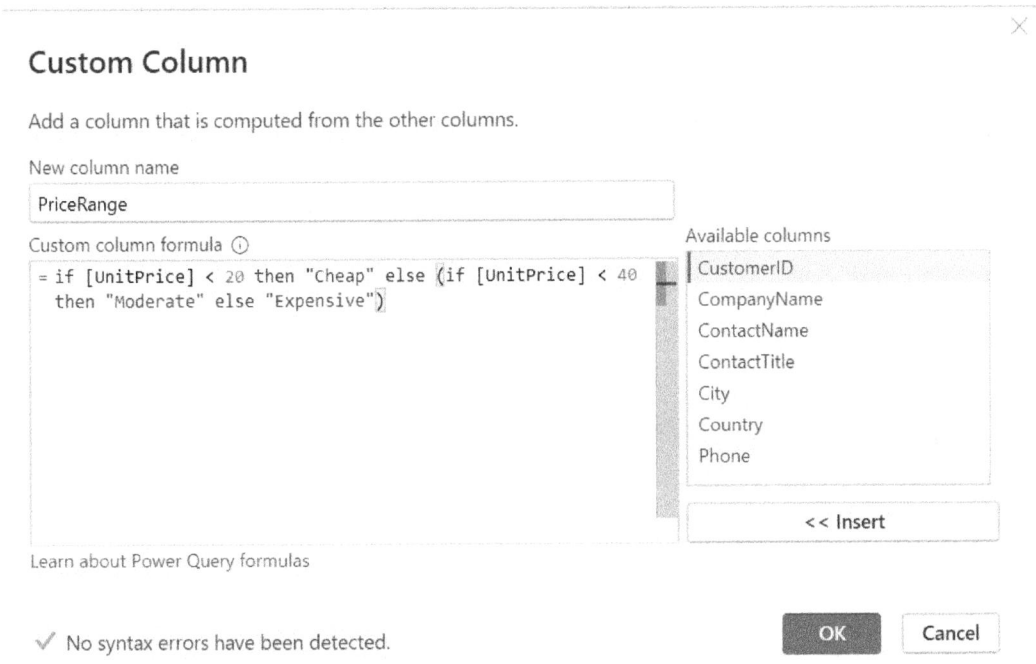

Custom Column

Add a column that is computed from the other columns.

New column name

PriceRange

Custom column formula ⓘ

```
= if [UnitPrice] < 20 then "Cheap" else (if [UnitPrice] < 40
   then "Moderate" else "Expensive")
```

Available columns

CustomerID
CompanyName
ContactName
ContactTitle
City
Country
Phone

<< Insert

Learn about Power Query formulas

✓ No syntax errors have been detected.

OK   Cancel

Figure 3.8: Custom Column

The language used here is called M for mashup language and is the language of Power Query. We will have a closer look at M-code in *Chapter 5, Advanced Techniques of Power Query*. For now, you need to understand that you can create new columns from existing ones by doing calculations on the existing columns. Our column **PriceRange** is just an example of that.

Note: **The column names should always by closed in square brackets. With normal brackets, you can nest expression. In the preceding example, an if is nested inside the else of the first if. M-code is always case-sensitive. If written with a capital 'I' it will lead to syntax errors.**

Power Query is a low-code/no-code ETL tool, and yet here we are writing an M expression.

A simpler way to do this is as follows:

1. With the query **Products** still selected, click on the button **Conditional Column** on the **Add Column** ribbon.

2. Fill in the dialog that opens as shown in *Figure 3.9*. You get the **Else If** option by clicking on the button **Add Clause**.

3. Click on **OK** when you finish filling in the dialog.

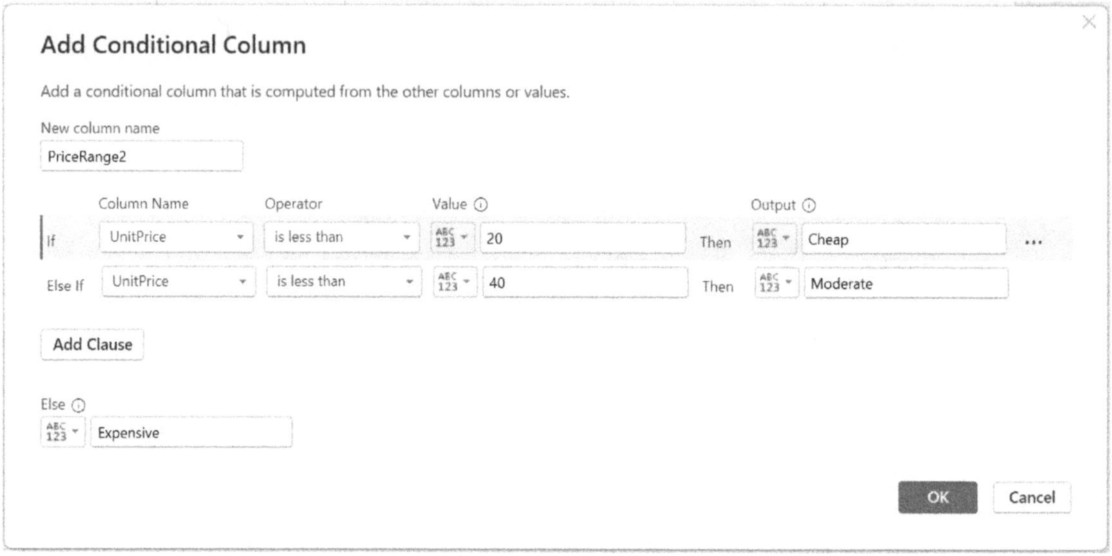

Figure 3.9: Add Conditional Column

4. Note that the result of what you just did is the same of the first custom column we created.

5. Click in the **APPLIED STEPS** list on the gear icon behind the step named **Added Custom**. This is the step where you added a column using an M-code expression.

6. Note that the **Add Conditional Column** dialog opens, and it is the same as *Figure 3.9* except the column name.

7. Delete the last step from the list of **APPLIED STEPS**. You do not need the same column twice.

8. Delete the column **UnitPrice** from the query. Now that you have a column **PriceRange** you do not need the column **UnitPrice** anymore.

This finalizes the **Products** dimension. The last table we need to create, referring to the Northwind examples from the previous chapter, is the fact table which is as follows:

Fact	Original table	Based on	Rule
CustomerID	Orders	CustomerID	
ProductID	Order_De-tails	ProductID	
ShipToID	Orders	OrderID	
ShipperID	Orders	ShipperID	

OrderDate	Orders	OrderDate	
DiscountAmount		Discount	[Quantity] * [UnitPrice] * [Discount]
Quantity		Quantity	-
UnitPrice		UnitPrice	-
GrossSales		Quantity UnitPrice	[Quantity] * [UnitPrice]
NetSales		Quantity UnitPrice Discount	[Quantity] * [UnitPrice] * (1 - [Discount])
Freight		Freight	[Freight] / # of order lines
Margin		NetSales Freight	[NetSales] - [Freight]
DaysToShipment		OrderDate ShipDate	[ShipDate] - [OrderDate] (in days)

Table 3.2: factSales table

Note: Compared to the table as shown in Chapter 2, Dimensional Modeling we added a few columns. The first five columns in this table are foreign keys to dimension tables. You already created the dimension tables, except for a Date table. We will add the Date table later.

The fourth column of *Table 3.2* shows the (generic) rule for how the computed column should be computed. Some of the rules can be copied directly to Power Query custom columns. Some are slightly more difficult to implement.

9. Select the query **Order_Details**.

10. Click on the button **Custom Column** on the **Add Column** ribbon.

11. Create a custom column called **DiscountAmount** and use the rule from the table as the expression to calculate this column.

Have a look at the values inside the newly created column. You see values with a lot of decimal places, like *222,6000088*. This does not look right. Before continuing, we need to discuss data types.

Data types

In this chapter, you have been creating tables based on the data we imported. With Power BI, you basically create an in-memory database, which is called the Power BI semantic model. The semantic model has a lot of properties that will help us when we start creating visualizations using Power BI's drag-and-drop functionality. However, the basis of the semantic model is tables and their relationships. A very important part of creating tables in a database is choosing the data types of all columns.

Data types basically determine two things:

- The values you can store in a column.

- The manipulations you can do with the data in the column.

A column of data type text can store anything. It is meant to store data like names and codes. A lot of dimension attributes will be of these data types. The dimension attributes are the readable labels we use to analyze facts. *Readable* will often mean textual, although that is not necessarily the case.

Text is also called **alphanumerical** as opposed to numerical data. Numerical data are numbers. You can perform mathematical operations on numbers. You can calculate new numbers using existing ones. Most facts in the fact table will be numerical.

Power BI has four different data types that all fall into the category of numerical. These are:

- Decimal number

- Fixed decimal number

- Whole number

- Percentage

A decimal number is what, in a lot of programming languages, is called **float** or **real**. You can store big numbers as well as numbers with a lot of decimal places (digits behind the decimal point). This is the data type you must use when working with numeric data that needs more than four digits after the decimal point. The price you pay for this is possible inaccuracy. It is an approximate data type, and that results in values like the *222,6000088* we saw earlier.

A fixed decimal number is equivalent to money in SQL Server and currency in a lot of other databases. It stores decimal numbers with four digits after the decimal point. Always four. When doing arithmetic with it, you may get rounding issues at the fourth decimal place, but not at the second (cents). You can recognize this data type by the $ icon used for it within Power BI. When you do not need more than 4 digits after the decimal point, this data type is preferable over a decimal number, even when not working with money:

1. In the query **Order_Details,** go to the **APPLIED STEPS** list and select the step called **Navigation** (above **Added Custom**).

2. Find the column **Discount** and note the values in this column. 15% discount shows as *0,150000006*. You do not want to perform calculations with these values.

3. Click on the little icon **1.2** in the column header of the column `Discount` (before the column name).

4. Select the data type **Fixed decimal number** in the popup menu that appears.

5. Click on **Insert** in the dialog box that shows (Power Query warns that you do not add a transformation to the end of your query but that you are inserting a step somewhere in the middle of the query. This can potentially break the rest of the query).

6. Note how the values in the column `Discount` change.

7. Select the step called **Added Custom** in the **APPLIED STEPS** and look at the values you now see in the column `DiscountAmount`. The value *222,6000088* became *222,6*.

Let us go back to discussing the available data types. The data type **Whole number** speaks for itself. **Percentage** is another story altogether. Our column `Discount` is a percentage, but we did not use this data type. We may try though, and see what happens.

8. Delete the step **Changed Type** in the **APPLIED STEPS**, and now change the column `Discount` into `Percentage`. Check the values in the computed column `DiscountAmount`.

Using `Percentage` as the data type did not solve the problem of inaccuracy in the values of the column `DiscountAmount`. Percentages are more of a formatting of numbers than a real data type. Formatting should be done on the report when showing values. Not in columns when you might still need to perform calculations with the values. You will almost never need this data type. You will use formatting on the report.

9. Change the data type of the column `Discount` back to **Fixed decimal number**.

There are some other data types to mention quickly before continuing to create our fact table. Power BI knows the data types **Date/time, Date,** and **Time**. They store the date and time combined in a single column or the data and time separately. Pay extra attention to the data type **Date/time**. This data type is used a lot. However, on reports, very often only the date part is used. When you do not use time in any of the visuals or calculations you create, use **Date** instead of **Date/time**. It is more efficient.

The data type **Date/Time/Timezone** is a special one. It exists in the Power Query Editor. Once loaded into the Power BI semantic model, it becomes a **Date/time**. Inside Power Query this data type helps to convert datetimes coming from different time zones into a local time zone for comparison (and linking). 8 AM in Amsterdam is not the same as 8 AM in New York. However, you may have to compare events that happened in Amsterdam and events that happened in New York to see if they occurred at the same time, and if not, which event occurred earlier.

The data type **Duration** is a bit similar to **Date/Time/Timezone**, as that it only exists inside Power Query. It becomes a **Decimal number** when loaded into the semantic model. During calculations, it lets you easily subtract or add periods from dates and **Date/time** data types. Let us use a simple example. We need a column called **DaysToShipment** that, according to the table showing the design of our fact table, is calculated by subtracting the order date from the ship date.

10. Expand the column **Orders** in the query **Order_Details** (Expand button in the right-hand side of the header of the column **Orders**).

11. Select the following columns (these columns all form foreign keys to the dimension tables we created earlier. Plus, we added both date columns we need for the custom column **DaysToShipment**).

   a. **CustomerID**
   b. **EmployeeID**
   c. **Freight**
   d. **OrderDate**
   e. **ShippedDate**
   f. **ShipVia**

12. Click on the button **Custom Column** on the **Add Column** ribbon. Use the formula given and name the new column **DaysToShipment**.

   = Duration.Days([ShippedDate] - [OrderDate])

   This formula uses the **Duration** data type to calculate the difference between two dates in days. The resulting data type, however, is not a **Duration**. If you look in the header of the column **DaysToShipment** you see an icon showing *abc* and *123* under it. This is Power Query letting you know that it could not determine the data type of this column.

13. Change the data type of the column **DaysToShipment** to **Whole number**.

   The last two data types remaining to discuss are **True/false** and **Binary**. **True/false** (Boolean) stores just the values true and false. This can be very useful. For instance, you can keep track for every day on the calendar, whether that day is a holiday or not. You use the data type **True/false** for a column like that.

   Be careful with the data type **Binary**. You can store anything in that type of column. However, it is inefficient and often may not have a lot of analytical value. Images may be an example where you may need to use **Binary**.

   With all data types discussed, let us continue to implement our fact table. We still need to create a couple of custom columns.

14. Create the following custom columns. Make sure the data types of the resulting column are **Fixed decimal number**.

   a. **GrossSales**: **[Quantity] * [UnitPrice]**

    b. **NetSales**: `[Quantity] * [UnitPrice] * (1 - [Discount])`

We are almost there, but the custom column `Freight` is slightly more difficult to implement. We need to divide the column `Freight` by the number of order lines. We will have to calculate the number of orderliness first, and we need to aggregate the query **Order_Details** to do that.

Aggregating tables

Let us look at how to aggregate a table:

1. Make a duplicate of the query **Order_Details**.

2. Delete all columns except the column `OrderID`.

3. Rename the query to **CountOrderLines**.

    Aggregating data is combining rows that have a common value for a column (or columns) into a new row. In our query **Products**, we have, for instance, a column `CategoryName`. You can transform this table to hold a single row for each category. You would use the **Group by** transformation using the `CategoryName` column to literally, group by. You can then, for instance, count how many rows you add together in a group to create a new row.

4. With the new query **CountOrderLines** still selected, click on **Group by** on the **Transform** ribbon.

    You will see the **Group by** dialog. In here, you specify what criterion (column or columns) to use to group by on and what columns to calculate over the combined rows. You always need an aggregation function to calculate rows. Aggregation functions are functions like `Count rows, Sum, Min, Max, Average`, etc. They have in common that they calculate a single value using multiple input values.

    A `Count rows` column is automatically added when the **Group by** dialog opens. That column is all we need for now.

5. Click on **OK** to close the dialog.

6. Select the query **Order_Details**.

7. Click on the button **Merge Queries** almost all the way to the right in the **Home** ribbon. The **Merge** dialog appears.

8. Select the query **CountOrderLines** in the drop-down list halfway down the **Merge** dialog.

9. Select the column **OrderID** in both queries within the dialog.

10. Select the **Inner join**.

11. Click on **OK**.

12. Expand the new column called **CountOrderLines** and select only the column called **Count** (keep **Use original column name as prefix** unselected).

    Now that you have calculated the number of rows (lines, details) for each order, you can create the two final custom columns.

13. Create the following custom columns. Make sure the data types of the resulting column are **Fixed decimal number**.

    a. **Freight**: **[Freight] / [Count]** (because there already is a column called **Freight** you cannot create one with the same name. So, give it another name at first, then delete the original column **Freight**, and then rename the custom column.)

    b. **Margin**: **[NetSales] - [Freight]**

14. Make both new columns of data type **Fixed decimal number**.

15. Make sure the table **CountOrderLines** will not be loaded into the semantic model.

    There is one last issue to solve while implementing the fact table. We need the key of the **ShipTo** dimension to be able to create a relationship to the **ShipTo** dimension later.

16. Click on the button **Merge Queries** almost all the way to the right in the **Home** ribbon. The **Merge** dialog appears.

17. Select the query **ShipTo** in the drop-down list halfway down the **Merge** dialog.

18. Select the column **ShipName** in the query **Order_Details** and **Name** in **ShipTo**.

19. Select the **Inner join**.

20. Click on **OK**.

21. Expand the new column called **ShipTo** and select only the column called **Index** (keep **Use original column name as prefix** unselected).

22. Rename the column **Index** to **ShipToID**.

    This almost finishes creating the fact table. We still need to rename it, and we must delete all columns we do not need. The very last step should always be to check the data types of all columns and change them if they are not correct.

23. Rename the query to **Sales**.

24. Make sure your query only has the following columns (delete all other columns):
    a. **CustomerID**
    b. **ProductID**
    c. **ShipToID**
    d. **ShipVia**

    e. `EmployeeID`

    f. `OrderDate`

    g. `ShippedDate`

    h. `DiscountAmount`

    i. `Quantity`

    j. `UnitPrice`

    k. `GrossSales`

    l. `NetSales`

    m. `Freight`

    n. `Margin`

    o. `DaysToShipment`

25. Make sure all columns have the correct data types.

    Even though we are done, let us do one more transformation. Northwind is a great example database to learn Power BI with. However, it is so old. All orders took place in the years 1996, 1997, and 1998. Let us add 25 years to those dates, just to have a more up-to-date feeling for the remainder of the book.

26. Create a new custom column. Name it **OrderDate1**. Use the formula:

    `= Date.AddYears( [OrderDate], 25)`

27. Delete the column **OrderDate**.

28. Rename **OrderDate1** to **OrderDate**.

29. Do the same for the column **ShippedDate**.

Filtering rows

In our example, we needed all rows that we read from the source system. In real life, the first thing to consider is which rows of a query you need and, more importantly, the ones you do not need. Suppose you analyze operations performed on patients in a hospital over the last two years. Obviously, you only need operations from the last two years. It is important to note, though, that you could read in all operations from the entire history of the hospital and then use filtering on the report while analyzing the data. This may be a large number of rows that you are going to use. Import all rows when you are going to use all rows. Import only those rows that you are actually going to use.

The **Patients** dimension needs filtering, too. When reading in a **Patients** table from an **electronic patient dossier (EPD)** system, you get all patients. Patients who were not in the hospital for the last two years are imported as well or consider staff that quit more than two years ago. They did not operate on patients within the last two years and can be filtered out.

Think about your data and work with only rows that you are going to use.

Filtering in Power Query Editor is straightforward. Have a look at *Figure 3.10*:

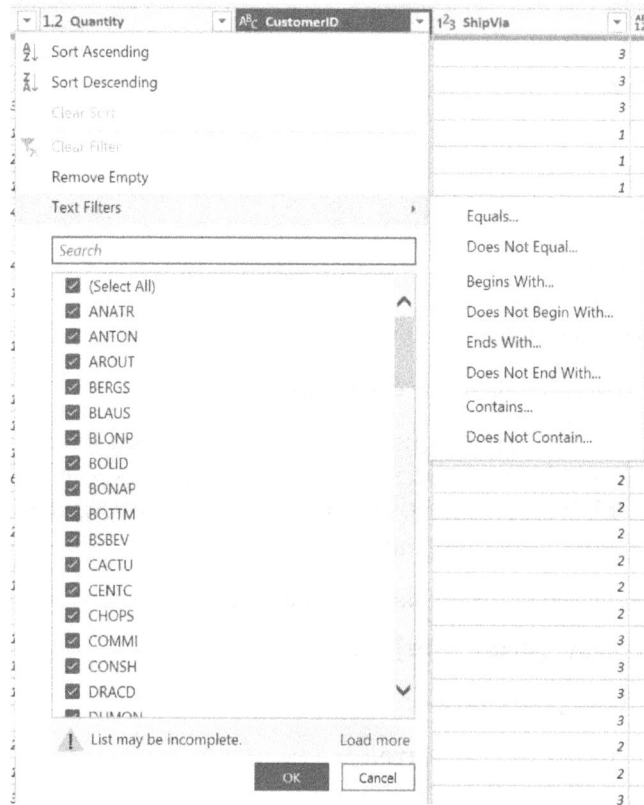

Figure 3.10: Filter rows

You will see a drop-down arrow button in the header of each column in all queries. In the screenshot, the icon in the column **CustomerID** was clicked. You will get a list of values, and you can just select, and or deselect the values you want. However, there are two important considerations to make here.

The first is the warning displayed at the bottom of the screenshot. With larger datasets, the list may be incomplete. You can click on **Load more**, but that may have performance implications. The second thing to consider is that a list may never be complete. You may, for instance, refresh your Power BI every night. After refreshing, there may be different data in the database, and future values will, of course, not show up today to be selected or unselected.

You also see An option called **Text Filters** in the drop down menu shown in *Figure 3.10*. Hovering your mouse over the text **Text Filters** will display the menu as shown in *Figure 3.10*. Using these options, you can create more dynamic filters. The options are self-explanatory.

The last thing to note is that the option **Text Filters** only appears when you select columns of data type **Text**. The option will read **Date/time filters** or **Number filters** when used on **Date/time** data types and number data types, respectively.

The button **Remove Rows** is a handy option used to remove the top *n* rows from your query. Please check the other options.

Other transformations

We have seen a lot of transformations and options to transform/prepare our data. There are a lot more options available to you to prepare your data. Let us mention a few of them, but keep in mind that the list is not exhaustive.

- You can split columns into two or more separate columns in a few different ways.
- You can merge two or more columns into a new column, replacing the original columns or creating a new merged column in addition to the existing columns.
- You can format data, for instance, by capitalizing text data.
- You can remove rows where values give you errors, or you can replace the erroneous values with some other values. Errors occur when data values do not adhere to the configured data type.
- You can replace values, for instance, replacing *Mr.* with *mister*.

Most of the options available to you can be found by right-clicking on a column header. All options can be found on the ribbons **Home**, **Transform**, and **Add Column**. A lot of the options can be found on both the ribbon **Transform** and the ribbon **Add Column**. The difference is that using buttons on the **Add Column** ribbon will add a new column to the query. **Transform** means change an existing column(s) into a new one that replaces the old one.

Challenge

You may have noticed when you paid close attention to the last chapter that we missed two dimensions in this chapter. In *Chapter 2, Dimensional Modeling*, the **Date** dimension and the **Employee** dimension were discussed. We will add the **Date** dimension later. For now, try to add the **Employee** dimension. You can click on **Recent Sources** to find the OData URL. Clicking it will bring up the **Navigator** window again, allowing you to select additional tables. Refer to the following table to create your employee dimension. Add 25 years to both date columns before creating the custom columns:

Attribute	Original column	Rule
EmployeeID	EmployeeID	
LastName	LastName	
FirstName	FirstName	

TitleOfCourtesy	TitleOfCourtesy	
FullName	TitleOfCourtesy FirstName LastName	Merge [TitleOfCourtesy], [FirstName], [LastName] with spaces in between
BirthDate	BirthDate	
AgeGroup	BirthDate	= if (Duration.Days(DateTime.LocalNow() - [BirthDate]) / 365.25 < 50) then "Young" else "Old"
HireDate	HireDate	
YearsInService	HireDate	= (Duration.Days(DateTime.LocalNow() - [HireDate]) / 365.25)
ReportsTo	ReportsTo	

Table 3.3: dimEmployee table

Close & Apply

When you are done preparing your data, it needs to be loaded into the Power BI semantic model, or the meta data needs to be loaded when you are not using import. You do that using the **Close & Apply** button on the **Home** ribbon. You can just close the Power Query Editor and apply your work later or you can just apply. Both close and apply do not mean save. Applying means loading the data as you prepared it into the Power BI semantic model. You save all your work when you are back in the Power BI Desktop. All work done in this chapter will be part of the Power BI Desktop file.

1. Click on **Close & Apply**.

    After writing or changing queries, you will want to check the data model you created.

2. Back in the Power BI Desktop, click on the Model view icon in the left-hand side of the Power BI Desktop. (It is the third from the top of four icons in total shown in the margin).

Power BI tries to automatically detect relationships between tables. You can turn this off in the Power BI settings (the same place that you can change the language settings). With the automatic detection turned on, Power BI may or may not detect the relationships; therefore always check it.

In our case, we need to do some of the work manually. You want your model to look like *Figure 3.11*:

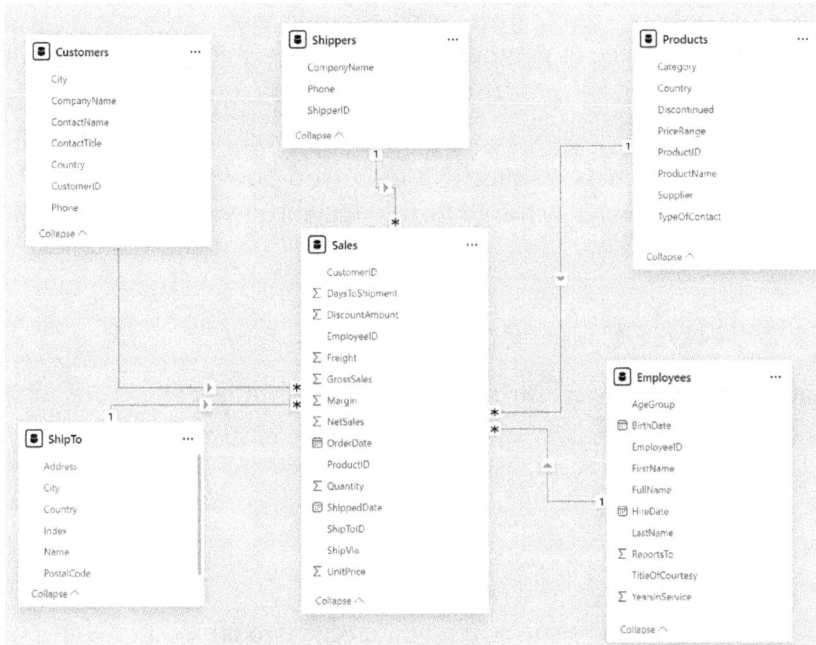

Figure 3.11: ERD Northwind star schema

Whenever there is no relationship between the tables in your solution, create them. It is as easy as dragging a column from a table and dropping it on the corresponding column in the other table. The relationships that you should have are as follows:

Dimension table	Column primary key	Fact table	Column foreign key
Employees	EmployeeID	Sales	EmployeeID
Products	EmployeeID	Sales	ProductID
ShipTo	Index	Sales	ShipToID
Shippers	ShipperID	Sales	ShipVia
Customers	CustomerID	Sales	CustomerID

Table 3.4: Model relationships

3. Create the relationships by dragging the key column from the dimension table and dropping it onto the **foreign key** column of the fact table. (the other way around works the same). Click on **Save** in the dialog that appears each time you drop a column.

Conclusion

The added value of Power Query completely depends on the data you get to work with. When you connect to data that is already in perfect shape for your use case, you can skip Power Query altogether.

In the scenario, we mainly needed to turn the data into facts and dimensions. We also needed to create some custom columns to get more out of our analysis in later stages. Transforming data can be a time-consuming job. Transforming data may very well prove to take most of the time of your overall Power BI project.

With the data prepared, the next chapter will teach you how to use the data. Power BI is a data visualization tool. You want to turn data into insightful visualizations. The next chapter teaches you how to do that.

Multiple choice questions

1. **What data type is best for storing a salaries of employees?**

    a. Whole number

    b. Decimal number

    c. Fixed decimal number

    d. Percentage

2. **Which join kind do you want when you merge two tables and you want a resulting row only if the matching column is present in both tables?**

    a. Left outer

    b. Right outer

    c. Inner

    d. Full outer

3. **Which transformation do you use when you need to aggregate a fact table to store less detailed rows?**

    a. Group by

    b. Merge tables

    c. Filter

    d. Merge columns

Answers

1	c
2	c
3	a

CHAPTER 4
The Basics of Visualizations

Introduction

Power BI is a data visualization tool. We want to visualize the data and turn it into insights. As Microsoft says, they are called usable insights or actionable insights.

In this chapter, you learn how to create visuals. Creating insightful reports turns out to be more complex than you might think initially. Creating visuals is easy in Power BI. Good visuals help people understand what is going on, and enable them to make the right decisions based on the data. *Chapter 6, Create Interactive Reports,* will focus on the theory of what makes a report a good report. This chapter focuses just on creating visuals from your data.

If you want to follow along with the examples presented in this chapter, Power BI Desktop needs to be installed on your workstation. You can continue in the Power BI Desktop file you created in the previous chapter. If you did not follow the steps in the previous chapter, you can use the file **Solution chapter 3.pbix** from the downloads folder of this book.

Structure

This chapter covers the following topics:

- A tour of the interface
- Creating a bar chart

- Setting visualization properties

- Adding a slicer to the report

- Table visuals

- Adding filters to your report

- Pie chart

- Visual interactions

- Configuring report page

- Paginated reports

Objectives

By the end of this chapter, you will be able to create reports in Power BI Desktop. It will also show a lot of settings available to report developers to change the look and feel of the visuals. You will be able to create bar charts, pie charts, tables, and other visualizations. You will be able to add slicers and filters to your report and will also be able to define interaction between different visuals.

A tour of the interface

Figure 4.1 shows a screenshot of the report we will create in this chapter. Before starting to build the report, let us introduce the key parts of the Power BI Desktop interface. Power BI Desktop is composed of different parts. Understanding these parts and knowing what functionality is located where in the Power BI Desktop is key to creating reports efficiently.

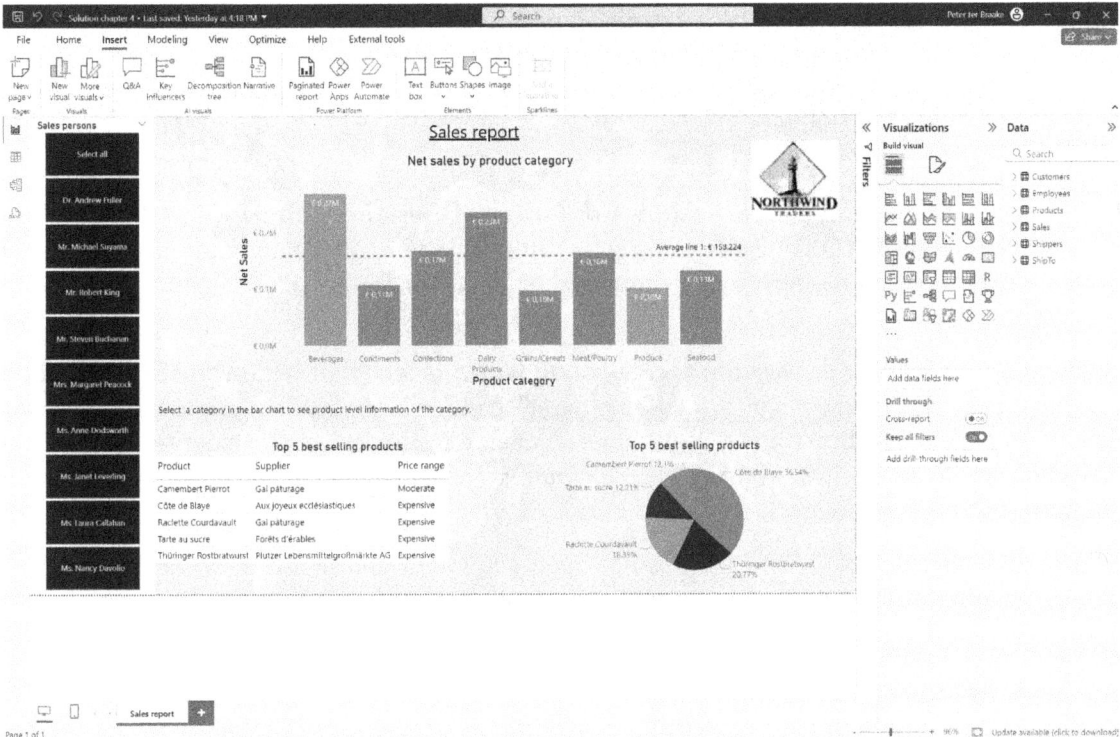

Figure 4.1: *Power BI Desktop with first report*

The ribbons on top of the screen are comparable to what Microsoft Office applications have. Each menu is a ribbon with a lot of buttons that give access to all the required functionality. You will get to know the ribbons along the way. Besides the ribbons, there are also four small icons on the left-hand side of the Power BI Desktop window. These icons are:

- **Report view**: This is the page that is currently selected, indicated by the small green line in front of the icon. The Report view is where you create your reports. You will study this in detail in this chapter.

- **Table view**: On this page, you can see the tables that you loaded with the data. A list of tables is shown in the right-hand side of the window in the **Data** pane. Selecting a table will show the data of that table in the central pane of Power BI Desktop. It can be useful to have a look at the data you are working with.

- **Model view**: The third icon represents the model view. It shows the **entity relationship diagram** (**ERD**) of your data. It was shortly introduced in the previous chapter. This pane is crucial. Power BI reports are based on a semantic model, which is sort of a database with additional settings to enable drag-and-drop reporting. The Model view represents the semantic model. The semantic model will be discussed in detail in *Chapter 7, The Basics of Semantic Models*.

- **DAX query view**: **Data Analysis Expressions** (**DAX**) is the language behind the Power BI semantic model. You can query this model (database) using DAX. You can write your DAX queries on the DAX query view page. You will learn about DAX in the upcoming chapters.

- **TMDL view**: At the time of writing of this book, this view is only visible when you activate it in the preview settings of Power BI Desktop. **Tabular Model Definition Language** (**TMDL**) view lets you script, modify, and apply changes to semantic model objects with a modern code editor. Scripting Power BI objects is outside the scope of this book.

The interface of Power BI Desktop is contextual, which means that what you see is based on the page you are on and even on what you have selected on that page. However, the **Data** pane is always present. It shows a list of all tables available in the Power BI semantic model. You can click on the little **>** icon in front of a table name. The table will expand to show a list of all columns within that table:

1. Open Power BI Desktop if it is not open yet. Open your solution from the previous chapter or open **Solution Chapter 3.pbix**.

2. Have a look at all four (or five) pages described above. Notice that each page has the **Data** pane on the right-hand side.

The **Visualizations** pane is next to the **Data** pane in the Report view (see *Figure 4.2*):

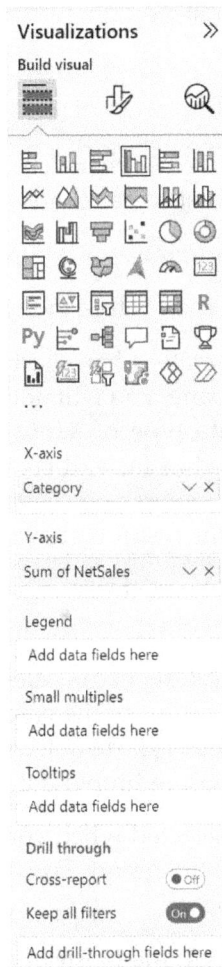

Figure 4.2: Visualizations pane

It is where you see all the different icons of all sorts of visualizations. This is where you both choose which visualization type you want, as well as where you configure your visual. The options and tabs available in the **Visualizations** pane depend on what you have selected (the entire report page or a specific visual and the type of visual selected). You will see the different options when we go along.

The **Filters** pane is on the left-hand side of the **Visualizations** pane. This pane is used to define filters to show only specific data. Filters can be defined for the entire report, or for a single page, or even a single visualization. You can keep it hidden from the menu bar.

Lastly, you can see some tabs at the bottom of the screen. A Power BI report can contain multiple report pages. You create and name the pages at the bottom of the Power BI Desktop window. Each new Power BI Desktop file always automatically has one report page called **Page1**.

Let us begin with creating the first visual.

Creating a bar chart

One of the most used visualizations is the bar chart. Therefore, let us start with a bar chart and get to know all the different ways to create a bar chart.

1. Make sure you are in the Report view.

2. Place a check mark in the checkbox before the column **NetSales** in the table **Sales**.

   Power BI will automatically create a bar chart with a single bar. If you look at the column **NetSales** in the **Data** pane, you will notice a sigma sign in front of the column name. This is because the data type of **NetSales** is numerical. Power BI assumes numerical columns will be used as facts. It creates an implicit measure that uses the **SUM** function to calculate the numbers you see in the visual. All net sales values for all rows are added together, and the result is shown in the bar chart.

3. Place a check mark in the checkbox before the column **Category** in the table **Products**. Here, there are two possibilities of what may happen:

   a. When the bar chart on the report is selected, the categories are added to the **X-axis** of the bar chart. In front of the column **Category** in the **Data** pane, there is no sigma sign. It is of data type text, making Power BI assume this column is a dimension attribute. Choosing proper data types helps in creating visuals easily.

   b. If the bar chart was not selected when you placed a check mark by **Category**, a new visual was added to the report. You can see whether a visual is selected by the thin lines surrounding it.

4. After selecting the bar chart, press the *Delete* button on your keyboard.

5. To recreate the deleted bar chart, drag to column **NetSales** from the table **Sales** in the **Data** pane and drop it somewhere on the report canvas.

6. Drag the column **Category** from the **Data** pane and drop it somewhere in the bar chart.

   The difference between selecting columns and dragging them is the position on the report canvas where the visual appears first. You can change the position and the size of the bar chart.

7. Click somewhere inside the bar chart and drag the bar chart to another location on the report. Release the mouse button when the visual is on the location you want.

8. Hover your mouse over one of the slightly thicker parts of the line surrounding the bar chart. Notice that the mouse icon changes. This indicates that when you hold your mouse button down, you can resize the visual by moving it.

You may have noticed that when moving or resizing the bar chart, red dotted lines appear on the canvas. They indicate that the side of the visual is exactly in the middle of the report canvas.

The third option to create a visual is to choose a visualization type first by selecting one, and then drag your columns to it.

9. Click on the report canvas, but outside your bar chart, and check if the bar chart is now not selected.

10. Click on the icon of the clustered column chart in the **Visualizations** pane. (This is the fourth icon from the left in the top row of icons displayed. When you hover your mouse over an icon, the visualization type will show in a tooltip).

11. Now, drag both **NetSales** and **Category** to the empty visual that has been created on the report.

Quick recap: Dragging columns onto your report canvas works. Selecting columns in the **Data** pane works just as well. A third way to create a visual is to create an empty visual first by selecting it in the **Visualization** pane. It is up to you to decide which method to use.

There is yet another alternative. Once you have a visual on the report (empty or not), its basic settings are displayed in the **Visualizations** pane under all visualization icons. With the bar selected, you can see the column **Category** is placed inside the text box called **X-axis**, and **NetSales** is inside **Y-axis**. **NetSales** shows as **Sum of NetSales** because that is what is happening in the visual. Individual net sales values are summed up to form the bars. You can drag columns from the **Data** pane directly to the text boxes (often called wells) in the **Visualizations** pane.

You can delete visuals using multiple methods. When a visual is selected, you will see a little icon showing three dots (**...**) either in the upper right corner or in the bottom right corner. When you click on it, a menu appears that has an option **Remove**.

12. Remove one of the bar charts currently on the report.

It matters in which order you drag columns to the report canvas. Dragging a fact first creates a bar chart. Starting with a dimension attribute of data type text creates a table visual.

13. Drag the column **Category** from the **Data** pane and drop it somewhere on an empty spot on the report canvas to create a new visual.

14. Now drag the column **NetSales** from the **Data** pane and drop it onto the newly created visual.

A table visual is created when the first column you select or drag has the data type text or date. The second column you add is added to the table visual as a new column. When the first column you use is numerical, Power BI assumes a bar chart is better. When you add a text column to the bar chart, Power BI will assume you want to use this as the x-axis of the visual. When your second column is numerical, it will add another bar to the existing bar chart. The data type of the column you add to a visual determines what happens. Whatever Power BI assumes, however, is only the default and can be changed when needed. To change the default visual, follow these steps:

1. Select the table visual on the report.

2. With the table visual selected, click on the icon of the clustered column chart in the **Visualizations** pane.

   You see how easily you can change a visual into another visualization type.

3. Remove one of the bar charts currently on the report.

Now that we have our first visual, let us look at some settings to change it appearance.

Setting visualization properties

You should now have a report with one basic bar chart in it. With Power BI's contextual menus, it can make a difference in the interface whether a visual on the report is selected or not:

1. Make sure the bar chart on the report is selected.

   With a visual selected on the report, the **Visualization** pane consists of three different tabs. You find them all the way on the top of the **Visualization** pane. Let us go over them before we continue:

   a. **Build visual**: This is the first tab. You already know this one. It shows all the visualization types, letting you easily switch from one type to another. Below the visualization icons are the basic settings where you define what columns you want to show on the axis, as legends, as values on so on. These settings will differ by visualization type.

   b. **Format visual**: This is the middle tab. It has the pencil in the icon. This refers to all formatting options that can be found on this tab. The tab is divided into two sub tabs, and each tab is divided into sections that you can expand or collapse. Most sections have names that are self-explanatory. Before going into the sub tabs, we complete the three main tabs of the **Visualization** pane.

   c. **Analytics**: This is the third and last tab and can be recognized by the magnifying glass icon. What you find on this tab depends on the selected visual. It does have functions like showing an average line for comparison. Not all visuals have this tab available.

The **Format visual** tab deserves a few more words. It has two sub tabs: **Visual** and **General**. To start with, the last: a lot of settings do not depend on the type of visualization you have selected. These settings include (but are not limited to) the size and position of the selected visual. You can provide a title for a visual and apply formatting to it. There are many settings to apply formatting to numbers. Etcetera. This tab will be the same for all visuals.

The **Visual** tab has all the settings specific for the type of visual selected. It will be different for different visualization types.

Let us format the bar chart we have in the report. We start by changing to report title and the title of the axes. The steps are as follows:

2. Select the **General** tab of the **Format visual** tab and open the section called **Title**.

3. Change to visual title to **Net sales by product category**.

4. Make the font **16** pt in size (leave the default font type).

5. Place the title in the middle of the visual.

   Notice that there are a lot of settings that can be used to create compelling reports. Especially notice that many settings have a little button next to them with the **fx** icon in it. This symbol denotes functions. Each setting with this button present can have conditional formatting applied to it. That means that you do not need to specify a fixed value at the time of report creation, but you can use another column or a formula to determine the value at report render time (when it is shown).

   Settings that are applicable to every visual can be found on the **General** tab. More specific settings can be found on the **Visual** tab. Since not every visual has axes, finding and changing the title of an axis can be done using the **Visual** tab of the **Format visual** tab.

6. Select the **Visual** tab of the **Format visual** tab and open the section called **X-axis**.

7. Open the sub section, **Title**.

8. Change the text **Auto** under **Title text** into **Product category**.

9. Change the font size of the title of the **X-axis** into **14** pt.

10. Open the section called **Y-axis**. Open the sub section, **Title**. Change the **Y-axis** title into **Net sales**.

11. Change the font size of the title of the **Y-axis** into **14** pt.

    The **Y-axis** has an interesting setting. In the sub section **Range**, you see a setting for **Minimum** and **Maximum**. Both are by default set to **Auto**. This means that the scale of the **Y-axis** will be determined automatically in such a way that the entire space allocated to the visual on the report is used. You give the bar chart a certain height, either by dragging the resize handles of the visual on the canvas or by setting the **Height** property (**Properties** section and **General** tab). This height will be used by the largest bar it needs to show, and the scale of the axis is automatically adjusted.

In most scenarios, the default setting of automatically adjusting the scale works fine. It can also be confusing and may lead to wrong conclusions when readers do not realize the scale has been adjusted. You can use the settings **Minimum** and **Maximum** to avoid the auto-adjusting. Both values can be hard-set or can be calculated during report rendering using the conditional formatting (**fx** icon). As an alternative, try out the zoom slider section!

With the visual title set and both axes formatted, we will focus on the bars next. First, we need them sorted differently. We also want two bars to have a different color as shown in the screenshot of *Figure 4.1* at the start of the chapter.

Sorting is done in the visual itself.

12. Click inside the visual on the small button with the three dots (**...**) in the upper or lower right corner of the bar chart.

When you hover your mouse over the option **Sort axis**, you see a popup. You can choose whether the bar chart should be sorted on the labels on the **X-axis** or on the value shown on the **Y-axis**. The latter is the default. In most cases, this is the better option. Only when you show periods on the **X-axis** do you want to sort it by these periods. In this case, however, we do want to sort the bar chart using the categories. We also want to use an ascending sorting order and not the default descending order.

13. Click on **Category** in the popup menu that shows after you clicked on the small button with the three dots (**...**).

14. Click again on the button with the three dots (**...**) to change the sorting order to **Sort ascending**.

With the sorting done, we continue our improvements to the bar chart. In our case, we will highlight the categories **Beverages** and **Produce**. We will also show the value the bar represents to show inside the top of the bar. Lastly, we want an average line to show in the bar chart for reference.

15. Open the section **Columns** inside the **Visual** tab of the **Format visual** tab.

The **Columns** section starts with a list box. It has **Show all** selected by default. This allows you to choose another color than the default for all the bars. Of course, you can apply conditional formatting here as well. We need to change the colors of only to specific categories. You can select specific categories in the list box at the top of this section.

16. Select **Beverages** in the list box. Change to color to **Orange**.

17. Select **Produce** and make it **Green**.

18. Turn on the toggle for the **Data labels** section of the **Visual** tab.

19. Change the **Position** to **Inside end**.

20. Open the sub section value and note all the formatting options to format how values are shown.

    Your bar chart should now show two categories with different colors than the default **Blue**. Also, the net sales values are shown inside each bar. The last formatting we will do here is to add a line showing the average net sales.

21. Select the **Analytics** tab.

22. Open the section **Average line**.

23. Click on the link **+ Add line**.

24. Use the sub section **Line** to make the added line black and change it is **Position** to **Behind**. Keep it dashed (unless you prefer one of the other options).

25. In the sub section **Data label** turn the data label on. Make it **Black** and show it in the right-hand side of the visual. Set **Style** to **both**. Set the number of decimal places to show to 0.

There are a lot more settings to play with to change the appearance of the bar chart. We leave it to the reader to check out all options.

Adding a slicer to the report

Often, people need to be able to quickly and easily change how data is filtered. The bar chart we created in the previous section shows the overall net sales by product category. However, we might be interested in a specific year or how our salespersons (employees) are doing. Let us focus on an analysis of how our employees perform. We measure the performance of employees for now by net sales through the following steps. We might, for instance, look at differences in the discount they give away at a later stage. To start with, we simply need to be able to analyze net sales by product category per employee.

1. Click somewhere on the report canvas but outside the bar chart. Make sure the bar chart is now not selected.

2. Place a check mark in the check box in front of the column `FullName` in the table `Employees` in the **Data** pane.

3. Change the table that Power BI creates on the report into a slicer by clicking on the corresponding icon in the list with visualization types (it is the icon with the little funnel in it ($\triangledown$)). Note that the table changes into a list of selectable labels.

4. Make sure none of the visuals on your report are selected.

5. Click on the slicer visualization type in the **Visualizations** pane to add a new empty slicer.

6. Drag the column `YearsInService` from the table `Employees` to the new empty slicer visual.

   As you can see on the report, you now have two very different slicer visuals. The difference comes from the difference in data types of the columns you chose to filter on. `FullName` is a text column, whereas, `YearsInService` is a numeric column. Based on the data type, Power BI defaults to creating a list or a slider bar that lets you select a range. Both forms can be customized to your liking. Let us understand the slicer you created for `FullName` first.

7. Select a name within the slicer, for instance, **Andrew Fuller**. Note that the bar charts changes. It now only shows data pertaining to Andrew Fuller.

8. Click on another name in the slicer, for instance, **Robert King**. With another person selected, the bar chart changes to show the sales data of that person.

9. Now hold down the *Ctrl* key on your keyboard and select **Andrew Fuller** again. Multi-select is possible.

10. Note that clicking on a selected item in the list will de-select everything. The report will show the data without a filter applied.

    The first setting to consider when using a slicer is the appearance of the slicer.

11. Make sure the slicer with names is still selected.

12. Select the **Format visual** pane of the **Visualizations** pane and then select the **Visual** pane.

13. Open the section **Slicer settings**.

14. Change the **Style** to **Dropdown** and note the appearance of the slicer on the report.

    Using a **Dropdown** slicer takes a lot less real estate on the screen than a vertical list. That can be an advantage. On the other hand, it takes an extra mouse click from users when they need to change the selection made. Users may get irritated when they use the slicer a lot.

15. Use the third option for style: **Tile**. This option creates buttons.

    Note that the slider used for the `YearsInService` slicer is not an option. It simply does not make sense for the data type **Text** to use a slider to select a range.

16. Set the slicer for `Fullname` back to **Vertical list** for now.

17. Open the sub section **Selection** and toggle on **Single select**. Note that the slicer now shows radio buttons instead of check boxes, and multi-select is no longer possible.

18. Turn **Single select** off again. Turn the setting **Multi-select with CTRL** off and turn **Show "Select all" option** on. Note the changes to the slicer.

19. For now, change the style to **Tile**.

20. Open the section **Slicer header** and then the sub section **Text**, and change the header to **Salespersons**.

21. Place the slicer in the left-hand side of the report filling the report page from top to bottom. You should get a single row of buttons all under each other.

    Let us return to the **YearsInService** slicer. It looked different than the **Salesperson** slicer simply because the data type of the column used is different. However, there are options. First, note that the current form lets you use the circles to change the selected range by dragging the circles to the minimum and maximum value of the desired range to filter on. As an alternative, you can type the new minimum and maximum value as well.

22. Go to the slicer settings of the **YearsInService** slicer in the **Visualization** pane.

23. Note the different options available. Test some options if you want.

    You have now seen that the slicer has extra possible forms when using numeric columns to filter on, as opposed to textual filters. How about using columns of data type **Date** to filter on?

24. Delete the slicer for **YearsInService**.

25. Create a new slicer on the report based on the column `OrderDate` from the table `Sales`.

    In this case, how you create your slicer matters. The easiest way is to create an empty slicer visual first and then drag the column `OrderDate` to it. The slicer will appear in style **Between** (the range). If you start by dragging the column `OrderDate` to the report canvas, to then turn the visual into a slicer, you will get a vertical list. Power BI created a textual date hierarchy.

    Filtering on dates should be done from a special date table. We have not created one yet. If we had done so, using the slicer would be slightly more intuitive because you choose whether to filter on a date or on a date hierarchy yourself. We will create a date table in the next chapter. For now, we just want to show the relative date options.

26. If you got the vertical list with the date hierarchy instead of the range, delete the slicer and recreate it by starting to create an empty slicer.

27. Check the different styles available for the slicer.

As you can see, there are even more options available when using dates compared to using numerical values. Often, you will want to filter on a period. A period is, in essence, a range of dates. The range (style **Between**) is the default appearance. The most interesting options to note are the relative filters: **Relative Date** and **Relative Time**.

28. Select the style **Relative Date**.

29. Configure the **Relative Date** to show **Last 1 Months** (three settings).

    This option shows the last month from the current day. So, if you use the report on the 16th of December 2024, it will show you the dates in the range from the 17th of November until the 16th of December 2024 (today).

    When you configure the slicer to show **Last 1 Months (Calendar)**, it will show entire months. So, when you use the report on the 16th of December 2024, like in the previous example, it will show the data for the entire month of November 2024.

30. For now, remove the date slicer.

Your report should now have a bar chart and a single slicer. The slicer shows buttons for salespersons and is positioned on the left-hand side of the report.

Slicers and bar charts are both often-used visualization types. Another very common one is the table. So let us move on and add a table to the report.

Table visuals

Tables are a great visualization type because almost everyone interprets them correctly. However, showing hundreds or even thousands of lines in a table on a Power BI report is not effective. When you do need to create a table-style report, consider using Power BI paginated reports or Excel. When showing a limited number of rows, the table can be effective on a Power BI report.

Let us go ahead and actually add a table visualization to our report:

1. Drag the column **ProductName** from table **Products** inside the **Data** pane and drop it on an empty spot in the report.

2. Add the columns **Supplier** and **PriceRange** to the table.

3. Make the table visual wide enough to show all three columns.

    Interpreting data correctly starts by using readable names. That means titles of visuals, titles of axes, and, in this case, column names.

4. Look for the three columns you just added to the table in the **Visualizations** pane on the **Build visual** tab. Make sure the table visual is selected. You find all three columns

directly under all the icons of all the visualization types in the well called **Columns**.

5. Right-click on the column `ProductName` and select the option **Rename for this visual** in the popup. Rename to the column to `Product`.

6. Rename `PriceRange` to `Price range`.

    It is useful to know that you can change the name of a column inside a visual. Having said that, defining good column names in the data model itself is the better option. You do not have to change the names in the visual if they are already what you need, making it easier to make reports and making your reports more consistent.

    As with the slicer, there are predefined styles to choose from that determine the appearance of the table.

7. Go to the **Format visual** tab inside the **Visualizations** pane and open the section **Style presets**.

8. Check out the different options and choose the one you like. We will continue with the **Style** set to **Minimal**.

9. Change the font size of the table header to **11** (**Column headers** section).

    The **Visual** tab of the table has a lot of settings. Almost every individual cell can be formatted to your liking. Go ahead and try it!

    When we added slicers to the report, it went almost without saying that selecting items in the slicer would filter the values shown in the bar chart. That is the entire reason for having slicers on a report. By default, every visual reacts to other visuals on the same report page as well. Interaction is not limited to slicers.

10. Click on the bar **Beverages** in the bar chart.

11. Note that the table visual only shows products in the category **Beverages**. (The slider bar on the right-hand side inside the table is an indication of how many rows are in the table.)

12. Also, note that all categories that you did not click on are now somewhat *grayed*.

13. Click again on the bar **Beverages** in the bar chart to undo the selection.

14. Now, find the product **Camembert Pierrot** on the table and click on it.

15. Note in the bar chart that it has a net sale of 0.05 million, and it is a dairy product.

You can change the way visuals interact with each other. You will learn to do that later in this chapter.

Northwind sells 77 different products that are all present in the table visual when no category is selected in the bar chart. Most of those 77 rows are not visible because you must scroll down to get to those rows. Even with a category selected, some products still do not show on the screen. It is time to set a filter.

Adding filters to your report

There are three ways in which data can be filtered in your report and in visuals:

- Slicer visuals
- Select something in a visual on the report
- Configure filters

You can find the filters in the **Filters** pane just to the left of the **Visualizations** pane. The **Filter** pane may or may not be visible. On the **View** ribbon (all the way at the top of Power BI Desktop), you will find a button called **Filters**. You toggle between having the **Filters** pane visible in Power BI Desktop or not with this button.

When you look at the top of the **Filters** pane, you will notice an icon resembling an eye. A diagonal line is placed through it upon clicking. This is an icon that represents hidden items. Hidden items will be hidden when the report is published to the cloud. You will learn about publishing to the cloud in *Chapter 12, Working with the Power BI Service*. Hiding the **Filters** pane in the cloud means that users will not be able to see or change the filters you set. This is an obvious difference from slicers that are on a report page meant to be used by users. In some reports, you need to set filters without report users being able to change those filter settings. In that case, you hide the filters pane. When report users may change filter settings, you leave the filter pane visible.

What you see inside the **Filters** pane depends on what is selected in the report. With the table visual selected, the Filters pane looks like *Figure 4.3*:

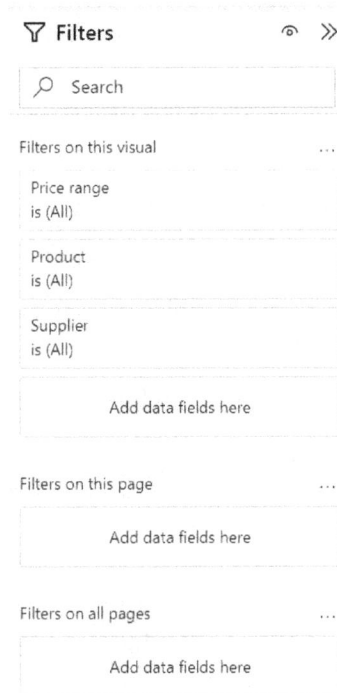

Figure 4.3: *Filters pane*

You can see the three columns that make up the table visual in the **Filters on this visual** section. Clicking on any of them allows you to define filters on these columns. In the section, **Add data fields here** you can define filters using other columns. Just drag a column from the **Data** pane and drop it in the section **Add data fields here**.

The section **Add data fields here** is shown multiple times inside the **Filters** pane. The accompanying text explains it all. Filters can be set for individual visuals, for the current report page, or for all pages of the current Power BI report we are working on.

Be cautious when applying different filters to different visuals. The possibility of doing so is a nice feature. However, the chances that a user misinterprets the report are high because they are not aware of the different filters in place.

Let us create a filter for our table visual. The steps are as follows:

1. Make sure the table visual is selected.

2. Click inside the **Filters** pane on the section for the column **Product**.

    Note the **Filter type** setting. Basic filtering lets you simply select the values you want to use on your visual. Advanced filtering is more advanced. There are a lot of options under the setting **Show items when the value**. Options like **Contains** and **Starts with** let you create more generic filters then just selecting values. When you create an advanced filter on a numerical column, you get different options. With numerical data, you get options like **Greater than** and **Smaller than**. The third filter type is **Top N**. We will use that option in our report.

3. Select the option **Top N** for the **Filter type**.

4. Keep **Top** selected under **Show items**. Type **5** in the text box behind **Show items**.

5. Drag the column **NetSales** from the table **Sales** in the **Data** pane and drop it onto **Add data fields** here under **By value**.

6. Click on **Apply filter** under the section where you just configured your **Top N** filter.

    The table now only shows five rows. It always shows the five products with the highest net sales. When you click on a category in the bar chart, the five products with the highest net sales of that category are shown. A filter icon shows when you hover your mouse over a visual. Clicking on it will provide a quick insight into which filters are active on this visual.

    To make it clear for readers of the report that the table shows the top five products, we will change the visual title.

7. Make sure the table visual is selected.

8. Find the section **Title** on the **General** tab of the **Format visual** tab.

9. Change the title into **Top 5 best-selling products** and align it to show in the middle of the table.

Let us add one more visual to the report.

Pie chart

Most visualization theories advise against the use of pie charts. You will learn a bit about visualization theory in *Chapter 6, Create Interactive Reports*. Pie charts are used a lot, even though they are not recommended. People like them mainly because they are used to working with pie charts. Thus, against best practices, we will add one to our report:

1. Make sure nothing is selected on your report and click on the pie chart icon in the **Visuals** tab to add an empty pie chart to the report.

2. Drag the column **NetSales (Sales)** from the **Data** pane and drop it onto the empty pie chart.

3. Add the column **ProductName** to the pie chart.

    You can see why pie charts are not a best practice. Let us improve the pie chart visual.

4. Add the same top five filter to the pie chart as the one filtering the table. Add this filter to the column **ProductName**, not to the column **NetSales**.

   Pie charts become a lot better with a limited number of categories shown.

5. Change the title of the pie chart into **Top 5 best-selling products** and align it centrally.

   Clear visual titles help interpret the data correctly.

6. Open the section **Detail labels** on the **Visual** tab. Change the setting **Label contents** to **Category**, percent of total.

7. Turn off the legend in the section **Legend** on the **Visual** tab.

With less categories shown and the legend gone as well, the pie chart looks a bit nicer. However, it does not work as expected. Whatever category you click on in the bar chart, it always shows the top five best-selling products overall. When you select a category that one of those five products belongs to, the corresponding part of the pie chart is highlighted. This is because the pie chart is not filtered by the bar chart. It only highlights the part selected in the bar chart. This behavior can be changed using visual interactions.

Visual interactions

Visual interactions define how visuals react to users making selections on other visuals:

1. Make sure the bar chart is selected on the report.

2. Open the **Format** ribbon and click on the button **Edit interactions**.

Notice the three little icons displayed in the top or bottom right corner of the pie chart. The right one (a circle with a line through it) turns off all interactions. Clicking on this icon means that the pie chart does not react in any way to what you select in the bar chart. The middle icon, a little bar chart icon, is the default behavior. The pie chart will show the data belonging to the selected bar in the bar chart highlighted. All other data is still present, but sort of *grayed*. The leftmost icon, the bar chart with the little funnel in it, represents filtering. The pie chart will be filtered based on the selection in the bar chart. So, when you select **Beverages** in the bar chart, the pie chart will only show products in the category beverages. The **Top N** filter will do the rest:

1. Click on the leftmost icon in the pie chart.

2. Test the pie chart now works as expected, showing the top five products of the product category you select in the bar chart.

   When you look at the table visual with the bar chart still selected, you will only see two icons to change the default interaction. Highlighting is not an option for the table. The corresponding icon is not shown. The default behavior of the table is that it is filtered by other visuals, but you can turn that off.

You just changed how the pie chart reacts to selections made in the bar chart. However, what happens when you click on a part of the pie? Both the table and the bar chart react to it, both in their own default way. For this report, we did not mean that. We want both the table visual and the bar chart to be unaffected by selections made in the pie chart.

3. Make sure the pie chart is selected, and the **Edit interactions** are still turned on (the icons defining interactions should still be visible).

4. Click the circle icon in both the table visual as well as in the bar chart.

5. To finalize setting interactions, select the table visual and turn of interactions in the pie chart. The pie chart should not react to selecting a product in the table visual.

6. Click again on the button **Edit interactions** in the **Format** ribbon. The icons defining interactions between visuals disappear.

We are almost done creating our first report page. Just a couple of settings more, and it is finished.

Configuring report page

When you create a report, you probably have an idea about how it is meant to be used. Adding some descriptive text on the report may help users understand what you had in mind. A good title for the page might be a first step:

1. Select the **Insert** ribbon and click on the button **Text box**.

2. Click in the text box and type **Sales report**.

3. Select the text you just typed and then change the font size to **20** and make it underlined using the formatting options shown directly on your screen.

4. Resize the text box to your liking and position it at the top of the page in the middle.

5. Position the visuals as shown in *Figure 4.1,* shown at the beginning of the chapter.

6. Add a text box with the text `Select a category in the bar chart to see product level information of the category`. Place it between in the bar chart and the table and pie visuals.

    A company logo might be the first thing a manager asks for.

7. Click on the button **Image** in the **Insert** ribbon.

8. Browse to the file `Logo Northwind.png` that is part of the downloads for this book in the windows file explorer that opens.

9. Resize the logo to your liking and place it in the upper right corner of the report page.

    Not only can you configure the look and feel of each visual on a report, but the report page itself is configurable as well.

10. Click somewhere in the report, but not on a visual.

The report page itself is now selected. The second tab of the **Visualizations** pane is now called **Format page** instead of **Format visual**. It shows all sorts of settings to change the look and feel of the page itself.

11. Open the section **Page information** and change the name in the **Sales report**.

12. Open the section canvas background and click on **Browse.**

13. Browse to the file **world.jpg** that is part of the GitHub Repo for this book in the windows file explorer that opens.

14. Change to setting **Image fit** to **Fill** and **Transparency** to **90%**.

Having a picture in the background may not be the best idea. However, sometimes having a repeating logo vaguely in the background is what companies want. We just want to show it here. It, however, looks a bit strange with the visuals having their own background.

15. Select the bar chart on the report.

16. Open the section **Effects** on the **General** tab of the **Format visual** tab.

17. Turn the **Background** off.

18. Turn off the **Background** of all other visuals as well, including the text boxes, but excluding the slicer.

Your report should now look exactly like in *Figure 4.1* unless you made some other formatting choices along the way. We did learn about the interaction between visuals on the page. There is a lot more in Power BI in terms of interactions in the report. You will learn about that in *Chapter 6, Create Interactive Reports*. Before that, we return to Power Query to add some more data to our semantic model.

Paginated reports

There is a completely different type of report that you can make as compared to what we have done so far in this chapter. These reports are called **paginated reports** as compared to the analytical report we have created so far.

Paginated reports are the old **SQL Server Reporting Services** (**SSRS**) reports. In theory, they are sometimes called **pixel perfect reports**. They focus more on pages that can be printed and should have a very well-designed and precise layout when printed. They do not necessarily need to be printed; it is where they are a better fit than Power BI analytical reports. If you need a printed list of items, as in a waybill, a paginated report is great. It is a static list. You do not need clickable charts.

When you need to create paginated reports, you have to download the Power BI Report Builder. You can either *Google* for it or download it from the Power BI portal. Creating paginated reports is outside the scope of this book.

Conclusion

In this chapter, you created your first report. It showed a lot of settings available to you to make compelling reports.

The first and most important step in creating a report is to choose the right visualization type, which you will learn about in the next chapters. This chapter was to get to know the Report view interface, find the properties available to you, and create visuals and reports. Not all settings have been discussed because there are simply too many settings to discuss them all. You should, however, have a feeling about the possibilities Power BI provides for creating effective reports.

Multiple choice questions

1. **For which data types is the range the default slicer form?**
   a. Numerical data
   b. Textual data
   c. Dates
   d. All of the above
   e. None of the above

2. **Filters allow for more complex filters when compared to slicers.**
   a. True
   b. False

3. **A table visual can be configured to highlight data selected in another visual.**
   a. True
   b. False

Answers

1	a, c
2	a
3	b

CHAPTER 5
Advanced Techniques of Power Query

Introduction

In this chapter, you will learn some new transformations, read data from multiple files, and automate the solution to automatically read in all files. More importantly, we will have a look at the M-code language that is behind all these transformations.

In *Chapter 3, The Basics of Power Query*, you learned to use Power Query. Normalized tables were turned into fact and dimension tables. Custom columns were created and you learned about the often-used transformations in Power BI. This chapter picks up where *Chapter 3, The Basics of Power Query*, left of to make you more proficient in using Power Query.

If you want to follow along with the examples presented in this chapter, you need Power BI Desktop to be installed on your workstation. You can continue in the Power BI Desktop file you created in the previous chapter. Alternatively, you can use the file **Solution chapter 4.pbix** from the GitHub Repo of this book.

Structure

This chapter covers the following topics:

- Date dimension
- Analyzing the raw data

- Unpivot data

- Creating a custom function

- Reading multiple files from a folder

- Understanding M-code

- Understanding the date table code

- Using parameters

- Organizing queries

- Exam tip

Objectives

After this chapter, you can read and understand the code behind Power Query. You can create custom functions in Power Query and use them to automate your solutions and work with multiple files. You also learn to unpivot data that comes in as pivot tables. You finally learn what parameters are and how to use them.

Date dimension

Before we continue to build the report you created in the previous chapter, we will create a date table (also called a **date dimension**). Almost every Power BI solution has a date table. This has two reasons: almost all the analysis that we people do involves time in some way. If we want to analyze our data over time, dimensional modeling prescribes that we need a dimension table to do that. Power BI has powerful **Data Analysis Expressions** (**DAX**) functions, known as **time intelligence functions**, that can help do this type of analysis. However, those functions require a Date table. That is the second reason almost all Power BI solutions have a Date table. Sometimes, even multiple Date tables can be used. This is known as **role-playing dimensions**.

There are three ways to get a Date table. The preferred way is to create one and store it somewhere centrally so it can be used by all Power BI reports you are going to make. It is the easiest way and assures consistency across all Power BI reports. Places to create a central Date table would be inside a SQL Server data warehouse, in a Fabric warehouse or lakehouse, an Excel workbook saved on a file share or on OneDrive, and so on.

When you do not have a central Date table to use, you can generate one using either Power Query or DAX. We will look at a DAX-generated Date table later in the book. We will create a Date table using Power Query in this chapter. The main difference between using Power Query, or DAX is that Power Query can get data from the internet, and DAX cannot. You might want to reach out to a government site to get information on which days on the calendar are considered holidays. You can use this information to enrich your Date table.

Let us begin creating our Date table:

1. Open Power BI Desktop if it is not opened yet. Open your solution from the previous chapter or open **Solution Chapter 4.pbix**.

2. Click on the **Get data** button in the **Home** ribbon.

3. Choose **Blank query**.

   The Power Query Editor will open. A blank query has no data, so there is not a lot to see. However, note that a query called **Query1** is in the list of queries on the left-hand side of the screen. This is the query you just created. It is a starting point.

4. Click on the button **Advanced Editor** on the **Home** ribbon.

5. Delete everything you see in the **Advanced Editor**.

6. Copy the code from the file **Power Query date dimension starter.txt** into the **Advanced Editor**.

7. Click on **Done**.

   We will come back to this code later in this chapter to explain it. For now, notice that the result is a table with a single column called **Date**. The smallest date is January 1^{st,} 2021, and the latest date is December 31st, 2023. This is the range of dates our sales data falls in. From this single-column table, we can create a more useful Date table.

8. Select the column **Date** by clicking in the header of the column.

9. Click on the button **Date** on the **Add Column** ribbon.

10. Select **Year** and then again **Year**.

11. Add columns for **Quarter**, **Month**, and **Month Name** in the same way. Make sure to select the **Date** column each time you try to add a column.

    The values you see in the column **Month Name** depend on your regional settings. It will pick up the language from your workstation. You may need to change the language of the month names.

12. Make sure the option **formula bar** on the **View** ribbon is checked.

13. Select the step **Inserted Month Name** in the list of **APPLIED STEPS** on the right-hand side of the Power Query Editor. You should now see the code of this step between the ribbon and the data preview.

14. Change **Date.MonthName([Date])** into **Date.MonthName([Date], "en-US")** in the code in the formula bar.

    You can, of course, use other language codes to get the name of the month in another language.

There are a couple more columns that we need.

15. Merge the columns **Month** and **Year** in this order with a comma and space between them, and add the merged column as a new column named **MonthYear**.

16. Create custom columns with the names **MonthKey** and **QuarterYear** using the following expressions:

    a. `[Year] * 100 + [Month]`

    b. `"Q" & Text.From([Quarter]) & ", " & Text.From([Year])`

17. Rename the **Query1** to **Date**.

    Your table should look like *Figure 5.1*. You can copy the code from the file **Power Query date dimension complete.txt** that has the code for the complete **Date** table.

    To finish the **Date** table:

18. Rename the column **Month** to **MonthNo**.

19. Change the data type of column **QuarterYear** to **Text** and change the data type of column **MonthKey** to **Whole number**.

    Refer to the following figure for the resulting date table:

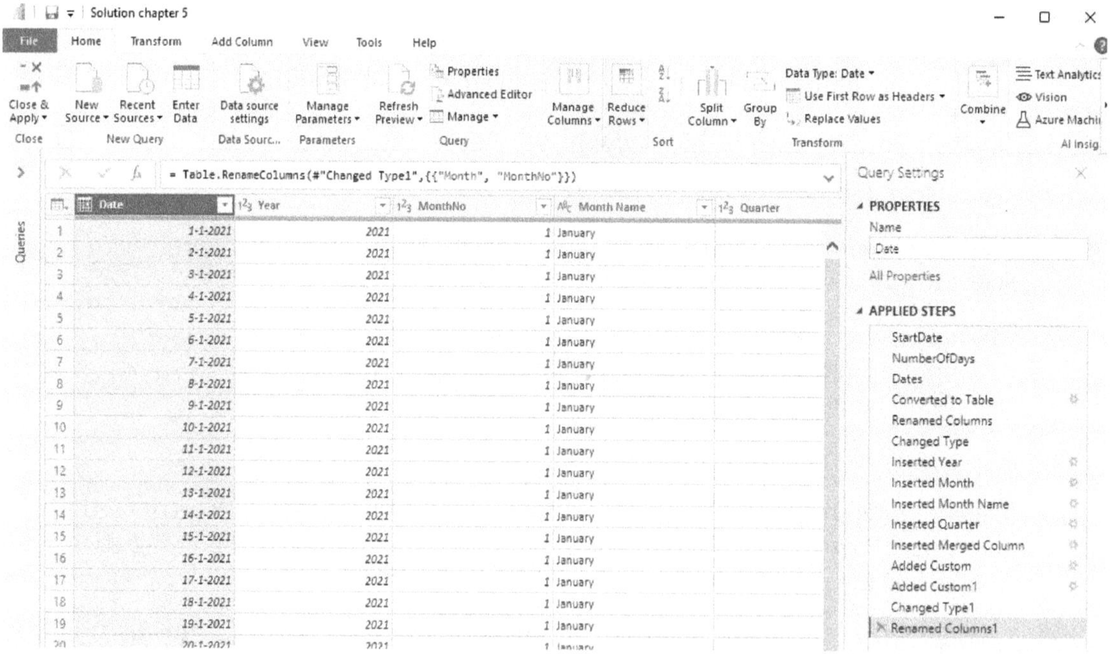

Figure 5.1: Date table

The columns created here will become clear when we start using them on the report. Now that we have finished creating a date table, let us load the data into the Power BI semantic model and add it correctly to that model.

20. Click on **Close & Apply** on the **Home** ribbon to close the Power Query Editor and load the data into the Power BI semantic model.

21. Back in Power BI Desktop, select the Model view (third icon from the top in the left-hand side of Power BI Desktop).

22. Drag the column `OrderDate` from the table `Sales` to the new table `Date` and drop it onto the column `Date`. Click on **Save** in the dialog that shows.

    You should have a relationship between the tables `Sales` and `Date` similar to the already existing relationships. You can now start to create visualizations that use your `Date` dimension.

23. Switch to the Report view of Power BI Desktop.

24. Click on the plus icon at the bottom of the Report view to add a new report page.

25. Right-click in the newly created tab where the plus icon was and rename the page to `Sales by Year by Salesperson`.

26. Drag the column `NetSales` (table `Sales`) from the **Data** pane onto the report canvas to create a new bar chart.

27. Add the column `FullName (Employees)` to the bar chart.

28. Change the bar chart into a horizontal bar chart.

29. Add a slicer to the report based on the column `Year` from the `Date` table. Turn the slicer into a vertical list.

You can improve that look and feel as you see fit. The report shows the sales by salesperson with an option to select a specific year. However, when is the sales manager happy? Just numbers are not very informative. Maybe we should add a target to the bar chart to see who did and who did not reach the set target.

We will add target data to the model.

Analyzing the raw data

You can find the target data we will use in the downloads for this book. There are three target files, one for each year of sales data in our report. When you open one of the files with *Notepad*, it looks like *Figure 5.2*:

EmployeeID	M1	M2	M3	M4	M5	M6	M7	M8	M9	M10	M11	M12
1	0	0	0	0	0	5.000	5.000	5.000	5.000	10.000	10.000	
2	0	0	0	0	0	1.000	2.000	2.500	5.000	5.000	7.500	
3	0	0	0	0	0	2.000	3.000	4.000	5.000	5.000	5.000	
4	0	0	0	0	0	10.000	3.000	3.000	10.000	10.000	5.000	
5	0	0	0	0	0	2.000	2.000	1.000	1.000	3.000	10.000	
6	0	0	0	0	0	2.000	2.000	3.000	2.000	2.000	5.000	
7	0	0	0	0	0	2.000	2.000	1.000	3.000	10.000	2.000	
8	0	0	0	0	0	1.000	8.000	4.000	2.000	2.000	6.000	
9	0	0	0	0	0	4.000	2.000	2.000	5.000	2.000	2.000	

Figure 5.2: Target file

There are two issues with the target data that we need to overcome. The first is that the data is not neatly in a single file or table. We will have to combine data from multiple files. We want to consider that we will get more than three files in the future. We expect a new file every year when the targets for next year are determined. Power BI should automatically read in all target files, no matter how many there are. You do want to manually add another file to Power BI each time new data becomes available.

The second issue with the target data is the format. Each line in the files holds the data of 12 months for the same employee. The year the targets belong to can only be derived from the file name. With multiple months on the same line, this file has a pivot format. Power BI needs tables.

Thinking about the grain of fact tables, the grain we have here is a target amount per employee per month. That means we need a row per employee per month.

For our target data to be integrated with the sales data, it should use some of the same dimensions. In this case, we have targets per employee per month. The files do have an **EmployeeKey** column that can be used to link target data to the **Employee** table. We also need it to link to the **Date** table to ensure the year slicer on our report works. We will create a date column by using month numbers derived from the column names in the target files. We will use the year from the file names. Lastly, we will use day number 1 for all targets. It is a common practice to link targets defined for a period to the first day of that period.

We now know what we need. A table with three columns: **EmployeeKey**, **Date**, and **TargetAmount**. The table should store data coming from multiple files.

Let us get to work.

Unpivot data

We will first transform a single file before worrying about how to read in multiple files, through the following steps:

1. Click on the **Get data** button in the **Home** ribbon of Power BI Desktop.

2. Choose the option **Text/CSV** and browse to the file `targets2021.txt`.

3. Click on **Transform Data** in the data preview window.

   It is not uncommon for data to be in a pivoted format. That means that Power Query knows about the pivot format and lets you unpivot with a single click of the mouse.

4. Right-click in the header of the column `EmployeeID`. Select **Unpivot Other Columns** in the drop-down menu that appears.

   Note: **Notice the other two options to unpivot data. Depending on how many columns of the total columns need unpivoting, these other options may be simpler.**

   Unpivot creates two new columns. The first is called `Attribute` and contains the column headers of the original file. The second column is called `Value` and holds the values that were in the cells of the pivot table. You can rename these two columns in the way already learned in *Chapter 3, The Basics of Power Query*.

5. Rename both columns to better names by double-clicking in the header and typing in the new name.

6. Notice the **Renamed Columns** step in the **APPLIED STEPS** on the right-hand side of the Power Query Editor.

7. Delete the **Renamed Columns** step.

8. Look at the code in the formula bar with the step **Unpivoted Other Columns** selected in the **APPLIED STEPS**.

9. Change `Attribute` in the formula into `Month` and change `Value` into `TargetAmount`.

   Note: **You did not get an extra step in your query, but you have the desired column names anyway.**

You may have noticed that we had some queries with quite some steps in *Chapter 3, The Basics of Power Query*. There are often opportunities to optimize your code. Less steps might be easier when you need to make changes to a query. Besides, the query might be more efficient this way, which may save some Fabric capacity units. Whether this is true depends on a lot of factors. However, changing the names inside the code of the **Unpivoted Other Columns** step will certainly not make it less efficient.

We are not done preparing the data for this single file. Let us first look at the column `TargetAmount`. You can see a lot of zeroes in this column. A zero can mean two things here. Either a person has a target that equals zero for this month, or zero was used as a filler in the file, but there is no actual target for this month.

The main difference, once we start analyzing the data, is what the average target amount is. It will be a lot lower if we keep all rows with a zero. For now, let us assume rows with a zero as the target amount can be deleted because the zero does not constitute an actual target amount.

10. Click on the little downward arrow in the column header of the column **TargetAmount**.

11. Remove the check mark in front of the **0**.

The last step for now is to remove the letter **M** in the **Month** column to create actual month numbers.

12. Right-click in the header of the column **Month**. Select **Replace Values...** in the drop-down menu that appears.

13. Type a capital **M** in the textbox under **Value To Find**. Leave the second textbox empty and click on **OK**.

Note: **Power Query is always case sensitive.**

This is how far we get in preparing the data using a single file. The next challenge is to apply the same transformations on all files. You should consider a query to be a script. In any language, when you need to reuse the same script multiple times, you turn your script into a function. The same is true for Power Query. To easily apply the same transformations to the other two target files without copying and pasting code, we will turn the query into a function.

Creating a custom function

Even though there is a button to change a query into a function, we will dive into the M-code behind Power Query through the following steps:

1. Click on the button **Advanced Editor** on the **Home** ribbon.

When you want to, the code you now see is (almost) understandable. The first line after the word **let** reads **Csv.Document** after the equals sign. We started our query with **Get data**, from **Tex/CSV**. The second and third lines were automatically added by Power Query. However, when you look at the rest of the lines above the word **in** and especially what is in front of the equals sign, you can recognize the steps we performed when transforming the data. Each time you perform a transformation on the data, a line of code is added here.

Turning this query in a function is straight forward.

2. Create a new empty line above the word **let**.

3. In the newly created line type **() =>**

Your query just became a function. However, it is not a very useful function yet. Let us have a closer look at the first line. We saw the part **Csv.Document**. That is followed by **File.Contents**. That makes sense because it needs to get the contents of the files we are working with. Behind **File.Contents,** you can see (between braces and quotes) the name of the target file we used, including the entire path to the file. This means that this code always reads in the same file. However, we need to perform this code on a different file every time.

4. Replace the entire path plus file name including the quotes by the single word **FileContents.** The line should now be similar to **Csv.Document(File. Contents(FileContents).** (see *Figure 5.3*)

5. Put the same word **FileContents** in between the braces at the top of your code. Your code should now look like *Figure 5.3*. When you have trouble getting this to work, you can find the code in the file **GetTargets M-code.txt** in the **Downloads** folder. Delete everything from your **Advanced Editor** and paste the code from the file in it:

Advanced Editor ☐ ✕

GetTargets

Display Options ▾ ❓

```
1  (FileContents) =>
2  let
3      Source = Csv.Document(FileContents,[Delimiter=" ", Columns=13, Encoding=1252, QuoteStyle=QuoteStyle.None]),
4      #"Promoted Headers" = Table.PromoteHeaders(Source, [PromoteAllScalars=true]),
5      #"Changed Type" = Table.TransformColumnTypes(#"Promoted Headers",{{"EmployeeID", Int64.Type}, {"M1", Int64.Type}, {"M2", Int64.Type},
6      #"Unpivoted Other Columns" = Table.UnpivotOtherColumns(#"Changed Type", {"EmployeeID"}, "Month", "TargetAmount"),
7      #"Filtered Rows" = Table.SelectRows(#"Unpivoted Other Columns", each ([TargetAmount] <> 0)),
8      #"Replaced Value" = Table.ReplaceValue(#"Filtered Rows","M","",Replacer.ReplaceText,{"Month"})
9  in
10     #"Replaced Value"
```

✓ No syntax errors have been detected.

Done   Cancel

Figure 5.3: M-code

6. Click on **Done** in the **Advanced Editor** to close it.

   You will see that Power Query does not show a data preview anymore. It now tells you that you have a function. Let us rename the function to something more descriptive of what it is doing.

7. Change the name of the function to **GetTargets** by right-clicking on **targets2021** in the list of queries.

This is all well, but how to use this function on all files and create a single **Target** table? We will use the **From folder** option for that.

Reading multiple files from a folder

Refer to the following steps:

1. With Power Query Editor still open, click on **New Source** in the **Home** ribbon.

2. Click on **More...** to open the **Get Data** dialog and select the option **Folder**. Click on **Connect**.

3. Browse to where you saved the three target files and click on **OK** until you see the preview dialog.

   In the data preview, you see a list of all the files and their metadata in the folder that you browsed to. At the bottom, you see two interesting buttons. The first is the button **Combine & Transform Data**. When using this option, Power Query will create a function and two queries for you. One query to transform a single file, and another two apply transformations after the data is combined into a single table. We will use the **Transform Data** button and do all that work ourselves. Doing it yourself the first time makes it easier to understand what is really happening. Once you do understand, use the option you like best.

4. Click on **Transform Data** to close the dialog and return to the Power Query Editor.

   In Power Query Editor, you see a list of all the files in the folder you selected. It also includes all files from all subfolders if you have subfolders. We will assume here that you do not have any subfolders. We will also assume that you have other files than the three target files in this folder. Since you want to work with the target files only, we need to filter out all other files.

5. Click on the filter icon in the header of the column **Name**.

6. Select **Text Filters** in the popup that appears, and then select **Begins With...**.

7. Behind the option **begins with** in the **Filter Rows** dialog, type **targets**.

8. Complete the dialog as in *Figure 5.4:*

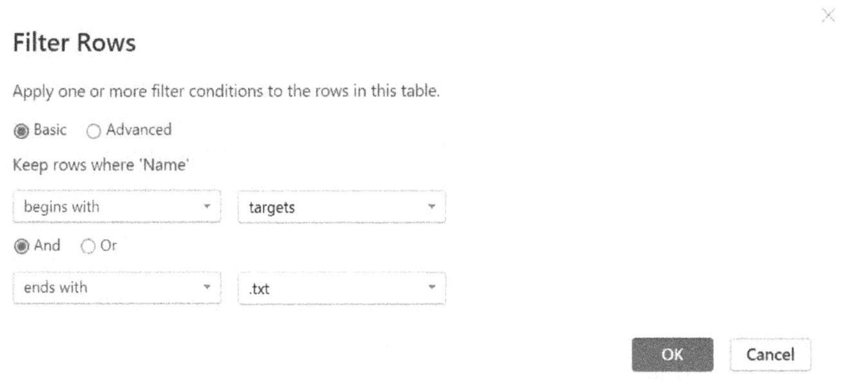

Filter Rows

Apply one or more filter conditions to the rows in this table.

⦿ Basic ◯ Advanced

Keep rows where 'Name'

| begins with ▾ | targets ▾ |

⦿ And ◯ Or

| ends with ▾ | .txt ▾ |

OK   Cancel

Figure 5.4: Filter Rows

By configuring a filter like in *Figure 5.4,* you create a type of dynamic filter. If in the future a file named **targets2024.txt** is added, it will be part of the files selected. If files with other file names are added to the folder, they will be ignored. After a new target file is added to this folder, all you need to do is refresh your Power BI semantic model. Inside Power BI Desktop, you must click a button for that. However, once the report is uploaded to the Power BI service, we will automate data refreshes. This means that new target data will be added to the report automatically as long as the naming convention for files with target data stays the same.

We are getting a bit ahead of ourselves. We now have the three files selected but we need the contents of these files.

9. Click on the button **Choose Columns** in the **Home** ribbon and select only the columns **Content** and **Name**.

10. Click on the button **Invoke Custom Function** on the **Add Column** ribbon.

11. Under **New Column name**, type **Target**.

12. In the drop-down list, under **Function query**, select our function **GetTargets**. Make sure the column **Content** is selected in the bottom drop-down list. Click on **OK**.

    You should now have three rows and three columns. The second column is called **Target** and has the word **Table** in the cells. More importantly, it has the **Expand** button in the column header.

13. Click on the **Expand** button in the header of the column **Target**.

14. Unselect the option **Use original column name as prefix** before clicking on **OK**.

    You now have a single table with the data of all three target files. We need just a couple more steps to reach the desired result of a table with three columns: **EmployeeID**, **Date**, and **TargetAmount**. We still miss the column **Date** and need to get the year out of the file name to then combine it with **Month** to create a date.

15. Right-click in the header of the column **Name** and select **Split Column** followed by **By Delimiter....**

16. In the top drop-down list under **Select or enter delimiter** leave (or select) the option **–Custom—**and type a dot (**.**) in the textbox underneath the drop-down list.

17. Under **Number of columns to split into** type **1**.

18. Click on **OK**.

19. Remove the last step, **Changed Type** from the **APPLIED STEPS**. (This step was automatically added).

20. Right-click again in the header of the column **Name.1** and select **Split Column** followed by **By Number of Characters....**

21. Type **4** under **Number of characters** and select **Once, as far right as possible** in the **Split Column by Number of Characters** dialog.

22. Remove the last step, **Changed Type** from the **APPLIED STEPS** (again).

We now have a column with just the year in it. Time to combine it with month into a date.

23. Select both columns **Name.1.2** and **Month** by clicking in the header while holding down the *Ctrl* key on the keyboard.

24. Click on the little down-arrow in the button **Column From Examples** on the **Add Column** ribbon.

25. Click on **From Selection** in the popup.

To the right of the data preview, a new column named **Column1** is created. It is still empty. With the option **Column From Examples**, you can type in the value you need and let Power Query generate the expression needed for this custom column. You start typing in a value for the first row. You might have to enter a value for the second and third row as well. If Power Query does not show the values in the other rows after providing it with three examples, it will probably never guess it.

26. Type **1-7-2021** in the first row and press enter. (This assumes that the column **Month** has value **7** and column **Name.1.2** has value **2021** in the first row. You may have to change what you type accordingly.

27. When the values in all other rows seem all right, press **OK**, change the name of the column to **Date** (click in header) and click on **OK**.

You may have to check the formula used by Power Query. The formula may contain the following code:

```
each Text.Combine({"1-", [Month], "-2021"})
```

When you see this code, it means it took a hard-coded value instead of using the value from the column **Name.1.2**. The code should be similar to:

```
each Text.Combine({"1-", [Month], "-", [Name.1.2]})
```

28. Change the partial code inside the formula bar, if necessary.

29. Select the columns **EmployeeID**, **TargetAmount** and **Date**. Remove all the other columns.

30. Change the data type of the column **Date** into **Date**. **EmployeeID** should be **Whole Number,** and **TargetAmount** should be **Fixed decimal number**.

31. Change the name of the query into **Targets**.

32. Click on **Close & Apply** in the **Home** ribbon.

    As always, after adding a table in Power Query, you need to check (and possibly create) relationships.

33. Go to the Model view of Power BI Desktop.

34. If necessary, create relationships between the table **Target** and **Date** (drag the column **Date** from one table to the other) and between **Target** and **Employees** (based on **EmployeeID**).

35. Got to the Report view of Power BI Desktop.

36. Drag the column **TargetAmount** from the table **Targets** in the **Data** pane and drop it onto the bar chart showing net sales by employee.

Your report should now look like *Figure 5.5*. It shows that actual sales by year by employee and puts the sales in perspective by showing the targets as well:

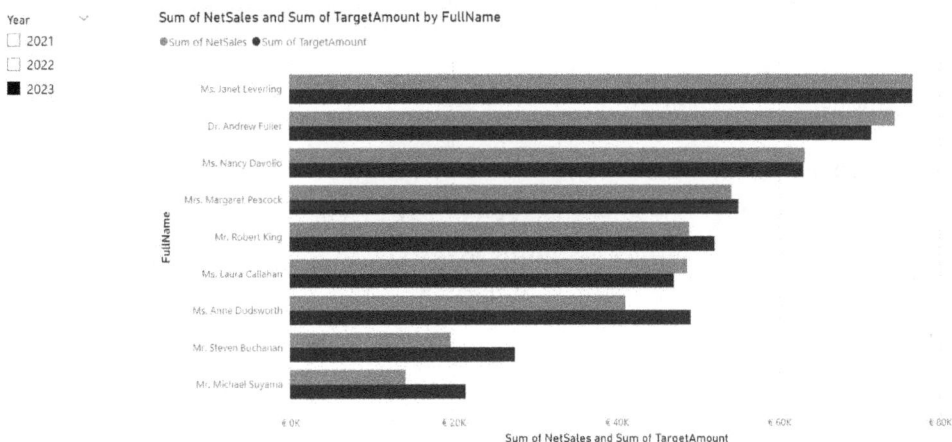

***Figure 5.5**: Sales and targets*

We added a second fact table to the Power BI semantic model. For that, we had to read multiple files and combine that into a single table. Using a function to do so makes for an automated solution. Data from new files will be added automatically on refresh of the Power BI semantic model.

By now, we came across quite some M-code. It is time to get a closer look at it.

Understanding M-code

Let us start at the beginning and create a blank query through the following steps:

1. Click in Power BI Desktop on the **Home** ribbon in the button **Get data**, followed by **Blank query**.

2. Once inside the Power Query Editor, open the **Advanced Editor** (**Home** ribbon).

   The code you see is as follows:
   ```
   let
        Source = ""
   in
        Source
   ```
   A Power Query query always starts with the keyword **let** (small letters). This basically creates a variable. A variable is a bit of memory that you can store a value in, temporarily, that you reference by a self-chosen name. In the blank query, that variable is **Source,** and the value stored in it is **""** (blank).

   A Power Query query always ends with the keyword **in**. After, the keyword **in** is a variable. The value in that variable is the result of the entire query. In this case, the blank value is the result. This means we have a blank query.

   We can change the query. We could, for instance, write the following M-code:
   ```
   let
        Number1 = 5,
        Number2 = Number1 + 6
   in
        Number2
   ```
   In this code, the first line after the keyword **let** creates a variable called **Number1** and assigns it the value **5**. Note the comma at the end of this line. It tells Power Query that there will be another variable. The next line creates that variable and names it **Number2**. This variable uses the variable created in the previous line and adds **6** to the value of **5** stored inside **Number1**. Now, since the line that creates the variable **Number2** does not end with a comma, it is the last line of variable declarations. The next line will always be the keyword **in**. After the **in**, you will almost always see the variable created in the last line before the **in**.

Have a look at the following code (*Figure 5.6*). It is the function we created earlier to unpivot a target file:

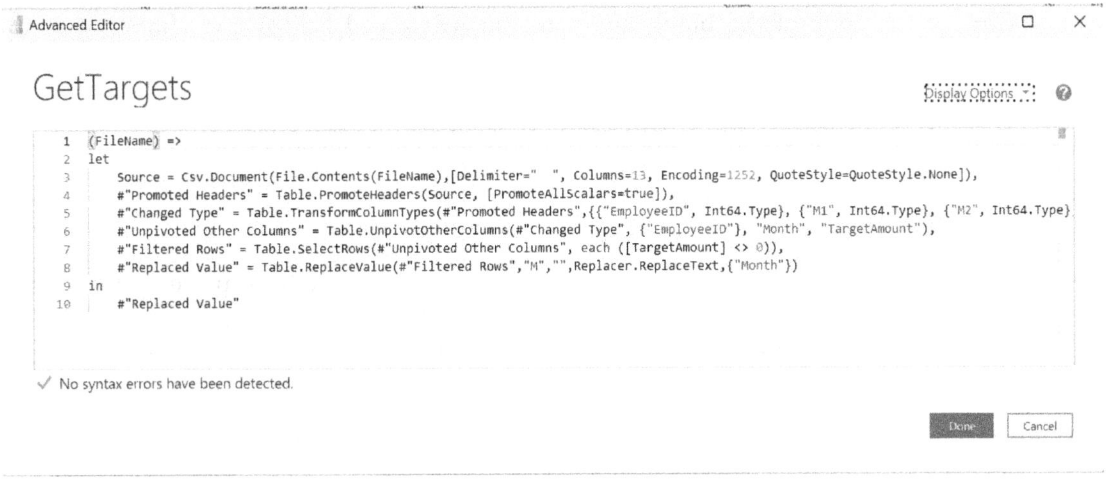

Figure 5.6: *Advanced Editor*

In *line 3,* a variable **Source** is created reading the file contents of a **Csv.Document**. Remember that we started with the **Get data** button and chose to import a **Text/CSV** file. This means that our mouse actions translate almost literally into code.

In *line 4,* a variable name **#"Promoted Headers"** is created and assigned a value. Interpreting the name of the variable already gives you a pretty good idea of what the code does. Our file had column names in it. Promoted headers means the first line of the file (the column names) are used as column names of the data in Power Query.

With code generated by Power Query itself, you will almost always see **Table. SomeThing** right behind the **=** sign. The **.SomeThing** denotes the transformation performed on your data in this step. It will have braces, and the first thing inside the braces is the variable created in the previous line. In *line 4,* you can see **Table. PromoteHeaders(Source, [PromoteAllScalars = true])**. Note the use of the variable **Source** just inside the braces. **Source** is the table from the previous step. This line of code will transform that table into a new, altered table.

Although this explanation may sound abstract, it is exactly how the interface works as well. When Power Query Editor opens, you see data in the screen in most cases. This is a table. You then apply a transformation that slightly alters the table into a new table. You repeat applying steps (or adding lines of code) until you are happy with the table you created.

Knowing M-code allows us to do some nice tricks. Let us think about the target data from the previous section. Each time a new target file is stored in the folder that we read from, that data is imported. After 10 years, we potentially read 10 years of data.

However, what if the report only uses the last three years of data? Should not we be able to automatically read in only the last three years of data?

Change the code of the blank query in the **Advanced Editor** and change it to the following code:

```
let
    Years = {2021, 2022, 2023}
in
    Years
```

3. Click on **Done**.

    M-code creates a list of values when using the curly brackets. You see that list when back in the Power Query Editor. The **List Tools** ribbon is automatically activated inside the Power Query Editor. One option you see on this ribbon is the **To Table** option that changes the list into a table.

4. Click on the button **To Table** in the **List Tools – Transform** ribbon. Click on **OK** in the dialog that appears.

    You now have a table, and every transform we have learned so far throughout this book is available to turn it into something more useful.

5. Open the **Advanced Editor**.

    Note that clicking on **To Table** added a step to your code. The name of the variable tells the story. It is worth noting that you can mix writing M-code and performing transformations using the GUI.

6. Change the M-code step you wrote into **Years = {2000 .. 2025}**.

7. Click on **Done** to check the result of the code. Using **..** creates a list using a range.

    Like any programming language, M-code has a lot of functions you can use. The function **DateTime.LocalNow()** gives you the current date and time. The function **Date.Year()** can calculate the year from any given date.

8. Change the code of the query to match *Figure 5.7*. Click on **Done** to see the result:

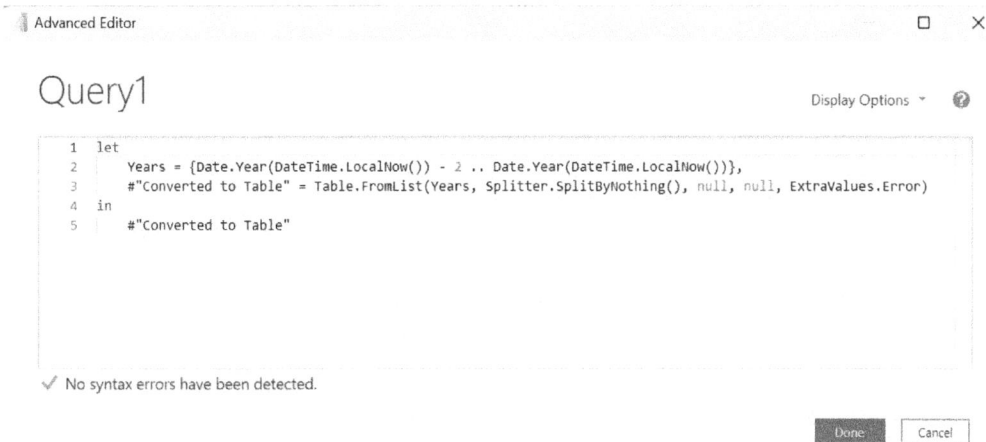

Figure 5.7: *Last three years*

With the targets example in mind, let us perform one more action.

9. Change the data type of **Column1** to **Text**.

10. Click on the button **Custom Column** in the ribbon **Add Column**.

11. Call the column **FileName** and use the following expression = **"targets" & [Column1]
    & ".txt"**.

    You just generated the filenames for the three most current target files. All you have to
    do now is add the file path to the name and then use our custom function **GetTargets**
    to read in the data inside those three files.

12. Since we will not use this query in our further solution, you can delete it.

Understanding the date table code

Figure 5.8 shows the code we used earlier to create a **Date** table. You can also find the code in
the solutions map of the downloads of this book. Let us have a closer look now that we know
M a bit.

Advanced Editor □ ✕

Date

Display Options ⌄ ❓

```
1  let
2      StartDate = #date(2021,1,1),
3      NumberOfDays = Duration.Days( #date(2023,12,31) - StartDate ),
4      Dates = List.Dates(StartDate, NumberOfDays+1, #duration(1,0,0,0)),
5      #"Converted to Table" = Table.FromList(Dates, Splitter.SplitByNothing(), null, null, ExtraValues.Error),
6      #"Renamed Columns" = Table.RenameColumns(#"Converted to Table",{{"Column1", "Date"}}),
7      #"Changed Type" = Table.TransformColumnTypes(#"Renamed Columns",{{"Date", type date}}),
8      #"Inserted Year" = Table.AddColumn(#"Changed Type", "Year", each Date.Year([Date]), Int64.Type),
9      #"Inserted Month" = Table.AddColumn(#"Inserted Year", "Month", each Date.Month([Date]), Int64.Type),
10     #"Inserted Month Name" = Table.AddColumn(#"Inserted Month", "Month Name", each Date.MonthName([Date], "en-us"), type text),
11     #"Inserted Quarter" = Table.AddColumn(#"Inserted Month Name", "Quarter", each Date.QuarterOfYear([Date]), Int64.Type),
12     #"Inserted Merged Column" = Table.AddColumn(#"Inserted Quarter", "MonthYear", each Text.Combine([[Month Name], Text.From([Year], "nl
13     #"Added Custom" = Table.AddColumn(#"Inserted Merged Column", "MonthKey", each [Year] * 100 + [Month]),
14     #"Added Custom1" = Table.AddColumn(#"Added Custom", "QuarterYear", each "Q" & Text.From([Quarter]) & ", " & Text.From([Year])),
15     #"Changed Type1" = Table.TransformColumnTypes(#"Added Custom1",{{"QuarterYear", type text}, {"MonthKey", Int64.Type}}),
16     #"Renamed Columns1" = Table.RenameColumns(#"Changed Type1",{{"Month", "MonthNo"}})
17 in
18     #"Renamed Columns1"
```

✓ No syntax errors have been detected.

Done Cancel

Figure 5.8: Date table M-code

Line 2 of the code creates a variable called **StartDate** that is hard-coded, initialized with the date **1-1-2021**. Replacing **2021** with **Date.Year(DateTime.LocalNow()) - 2** would turn the start date in the first of January two years ago.

Line 3 creates a variable **NumberOfDates** and uses the data type **Duration** to calculate how many days we have between the start date and **31-12-2023**. Again, you can replace the hard-coded value **2023** by functions to make it more dynamic.

Line 4 creates a list of dates from the start date, with as many rows as we have days between the start date and **31-12-2023**.

Then, the list gets converted into a table. The sole column in the table is renamed to **Date**, and its data type is changed into **Date**.

From there on, all other columns are added to the table to create a proper **Date** table.

There is more you can do now that you know M-code a bit. Look at *Figure 5.9*. The code generated a table with two columns **MonthNumber** and **MonthName**. It then adds twelve rows to the table.

Advanced Editor □ ✕

Query1

Display Options ▾ ❓

```
 1   let
 2       Source = #table(
 3           {"MonthNumber", "MonthName"},
 4           {
 5               {1 , "Jan"},
 6               {2 , "Feb"},
 7               {3 , "Mar"},
 8               {4 , "Apr"},
 9               {5 , "May"},
10               {6 , "Jun"},
11               {7 , "Jul"},
12               {8 , "Aug"},
13               {9 , "Sep"},
14               {10 , "Oct"},
15               {11 , "Nov"},
16               {12 , "Dec"}
17                   }
18       )
19   in
20       Source
```

✓ No syntax errors have been detected.

Done   Cancel

Figure 5.9: *M table*

Using a table like this can be handy, for instance, when you need a custom sorting order for categories. Create a row for each category. Add a column for the categories and a number column that has numbers that sort correctly.

We are almost done learning Power Query and M. There is one important thing left to learn about: parameters.

Using parameters

Eight of the queries we created so far read data from the URL to the Northwind OData feed. Refreshing the data will fail when that URL changes. Another query uses a local folder and will likewise fail when the folder name changes or when the files are moved to another folder. It should be easy to deal with changes like this.

Some things will change over time. Server names, database names, file names, file locations, and so on. At some point, they will change. It should be easy to deal with such a change. In our current solution, we will have to go to the advanced editor of eight queries to change the hard-coded URL in the M-code when the OData URL changes. That is not easy.

Also consider the following scenario. You work at a bank, and for privacy regulation reasons, you are not allowed to work with real data. You get anonymized data and maybe even a small subset of anonymized data. When you finish developing the report, a test department will test the report on test data. After successful testing, we move to the next phase, where a select group of people work with the report to see whether it is acceptable for use in real life. They have a special environment for this to be sure they do not impact the business. The last phase is when we use the report in the organization on real data. We call this scenario **Development, Test, Acceptance, and Production (DTAP)**. In each phase, the data used comes from a different source. How to facilitate easy moving from one phase into the next?

Parameters are the answer.

1. Click on the upper part of the **Manage Parameters** button on the **Home** ribbon of the Power Query Editor.

2. Click on **New**.

3. Under **Name** type `ODataURL_Northwind`.

4. Under **Current value** type `http://services.odata.org/V3/Northwind/Northwind.svc`.

5. Select **Text** for the **Type**.

   Note the list **Suggested Values**. When you leave the default option **Any value** selected, you just type any value in **Current value**. In a DTAP scenario, you might choose **List of values** and provide, for instance, server names for all four phases. This allows for easy selecting later. With the option **Query** you can select a Power Query query that has the values to use. This allows for easy maintenance. Create a table in SQL Server or an Excel workbook with valid values and import that into a query. Now, when things change, change the SQL table or Excel workbook. The new values will be picked up by Power Query automatically.

6. Click on **OK**.

   You should now see the parameter in the list of queries (left-hand side of the Power Query Editor). Now that you have a parameter, you must still start using it.

7. Select the query **Customers** and select the first step in the **APPLIED STEPS** list in the **Query Settings** pane.

8. Note the URL to the OData feed in the formula bar. Replace the URL (including the quotes) with `ODataURL_Northwind`.

9. Nothing should happen.

   The query now uses the value stored in the parameter to connect to the data source. Whenever the URL changes, change the value of the parameters. The query picks up the new value automatically. You should, of course, change all the queries connecting to the OData feed to use the parameter.

10. Click on the button **New Source** and select **OData** as the source.

11. Note the option to select a parameter in the **OData feed** dialog.

12. Click on **Cancel**.

Create parameters for all sources that you connect to. Start with creating parameters and use them with every new query you make. Otherwise, you will have to change a lot of queries afterwards.

Parameters can be used for other things as well. You can filter rows using parameters, for instance. We will see an example of that in *Chapter 10, Scalable Power BI Solutions*.

Once you publish a report to the cloud, the parameters are published as well, and they are accessible through the portal. So even after publishing a report, it is still easy to change parameter values. You will learn this in *Chapter 12, Working with the Power BI Service*.

Organizing queries

You might end up with a long list of queries, functions and parameters in the list of queries. It is possible to organize the list a little bit.

1. Right-click in the list of queries on **Customers** and select **Move To Group**, followed by **New Group...**.

2. Name the new group **Imported tables**.

3. Drag the queries, **Shippers**, **ShipTo**, **Employees**, **Date**, **Products**, **Sales**, and **Targets** to this newly created group.

4. Create separate groups for parameters and functions, and add the parameter and function to the appropriate group.

5. Create a group **Support queries**, and add the queries **Suppliers** and **CountOrderLines** to it.

Creating groups here has no functional meaning. It is just to make your life easier.

Optimizing queries and query folding

Have a look at the steps it took to create the Sales query. It has a lot of steps. When looking more closely, you can see several **Changed Type** steps or **Renamed Columns** steps, for instance. More steps in a query can have two negative effects: readability and maintainability for humans, and bad performance of data refreshes.

With all the steps, it becomes difficult to quickly see what is going on. At some point, you might have to change the query because something has changed. Report requirements may change, file structures may change, anything can change. The easier your query is to understand, the easier it will be to change.

The more complex a query becomes, the longer it might take to refresh your data later. A lot of steps do not necessarily make a query complex for Power Query. Power Query analyzes the steps and will execute an optimized plan. However, with more complexity and steps added, there will be an increasing chance that you do not get a really well-optimized plan. We may have to help Power Query where possible.

Suppose you have filters on two columns, and you need to rename both columns. You can create a filter on one and then rename the column. You then do the same with the second column. This results in four steps added to your query. If you create filters on both columns and then rename them both, you get only two steps. The two filters are combined into a single filter step. There is also just one step to rename both columns.

Try to plan your steps and perform them in a smart order. It will reduce the number of steps and keep your query easier and may be faster.

When working with a relational database, there is an extra optimization that Power Query tries to do automatically. When you perform a transformation, it will try to translate that in SQL code and let the database do the transformation. This is called **query folding**. The assumption is that the database server is more powerful than Power Query. It can also mean that less data must be transferred from the database to Power BI.

How well Power Query can apply query folding depends on your query. At some point it may not know how to generate the correct SQL, and it will do the work by itself. An indication can be seen in the step. When you right-click on a step, you can see the native query or not!

Keeping things as simple as possible is always a good idea. Try to use foldable steps as early in the query as possible. Sometimes an action prevents later steps to be foldable. With that, Click on **Close & Apply** on the **Home** ribbon to close Power Query Editor.

Exam tip

You should understand what Power Query is and what it is capable of. In the exam, you may get asked how to read in multiple files or scenarios that they describe might use custom functions. At a high level, you must know it all.

You do not need to know all the buttons on all ribbons by heart. You will also not be tasked with writing M-code from scratch. You may however, get to see a bit of M-code where a part of the code is missing. You must specify from a list which option to use to make the code complete.

Practice with Power Query as much as you can. Each time you create a query, have a look at the M-code. With that, you should be able to answer Power Query questions correctly.

Conclusion

In this chapter, you learned some more basic transformations. More importantly, you learned to write a little M-code and you learned how to create custom functions. These kills can be used to automate Power BI solutions. You do not want to copy-paste queries when you have two or more similar files to import. You do not want to change your solution manually every time new data becomes available, and you do not want recurring manual labor because a simple thing like a new year happened. All of that is not necessary with a bit of smart Power Query coding.

In the next chapter, we return to creating visualizations. You learned the basics of creating visualizations in *Chapter 4, The Basics of Visualizations*. However, there is a lot more to creating effective reports than what you already learned. The next chapter focuses on how to use interactivity in the report to make it an effective report.

Multiple choice questions

1. **An advantage of using Power Query to generate a Date table is:**

    a. You can easily re-use the table in other Power BI Desktop files.

    b. It performs better compared to generating one using DAX.

    c. You can use the internet to enrich the table.

    d. Power Query has more functions to use than other options.

2. **The key word let in a Power Query query is followed by:**

    a. A list of variable assignments

    b. Steps that transform data

    c. Statements that together form a query

    d. Query clauses that combined form a query

3. **Parameters can be used to connect to:**

    a. Databases

    b. Excel workbooks

    c. OData feeds

    d. SharePoint lists

Answers

1	c
2	a, b
3	a, b, c, d

CHAPTER 6

Create Interactive Reports

Introduction

Chapter 4, The Basics of Visualizations, focused on all the settings of visuals, where to find them, and how to use them. Another important aspect is when to use these settings and how. This chapter focuses on creating effective reports. Creating effective reports starts with choosing an appropriate visualization type. You also need to choose colors that will help the reader understand the report more easily. Another thing to consider is the amount of information that you can present in a single visualization or on a single page.

After you learn about report development theory, we will apply the theory. We will create highly interactive reports using functionality like drill down, drill through, and more.

If you want to follow along with the examples presented in this chapter, you need Power BI Desktop to be installed on your workstation. This chapter continues where the previous ended. If you followed along in the previous chapter, you can continue in the Power BI Desktop file you created there. If you did not, you can use the file **Solution chapter 5.pbix** from the GitHub repository of this book.

Structure

This chapter covers the following topics:

- Pitfalls and considerations
- Preferred visualization types
- Hiding items on a report
- Using buttons
- Questions and answers
- Page navigator and bookmark
- Shapes and images
- Using visual calculations
- Conditional formatting
- Other visuals
- Themes and templates

Objectives

In this chapter, you will learn what it means to create an effective report. You will also learn to choose between visualization types and keep a report simple by using all sorts of interactivity options of Power BI.

Pitfalls and considerations

Let us start by discussing the two most frequently asked questions of users when creating a report (at least in my experience):

- Can you export this data to Excel?
- Can you add … to the report?

The answer to the first question is that data on a report can be exported to Excel. However, report users should not use that option. Power BI has several ways to export data to Excel. You can export data from visuals on a report or Power BI dashboard. This feature can be turned off for the report in the settings of Power BI Desktop. You can also allow or disallow it from the admin portal in the Power BI service. Users can also use the feature **Analyze in Excel**, available from a report published to the cloud or from a Power BI semantic model in the cloud.

Excel is a great tool for analyzing data. That makes the feature **Analyze in Excel** from a semantic model great as well. Build your own Excel report from the data we prepared in Power BI.

Keep in mind, though, that Power BI is not a data export tool. Power BI gets its data from somewhere. When people need that data but not your Power BI report, let them get that data directly from the source (if possible, of course) instead of using Power BI as an export tool.

In my opinion, there are two reasons why users ask for data to be exported to Excel. One reason is that they do not trust the Power BI report and try to check your values using Excel. Try working on this trust issue by giving them a more important role in the report development phase. The other reason is that they want another report. You created a bar chart, for instance, where they prefer a pie chart. Create the report they want, in this case.

The trust of your users is of critical importance to your success. In some scenarios, exporting to Excel is ok, but make sure you do it for the right reasons.

The second often asked question is: *can you add … to the report?* People always want more on the report. You create a report with net sales on it, and they want gross sales as well. When you comply, then they want you to add quantities sold to the report and so on. Your screen is always too small to fit the information on the screen, and still people want more. This leads us to two pitfalls.

Pitfalls

Almost all reporting tools suffer from the same two pitfalls:

- The wow-factor
- Report abundance

You can create really visually appealing reports, nicely colored visuals. A bunch of **key performance indicator** (**KPI**) on the report with nice traffic lights or other colored indicators for the status, and an even more nicely colored logo. Maybe a report background as well, and all the visuals are grouped using shapes. In addition to all the visually appealing elements, report users will ask for extra information on the report as well.

Consider walking into a room where a report like that is shown on a big TV screen. The first thing you may think is: wow, that is a cool report! That is what can be referred to as the wow-factor. However, ask yourself this: *what do you learn from the report?* and how long does it take to get the message? How much effort, interpretation, and coming to conclusions does it take? Nice colorful pictures that make you think, *Wow, they belong in art museums!* A report should be effective. Meaning it should be easy and quick to get the message that the report is supposed to deliver.

The second pitfall is report abundance. In most organizations, there are too many reports, not too few. This leads to people not knowing what information is available and on what report. So, they will create a new report or ask the reporting/BI department to make a new report. The result is even more reports.

The challenge here is to create a few simple reports that contain all the information we can possibly need. This is an almost impossible task, but we will try anyway.

Important considerations

With the preceding in mind, there are two important considerations to make:

- What is the message of the report?
- Who are you users?

Consider the three-bar charts of *Figure 6.1*. All three bar charts are based on the exact same data. Let us have a closer look to see which one we should use:

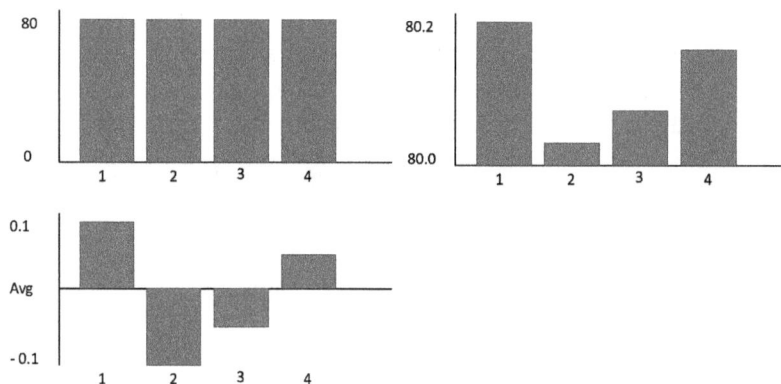

Figure 6.1: Bar charts

Determine the message

Let us suppose the x-axis shows week numbers. The top left bar chart shows four values on a scale of 0 to 80. All bars appear the same length. If the message of the report is that business is stable and the value shown in the chart is the same, week after week, this is a nice visual.

The top right bar chart shows the same values on a scale of 80.0 to 80.2. With this scale, you can see that all four weeks were different after all. The differences are small, but what if you were trying to analyze just these differences? The top left bar chart would be useless.

Bar charts are often (always?) interpreted by people in such a way that a bar with twice the length represents a number twice as big. The top right bar chart leads to misinterpretations. Due to the way people interpret the bar chart, it should always have a scale starting at zero.

When we analyze the week-to-week differences, the bottom bar chart is the correct one. It shows the week-to-week difference from the average. The y-axis shows the average as zero. Bars above the line have values greater than average, bars below show values smaller than average. The area of each bar is directly proportional to the difference.

The top right bar chart is wrong from a theoretical standpoint. Which of the other ones you want depends on the message you want to bring across: whether each week is the same or how different it is from week-to-week.

Often, data becomes more informative when you can compare it to something. In the bottom bar chart, each value is a difference calculated from the average value. So, it compares the raw value to the average.

Determine the user

The second important consideration to make is to ensure you know your audience. Users interpret your reports. Do they do that correctly, and are they able to do it correctly? Have a look at the box and whisker plot of *Figure 6.2*:

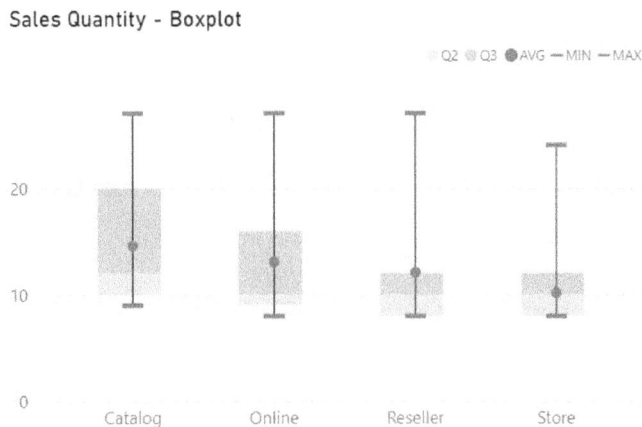

Figure 6.2: Box plot

A box and whisker plot is a great way to visualize the distribution of values in a column. In this case, it shows how many products are sold through different sales channels. Since an average is a very limited statistic, a box plot is used to show the distribution of the quantity instead of just something like an average.

This is great, but how many people can read and interpret this box plot? The box plot is great when all your users are econometrists or when all are good at statistics. There are a lot of people who are not. That is when a box plot will become a nice picture instead of an informative visual.

When you recognize the limited use for box plots (or just the risks of losing users), the question becomes which visualization types should you use.

Preferred visualization types

According to some visualization theories, there are three preferred visualization types. They are:

- Bar chart
- Line chart
- Table/Matrix

The reason why you should prefer one of these three visualization types is their simplicity. Almost everyone understands them natively and can use and interpret them correctly.

The bar chart is great for showing a fact split by a category. For instance, sales by sales channel. You should favor horizontal bars over vertical bars because people are better able to guess relative differences between the bars that way. You should sort the bar from the greater values to the smaller ones. The longest bar is the top one, the shortest the last one. The exception is when you have periods on the x-axis. You should now have standing bars, and you should sort on the periods to make them chronological.

Line charts are great for showing trends. Always use the line chart with periods on the x-axis. The y-axis does not need a scale that starts at zero, as the bar chart does.

Tables are not really preferred because they need a lot of focus from the user to read and interpret. That leads to a higher risk of misinterpretation. However, everyone is capable of understanding tables and matrices.

You may have noticed the pie chart is not in the list, even though in real life, it is an often-used visualization type. People like them often because they are used to them. They think they can read them well. As it turns out, however, people are bad at estimating the relative sizes of different parts of the pie, even though that is the main focus of the pie. It is way less effective than most people think. With a limited number of categories and the percentages shown in the visual, a pie chart might be ok.

All other visualization types are good if you know that your target audience knows how to interpret them and get the message you wanted them to get from it.

The same data can be visualized in many different ways to convey other information. As an example, look at *Figure 6.3*:

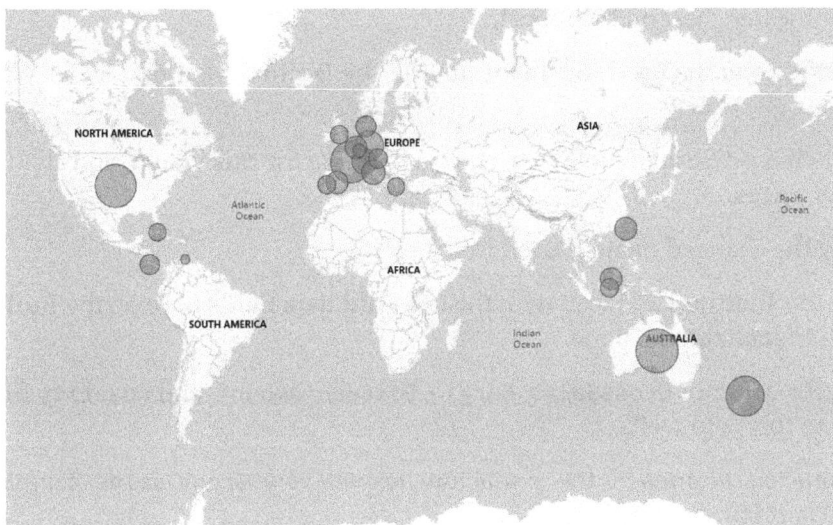

Figure 6.3: Map visual

When you want to show where in the world you do business, and you are trying to convince an investor that you already are a multinational, this is a great visual. You can see business in multiple countries in multiple parts of the world. You also see a concentration of countries in Europe. If you want to compare countries to each other based on whatever measure creates the circles, this visual is bad. A bar chart would do a much better job.

This is enough for this book. There are five-day courses about storytelling with data and formatting reports which are outside the scope of this book. It is, however, relevant to good report development. We will now continue to develop Power BI reports, with in the back of our minds: create a few simple reports that contain all the information we possibly need.

Using tooltips

Power BI automatically creates a tooltip for almost every visual you create. Let us look at tooltips with the following steps:

1. Open Power BI Desktop if it is not open yet. Open your solution from the previous chapter or open **Solution Chapter 5.pbix**.

2. Select the report page, **Sales report**.

3. Hover your mouse over one of the bars in the bar chart.

A popup (the tooltip) appears whenever you hover your mouse over a visual. It shows you two things: the category you are hovering over and the value of the fact visualized in the visual. It shows the column names used to create the visual. Let us make some improvements to the tooltip:

1. Select the bar chart on the report.

2. Find the columns used for this visual on the **Build visual** tab of the **Visualizations** pane.

3. Right-click on **Sum of NetSales**, choose **Rename for this visual**, and change the name to **Net sales**.

4. Verify the changed name is used in the tooltip.

5. Note the **Tooltips** field well with the text **Add data fields here** on the **Build visual** tab of the **Visualizations** pane.

6. Drag the columns **GrossSales**, **Margin**, **DiscountAmount**, and **Quantity** from the **Data** pane to this field well.

7. Rename the columns for this visual into, respectively: **Gross sales**, **Margin**, **Discount**, and **Quantity**.

8. Hover your mouse over the bar chart to see the result of what you just did.

   Instead of adding extra columns directly into a visual, consider using tooltips. It keeps the report clean and easy. However, you invite users to get the extra information by hovering the mouse over a category that triggers their interest. Since you make them interact and consciously choose a column to hover over, they process the information better. Tooltips keep the report simple and help users process the information more effectively. When you use tooltips for most visuals, users will come to learn that there is always something extra to get.

   We can do even better. You can show an entire report page as a tooltip.

9. Click on the plus icon at the bottom of the Report view to add a new report page.

10. Right-click in the newly created tab where the plus icon was and rename the page to **Net sales tooltip**.

11. Go to the page properties of this new report page (**Format page** tab of **Visualizations** pane).

12. Open the section **Page information** and toggle **Allow use as tooltip** on.

13. Open the **Canvas settings** section. Choose **Custom** in the **Type** drop-down list and enter **500** for **Height** and **800** for **Width**.

14. Click on the icon of the clustered bar chart in the list of visualization types on the **Visualizations** pane to add a visual to the report. (Hover your mouse over the icons to get the name of the visual in a tooltip. You need the third icon from the left in the top row).

15. Drag the column **NetSales** from the **Data** pane and drop it onto the visual. Add the column **Year**.

16. Since the column **Year** has a numerical data type, it is added to the **X-axis** as an extra bar. Drag it in the **Build visual** tab of the **Visualizations** pane from the **X-axis** to the **Y-axis**.

17. Delete the title for both the **X-axis** and **Y-axis**. (**Visual** tab of the **Format visual** tab in the **Visualizations** pane).

18. Change the visual title to **Net sales by Year**. (**General** tab of the **Format visual** tab in the **Visualizations** pane).

19. Make the size of the bar chart to cover exactly the upper left quarter of the report canvas. Use the red lines, indicating when you are in the middle of the canvas.

20. Create a second bar chart in the lower left quadrant of the report showing **Net sales by Age group**.

21. Create a third bar chart in the lower right quadrant of the report showing the **Top 5 Customers by Net sales**.

22. Click in the upper right quadrant of the report and make sure none of the bar charts are selected.

23. Note the **Tooltip** field well on the **Build visual** tab of the **Visualizations** pane. Drag the column **NetSales** from the **Data** pane and drop it in the field well on the text **Drag tooltip fields here**.

24. Switch back to the report page, **Sales report**, and hover your mouse over the bar chart.

    When you hover your mouse over the bar chart, Power BI should now show your newly created report page as a tooltip. The data on the tooltip is filtered by the category you hover over. When a salesperson is selected in the slicer, the tooltip is filtered on that employee as well.

    Let us finish the tooltip. The tooltip should clearly show what category it uses to filter the tooltip. We will need a little bit of **Data Analysis Expressions** (**DAX**) for that. DAX will be explained extensively in *Chapters 8, DAX*, and *Chapter 9, Advanced DAX Concepts*.

25. Switch back to the report page, **Net sales tooltip**.

26. Right-click on the table **Products** in the **Data** pane. Select **New measure** in the popup.

27. Enter the following in the formula bar that appears between the ribbon and the report:

```
Selected category = SELECTEDVALUE(Products[Category])
```

28. A column named Selected category will be visible in the table **Products** in the **Data** pane. Drag this column to the report page. Turn the visual Power BI created into a card visual. (Icon showing **123**).

29. On the **Format visual** tab of the card, in the **Visualizations** pane, turn **Category label for the card** off.

30. Lastly, right-click on the tab of the report page, all the way at the bottom of Power BI Desktop. Click on **Hide**.

31. Switch back to the report page, **Sales report**, and hover your mouse over the bar chart.

    The Card visual enables you to show a single value. DAX allows you to add calculations to your Power BI semantic model. So, we *calculated* which category is selected and show it in the card.

    The report page **Sales report** is not meant to be used other than as a tooltip. That is why we set it to hidden. It will not be visible after publishing this report to the Power BI service. It will continue to show as tooltip.

    You should have a result as shown in *Figure 6.4*:

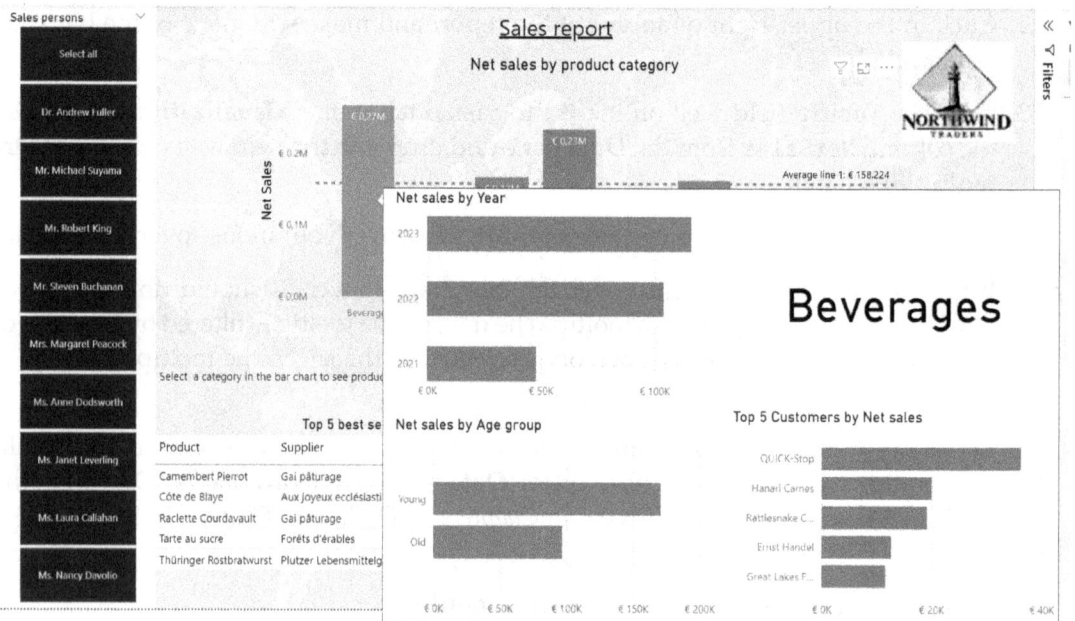

Figure 6.4: Tooltip

Every visual showing net sales will use the newly created tooltip. You can create a different custom tooltip for every visual if you want to. In that case, you need to configure each visual to use the tooltip meant for that visual.

32. Hover your mouse over the pie chart to see that the tooltip works for the pie chart as well.

33. Select the pie chart by clicking in it. Go to the **General** subtab on the **Format visual** tab of the **Visualizations** pane.

34. Open the section **Tooltips**. Note that you can turn **Tooltips** off altogether.

    When you leave the option **Type** on **report page**, you can select the report page to use as a tooltip from the next drop-down list.

35. Select **Default** as **Type** in the **Options** sub section of the **Tooltips** section.

36. Check the tooltip of the pie chart.

When you explicitly link a tooltip-page to a visual, you do not need to specify the tooltip fields in the settings of the tooltip-page. That is just a convenient way to link a tooltip to all visuals that show the same facts.

Tooltips are a great way to add a lot of information to a report page end, keeping that page simple at the same time.

Let us now investigate some other interactivity you can use. We start with hierarchies.

Using hierarchies

Hierarchies are a very important aid in data analysis. They allow us to start looking at highly aggregated data and then move towards more detailed data. In Power BI, we can use natural hierarchies to this end. A natural hierarchy is a hierarchy where a level of the hierarchy naturally breaks down into multiple items. One of the most used and intuitive natural hierarchies is in the **Date** dimension. A year can be split into four quarters. A quarter can be divided into three months. A month consists of multiple days. This is a five level hierarchy: all – year – quarter – month – day.

With a natural hierarchy, each level has a one to many relationship with the level below it. Let us see how that works in Power BI by going through the following steps:

1. Create a new report page and call it **Sales over time**.

2. Add a new **Clustered Column Chart** to the report page.

3. Drag the column **Month Name** to the **X-axis** field well in the **Build visual** tab of the **Visualizations** pane.

4. Drag the column **NetSales** to the **Y-axis**.

    You now have a bar chart with two problems. The first problem is the sorting. Power BI by default sorts bar charts descending on the fact. This is well chosen except when we analyze a fact over time. With time, sorting ascending on the periods on the **X-axis** is way better.

5. Click on the icon with the three dots (**...**) in the upper or lower right corner of the bar chart. Change the **Sort axis** to `Month Name`. Click again on the icon with the three dots (**...**) to change the sort order to **Sort ascending**.

   These steps introduced a new problem. Power BI did exactly what you asked it to do: it sorted the labels on the **X-axis** alphabetically but this can be solved.

6. Click somewhere on the name of the column `Month Name` in the **Data** pane (not the check box in front of the name, but on the name itself). The **Column Tools** ribbon should become activated.

7. Click on the **Sort by Column** button in the ribbon and select `MonthNo`.

   From now on, each visual that you sort on the column `Month Name` will, under the covers, use the `MonthNo` column to do the sorting.

   Now that we have solved the first problem, let us turn our attention to the second problem. This problem can become obvious when you hover the mouse over a bar in the bar chart. Since we linked our tooltip-page to `NetSales`, the tooltip is shown on this visual as well. When hovering over a bar of a single month, the tooltip shows data for two or three years. Each bar shows a month, but because each year has the same months, all years are added together.

   There are several solutions to this problem. We could have used the column `MonthYear` instead of `Month Name`. This column was made to mitigate this problem. You can also add a single select slicer on the report page using the column **Year**. Now there is only a single year to show. A third option is to use a hierarchy. That is what we will do now.

8. Drag the column **Year** to the **X-axis** of the bar chart in the **Build visual** tab of the **Visualizations** pane. Make sure it is above the column `Month Name` that is already there.

   When you have two or more columns on a single axis, some extra icons appear in the visual. More columns on an axis are interpreted by Power BI as a hierarchy. The buttons (icons) allow you to navigate this hierarchy.

9. Click on the upward-pointing arrow inside the bar chart. The bar chart now shows net sales by year.

10. Click on the downward-pointing arrow inside the bar chart. The appearance of the icon changes into a black circle with an arrow inside. This denotes that traversing the hierarchy is now enabled.

11. Click on the bar for 2022. You will now see net sales by month. Hover your mouse over a bar and confirm in the tooltip that you see only 2022 data.

12. Click on the upward-pointing arrow inside the bar chart. You are back at net sales by year.

13. Add the column **QuarterYear** to the **X-axis** of the bar chart in the **Build visual** tab of the **Visualizations** pane. Make sure **QuarterYear** is in between **Year** and **Month Name**.

14. Click on the bar for **2022**. You now see net sales by quarter. Click on **Q1, 2022** to see a bar chart with just three months.

15. Go back to **Sales by Year**.

16. Click on the forked downward arrow in the visual. You go down one level in the hierarchy without selecting a specific year.

17. Click on the upward-pointing arrow to go back to **Sales by Year**.

18. Now try the double arrow icon.

   The forked arrow preserves hierarchy. The double arrow does not. The main difference is the resulting sorting order.

   Going from aggregated data to less aggregated data (or more detailed data) is called **drill down**. Back to more aggregated data is **drill up**.

   There are a few things to note about hierarchies:

   - By default, Power BI creates a date hierarchy automatically for each column of data type **Date**. Try creating a bar chart using the column **Date** from our **Date** table. However, even though convenient, we will turn this off later because it is not efficient to let Power BI do this.

   - You can create hierarchies on lots of things. In our data set, we have a natural hierarchy in the **Products** table as well. A category naturally breaks down into products, but a product always belongs to a single category. Know your data and find the hierarchies.

   - Creating a hierarchy, as we just did, is an ad-hoc hierarchy created in the visual. We will learn how to add hierarchies to the semantic model for easier use in the next chapter.

   - Table visualizations do not handle hierarchies well. Matrix visualizations do. Try changing the table you just created into a matrix and play with the settings.

19. Go to the report page **Sales report**.

20. Add the column **ProductName** to the bar chart showing **Net sales by product category**.

You must consider what happens with other visuals when you use drill down in a visual on a page with multiple visuals on it. Are they still filtered as before? Should they show data of the category that you drilled down to? Or should the visual show detailed data, and other visuals be unaffected by the drill down? This last option is not intuitive for most people but is possible. When you have a bar chart selected, you can see the Data/Drill ribbon. The **Apply drill down filters to** option gives you both mentioned options.

Imagine a bar chart with a bar per month showing five years of sales data. That is 60 bars. How readable is that? Using hierarchies and drill down, you can start with a really simple and easy-to-read visual showing only five data points. By interacting, users can easily access more detailed data that is automatically filtered by the category they click on. Again, we want to keep the initial report as simple as possible, but add lots of details anyway. Drill through is another way to accomplish that.

Using drill through

A disadvantage of tooltips is that tooltip-pages themselves are not interactive anymore. Drill down shows the same data, just more detailed. What if you want more detailed data in another type of visual or in another way (another perspective) of looking at the same data? Or do you need interactivity on the extra provided information? These are all arguments to implement drill through. It allows users to click to another report page.

The main page of our report so far is the page called **Sales report**. Let us keep it that way. You start by looking at overall sales by category, with the ability to see the sales for specific salespersons using the slicer. When you notice something, you should be able to track how sales evolved over time using the bar chart with drill down we created in the previous section.

1. Select the **Sales over time** report page.

2. Make sure no visual is selected on the report page. There is now an option **Drill through** available in the **Build visual** tab if the **Visualizations** pane.

3. Drag the column **Category** from the **Data** pane and drop it in the field well, displaying the text **Add drill through fields here**.

4. Make the entire report page hidden.

5. Switch to the report page **Sales report**.

6. Right-click on any bar in the bar chart **Net sales by product category**. Select **Drill through** followed by **Sales over time**.

7. Confirm using the tooltip that the report page **Sales over time** shows data of the category you clicked on.

   Drill through takes all the filters applied on a page to the drill through page, not just the category of the item you activate drill through on. When you have a salesperson selected in the slicer when activating drill through, the **Sales over time** page shows data pertaining to this salesperson.

   It is a good idea to make the user aware of this. We can do that by creating a dynamic title.

8. Right-click on the table **Products** in the **Data** pane and select **New measure**.

9. Enter the following DAX expression in the formula bar that is now showing between the ribbon and the report:

```
SalesOverTimeReportTitle    =    "Showing    sales    of    "    &
SELECTEDVALUE(Employees[FullName], "multiple sales persons") & " and " &
SELECTEDVALUE(Products[Category]) & " over time"
```

10. Place this new measure in a **Card** visualization. Place the card on top of the report over the full width of the report. Apply formatting as desired to make it look nice.

11. Test the dynamic title by activating drill through from the **Sales report** using different selections in the slicer (use multi-select as well) and selecting different categories.

Drill through is defined in a column, `Category`, in our example. You can activate the drill through from everywhere in the report where the column `Category` is used in a visual. You can also make multiple report pages that have the column `Category` configured to be the drill through field. When you then activate drill through, you can choose from all those pages.

By making hidden drill through pages, you limit the number of pages a user sees when opening a report. Preferably, a single page is available. However, using interactions, the user can get to a lot of information on a lot of pages. We just help the user to get (to find) the information in a usefully filtered way. Bookmarks are yet another useful feature to help users.

Using bookmarks

We have focused so far on keeping the report as simple as possible. Although that is a sound approach, it is not always easy and sometimes even impossible to achieve.

Let us create a new report page just to show bookmarks and their use:

1. Create a new report page and call it **bookmarks**. Add three slicers based on **Fullname (Employees)**, **MonthYear (Date)**, and **ProductName (Products)**, respectively.

2. Add three cards to the report showing `NetSales`, `GrossSales` and `Margin`, respectively.

3. Select the **View** ribbon and click on the button- **Bookmarks**.

   Clicking on **Bookmarks** makes the **Bookmarks** pane visible next to the **Visualizations** pane. Using this pane, you can create and work with bookmarks.

4. Make sure none of the slicers have a selection made. Click on the button **Add** in the **Bookmarks** pane.

5. Double click on the created bookmark to change its default name **Bookmark 1** into **Default**.

6. Select something in each slicer.

7. Go to the report page, **Sales report**.

8. Click on the bookmark called **Default**.

By default, a bookmark saves the state of a report page at the time you create the bookmark. It remembers the page you were on and remembers slicer settings as well. It also remembers any selected items on the page and whether a visual was in focus mode (focus mode icon in the visual). Whenever you click on a bookmark, it will bring you back to the page in the state it was in when creating the bookmark. An often-used use case is bringing a report back into a default state.

You can see a couple of options when you click on the three dots behind the name of the bookmark in the **Bookmarks** pane: **Data**, **Display**, and **Current page**:

- **Data**: When unchecking this option, the state of filters is not part of the bookmark. Also, custom sorting on the report and applied drill downs in visuals are no longer part of the bookmark. The bookmark still remembers the page where this bookmark was made. The **Data** option is the most valuable option of the bookmark. So, consider carefully before turning this off.

- **Display**: As we will see in a later section in this chapter, you can hide or show visuals. With the option **Display** selected it remembers the visibility state. When a visual was hidden when the bookmark was created, it will be hidden again when selecting the bookmark. Without **Display** selected, this state is not remembered.

- **Current page**: With **Current page** not selected, clicking the bookmark will not bring you back to the original page. This can be useful when slicers are synced over multiple pages. You will learn about syncing slicers in the next section of this chapter.

Under the three options we just discussed is another option. Do you want to apply the options just discussed to the entire report or just to the selected visuals?

Before looking at hiding visuals and syncing slicers, there is one more use case for bookmarks to discuss. A user might need to present findings (insights gained from the report) to others in a meeting. You could create screenshots of the reports and copy them into a PowerPoint presentation. In the Power BI service, you can even export a report as a PowerPoint presentation. A third option is to use bookmarks to create a presentation of your report.

9. Create three new bookmarks. The settings do not really matter for this demonstration.

10. Select the three newly created bookmarks (*Ctrl* key), click on the three dots (**...**) behind the name of one of the bookmarks, and select **Group**. You can rename the group if you wish.

11. Select the group (one of the bookmarks within the group) and click on the button **View** at the top of the **Bookmarks** pane.

In the bottom of the report appears a grey bar. In it you can see the bookmark currently showing. In the far right of this bar are previous (**<**), next (**>**), and exit (**X**) buttons. These allow you to walk through the bookmarks as if they were your PowerPoint slides.

12. Click on exit to stop the presentation.

Power BI is about collaborating on data as much as on analyzing data. Bookmarks can help with collaboration by using bookmarks as talking points for a presentation. Note that during this presentation, the reports are still fully functional. Slicers, for instance, can be changed in response to questions asked in your audience.

With this said, let us quickly move forward to sync slicers.

Sync slicers

Syncing slicers was introduced when discussing the **Current page** option of bookmarks. It is a neat feature that warrants some careful consideration. Notice that the report page we created to show bookmarks has a slicer for employee **FullName**. The report page **Sales report** does as well. What happens when a user selects a salesperson on one page and ends up on the other page? Is the same salesperson selected on that page as well or not? It is when the slicers are synchronized:

1. Click on the button **Bookmarks** on the **View** ribbon. Also, click on **Sync slicers** in the same ribbon.

   The **Bookmarks** pane disappeared; the **Sync slicers** pane became visible.

2. Make sure the **FullName** slicer is selected in the report (it does not matter on which page you select it).

   The **Sync slicers** pane shows a list of all pages. For each page, there are two check boxes available. The second one, with the eye icon in the header, shows you on which page this slicer is visible. Currently, that should be on the pages **Sales report** and **Bookmarks**. Using the checkmarks in this column adds (or deletes) the slicer to (from) pages.

   The first checkmark determines whether slicers are synchronized (synced). Currently, the slicer is not synced. Selecting a salesperson on one page does not affect the settings on the other page (and vice versa). This can be confusing. A user sets a slicer and now interprets the data with the slicer settings in mind. If that user ends up on another page that is filtered differently, but he or she still has the slicer setting in mind, we end up with our data being interpreted incorrectly. Tooltips and drill through always take filter settings and apply them to where they bring you. That is for a reason.

3. Place checkmarks in the sync slicer columns for both **Sales report** and **Bookmarks**.

4. Check to see that when you change the selection on one page, the other page follows the selection.

You can make all sorts of combinations of not showing a slicer on a page, but still applying the filter to that page, or make the sync unidirectional instead of bi directional. Just make sure that whatever you do is clear to users. You do not want to confuse them or even worse: have them interpret the data wrongly without so much as a thought.

Hiding items on a report

Let us get back to a recurring theme of this chapter: keep it simple but show a lot of information at the same time. Hiding items can be helpful here as well:

1. On the **View** ribbon, click on **Sync slicers** to make the **Sync slicers** pane disappear and click on **Selection** to make the **Selection** pane appear.

   The **Selection** pane shows a list of all visuals on the report page. Selecting a visual in the **Selection** pane also selects the visual on the report page. Each visual has an eye icon behind it. Clicking on this icon hides the visual on the report page. The icon changes. A line is now drawn through the eye. Clicking again makes the item visible again.

   You can multi-select visuals and then show or hide the entire group with a single click.

   You may wonder why you would add a visual on a report and then make it invisible. However, you must see this in combination with bookmarks.

   Consider, for instance, a report with multiple slicers on it. All these slicers take up screen real estate, leaving less and less space for the actual visuals that convey the insights the report is about. You may have to make your visuals smaller. However, that can make them less effective and more difficult to read.

   A solution to this could be to make a group of all the slicers and hide them. At that point, we create a bookmark. Create a second bookmark with all slicers visible. The bookmarks toggle between the slicers being visible and hidden. The next section of the chapter is about buttons. That will make toggling even easier and more intuitive for users.

   The extra thing you need to understand here is that you can place visuals on top of each other. Use this by placing the slicers on top of other visuals. These visuals can now use the entire screen. When the slicers are visible, they are on top of the visuals (partially) hiding them. Use the **Layer order** tab of the **Selection** pane to configure which visual is on top of which other visual. We leave it up to you to play with this.

2. Hide the **Selection** pane.

   We mentioned buttons. Let us look at them.

Using buttons

You have come across buttons. As soon as you create a drill through page, a button is added to the page. Let us have a closer look at buttons:

1. Select the page **Sales over time** and notice the circle with a left pointing arrow in it.

    This is a back button. It brings you back to the previous page you were on. It was placed in the top left corner of the report automatically when configuring the page for drill through. It might be under the card showing the dynamic title.

2. Go to the **Sales report** and activate drill through.

3. On the **Sales over time** page, click on the button while holding down the *Ctrl* key on your keyboard.

    You must hold down the *Ctrl* key when in Power BI Desktop. Clicking it without holding down the *Ctrl* key is selecting it to do any necessary formatting. Once a report is published to the Power BI service, the button works as a button should: just click on it.

4. Go to the **Sales over time** report page and select the button. The **Visualizations** pane turned into the **Format button** pane.

5. Open the section **Style** on the **Button** tab of the **Format button** pane.

6. Toggle **Text** on. Enter `Go back to Sales report` as text.

7. Make the font color **Black**.

8. Toggle **Icon** off.

9. Toggle **Border** on.

10. Place the button in the bottom right corner of the report and resize it to show the text inside it on a single line.

11. Return to the sub section **Text** of the section **Style**. Note the **State** drop-down list in the top. Select the option **On hover**. Enter the text `Yes, go ahead`.

12. Navigate to the **Sales over time** page by activating drill through on the **Sales report** page.

13. Hover your mouse over the button and notice that the text changes. Now *Ctrl* click on it.

    There are more types of buttons you can use.

14. Click on the **Buttons** button on the **View** ribbon.

Note: **There are different types of buttons available. Most of them are not actual different buttons. They are the standard button with different default settings applied. Let us try some of them.**

15. Go to the **Bookmark** page.

16. Insert a **Blank** button.

17. Toggle **Action** on and open the section **Action** of the **Button** tab of the **Format button** pane.

18. Open the drop-down list **Type** and notice the available types.

Let us go through the different available types quickly.

Back, bookmark and page navigation

These three do not need much explanation. We have seen the **Back** button. The **Bookmarks** button brings the user to a bookmark when clicked. This makes using bookmarks easier than from the **Bookmarks** pane, that is (sort of) hidden away. With a clear text displayed in it, the use should be intuitive for the user. The same goes for the **Page navigator** button. Clicking on it will bring the user to another page. That may even be a hidden page. You can use this as a custom drill through. When clicked, learn more on the new page. With the use of measures, you can even make dynamic page navigation. The page you navigate to is calculated using a measure where you can define conditional logic.

Another useful use case for the **Page navigator** button is to make a page with a description of the report. How should the report be used? What is on it? Which data source(s) are used? What business rules are implemented? Then, add a **Help** button on each real page that brings the user to this documentation page. With a **Back** button on it, the user can easily navigate back to the original page.

You can make a page as described here by simply using textboxes and type what is needed in them. In more data-mature organizations, you should keep track of lineage (data sources being used) and business rules in a database. Connect to that database, use the information to create a help page, and make the table used for it hidden.

Another option with the same use case in mind is the **Web URL** button.

Web URL

As the name suggests, this button opens a browser and displays the web page that you configure in this button. A nice use case could be to use an intranet site or SharePoint to document data sources, business rules, definitions, and reports. A **Web URL Help** button opens this documentation.

Drill through

This chapter has been about the usability of a report, and although drill through is a really nice feature, a user might not be aware of the fact that drill through is implemented on a visual. When users are aware of the drill through being available, they may find the process of right-clicking a visual and then selecting the drill through, too much clicking. The **Drill through** button may help:

1. Go to the **Sales report** page.

2. Insert a **Blank** button on the report. Position it next to the **Net sales by product category** bar chart on the right of it.

3. Open the section **Action** on the **Button** tab of the **Format button** pane.

4. Select **Drill through** for **Type** and **Sales over time** for **Destination**.

5. Open the **Style section** and select **Disabled** in the drop-down list for **State**.

6. Enter `Select a bar and click here for more details` under **Text** in the **Text** sub section.

7. Change the **State** from **Disabled** to **Default**.

8. Enter `Click for more details` under **Text** in the **Text** sub section.

9. Make additional changes to your liking.

10. Click multiple times on a bar in the bar chart to select and de-select a category. Note the change in the text of the button. *Ctrl* click the button when it reads **Click for more details**.

You just made your drill through more intuitive on your report.

Questions and answers

As described earlier, Power BI has the Q&A feature. You can add this directly to a report, as done in the following steps.

1. Go to the **Bookmark** page and add a **Q&A** button to it.

2. *Ctrl* click on the button.

3. Enter `show net sales by customer by country` and press *Enter*. A bar chart with net sales by customer is shown.

As you can see, the Q&A functionality can be used to let a user ask any question about the data. It can be a cool feature, especially when combined with the bookmark presentation functionality described earlier. People will have questions when you present a report. Try answering them immediately.

You can also use the Q&A visual to help you create the visuals on your report. It is also available in Power BI dashboards in the Power BI service and from the **Insert** ribbon in Power BI Desktop.

How well Q&A works depends on the Power BI semantic model. We have not put a lot of effort into the model so far. It will be discussed in detail in the next chapter.

Apply all slicers and clear all slicers

These two buttons can be really helpful to users and may optimize performance and reduce costs in Fabric. Suppose there are a lot of slicers on a report page and suppose you need to change the selection in each of them. Every time you change a selection in a single slicer, the report page adjusts all visuals to this setting. This takes time and compute resources. All for nothing because you do not look at the result, you move on to change the next slicer. The **Apply all slicers** button can help. Let us see how:

1. Go to the **Bookmark** page.

2. Change the **Action type** of the **Q&A** button to type **Apply all slicers**. (section **Action** on the **Button** tab of the **Format button** pane).

3. Change what is selected in the **FullName** slicer.

   Nothing happens in your report. The same data is displayed. That is because the change has not been applied yet. The users get three visual cues as to what is happening. For starters, the **Apply all slicers** button became active instead of disabled. Using appropriate settings of the button, you can make this even more clear by applying different formatting for the **State Disabled** versus the **State Default**.

   You can see what is happening in the slicer itself as well. In the header, it displays the text (**Not yet applied**), and a little icon resembling a clock is shown.

4. Change your settings for the other two slicers as well.

5. *Ctrl* click on the **Apply all slicers** button to apply the slicers to the report.

   The **Clear all slicers** button should now speak for itself.

Page navigator and bookmark navigator

You find the **Page navigator** and **Bookmark navigator** under all options when inserting a button. Both are navigator objects and not buttons. You can see this when you insert one and have a look at the format pane. It is now called **Format navigator** instead of **Format button**.

When you insert one of them, you do not get a single button but a whole bunch of buttons. One for each page or bookmark that you created. In the settings, you can configure which pages or bookmarks to create buttons for and which not.

You may consider creating a start page in a report that consists of buttons only. By using clear descriptive texts in them, users start using the report by clicking on a button. When well set up this might be easier or more intuitive than having to select a page to start with from tabs.

Shapes and images

Shapes and images can be used as buttons as well. Sometimes an image is much clearer than an icon or text. An image can be a better button in that case than an actual button. Let us create an image that acts like a button, through the following steps:

1. Go to the **Sales report** page.

2. Select the Northwind logo.

3. Toggle **Action** to on in the **Image** tab of the **Format image** pane.

4. Select **Web URL** as **Type**.

5. Enter `https://en.wikiversity.org/wiki/Database_Examples/Northwind` as the URL.

6. *Ctrl* click on the logo and see what happens.

The URL used here brings you to a page that describes the Northwind database we are using throughout this book. Maybe this URL should be used for a Help button. The Northwind company's home page would be a nice URL for the logo.

This concludes the tour of features you can use to create interactive reports. Remember to use it to aid your user, not to confuse the user.

We still have a couple of items to discuss in this chapter. We start by looking at visual calculations.

Using visual calculations

Our report page **Sales by Year by Sales person** can use some improvements. Most notably, we are interested in whether sales persons reach their target or not. We are showing sales and targets. However, why not show the difference? That is what we were really interested in.

Let us create a new report page that is an improvement over the current **Sales by Year by Sales person** page.

Once done, it should look like *Figure 6.5*:

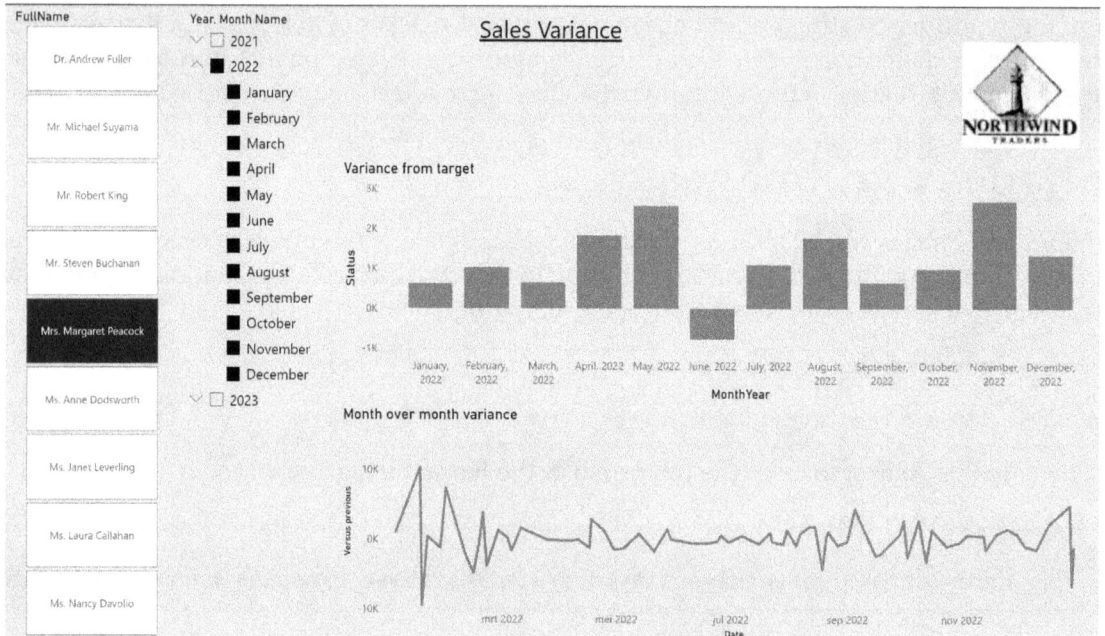

Figure 6.5: *Sales by Year by Sales person*

Let us create the **Sales by Year by Sales person** report of *Figure 6.5*:

1. Go to the **Sales report** page.

2. Select the **FullName** slicer and click *Ctrl + C* on your keyboard to copy the slicer.

3. Create a new report page.

4. Click *Ctrl + V* on your keyboard to past the slicer. Click **Sync** in the **Sync visuals** dialog the shows.

5. Add an empty slicer on the report and drag the column **Year** from the **Date** pane to it.

6. Add the column **MonthName** to the slicer to create a hierarchy in the slicer.

7. Add an empty clustered column chart to the report. Drag the column **MonthYear** to it.

8. Add both the columns **GrossSales** and **TargetAmount** to the bar chart.

9. Click on the three dots (...) in the bar chart and select **New visual calculation**.

We will learn how to create DAX calculations in *Chapter 8, DAX*. DAX calculations are part of the entire Power BI semantic model. Visual calculations are limited to a visual and, by that, to only the data used in that visual. That makes them easier to use. It also makes them limited in what you can do with them compared to DAX calculations added to the Power BI semantic model. Lastly, visual calculations are harder to maintain and can easily lead to duplication of code or even inconsistencies between different visuals. Using DAX at the level of the semantic model is the preferred option. However, sometimes visual calculations are simply easier to use.

The second part of your screen now looks like *Figure 6.6*, except for the formula in the formula bar shown:

MonthYear	Sum of GrossSales	Sum of TargetAmount	Status
January, 2022	€ 25.620,1	€ 25.000	620,10
February, 2022	€ 13.530,3	€ 12.500	1.030,30
March, 2022	€ 5.644,8	€ 5.000	644,80
April, 2022	€ 14.333,15	€ 12.500	1.833,15
May, 2022	€ 7.573,2	€ 5.000	2.573,20
June, 2022	€ 4.232,4	€ 5.000	-767,60
July, 2022	€ 6.104,8	€ 5.000	1.104,80
August, 2022	€ 16.766,79	€ 15.000	1.766,79
September, 2022	€ 8.147,63	€ 7.500	647,63
October, 2022	€ 10.996,53	€ 10.000	996,53
November, 2022	€ 7.684,75	€ 5.000	2.684,75
December, 2022	€ 18.843,25	€ 17.500	1.343,25
Total	**€ 139.477,7**	**€ 125.000**	**14.477,70**

Formula bar: `1 Status = [Sum of GrossSales] - [Sum of TargetAmount]`

Figure 6.6: Visual calculations

10. Enter the following formula:
    Status = [Sum of GrossSales] - [Sum of TargetAmount]

11. Click on the **Build visual** tab of the **Visualizations** pane on the eye icons behind the columns **GrossSales** and **TargetAmount** to hide them.

12. Click on **Back to report** in the top left corner of the screen.

    Your visual now shows the difference between the actual and the target. The users do not have to look for the difference themselves. They do not need to guess how big that difference is. We now show what they were interested in in the first place.

13. Add an empty line chart to the report page.

14. Add **GrossSales** to the **Y-axis** and **Date** to the **X-axis**.

15. Click on the icon resembling a down arrow behind the column **Date** in the **Build visual** tab and select **Date** (instead of **Date hierarchy**).

16. Click on the three dots (**...**) in the bar chart and select **New visual calculation**.

17. In the visual calculation pane, click on the **Fx** icon in front of the formula bar.

    Power BI Desktop has a lot of suggestions for visual calculations to improve reports. When you click on the **Fx**, you get a list of them. You can also open the visual calculation editor from the **Home** ribbon. Suggestions can be found there as well.

18. Select **Versus previous**.

19. In the formula, replace `[Field]` by `[Sum of GrossSales]`.

20. Hide the column `GrossSales` in the visual.

21. Click on **Back to report** in the top left corner of the screen.

   You now have a line chart that shows the difference of each month to the previous month. This helps analyze the variance in sales by month.

   To finish this page:

22. Copy the Northwind logo from the **Sales report** to the current report page.

23. Make the **Background color** of the report light grey.

24. Turn off the **Background** property of all visuals.

25. Change the title of the bar chart to `Variance from target`.

26. Change the title of the line chart to `Month over month variance`.

27. Add an overall report title with the same formatting as on the **Sales report** with the text `Sales Variance`.

28. Delete the report page **Sales by Year by Sales person** and rename the one you just created to **Sales by Year by Sales person**.

You created a much better version of the page **Sales by Year by Sales person** by using some simple visual calculations. Now, let us look quickly at some other visualization types.

Conditional formatting

There is a well-known saying: *A picture says more than a thousand words.* This is often true for reporting. In reporting, it means that, for instance, bar charts and line charts are often more effective than tables and matrices. However, sometimes tables are better. Suppose you need to show net sales and quantity sold in a single visual. Due to the different scales of the two facts, most visuals will not work. A table might. With conditional formatting, you may be able to add the power of pictures to the flexibility of the table. Let us see that in action:

1. Create a new report page and call it **Conditional formatting**.

2. Place a table visual on it with the column `Category` in it.

3. Add `NetSales` to the table visual and rename it for this visual to `Net Sales`.

4. Add `Quantity` to the table visual.

5. Right-click on **Net Sales** in the field well on the **Build visual** tab of the **Visualizations** pane. Select **Add a sparkline**.

6. Select the column **Date** in the **Add a sparkline** dialog in the drop-down list **X-axis** and click on **Create**.

    A sparkline is a little trend (a mini line chart) shown inside a table. As currently configured, it shows the net sales of a category over time.

7. Right-click on **Net Sales** in the field well on the **Build visual** tab of the **Visualizations** pane. Select **Conditional formatting** followed by **Data bars**.

8. Accept all the defaults in the **Data bars** and **Net Sales** dialog and click on **OK**.

9. Right-click on **Net Sales** in the field well on the **Build visual** tab of the **Visualizations** pane again. Select **Conditional formatting** followed by **Icons**.

10. Accept all the defaults in the **Icons** and **Net Sales** dialog and click on **OK**.

Your table should now look like *Figure 6.7*:

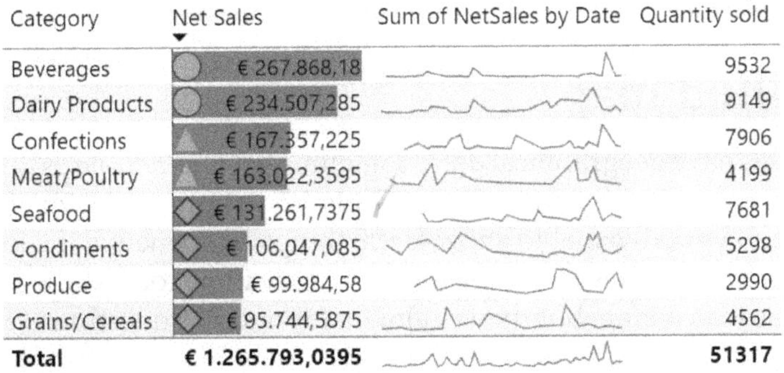

Category	Net Sales ▼	Sum of NetSales by Date	Quantity sold
Beverages	○ € 267.868,18		9532
Dairy Products	○ € 234.507,285		9149
Confections	△ € 167.357,225		7906
Meat/Poultry	△ € 163.022,3595		4199
Seafood	◇ € 131.261,7375		7681
Condiments	◇ € 106.047,085		5298
Produce	◇ € 99.984,58		2990
Grains/Cereals	◇ € 95.744,5875		4562
Total	**€ 1.265.793,0395**		**51317**

Figure 6.7: Conditional formatting

Other formatting options, like changing the foreground or the background, can be set conditionally as well.

The last option is **Web URL**. This option can change categories in your table into links to websites.

Note: **We accepted default settings in this simple demonstration. You can add a lot of logic to your conditional formatting. You can base colors or icons on other fields, even calculated fields. You can also change the rules of how and when you need which icon or color. We invite you to play with the possibilities.**

You can also apply the formatting described here to matrix visuals.

Other visuals

It is impossible to show all visualization types in detail in the book. Go through them and play with them. Just keep in mind: you have a message that your target audience should get. Tables, matrices, bar charts, and line charts are intuitive for almost everyone. That makes them important options to consider. Other visualization types may become less effective quickly. When a visual serves the goal of clearly conveying the message to the audience, it is a good visual. Otherwise, it is just an image. There are a lot of visual types that we have not discussed yet. Let us take a look at some popular visuals.

Gauge, KPI

A number by itself is rarely insightful. Comparing that number to a reference makes it much more informative. That reference may be a predefined target, the same number from another period, for instance, last year, the average value, and so on. You can show both the actual value and the reference value and let the user do the comparison, or you can do the comparison and show the result. Gauge and KPI visuals are good visualization types for this goal. They make it clear to the user immediately what the status is.

Map and filled map

Almost all businesses have geographical data. Sometimes, it is as simple as just the addresses of customers. Sometimes it may be as complex as **Global Positioning System** (**GPS**) coordinates of trucks in logistics. A good visual to show *where* things happened is the map. A map visual can answer questions like, *where* is it happening, with a single look at the visual. Comparing values is not that easy on a map, but then again, that is another question.

Scatter chart

Correlations between two or three numerical values can be visualized using the scatter plot. The margin, for example, could depend on the order size. Until now, in the book, we showed a fact and analyzed it by dimensions. However, correlations between facts can be very informative.

Get more visuals

Power BI has an open standard as it comes to visuals. This allows other people and companies to create visuals for Power BI. Via the option **Get more visuals** (three dots in the **Visualizations** pane), you can open a gallery with a lot of additional visualization types. Box and whisker, text search, and Gantt chart are just three examples of very useful visuals you might add.

Key influencers

Most visuals just show the numbers. Analyzing data goes beyond just showing numbers. Three special visuals in Power BI take the first step to really analyze the data. The first of them is the **Key influencers** visual. Let us look at this visual:

1. Create a new report page with the name **Analyze data**.

2. Click on the button **Key influencers** on the **Insert** ribbon. (The visual can also be found on the **Visualizations** pane.)

3. Drag the column **NetSales** from the **Data** pane and drop it in the **Analyze** field well on the **Build visual** tab of the **Visualizations** pane.

4. Drag the columns **YearsInService** (**Employees**), **PriceRange** (**Products**), and **Freight** (**Sales**) to the **Explain by** field well on the **Build visual** tab.

The key influencer tells you that the value of **Expensive** in the column **PriceRange** is indicative of high net sales. It reads: when **PriceRange** is **Expensive,** the average of **NetSales** increased by 1.15K. The **Sum of Freight** also has a correlation to net sales, but less so. **YearsInService** apparently does not matter and has no predictive power over net sales. So, the experience of our sales people, measured in how long they work for us, has neglectable influence on net sales.

The **Top segments** tab of the **Key influencers** visual shows clustering. Data is in this case simply divided into sales with **PriceRange Expensive** and another set of sales rows with **PriceRange** being **Moderate,** and **Sum of Freight** is greater than 37.23. Two similar sales rows were detected.

Note: **Interpreting this data is more complex than reading a simple line chart.**

Decomposition tree

Another interesting visual is the decomposition tree. Let us have a look at it:

1. Add a decomposition tree to the report page.

2. Configure it similarly to the **Key influencers** visual.

3. Click on the plus icon at the end of a bar inside the decomposition tree.

This visual may be easier to read than the **Key influencers** visual.

Narrative

The narrative visual analyzes your report or visual and explains it in human language. Try it out on the sales report page. Although great, ask yourself this: when this actually helps, was not your report too difficult to begin with? Create intuitive reports that people understand without the need for AI.

Themes and templates

Having discussed most visualization types and how to format them, there is one thing left to say. How you do the layout of your reports and how you do the formatting can be really important. Doing it consistently is even more important. Always use the same style. People get used to it. And that makes it easier to work with the reports.

Setting properties of visuals can take a long time, and doing it manually all the time will result in differences from report to report. Themes can help with that.

A theme is a formatting style that is automatically applied to all report pages and all visuals on them. You find a bunch of predefined themes on the **View** ribbon. Just select one and see how your entire report is affected by it.

Chances are that no predefined theme fits your needs. There are three options that may help. Firstly, you can choose the theme that is nearest to what you want and then customize it. Secondly, there is a gallery with even more predefined themes to choose from. The third option is to create a theme by yourself. This cannot be done in Power BI Desktop. When you Google on *Power BI Theme Generator,* you find a couple of sites that assist you in creating a custom theme. You can then import the theme you created in Power BI Desktop.

Themes apply standard formatting, like font types and sizes to use. They say nothing about the report layout. Maybe you want each report to have the slicers on top and a max of two visuals next to each other on the report page. You can make a template like this. Templates are Power BI Desktop solutions saved as `.pbit` files instead of `.pbix` file.

Conclusion

The key takeaway of this chapter is to know what a report should tell the users. Make sure that you can phrase the message of a report in a short, simple sentence. Keep the report simple and to the point, focusing on that core message. Use visualization types and formatting to help users understand what question is answered and help them interpret that data correctly. Creating reports is not about creating nice visuals. You may need nice visuals, but it is about your users learning something.

A second important lesson is to be consistent. Always use the same layout and the same formatting. Users get to know the setup and will find it easier to read reports, even new ones.

Power BI is making a lot of assumptions when you drag columns onto the report canvas. These assumptions come from the semantic model that Power BI reports are based on. Even when you are not aware of the semantic model, there always is one. The next chapter will teach you all about it.

Multiple choice questions

1. **Which visualization type do you use when you want to find correlations between two facts?**

    a. Bar chart

    b. Line chart

    c. Scatter plot

    d. Key influencers

2. **Where do you find properties that are equal for all visuals?**

    a. General tab of Visualization pane

    b. Visual tab of Visualization pane

    c. Format visual tab

    d. Format ribbon

3. **What are preferred visualization types?**

    a. Matrix

    b. Map

    c. Line

    d. Pie

Answers

1	c
2	a
3	a, c

CHAPTER 7
The Basics of Semantic Models

Introduction

Power BI reports rely heavily on the Power BI semantic model. We created relationships between tables at two occasions earlier in this book. If we had not done that, all the reports we created in the previous chapters would not have worked. The relationship between tables is a crucial part of the Power BI semantic model.

Power BI Desktop creates a default semantic model for us as soon as we connect to or import data. It enables us to visualize data as soon as we have the data. We should be aware of that model because it determines how the reports function. Additionally, you need to be able to change the defaults when the default settings do not work.

If you want to follow along with the examples presented in this chapter, you need Power BI Desktop to be installed on your workstation. This chapter continues where the previous ended. If you followed along in the previous chapter, you can continue in the Power BI Desktop file you created there. If you did not, you can use the file **Solution chapter 6.pbix** from the GitHub repository of this book.

Structure

This chapter will cover the following topics:

- Active and inactive relationships
- Types of relationships
- Cross-filter direction
- Attribute properties
- Table properties
- Other table properties

Objectives

In this chapter, you will learn what relationships are and the role that they play. You will learn about different types of relationships and their use cases, along with the settings that define the semantic model, both at the table level and the column level.

Introduction

The term semantic model is used to describe a set of properties that *translates* a database, that is technical by nature, to a more intuitive human-oriented data store. In database design, developers have best practices that they adhere to, which make sense for database technologies and developers. However, those best practices do not necessarily make sense to business users who create or consume reports.

For example: In the naming convention used by most developers, they do not use spaces in names. Looking back to *Chapter 3, The Basics of Power Query*, where we imported data from the Northwind OData feed, we imported a table called **Order_Details**. However, that is not correct English. Order details, with space, makes more sense. In a lot of businesses, people might talk about an order consisting of multiple order lines. If that is the case, order lines would be an even better name. Naming columns and tables using terms (names, words) used in everyday life by business users is a very simple but important part of creating a semantic model. For your reports to make sense to business users, you must first make sure the report uses their language. The jargon of the business.

Another example of a naming convention that might be strange to users is **UnitPrice**, one word with a capital *P* in the middle. In a semantic model, unit price, as in normal English, would be better. Note that we made the same mistake when creating tables in *Chapter 3, The Basics of Power Query* . For example, we created columns like **GrossSales** and **AgeGroup**. With spaces would make more sense.

Apart from naming conventions that we may or may not like, there is the issue of formatting. The most notable formatting that a database lacks is how dates are shown on screen or how dates are printed on paper. Inside a database, a date is a date. On a Power BI report, a date can be shown in a variety of formats. You can choose the American formatting with the month first and then the day followed by the year, like *12-31-2024*. Alternatively, you can use a European style where the day comes first, like *31-12-2024*. There are a lot of other options with the year coming first, month name instead of month number, and so on. In a semantic model, you can define your preferred format, which is automatically used whenever data is shown on a report.

A similar issue occurs with money. In a database, the amount is just a number. On screen, it is something else. Try to think of these questions: which currency symbol do you want to use? With or without decimals? With or without a thousand separator? Should thousand separators be a point or a comma? Formatting dates and currencies helps users to interpret data correctly. Always use the same formatting, as that is an important part of it. So, you will define formatting once in the semantic model and have the defined format used throughout your report.

Even more important is that we want drag-and-drop reporting. Creating a report should be as simple and straightforward as possible. Making report development easy allows non-technical people who know the business well to create reports. These people know better what reports are useful and how they should look than technical people who know about technical things but less about the business.

Apart from enabling as many people as possible to create reports, easy report development makes report developers more productive. Today, you can create maybe ten reports in the same amount of time that you needed to create just one prior to the existence of semantic models and drag-and-drop report authoring.

Lastly, a very important aspect of semantic models is that they naturally aggregate data. Most reports will somehow aggregate data. All the visuals that we created so far show aggregated data. Aggregation in a semantic model is way more dynamic than it is in a database. The language **Data Analysis Expressions** (**DAX**) that we will discuss in the next chapter is all about aggregating data. This means that the way a semantic model treats data is very close to what we need to create reports.

The important point here is:

A semantic model makes report authoring simple. It uses a structure optimized for analytical workloads where (most) sources do not.

Active and inactive relationships

Power BI reports can display visuals, such as sales by year, because of the relationships between tables. To get the correct sales numbers, we must first think about what we mean by something as simple as sales by year. Suppose an order is placed, and we keep track of the date on which the order was placed. Also, suppose that we create invoices for all orders placed the previous week on Monday. We do keep track of the invoice date. However, we do not receive any money until the invoice is paid. Payment results in a third date, which is the payment date. When you are interested in sales by month, you will have to specify whether to use the invoice date, the order date, the payment date, or any other relevant date.

In theory, this is called **role playing dimension**. The date dimension can play the role of order date, invoice date, and payment date. Power BI will need you to be explicit in what you want.

In our Northwind database, we have two dates inside the **Sales** table: **ShippedDate** and **OrderDate**. Let us look at the relationships between these two tables:

1. Open your Power BI Desktop solution from the previous chapter or open **Solution chapter 6.pbix**.

2. Go to the Model view page in Power BI Desktop to see the tables and their relationship.

3. Hover your mouse over the relationship between the tables **Sales** and **Date**.

4. Confirm the relationship is based on the columns **OrderDate** and **Date**.

    The previous means that all our time-related analysis in the book so far has been based on the order date.

5. Open the Report view and select the report page **Sales by Year by Sales person**.

6. Note the **Status** value for **Andrew Fuller** in **January 2022**. It should be **650.20**.

7. Go back to the Model view.

8. Right-click on the relationship between the tables **Sales** and **Date** and select **Delete**.

9. Check what happened to the **Variance from target** visual on the report page, **Sales by Year by Sales person**.

10. Create a new relationship between the two tables by dragging the column **ShippedDate** from the table **Sales** and drop it onto the column **Date** of the table **Date**. Click on **Save** in the **New relationship** dialog. We will discuss it shortly.

11. Note the **Status** value for **Andrew Fuller** in **January 2022**. It should now be **4826.20**.

    You can see how relationships affect the numbers on the report. The difference makes sense from a business perspective. When the order date and ship date are not the same, the sales amount can fall into a different month or even a different year. So, choose your relationship carefully.

    However, what if you need to be able to use both dates? You can, of course!

12. On the Model view page, click on the button **Manage relationships** in the **Home**

ribbon. The **Manage relationships** dialog, as shown in *Figure 7.1*, will show:

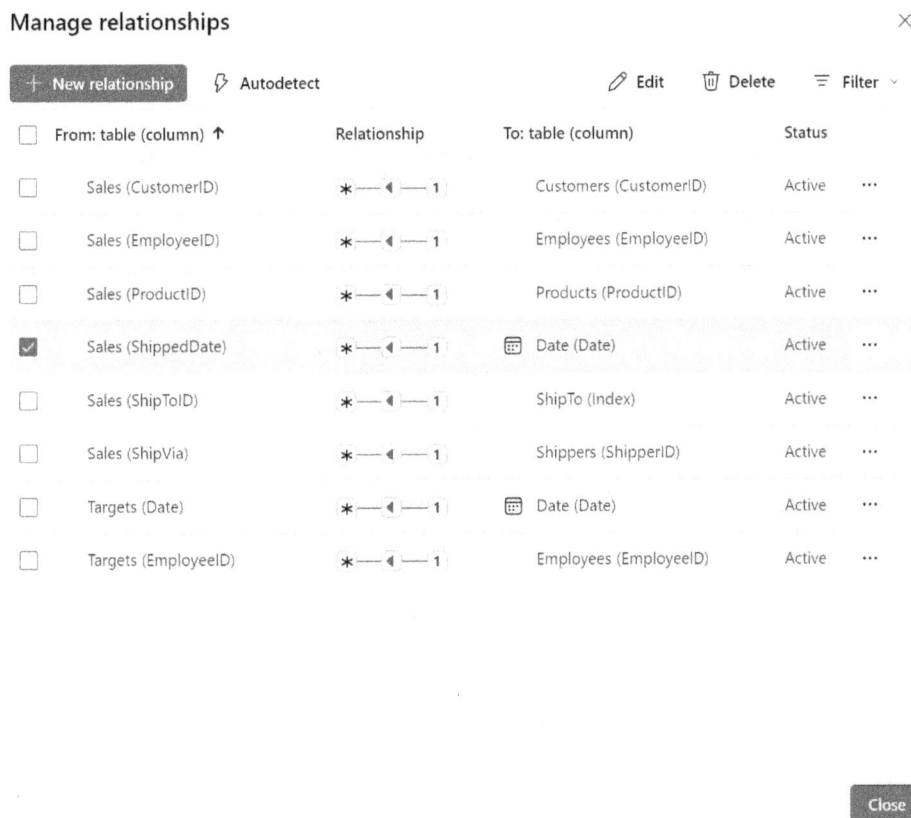

Manage relationships

	From: table (column) ↑	Relationship	To: table (column)	Status	
☐	Sales (CustomerID)	* ◄ 1	Customers (CustomerID)	Active	...
☐	Sales (EmployeeID)	* ◄ 1	Employees (EmployeeID)	Active	...
☐	Sales (ProductID)	* ◄ 1	Products (ProductID)	Active	...
☑	Sales (ShippedDate)	* ◄ 1	▦ Date (Date)	Active	...
☐	Sales (ShipToID)	* ◄ 1	ShipTo (Index)	Active	...
☐	Sales (ShipVia)	* ◄ 1	Shippers (ShipperID)	Active	...
☐	Targets (Date)	* ◄ 1	▦ Date (Date)	Active	...
☐	Targets (EmployeeID)	* ◄ 1	Employees (EmployeeID)	Active	...

Figure 7.1: Manage relationships

13. Select the relationships between the tables **Sales** and **Date**. Click on the three dots (**...**) in the far right of the line and select **Switch status to inactive,** and click on **Close**.

14. Create a new relationship between the two tables by dragging the column `OrderDate` from the table **Sales** and drop it onto the column **Date** of the table **Date**. Click on **Save** in the **New relationship** dialog.

    You should now have two relationships between the tables **Sales** and **Date**. One is denoted by a solid line; this is an active relationship. The other is a dotted line; this is an inactive relationship. You can have multiple relationships between two tables. Only one of them can be active. When you create visuals on a report without any extra considerations, the active relationship is used. You must write some DAX code to use the inactive relationship. Let us have a look at that.

15. Right-click on the table **Sales** in the **Data** pane and select **New measure**.

16. Use the following code for this measure:

```
NetSales by ShippedDate = CALCULATE(SUM(Sales[NetSales]),
USERELATIONSHIP('Date'[Date] , Sales[ShippedDate]))
```

17. To test the measure, create a new report page and call it **Ship versus Order date**.

18. Create a clustered bar chart and put the column **MonthYear** on the **X-axis** and **NetSales** plus **NetSales by ShippedDate** on the **Y-axis**.

You can clearly see the differences per month. When you take a closer look at the formula we used for **NetSales by ShippedDate**, it is explicitly clear that values are calculated by summing the values inside the column **NetSales**. When dragging in the column **NetSales** itself, Power BI uses the active relationship. However, the formula tells Power BI to use the other relationship. That relationship is named explicitly by specifying the columns that make up the relationship. For the function of **USERELATIONSHIP** to work, an inactive relationship must exist.

Inactive relationships are used for two scenarios. One is role playing dimensions as just described. Another is to avoid circular references. Relationships define how filters propagate through the data model. It is possible to have multiple paths from one table to another. In that case, Power BI will automatically create inactive relationships to avoid confusion. You should avoid this type of inactive relationship usage by creating a proper star schema. We will learn more about filter propagation in an upcoming section.

Now that we know a bit more about relationships and their importance, let us have a closer look at them.

Types of relationships

We have now created relationships on multiple occasions, ignoring the **New relationship** dialog all the times. Refer to the following steps to understand this dialog:

1. On the Model view page, click on the button **Manage relationships** in the **Home** ribbon to open the **Manage relationships** dialog.

2. Select the relationship between the tables **Sales** and **Customers** and click on **Edit** in the top of the dialog.

   The **Edit relationship** dialog that you now see is the same as the **New relationship** dialog:

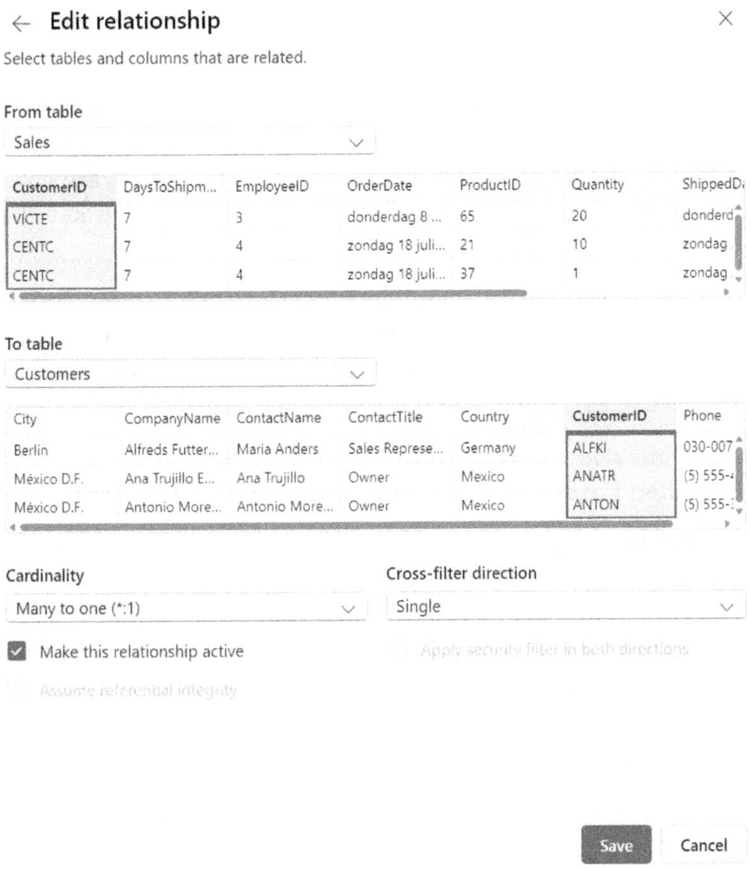

← **Edit relationship**   ✕

Select tables and columns that are related.

From table

Sales	⌄

CustomerID	DaysToShipm...	EmployeeID	OrderDate	ProductID	Quantity	ShippedD
VICTE	7	3	donderdag 8 ...	65	20	donderd
CENTC	7	4	zondag 18 juli...	21	10	zondag
CENTC	7	4	zondag 18 juli...	37	1	zondag

To table

Customers	⌄

City	CompanyName	ContactName	ContactTitle	Country	CustomerID	Phone
Berlin	Alfreds Futter...	Maria Anders	Sales Represe...	Germany	ALFKI	030-007
México D.F.	Ana Trujillo E...	Ana Trujillo	Owner	Mexico	ANATR	(5) 555-4
México D.F.	Antonio More...	Antonio More...	Owner	Mexico	ANTON	(5) 555-

Cardinality   **Cross-filter direction**

Many to one (*:1)	⌄

Single	⌄

☑ Make this relationship active   ☐ Apply security filter in both directions

☐ Assume referential integrity

Save   Cancel

Figure 7.2: Edit relationship

The dialog has a drop-down list at the top (**From table**) in which you can select a table. Currently, the **Sales** table is selected. A preview of the selected table is shown. A second drop-down list (**To table**) lets you select the table that the first one has a relationship with. The table **Customers** is selected here, and you see a data preview of this table as well.

Important here is that in both tables in the preview, the column **CustomerID** is selected. You can see this because it is grayed. By selecting columns in both tables, you define which columns make the relationship.

Let us explain some theory before we continue to further discuss the **Edit relationship** dialog. Databases are set up following some simple rules coming from the mathematical set theory. The first rule is that rows in a table should be unique. In most databases, this is enforced by using a primary key. The primary key is a column (or columns) that stores unique values. Each row has another value for the primary key column. Power BI does not enforce uniqueness and does not have primary keys. It is, however, a more than wise idea to make sure you have unique rows and a column with unique values in it. For most dimension tables, this primary key should be clear. The primary keys in our Northwind example are: `CustomerID`, `Index` (`ShipTo`), `ShipperID`, `ProductID`, `EmployeeID`, and `Date`.

Tables can reference other tables. Relationships are references to other tables. A column in a table can uniquely reference a row in another table by using the primary key of the other table. The column `CustomerID` in the table `Sales` is not unique. However, the column `CustomerID` in the table `Customers` is. That makes `CustomerID` in `Sales` a foreign key that references the `Customers` table.

Relationships are always primary key, foreign key relationships. You must make sure that your tables have the proper primary keys and foreign keys. Each dimension table should have a primary key. The fact table has foreign keys to the dimension tables. You have Power Query to make sure this is (becomes) true for your data.

Time to return to the **Edit relationship** dialog. The following data preview of the second table is a drop-down list called **Cardinality**. Opening the drop-down list shows four options:

- **Many to one (*:1)**: Primary keys are unique (1), foreign keys not (* or many). Many to one means that the first table displayed has a foreign key that references the primary key of the second table. In our example, the column **CustomerID** in the table **Sales** is the foreign key referencing the column **CustomerID** in the table **Customers**, aka the primary key.

- **One to many (1:*)**: This is the same relationship as many to one. It is just a matter of the order in which you mention the tables. When there is a one to many relationship between **Customers** and **Sales**, there is a many to one relationship between **Sales** and **Customers**.

- **One to one (1:1)**: With this cardinality, the many side of the previous two relationship types is limited to a maximum of one. One row in one table matches a single row in the other table. If this is always true for your data, you should merge the two tables using Power Query into a single table. That will be better for your model's efficiency.

- **Many to many (*:*)**: This is the dangerous one (and may be even the forbidden one). Database theory does not cater for this. When you create a many to many relationship, the warning shown in *Figure 7.3* is displayed. You should change your table structure in such a way that you do not need this type of relationship. The effect on your report is difficult to understand, and you risk getting incorrect results. Avoid many to many relationships.

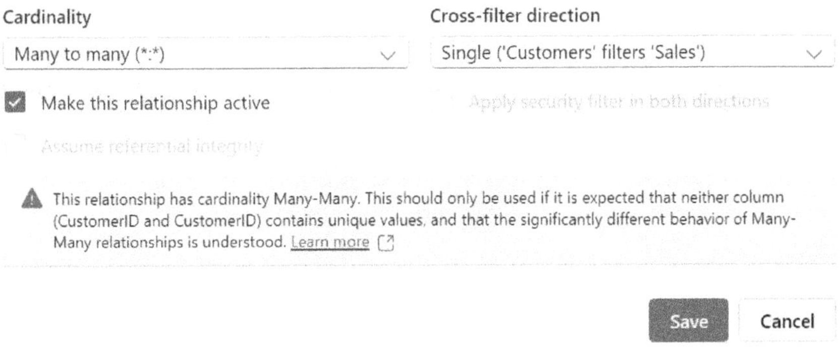

Cardinality

Many to many (*:*) ∨

☑ Make this relationship active

Assume referential integrity

Cross-filter direction

Single ('Customers' filters 'Sales') ∨

Apply security filter in both directions

⚠ This relationship has cardinality Many-Many. This should only be used if it is expected that neither column (CustomerID and CustomerID) contains unique values, and that the significantly different behavior of Many-Many relationships is understood. Learn more [↗]

Save   Cancel

Figure 7.3: Many to many

Relationships are always one to many relationships when using a proper star schema. The dimension table is always the one side of the relationship; the fact table is always the many side.

Next to relationship types, we should have a clear understanding of another important concept: cross-filtering.

Cross-filter direction

Next to the **Cardinality** option of a relationship is the drop-down list called **Cross-filter direction**. The two options to choose from are: **Single** and **Both**. Let us first see it in action before further discussing them:

1. Create a new report page called **Cross-filter direction**.

2. Create two slicers that both show as vertical list. One based on **Year,** the other based on **CompanyName** (**Customers**).

3. Create a clustered column chart with **MonthYear** on the **X-axis** and **NetSales** on the **Y-axis**.

4. Select the year **2021** in the year slicer. Select **Alfreds Futterkiste** in the **CompanyName** slicer.

   As you can see, there is nothing to show for the combination of **2021** and **Alfreds Futterkiste**. You can make customers who do not have any sales in the selected year disappear from the slicer to avoid selecting this not so useful combination.

5. Go to the Model view page. Right-click on the relationship between the tables **Customers** and **Sales**. Select **Properties**.

6. Change the **Cross-filter direction** to **Both**.

7. Go back to the Report view page. Clear both slicers (**Clear selections** button at the top of slicer, visible when you hover the mouse over the slicer.)

8. Now again select **2021** in the year slicer. Notice that **Alfreds Futterkiste** disappears from the **CompanyName** slicer.

9. Clear **2021** in the **Year** slicer, select **Alfreds Futterkiste** and then select **2021** again. In this order of selecting values, you can still select combinations of year and customer without sales.

10. Switch back to the Model view.

Your data model should look like *Figure 7.4*:

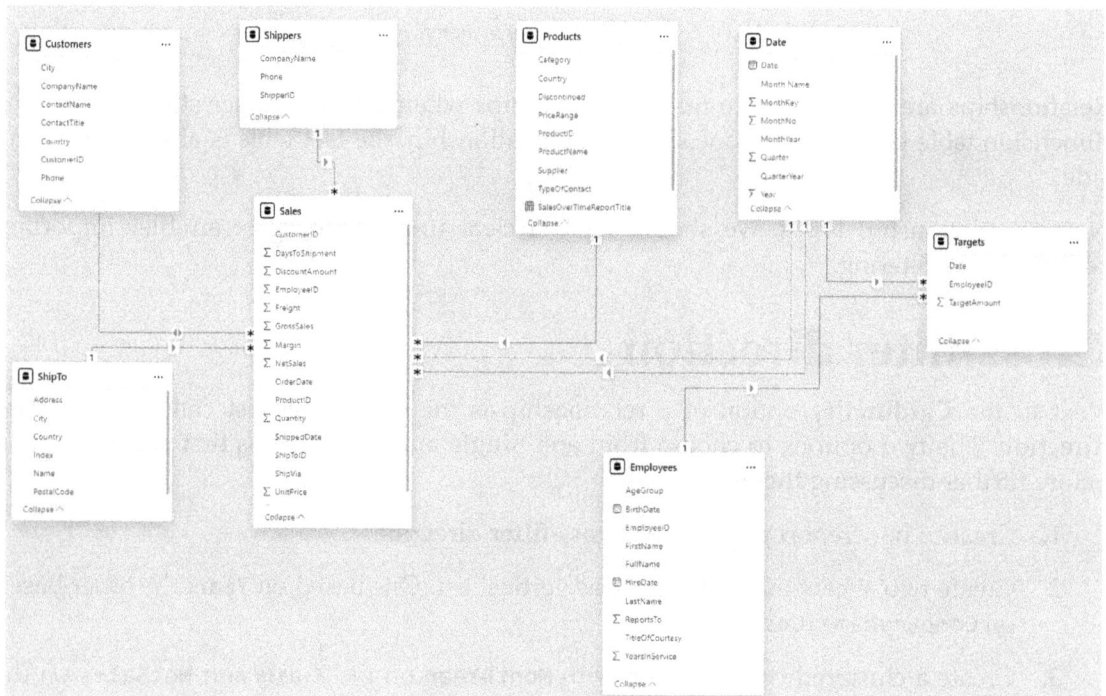

Figure 7.4: Structure of Northwind solution

Let us start explaining cross-filter direction by explaining how a report works. You create a slicer based on a dimension attribute (column from dimension table). When you select an item in the slicer, you want only data pertaining to the selected items to show on the report. This means: the report should be filtered, or, in other words, the data should be filtered.

Now look at the **Date** table, specifically the relationship between the **Date** table and the table **Sales**. There is a little arrow icon in the relationship pointing from the **Date** table towards the table **Sales**. This means that whenever the **Date** table is filtered (for instance by selecting a value in the slicer), the same filter is applied to the **Sales** table. That is exactly what we want:

dimensions filtering facts. Selecting **2021** in the **Year** slicers filter the fact table down to only rows from **2021**. This filtering is a one-way street. Whenever the table **Sales** is filtered, that filter is not also applied on the **Date** table.

When you changed the **Cross-filter direction** between the tables **Customers** and **Sales**, the arrow icon in the relationship also changed. It is now an arrow pointing in both directions. This means that filters on either table are propagated to the other table as well.

Changing the **Cross-filter direction** has the following impact on our example:

- When you select a year in the year slicer, the year table is filtered to only the year you selected. The same filter is applied to the **Sales** table. Only sales transactions that took place in the selected years remain. Then the filter is propagated to the **Customers** table as well because of the arrow in the relationships pointing towards **Customers**. Only customers with sales transactions in the selected year remain.

- **Going in the reverse direction**: When you select a customer in the customer slicer, the **Sales** table is filtered to show only rows with sales transactions of the selected customer. The **Date** table is unaffected by this filter because the arrow is not pointing towards the **Date** table. Hence, all three years still show in the year slicer.

This filtering and how filters are propagated through the data model is crucial for Power BI. By default, the filter direction is set to filter the many side of a relationship from the one side and not vice versa. That means for a proper star schema, dimensions filter facts!

You should never set the **Cross-filter direction** from the fact table to the **Date** dimension to **Both**. The **Date** dimension plays a special role. Setting the **Cross-filter direction** to **Both** will get you into trouble when using time intelligence functions. These functions are discussed in *Chapter 8, DAX*.

Some people even say you should never use **Cross-filter direction** set to **Both**. It has a big impact on DAX expressions and how they are calculated. So, you must be careful. Changing the **Cross-filter direction** when you already have DAX calculated measures added to your data model is dangerous because it may affect the outcome of those DAX expressions. However, if you know what you are doing, **Cross-filter direction** can be helpful. Having slicers with columns from different dimension tables that react to each other is a really important feature.

The **Cross-filter direction** option is also really important with many to many relationships between dimensions. Consider the following scenario:

You have a fact table (**factBalance**) with balances of all bank accounts. There is an account dimension **dimAccount**. Each row in the table **FactBalance** is linked to one bank account. You want to be able to analyze the overall balance by customer. However, a customer can have multiple accounts, but vice versa, can an account be owned by multiple people (customers)? For this, you will have to create a separate customer dimension and a bridge table (sometimes called **factless fact table** in dimensional modeling) in between the account and customer dimension. Refer to *Figure 7.5*:

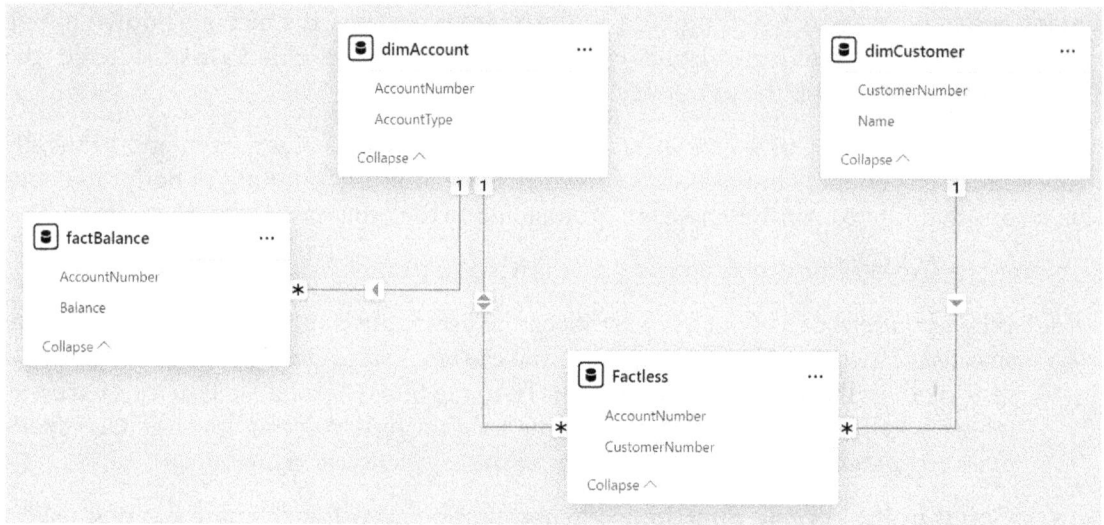

Figure 7.5: Many to many with factless fact table

In order to filter the table **factBalance** by customers you need to set the **Cross-filter direction** of the relationship between the **Factless** fact table and the table **dimAccount** to **Both**.

There are still two settings left to discuss on the **Edit relationship** dialog:

- **Assume referential integrity**: This option is only available when using either DirectQuery or Direct Lake connection mode. Both will be discussed in *Chapter 10, Scalable Power BI Solutions*. It tells Power BI that it is guaranteed that for every row in the many side of a relationship, a row in the one side exists. When you know this to be true, this setting optimizes how Power BI queries the underlying source.

- **Apply security filter in both directions**: This setting applies to **row level security (RLS)**, which is discussed in *Chapter 11, Security*. It basically says that you want filtering, as discussed, to happen to security filters as well.

The most important part of creating a semantic model is the tables you create and the relationships they have, but there is more to the semantic model.

Attribute properties

There are a lot of properties to consider when it comes to attributes (columns) in your semantic model. A lot of these properties can be set from the Report view page and will be set during report development. This is for convenience. From a theoretical standpoint, you should set them before creating a report in the Model view. Either way, the properties are the same. Let us go over these properties.

Data type and default aggregation

We already encountered this setting. Let us see it in action:

1. Create a new report page called **Attribute properties**.

2. Drag the column **Year** from the table **Date** onto the report canvas.

    Power BI creates a bar chart with a single bar. All years are added to a single value. This does not make sense, so why does Power BI do so? Power BI assumes that when you read in data, numerical columns are facts and that alphanumerical columns are dimensions. Facts are aggregated; dimensions are put on axis of visuals.

    Note the sigma sign (Σ) in front of the column **Year** in the **Data** pane. This indicates the data type of the column is numerical, and Power BI will, by default aggregate this column when used.

3. Select the column **Year** in the **Data** pane, not by selecting the check box in front of it, but by clicking anywhere in the name. This activates the **Column tools** ribbon.

4. Change the setting **Sum** in the **Summarization** setting to **Don't summarize**.

5. Remove the bar chart from the report page and drag the column **Year** from the table **Date** onto the report canvas again.

    You get a table with distinct years in it instead of a bar chart with all the years added together. You changed the default behavior. Note that you can also change the default aggregation of **Sum** to another aggregation function in the same way.

6. Change the table visual into a slicer.

7. The default slicer for numerical data is the **Range** (or **Between**). This will often make more sense than selecting individual values, especially when there are a lot of distinct values to show.

8. Go to the slicer settings (**Format visual** tab of **Visualizations** pane) and note the different styles available.

9. Select the column **Year** in the **Data** pane and change the data type from **Whole number** into **Text**.

10. Note that the appearance of the slicer changed. Check the available styles for the slicer.

The available styles for the slicer depend on the data type. It is again different for the **Date** data type. Especially note the relative date style. Try it out!

Whether you choose **Text** as the data type for **Year** or **Whole number**, together with **Don't summarize**, can be a personal preference. Keeping columns numerical when they are numerical in nature makes the most sense. So keep **Year** numerical end set **Don't summarize**.

Changing data types can be done in Power BI Desktop. A better option would be to carefully think about the data types and choose the proper ones in Power Query.

Formatting

The data type of a column specifies what you can do with the data. It says nothing about how values look on screen. Formatting determines the look and feel of values. The following steps will demonstrate formatting:

1. Drag the column **Date** from the **Data** pane into an empty area on the report canvas. Power BI creates a hierarchy and shows the four columns of the hierarchy in a table.

2. Right-click on the column **Date** in the **Columns** well on the **Visualizations** pane and select **Date** instead of **Date hierarchy**. The table changes into a single-column table showing the **Date**. How the date is shown depends on your Power BI regional settings.

3. Select the column **Date** in the **Data** pane to open the **Column tools** ribbon.

4. Change the format of the data to something you like using the **Format** drop-down list on the ribbon.

5. Add the column **NetSales** to the table visual.

6. Select the column **NetSales** in the **Data** pane to open the **Column tools** ribbon.

7. Keep **Currency** as the selected option for **Format**. Click on the Dollar sign under the **Format** drop-down list and choose the currency symbol of your country.

   Note: **Choosing the proper format is not a currency conversion, it is only formatting.**

8. Click on the comma icon to toggle thousand separators on and off.

9. Choose the number of decimals to show behind the comma.

Correctly formatting your data is important. It can help users interpret that data better.

Hierarchies

We saw in *Chapter 6, Create Interactive Reports*, how important interactivity in reports is in helping to keep reports simple. One way of doing that was the use of hierarchies. We used ad-hoc hierarchies, but we already mentioned that you can add hierarchies to the data model. Let us create two hierarchies in our model. Refer to the steps to create hierarchies:

1. Right-click on the column **Category** in the table **Products** in the **Data** pane and select **Create hierarchy**. You can click on the three dots behind the name of the column instead of right-clicking. The three dots appear when you hover your mouse over a column name.

2. Right-click on the column **ProductName** in the table **Products** in the **Data** pane and select **Add to hierarchy** followed by **Category hierarchy**.

3. Right-click on the hierarchy **Category hierarchy**, select **Rename**, and rename it to **Categories**.

   Note: **The hierarchy you just created is the first field in the fields list of the table in the Data pane. This way it is easier to see there is a hierarchy which will increase its use.**

4. On the Report view, delete the column **Date** from the table visual.

5. Drag the **Categories** hierarchy to the **Columns** well of the **Build visual** tab and drop it above the column **Sum of NetSales**. Note that two columns are added.

6. Change the table visual into a matrix. Note that you see only the top-level attribute, **Category**, but with + icons to drill down.

   In the **Data** pane, both the hierarchy and the individual columns **Category** and **ProductName** are visible. Now that we have a hierarchy, that hierarchy should be used. It is best practice to now hide the original columns.

7. Right-click on **Category** and select **Hide**. Do the same for **ProductName**.

8. Right-click again on any column. Notice the option **View Hidden** that toggles between hidden fields being hidden or not. Hidden fields will always be hidden once the report is published to the Power BI service.

9. Create another hierarchy in the **Date** table using **Year** -> **QuarterYear** -> **Month name**. Hide the individual columns. Name the hierarchy **Calendar**.

Note that when working on the Model view page, an alternative interface for creating hierarchies appears on the **Properties** pane as soon as you create a hierarchy. You may find this interface easier to work with.

Also, note that when you go to the Model view page, you can multi-select columns within a table. You can then set a property, like hiding the column, for all selected columns at once. Hiding can be done by clicking on the eye icon that appears behind a column name within a table as soon as you hover the mouse over the column name.

Hide columns

Hiding columns can be important. They keep the model simpler. Some columns are necessary in the model, but should not be used on the report. The most obvious ones being the primary and foreign keys. Foreign keys should never be used inside a report. Use columns from the table they reference. Primary keys are preferably meaningless numbers whose only function is to provide efficient, unique values. They have no reporting value. There are always exceptions.

Most notable is the date inside the date table that serves as primary key and is valuable for analysis. Hide all primary keys and foreign keys except the primary key **Date**.

Data categories

As we already understand by now, the properties we are talking about help Power BI make choices of how data is to be used. Setting these properties once makes developing reports easier and less time consuming. Another simple property is the **Data category**. Let us take a look at this property:

1. Go to the Report view.

2. Select the column **Country** from the table **ShipTo** in the **Data** pane to activate the **Column tools** ribbon.

3. In the drop-down list behind **Data category** on the ribbon, select **Country**.

4. Set the **Data category** for the other columns of the **ShipTo** table and categorize them.

These settings tell Power BI it is dealing with geographical data. When dragging these columns onto the report canvas, the map visual will be the default visual.

Also note the three non-geographical categories. Image URL tells Power BI that a column is an image. The other two are self-explanatory.

Grouping and binning

Yet another feature is the ability to create groups of data. Let us show that by an example.

- Right-click on the column **UnitPrice** in the **Data** pane and select **New group**.

- Leave all defaults and click **OK**.

- Drag the new column to the report canvas to create a table visual and add the original column **UnitPrice** to the table.

- Change the aggregation of the column **UnitPrice** to **Count** in the **Build visual** tab.

The top row in the table visual shows the numbers 0.00 and 478. That means there are 478 rows with a unit price greater than or equal than 0 and smaller than 10.06 (the value in the second row). Note that the values in the first row, the group, have equal increments from row to row.

Instead of leaving **Bin type** to be **Size of bins**, you can select number of bins. The bins size is then automatically calculated. With **Group type** set to **List** instead of **Bin**, you can create random groups based on what you select to be a group. Try them out for different data types.

Note: **What we are doing here resembles our calculated column AgeGroup. Creating groups and bins can be done during ETL. That is, whenever possible, the better solution.**

Display folder

As we said before, a lot of the settings we learn about in this chapter can be done during report development from the Report view page. Besides that, some settings are important for the functionality, like data types, and others not so much, like data categories.

There is a reason why the settings discussed here are semantic model settings and not reporting settings. Suppose a large(r) company with complex business processes and lots of disparate data sources. A good data engineer should be able to structure the data and make a nice model out of it. A business user who understands the business processes and understands what the business needs might be better equipped to create the correct (useful) visuals. In Power BI, all the work can be done by a single individual. In real life, you sometimes want to (or need) to have separate people with different skills to combine their skills to build a report. One does the work of creating a nice semantic model, the other uses it to create meaningful reports. All settings as described here are either necessary for Power BI to function correctly or they help to make the life of the report builder easier. The settings make a better model. A better model makes it easier to create useful reports.

Another setting that makes building reports easier is the **Display folder**. Some tables have a lot of columns. Opening that table in the **Data** pane shows the entire list. When the list of columns becomes too large, finding columns becomes troublesome. Creating folders and placing columns in appropriate folders can help.

1. Go to the Model view page.

2. Open the table `Products` in the **Data** pane.

3. Multi-select the columns `Country, Supplier, TypeOfContact`. In the **Display folder** textbox in the **Properties** pane, enter `Supplier info`.

4. Note the change in how columns are shown in the `Products` table in the **Data** pane.

5. Go to the Report view page and open the `Products` table in the **Data** pane.

Note: **If report developers do not find the columns easily anymore in the Data pane, the model may have become to complex. The entire idea of display folders is that it becomes easier again to find columns. You can create multiple display folders per table.**

Sort by column

A property too important not to mention here is the **Sort by column**. We saw this property in action back in *Chapter 5, Advanced Techniques of Power Query,* when we wanted month names to be sorted on the number of the month instead of on the alphabet of the month name. You can refer back to that chapter.

This concludes the properties of columns. We have not looked at tables yet.

Table properties

A table is an object to be used just as columns are. That means that tables have properties we can set as well. An important one is specific to the **Date** table. Let us start there.

Mark as date table

A **Date** table in Power BI is a table with a single row in it for each day on the calendar in a range you define. Once you start using time intelligence functions in DAX expressions, you need one. Until then, it is just convenient to have one.

However, for Power BI, a table is a table. It does not make a distinction between fact and dimension tables. It also does not know your date table is a date table, but you can tell Power BI that it is. The steps to define a date table are as follows:

1. Got to the Model view page inside Power BI Desktop.

2. Find the **Date** table and click on the three dots (**...**) in the right-hand side of the table header within the diagram.

3. Select **Mark as date table**.

4. Toggle **Mark as date table** on in the **Mark as date table** dialog.

5. Select **Date** in the drop-down list **Choose a date column**.

    Note that a message is displayed saying: Validated successfully. Power BI validates that you have a single row in the table for each day on the calendar.

6. Click on **Save**.

Although you cannot see an immediate effect, this setting has quite an impact. In the book, until now, we encountered on a couple of occasions that Power BI automatically creates a date hierarchy for you. This is great because you do not have to create it yourself. However, Power BI creates an invisible date table to accomplish this. Power BI does so for each date column in your data model. So, when you have 20 columns of data type **Date,** you will also have twenty hidden date tables. Not very efficient.

With your own **Date** table marked as **Date** table, Power BI will not create hierarchies anymore. More importantly, it will not add hidden tables to your model anymore, keeping your model more efficient. The drawback is that you must create your own date hierarchy if you want to use one, but you learned how easy that is in this chapter.

It is a best practice to always have a **Date** table and mark it as such.

Most other table properties have less impact. Let us go through them quickly.

Other table properties

You can find the table properties on the Model view page inside the **Properties** pane.

The following list shows the available table properties:

- **Name and description**: Naming is an important part of creating an intuitive semantic model. Stick to the jargon used in the business. Adding a description can help users that use the semantic model to better understand the data in a table.

- **Synonyms**: We came across the Q&A feature earlier in this book. That is where users ask questions in human language. Q&A uses table and column names to figure out what the question is about. However, some users will use the term employee while others use salesperson or sales representative. Choose one term as the table name and add the others as synonyms. Q&A will work better. Note that synonyms can be set at the table and at the column level.

- **Row label**: Row label is also meant to improve Q&A. The column defined as the **row label** best describes a table and will be used first by Q&A. `CompanyName` is a good candidate for the row label of the table `Customers`.

- **Key column**: Suppose you have two employees with `Peter` as their first name and you create a net sales by first name table. There will be just one row for `Peter`, and the sales of both the people will be added together. Setting the **Key column** of the `Employee` table to `EmployeeID` will change this. You will get two rows with `Peter`. Having two separate rows is better. However, it only solves the problem half. In the table visual, you cannot distinguish between the two rows because they show the same name: `Peter`. Better would be to create a column with unique labels using Power Query. For instance, the name with the `EmployeeID` in between braces appended to the name, like *Peter (5)*.

- **Is hidden**: Sometimes, you need tables in the semantic model that are not meant to create visuals from. Make these tables hidden. Tables used for dynamic RLS are an example. *RLS is discussed in Chapter 11, Security.*

- **Is featured table**: When toggling this on, users can find the table from Excel. Combining this property with the row label and key column helps Excel connect to the table.

- **Storage mode**: Storage mode is an important feature. We will discuss storage modes in *Chapter 10, Scalable Power BI Solutions*.

Conclusion

The Power BI semantic model is an invaluable part of Power BI reporting. It helps build better reports more easily. The most important part is the relationships you define between tables. The relationships determine how tables are filtered and, by that, what numbers are shown in the report.

In theory, you should create a semantic model before you start creating reports and visuals. In Power BI development, building visuals and creating the semantic model go hand in hand in an iterative way. You create a report by dragging in columns. At that time, you may get unwanted results because the semantic model is not yet what it needs to be. At that time, you change the semantic model settings, after which you proceed with your report development work.

The Power BI semantic model is more than the properties and settings described in this chapter. An important part of the semantic model is the addition of calculations to the model. You will learn about DAX calculations in the next chapter.

Multiple choice questions

1. **Which two relationship types are essentially the same?**

    a. Many to one

    b. One to one

    c. Many to many

    d. One to many

2. **Which property should you change when a value is correct but printed correctly on screen?**

    a. Data type

    b. Hide

    c. Data category

    d. Format

3. **What should you do when people often refer to sales as orders or transactions when using Q&A?**

    a. Rename the table sales to orders/transactions

    b. Create aliases orders and transactions for the table sales.

    c. Create extra tables for orders and transactions

    d. Create inactive role-playing dimension relationships

Answers

1	a, d
2	d
3	b

CHAPTER 8
DAX

Introduction

Data Analysis Expressions (**DAX**) is a formula expression language used in Analysis Services, Power BI, and Power Pivot in Excel. We came across DAX a couple of times already. It is now time to look into DAX in much more detail. You could say that Power BI follows the 80-20% rule. 80% of report creation is straightforward. You just drag columns to your report. DAX allows you to get to that extra 20%. You can create calculations that cannot be done otherwise. In short, you use DAX to enrich your semantic model.

If you want to follow along with the examples presented in this chapter, you need Power BI Desktop to be installed on your workstation. This chapter continues where the previous ended. If you followed along in the previous chapter, you can continue in the Power BI Desktop file you created there. If you did not, you can use the file **Solution chapter 7.pbix** from the GitHub repository of this book.

Structure

This chapter covers the following topics:

- Introduction to DAX
- Calculated columns

- Parent-child hierarchy
- Calculated measures
- Time intelligence

Objectives

In this chapter, you will learn about context. Context is another word for filter and is crucial in understanding DAX. You will understand how to create calculated columns and calculated measures using DAX. A section highlighting the difference between calculated columns and measures is there for further understanding. In the end, you will know how to apply the learned DAX knowledge to create some time intelligence measures.

Introduction to DAX

Way before the inception of Power BI, Microsoft had a product called Microsoft **SQL Server Analysis Service (SSAS)**. You could create what was then called **online analytical processing (OLAP)** cubes using this product. Today, an OLAP cube is called a **semantic model**. A data store meant to enable drag-and-drop reporting. The current version of the semantic model you create using Microsoft SSAS is called **tabular model**, and it is the same technology as used in Power BI semantic models.

The language behind the old SSAS was called **Multidimensional Expressions (MDX)**. MDX was a difficult language to master, even for software developers. So, when Microsoft moved its SSAS technology into Power BI to enable self-service BI, they needed a different language. Self-service does not go well together with a language that is difficult even for developers. A big target audience Microsoft had in mind for Power BI were Excel users. So, Microsoft created a language that looks like Excel formulas but with the power and functionality of MDX. This language is DAX.

DAX has the functionality of the old, but difficult language MDX, while it has the look and feel of Excel functions and formulas. DAX is meant to enable a lot of people, not just developers, to create compelling reports.

A brief note of caution is advised. *Alberto Ferrari*, one of the DAX gurus in the world, once wrote: *DAX is simple, but not easy*. DAX uses Excel syntax, which is easy enough. It, however, has the complexity of MDX and a multidimensional world in it. That can make it far from easy. However, it can be mastered, and we will set our first step towards mastering it here.

Three things that you can do using DAX are:

- Create calculated columns
- Create calculated measures
- Write queries

This chapter will focus on calculated columns and measures. You will learn about DAX queries in the next chapter.

We can make the distinction between calculated columns and calculated measures in two ways:

- Based on the usage of the result

- Based on technical implementation

In *Chapter 2, Dimensional Modeling,* we learned to categorize columns of tables into facts and dimensions. Dimension attributes (the columns in our dimension tables) are used on axes of visuals or as filters. Dimension attributes are used to analyze the facts. Facts, on the other hand, are aggregated values that tell us how well processes are doing. They determine the height of a bar in a bar chart, the size of a part in a pie chart, or the numbers in the cells of a matrix. When a calculation is used as a dimension attribute, you must create a calculated column. When it is to be used as a fact, you must create a calculated measure.

From a more technical perspective, you can say that calculated columns are static. They are calculated during data refresh and only then. They are static in between refreshes. Calculated measures are dynamic. They are calculated every time they appear on a report. That is why we could use them earlier to create dynamic report titles.

We will start by looking at calculated columns.

Calculated columns

The most important concept when starting to write DAX expressions is context. Calculated columns use what is called **row context**. Row context makes our lives easy. It basically means that each value is evaluated within a row. You cannot reference values from other rows. When you are used to working with tables, this makes perfect sense. When you have an Excel background, it basically means we have relative references when calculating a value; we do not have absolute references. Some examples will make this clear. We will use a new Power BI Desktop file to demonstrate the concepts before moving back to the solution we created before and enriching it using DAX. Perform the following steps to create the DAX examples yourself:

1. Open a new Power BI Desktop solution.

2. Click on **Get data** button in the **Home** ribbon and select **OData feed** as the type of source to use.

3. Enter the URL `http://services.odata.org/V3/Northwind/Northwind.svc`, which we used before, and click on **OK**.

4. Select the tables `Categories`, `Order_Details` and `Products` and click on **Load**.

5. Go to the Table view page and select the table `Order_Details`.

In *Chapter 3, The Basic of Power Query,* we used Power Query Editor to create computed columns. We can use DAX as an alternative. The following steps will show you how to use DAX to create calculated columns:

1. Right-click on the table **Order_Details** in the **Data** pane and select **New column**. Note the formula bar displayed between the report canvas and the ribbon.

2. Enter the following DAX formula in the formula bar to create a column called **LineTotal**:

   LineTotal = Order_Details[UnitPrice] * Order_Details[Quantity] * (1 - Order_Details[Discount])

3. Press *Enter* when done typing.

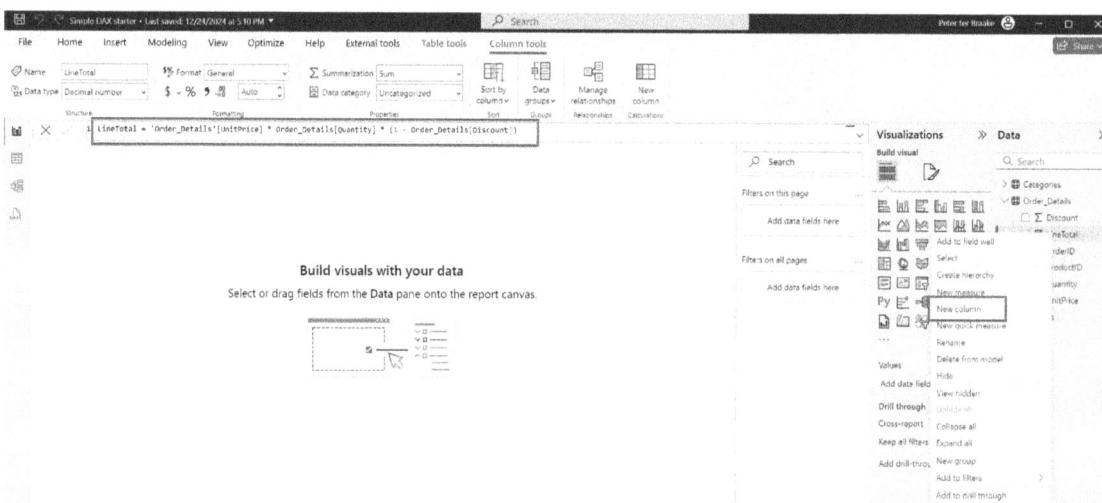

Figure 8.1: Calculated column

> **Note: It is a similar formula used before in Power Query.**

There are a couple of things to note here. First, a column name inside a DAX expression is always inside square brackets, e.g. **[UnitPrice]**. Before the name of the column, you may enter the name of the table the column is from, e.g. **Order_Details[UnitPrice]**. When you reference a column from another table, you must prefix the column with the table name. The table name can be written between single quotes like **'Order_Details'[UnitPrice]**. Use quotes when the name of the table contains spaces.

Apart from the syntax of the DAX, note the result. You see a value for every row in the table. These values are calculated now and every time you refresh the data. However, the values are not recalculated in between refreshes. The row context mentioned earlier simply means that the values for **UnitPrice**, **Quantity**, and **Discount** used are always the values as they are in the same row of the resulting value. You cannot refer to the value of a column in another row.

When a calculated column can be created just as easily in Power Query, prefer Power Query over DAX. In that perspective, the first example is a bad one. Please do this in Power Query. It was just a simple calculation to start our learning journey. The following steps will create some more DAX computed columns, working towards more useful examples:

1. Select the table **Products** in the **Data** pane on the Table view page.

2. Right-click on the table **Products** in the **Data** pane and select **New column**.

3. Enter the following DAX formula to create a column called **CategoryName**:

```
CategoryName = RELATED(Categories[CategoryName])
```

This calculated column uses the DAX function **RELATED** to get the column **CategoryName** from the table **Categories** to add it to the table **Products**. The name of the category a product belongs to should be in the **Products** table according to the theory of good dimension design. We did that before using Power Query, which is, again, the better solution.

However, this example shows the use of the function **RELATED**. It uses a relationship to reference a row on one side of the relationship and uses that row on the many side of the relationship. It uses the relationship definition from the semantic model. You do not have to specify the relationship to use as it is known because of the semantic model we have created already. For people with Excel experience, it is very similar to the Excel **VLOOKUP** function, only simpler because it uses the semantic model.

Let us do a third example, but now one that should be done using DAX instead of Power Query:

1. Select the table **Categories** in the **Data** pane on the **Table view** page.

2. Right-click on the table **Categories** in the **Data** pane and select **New column**.

3. Enter the DAX formula to create a column called **# of Products**:

```
# of products = COUNTROWS(RELATEDTABLE(Products))
```

The table **Categories** should now look like the following figure:

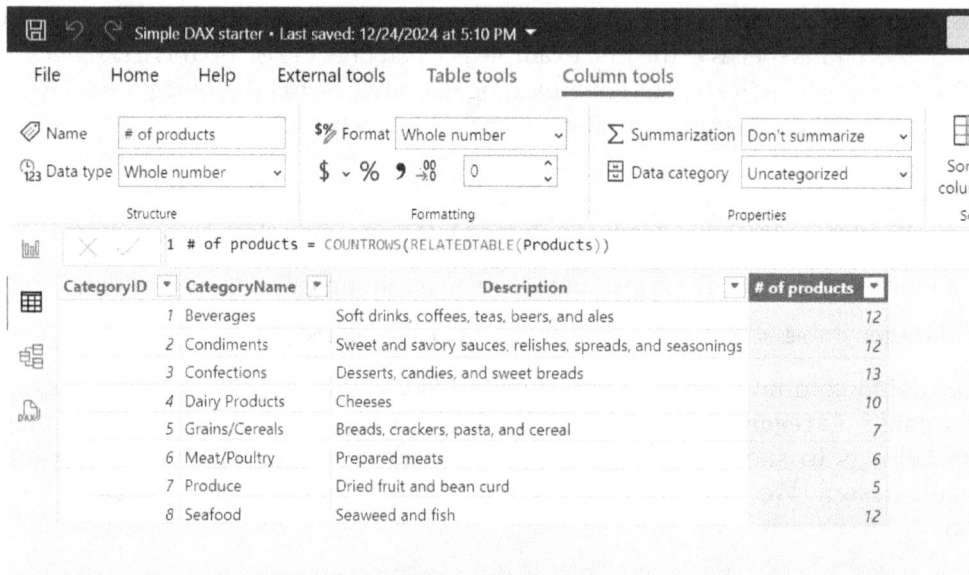

Figure 8.2: Number of products

This formula uses two nested functions. When we read the formula from inside out, we first see the function **RELATEDTABLE**. This function is similar to the function **RELATED,** with the difference that it traverses a relationship from the one side of the relationship to the many side. Inside the parentheses behind the name of the function, you specify parameters. In this case, the name of the table **Products**. The function now knows you want to do something with the table **Products**. Since you reference an entire table while calculating a single value for each row, you must reduce that table into a single value. An easy way to do that is by simply counting how many rows there are in the table: **COUNTROWS**.

Note that the formula sort of translates to: count all the rows in the related table **Products**. We get different values for each row because of row context. Power BI will first calculate the value for the first row. This is the row of the category **Beverages**. Power BI will filter the table **Products** down to only products that belong to the category **Beverages**. Only after that filter is applied will DAX start counting rows. It does not count the rows of the table; it counts the row of the filtered table.

DAX will filter tables before calculating aggregations.

For each category (for each row in the table **Categories**), a filter is applied to the table **Products**, and only then the rows are counted. This is row context at work.

The reason that this example should be done using DAX instead of Power Query is the aggregation **COUNTROWS**. Power Query is good for working with rows. DAX is good in aggregating data. As a rule of thumb, aggregations should be made in DAX (unless it is for defining the grain of your fact table). Calculated columns that do not use aggregations should be done using Power Query. Using Power Query, both the storage compression and the performance will be better.

Even though the example is a good DAX example, the resulting column is not very useful. Remember, we created a calculated column that is to be used as a dimension attribute. A slight change in the formula can make it more useful:

4. Change the formula for **# of products** into the following formula:

```
# of products = IF ( COUNTROWS(RELATEDTABLE(Products)) < 10 , "Small
category" , "Big category" )
```

All categories are now labelled as either a big or a small category. Your table should now

look like *Figure 8.3*. You can use this to analyze whether more choice leads to different customer behavior.

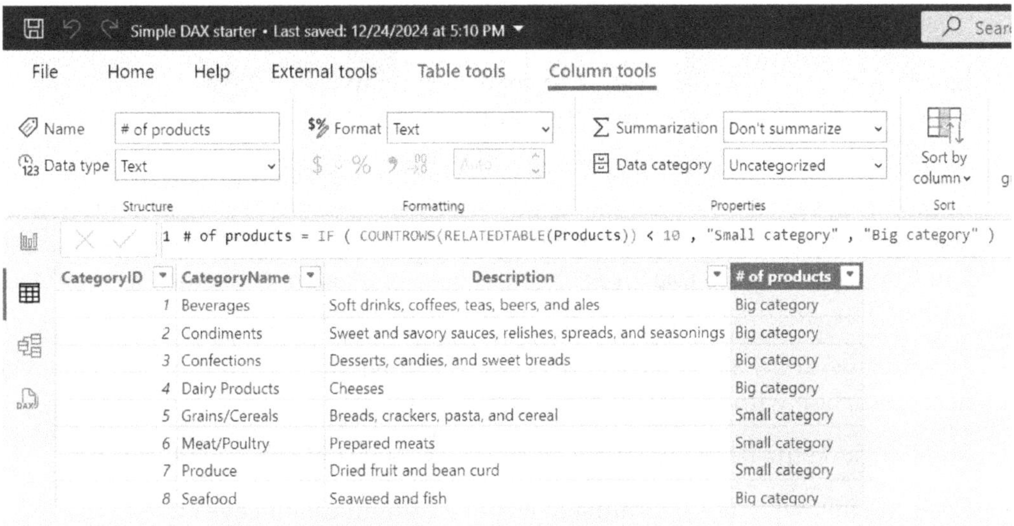

Figure 8.3: Categories categorized

Parent-child hierarchy

We learned about hierarchies in *Chapter 6, Create Interactive Reports,* and *Chapter 7, The Basics of Semantic Models*. All hierarchies used thus far were natural hierarchies. In natural hierarchies, there is a one to many relationship between an element and the elements one level down in the hierarchy. The most detailed level is always the same number of levels down from the top level, no matter the path you follow. There are always four levels—year, quarter, month, and day—regardless of which year you are referring to.

Parent-child hierarchies are different. There is a one to many relationship between an element and the elements one level down in the hierarchy, like for natural hierarchies. Only the number of levels may not be fixed. The number of levels depends on the path chosen. An employee hierarchy where employees report to a *boss* is an example of this. We do have just this hierarchy in our Northwind data. Creating a parent-child hierarchy in Power BI does involve quite some DAX. The following steps create the hierarchy:

1. Open your own Power BI solution from the previous chapter or open the files **Solution chapter 7.pbix** from the Github repository

2. Go to the Table view page and select the **Employees** table. Note the column **ReportsTo**.

   The column **ReportsTo** stores the **EmployeeID** of the person an employee reports to, his or her boss. However, this boss reports to someone as well, who reports to someone, and so on. The first thing to do is *figure out* this path to the top. That is exactly what the **PATH** function is for.

3. Right-click on the table **Employees** in the **Data** pane and select **New column**.

4. Enter the following DAX formula to create a column called **Path**:
   ```
   Path = PATH( [EmployeeID] , [ReportsTo] )
   ```

   Look, for instance, at the value of the new column for **Robert King**. The value in the column is **2|5|7**. The last number is the **EmployeeID** of **Robert King** himself. The **5** in front of the **7** is the **EmployeeID** of the boss of **Robert King**, **Steven Buchanan,** and the **2** in front of that is the **EmployeeID** of the boss of **Steven Buchanan**, **Andrew Fuller**. **Andrew Fuller** is the CEO; he does not report to anyone.

   Now that we know all the *bosses*, we need to get their names. The function **LOOKUPVALUE** in combination with **PATHITEM** can do that.

5. Right-click on the table **Employees** in the **Data** pane and select **New column**.

6. Enter the following DAX formula to create a column called **Level1**:
   ```
   Level1 = LOOKUPVALUE (Employees[FullName], [EmployeeID], PATHITEM (
   [Path]  , 1 , 1))
   ```

   Note that the preceding expression returns **Andrew Fuller** for all rows because **Andrew Fuller** is the CEO of the company. Let us explain the formula from the inside out.

   The function **PATHITEM** uses the column **[Path]** that we created in the previous step. It takes the first value from the |-separated list that the column **[Path]** stores. The last parameter, the **1**, tells Power BI to consider this a number. The column **[Path]** itself is of data type **Text**. We want numbers to compare the result of the function **PATHITEM** to the **EmployeeID** column, which is a **Whole number** data type.

   The function **LOOKUPVALUE** gets the column passed as the first parameter (**Employees[FullName]**), returning the value where the **EmployeeID** (second parameter) equals the third parameter (the value we got from `PATHITEM ( [Path] , 1 , 1)`).

Now, let us create the next level of the hierarchy.

7. Right-click on the table `Employees` in the **Data** pane and select **New column**.

8. Enter the following DAX formula to create a column called **Level2**:
   ```
   Level2 = LOOKUPVALUE (Employees[FullName], [EmployeeID], PATHITEM (
   [Path] , 2 , 1))
   ```

9. Create a calculated column called **Level3** in a similar way.

   The longest list found in the column **Path** contains three numbers. That is why we want to make three columns: to translate the numbers into corresponding names.

   The last thing to do is to make a hierarchy using the columns **Level1**, **Level2**, and **Level3**.

10. Create a hierarchy called **Staff hierarchy**.

11. Hide the columns **Path**, **Level1**, **Level2** and **Level3**.

12. Test the hierarchy yourself. Using a matrix it could look like *Figure 8.4* Employee hierarchy:

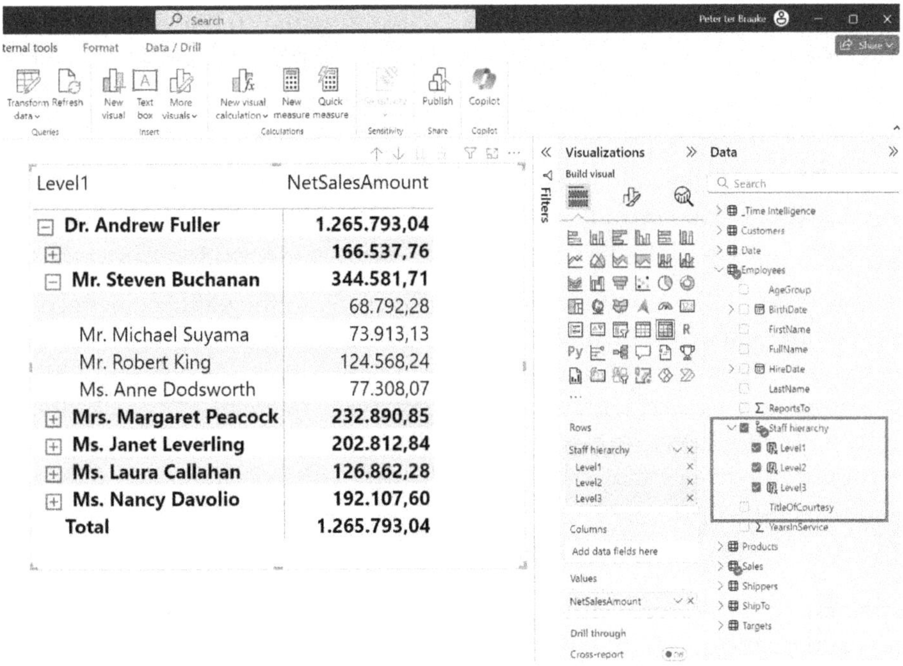

Figure 8.4: Employee hierarchy

With all this, it is time to have a first look at calculated measures.

Calculated measures

A calculated column has a value for every row in the table it is added to. That is why we created them while on the Table view page. Calculated measures do not exist until used in a visual on your report. As you learned in the introduction section of this chapter, calculated measures are calculated dynamically each time they are used. Calculated measures are used in visuals on report pages and need to be calculated every time a report page is shown on your screen.

One reason for this is that measures need context. They get their context from the report. Consider a simple measure sales. How many different values can possibly be calculated, all being sales? There is the overall sales amount, which is a single value. Sales by category is eight different values because we have eight different categories in this example. Sales by product is another 77 values with 77 products in the dataset. Sales can also be analyzed by product, by year, or by any combination of dimension attributes. What sales actually means depends on the context of how it is being used. Calculating the correct values only makes sense when that context is defined. In other words, calculating the correct values for sales only makes sense when you know what you want to show on the report.

As soon as you drag a calculated measure onto a report, Power BI will analyze the report. Are there selections made in slicers? Are filters applied? Is something in another visual selected? What dimensions are used alongside your calculated measure in the visual you are creating? All this is context. The context in which the values of the measure are calculated. It is called the **filter context**.

Filter context is what makes Power BI work as it does. Until now, we did not know about filter context, but it was there all along. The first visual we created was a bar chart showing **NetSales by Category**. The result is eight bars, all with different heights. That is because the context is different for each bar. Each bar represents another category.

Filter context is great until it is not. What if you do not get to the values you need with Power BI's automatic filter context? Then, you change that context. You apply your own context. The context you write is called the **query context**. To articulate more accurately, Power BI combines its automatic context with the context you write to create a query context. Power BI automatically applies filter context whether you like it or not. You change or overrule the filter context by providing extra context that leads to a query context. Let us see this at work.

Implicit vs. explicit measures

Until this point in the book, we were able to create reports because Power BI implicitly creates measures. That begs the question of what a measure is. A measure is the aggregation of a fact. A fact is (often) a numerical value, like an individual sales amount. In our table, we have the column **NetSales** storing an amount for each row in the **Sales** table. The column **NetSales** is a fact.

When you drag the column **NetSales** to a report, those individual values are summed. In the afore-mentioned bar chart, **NetSales** values of all rows that are linked to products in the same category are summed into a single value. In the field well of the visual, you can see the text **Sum of NetSales** to indicate this behavior. **Sum of NetSales** is an implicit measure. Power BI assumed you wanted to sum all values together. Let us look at this more closely:

1. Go to the Report view page.

2. Create a new page called **Simple DAX**.

3. Select the column **Category** from the **Categories** hierarchy in the **Products** table in the **Data** pane to create a new table visual.

4. Add the column **NetSales** to the table visual.

   You get a table visual with eight rows plus a total row. Notice that the visual shows nine different values for **NetSales**, and the column in the visual is called **Sum of NetSales**. This is your implicit measure.

   Continuing with the example:

5. Right-click on the table **Sales** in the **Data** pane and select **New measure**.

6. Enter the following DAX formula in the formula bar to create a measure called **Sales**:

   NetSalesAmount = SUM(Sales[NetSales])

   Notice that the measure shows as a column in the table Sales in the Data pane. There is a special icon in front of the name indicating it is a calculated measure. Also note that you will not see this column in the data preview on the Table view page.

7. Drag the new measure from the **Sales** table in the **Data** pane into the table visual on your report.

   You should now see the same values twice. The formatting may be different; the values are the same. **NetSalesAmount** is an explicit measure. You explicitly defined it using a DAX **SUM** function.

8. Right-click on the column **Sum of NetSales** in the field well **Columns** in the **Build visual** tab of the **Visualizations** pane.

   There is a list of (aggregation) functions to choose from. Power BI chose the default aggregation as set within the semantic model, but you can choose any function you like.

9. Right-click on the column **NetSalesAmount** in the field well **Columns** in the **Build visual** tab of the **Visualizations** pane to see that you cannot change the function.

An explicitly defined measure cannot be changed in the report. You will have to change the DAX code and, by doing so, change the definition of your explicit measure.

For both the explicit and implicit measures, we see eight different values plus a ninth for the total row. Both get calculated row by row when the report is built to show on screen. Rows of the table visual to be precise. Each row shows another category, meaning the context of each row is different. Power BI filters the data model on the category of the row it is calculating before it executes the **SUM** function. First filter, then aggregate. Power BI will always use this order.

All this is just to get familiar with how Power BI works. Let us continue and see some more useful calculated measures.

% of parent

Numbers are just numbers and by themselves are often not very informative. Comparing a number to another number helps put it into perspective. For now, we want to add a column to the table that shows the sales amount as a parent of the grand total. We work towards a calculated measure called **% of parent**, but will do so in a couple of little steps:

1. Create a new measure in the table **Sales** by using the following DAX code:

   ```
   % of parent = CALCULATE( [NetSalesAmount] , ALL ( Products[Category] ) )
   ```

2. Delete the column **Sum of NetSales** from the table visual on your report and add the newly created **% of parent** to it.

Your table visual should look like *Figure 8.5:*

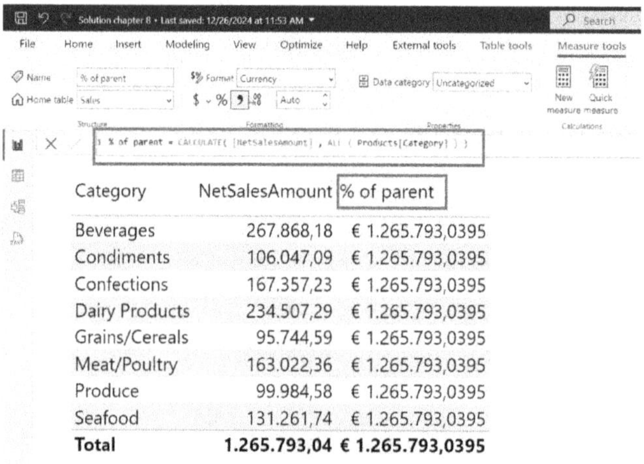

Figure 8.5: ALL

There are a couple of things to note here.

First, the use of the function **CALCULATE**. When Power BI, with its automatic filter context, does not do what you want, you will have to do the calculations yourself. Hence, calculate. A better description will be given in the next chapter.

A measure is always an aggregation. You will always have to use a function like **SUM**, **COUNT**, **MIN**, **MAX**, **AVERAGE**, or another aggregation function. The use of the aggregation distinguishes the measure from the fact. The first parameter inside the parentheses following **CALCULATE** is this aggregation. In this case, the aggregation is implicit. The formula states it wants to calculate **NetSalesAmount**. This is, however, the same as **SUM(Sales[NetSales])**, which uses the **SUM** aggregation function. We could have used the original formula for NetSalesAmount instead of **NetSalesAmount** itself.

The second argument of the **CALCULATE** function is **ALL (Products[Category])**. Here, we tell Power BI to calculate this over all categories. This means that Power BI should ignore the filter context that would calculate **NetSalesAmount** for each row after filtering on the category. We tell it not to do **NetSalesAmount** by category, but to calculate it for all categories. That is our context. Our context overrules Power BI's filter context to create a new query context.

All together, this leads to having the overall sales amount calculated for each row. Dividing sales by overall sales gives the percentage:

1. Change the formula for **% of parent** into: (you can do multi-line code by pressing *Shift + Enter*):

2. Select the measure **% of parent** in the **Sales** table in the **Data** pane.

3. Change its formatting to **Percentage** with just a single decimal. (**Measure tool** ribbon, % icon).

   Your table visual changed into the one shown in *Figure 8.6*:

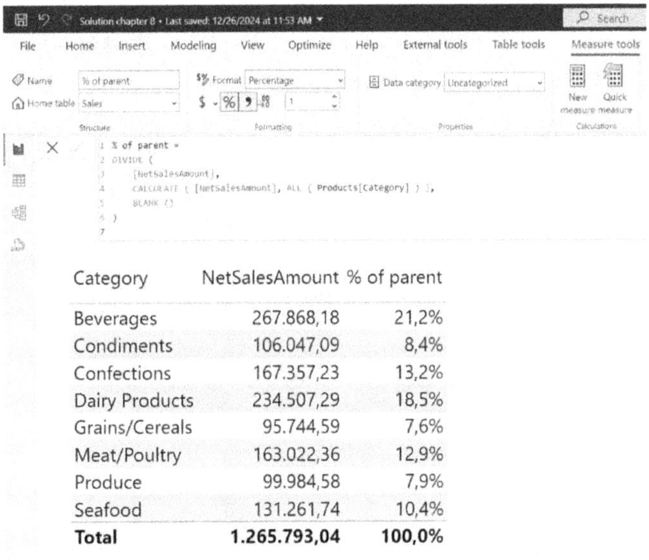

Category	NetSalesAmount	% of parent
Beverages	267.868,18	21,2%
Condiments	106.047,09	8,4%
Confections	167.357,23	13,2%
Dairy Products	234.507,29	18,5%
Grains/Cereals	95.744,59	7,6%
Meat/Poultry	163.022,36	12,9%
Produce	99.984,58	7,9%
Seafood	131.261,74	10,4%
Total	**1.265.793,04**	**100,0%**

Figure 8.6: % of Total

The formula we just used is straightforward. We let Power BI calculate **NetSalesAmount** and **DIVIDE** that value by the total we calculated ourselves in the previous step. The third parameter, the function **BLANK ()**, returns a blank value when we divide by zero.

To continue with the example, perform the following:

4. To see how cool DAX is, add a vertical list slicer based on the column **Year** to the report.

5. Select a year in the slicer to see what happens.

    We know how a slicer works for the implicit measures we have used so far in the book. Values on the report will be filtered. The same is true for calculated measures. Power BI automatically detects new context on the report, in this case, the new slicer. It filters everything, including our explicit measures, by that context. Since our expression **CALCULATE ([NetSalesAmount], ALL (Products[Category]))**, says nothing about what to do with years, the default behavior applies. When you want Power BI to ignore the slicer, you will have to tell the function **CALCULATE** what to do with the column **Year**.

Let us take this knowledge one step further:

1. Add the column **ProductName** to the table visual.

    Can you understand why the measure **% of parent** is now showing 100% for each row in the table visual?

    Adding slicers or filters to a report changes the context in which measures are calculated. Adding a column to an existing visual changes the way the visual are evaluated. For each row in the visual, the context is defined by the category displayed in the row and the product name displayed in the same row. The expression **CALCULATE ([NetSalesAmount], ALL (Products[Category]))** over rules the context on category. However, like with the year slicer, it says nothing about the column **ProductName**. Power BI will use **ProductName** as context and filter on it. The **CALCULATE** now calculates the **NetSalesAmount** for a product, just as **NetSalesAmount** itself. Hence, the 100%. However, we can change the context for **ProductName** just like we did for **Category**.

2. Change the formula for **% of parent** into:

```
% of parent =
DIVIDE (
    [NetSalesAmount],
    CALCULATE (
        [NetSalesAmount],
        ALL ( Products[Category] ),
        ALL ( Products[ProductName] )
    ),
```

```
        BLANK ()
)
```

The function **CALCULATE** can take as many arguments as needed. We just added **ALL (Products[ProductName])** to it to overrule any filter context on the column **ProductName**.

Let us change the table visual into a matrix to better see what is going on with our measure.

3. Change the table visual into a matrix. Make sure you have the **Categories** hierarchy on the **Rows** of the matrix and the **NetSalesAmount** and **% of parent** as **Values**.

With only categories showing with plus icons in front of them, everything looks ok but what if you open a category?

The definition of **% of parent** when using a hierarchy is to divide a value to the total one level up in the hierarchy. All products in a category add up to 100%. The category is the parent, and all products within a category make up 100% of the total net sales of that category. So, the values in bold face are correct, the non-bold face values are not. The **IF** function, together with the **ISINSCOPE** function, can help:

1. Change the formula for **% of parent** into:

```
% of parent =
IF (
    ISINSCOPE ( Products[ProductName] ),
    DIVIDE (
        [NetSalesAmount],
        CALCULATE ( [NetSalesAmount], ALL ( Products[ProductName] ) ),
        BLANK ()
    ),
    DIVIDE (
        [NetSalesAmount],
        CALCULATE (
            [NetSalesAmount],
            ALL ( Products[Category] ),
            ALL ( Products[ProductName] )
        ),
        BLANK ()
    )
)
```

The result has now become like *Figure 8.7:*

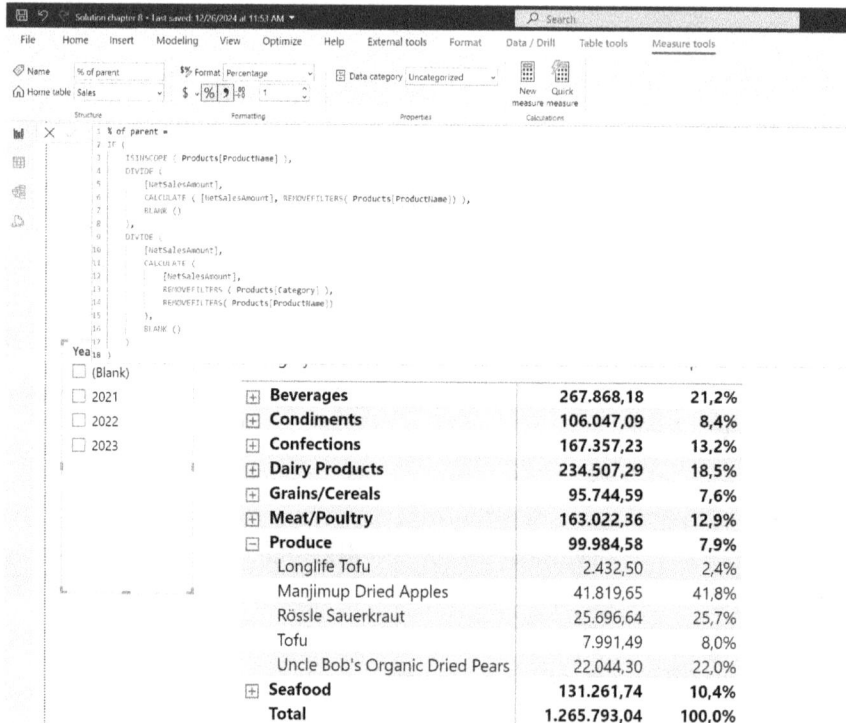

Figure 8.7: % of parent

DAX is all about context. It is about creating your own context, but also about figuring out the filter context Power BI is using. When you have a category expanded in the matrix visual, you can see a row for each product. That means that there is a product in the context, or, in other words, a product is in scope. When calculating the values for our measure for these rows, the function **ISINSCOPE (Products[ProductName])** returns **TRUE**. In this case, we calculate the **NetSalesAmount** over all products (**CALCULATE ([NetSalesAmount], ALL (Products[ProductName]))**). Since nothing is said about the category and since the row is about a category as well (because we have the drill down enabled), **Category** is still part of the Power BI filter. This means that **CALCULATE([NetSalesAmount], ALL (Products[ProductName]))** calculates a category total, not the overall net sales total.

The function **IF** is like you would expect. It checks the **ISINSCOPE (Products[ProductName])** and performs either of the calculations.

When writing multi-line expressions like we just did, the formula bar in Power BI Desktop is not nice to work with. You can download DAX Studio for free. DAX Studio is an application that makes it easier to write DAX queries and expressions. It is a simple code editor. It works a lot better when writing complex DAX than the Power BI Desktop formula bar.

Once you get to know more DAX functions, you may see that often there are alternatives to get the same result. In the preceding example, we could have used the **REMOVEFILTERS** function instead of the **ALL** function. **REMOVEFILTERS** will be better for performance.

Change the DAX for **% of parent** to use **REMOVEFILTERS** instead of **ALL**.

The chapter started by saying that DAX can enrich our semantic model. Showing the percentage a product or category contributes to a larger whole, makes the matrix more informative. We enriched the model, enabling us to compare products and categories to each other more easily.

DAX is about context, and context is about how data is filtered before DAX calculates aggregations. You figure out what the context is by knowing your report in simple scenarios or by using DAX info functions inside your expressions that provide the needed information dynamically, like the function **ISINSCOPE**. Let us look at another (useful) scenario that will make us understand DAX even better, and shows that it does not have to be complex in many cases, time intelligence functions.

Time intelligence functions

In most analyses, people do involve time in some way. Power BI has a lot to offer to help us to perform time-based analysis. The functions that provide this functionality are called **time intelligence functions**.

For now, we want a year to date calculation. We will do it the hard way first to get a better understanding of DAX. Then we will see there are simpler alternatives:

1. Create a new report page and call it **Time Intelligence**.

2. Select the column **MonthYear** from the **Date** table in the **Data** pane to create a new table visual.

3. Add the measure **NetSalesAmount** to the table visual.

   Since measures do not really exist in a table (they only exist on your report), it does not really matter where they are created. It can be intuitive to create a special table for measures. With **% of parent** it made sense to just add it to the fact table **Sales**. Time intelligence calculations are often places separately.

4. Click on the **Get data** button in the **Home** ribbon and create a new Blank query.

5. Rename the new query **_Time Intelligence** and click on **Close & Apply** in the **Home** ribbon of Power Query Editor.

   The underscore in the name is just a trick to make the new table appear at the top of the list in the **Data** pane. This makes it easier to find and use.

6. Create a new measure inside the new table **_Time Intelligence** using the following

DAX:

```
YTD Sales =
CALCULATE (
    [NetSalesAmount],
    FILTER (
        ALL ( 'Date' ),
        'Date'[Year] = MAX ( 'Date'[Year] )
            && 'Date'[MonthYear] = MAX ( 'Date'[MonthYear] )
    )
)
```

7. Add the measure to the table.

Refer to *Figure 8.8* for the result (note that more time intelligence measures have been added already; you will also add them in the upcoming sections):

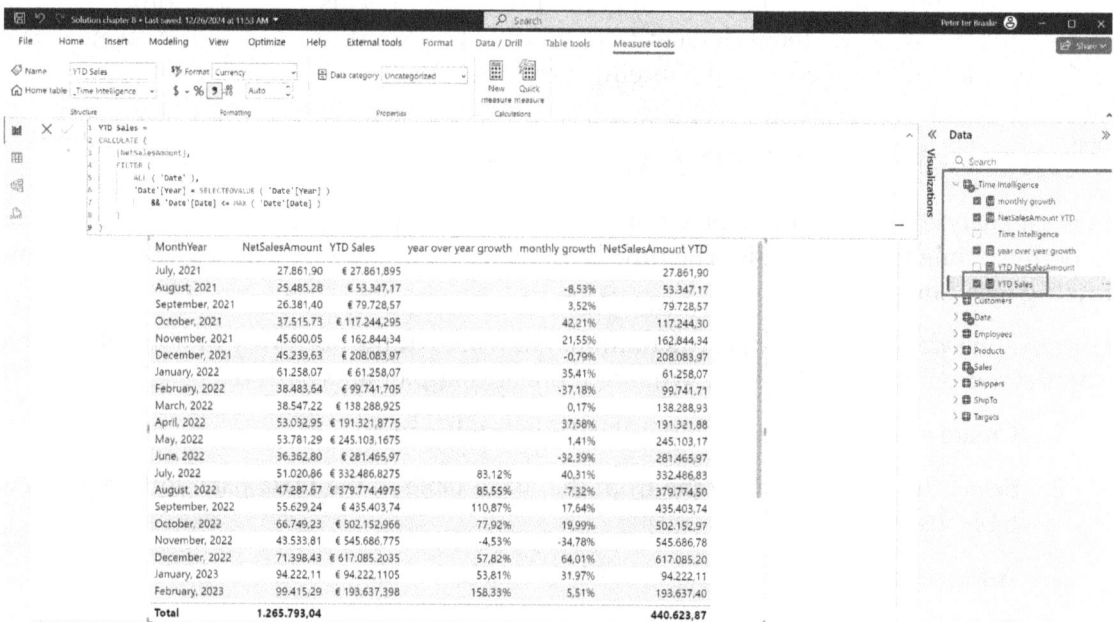

Figure 8.8: Time intelligence

The measure we just created gives the exact same values as the simple measure **NetSalesAmount**. Let us try to understand this by reading from the inside out. It starts, like our previous example, with the function **ALL**. Note that we provided the entire table **Date** as parameters to **ALL** and not just a column like before. We then filter the entire **Date** table using the **FILTER** function. The filter we use consists of two parts combined with a logical and, the **&&** operator.

The first part of the condition is `'Date'[Year] = MAX ( 'Date'[Year] )`. This means that from the entire **Date** table, we only want rows where the column `'Date'[Year]` is equal to `MAX ( 'Date'[Year] )`. The function **MAX** is a bit strange here. However, remember: DAX filters first and then calculates aggregations like **MAX**. It gets the maximum value for the year out of the existing context. Each row in our table visual is about a single month within a single year. **MAX** is just a trick to get the value of that year.

The second part of the condition is **'Date'[MonthYear] = MAX ('Date'[MonthYear])**. This means we filter the **Date** table further to include only the month coming from the context. So, with **ALL**, we tell Power BI to ignore the context. Then we use **FILTER** to re-create the context we just ignored! Without the automatic filter context of DAX, the simple measure **NetSalesAmount** would have looked like the formula we used for **YTD Sales**.

8. Change the formula for **YTD Sales** into:
```
YTD Sales =
CALCULATE (
    [NetSalesAmount],
    FILTER (
        ALL ( 'Date' ),
        'Date'[Year] = MAX ( 'Date'[Year] )
            && 'Date'[Date] <= MAX ( 'Date'[Date] )
    )
)
```

Note that this time we used the column **'Date'[Date]** instead of **'Date'[MonthYear]** to get the maximum date from the month in the context. Also note the **<=** operator. This operator ensures we get all dates smaller than or equal to the maximum date in the month that is on the row the calculation is performed in.

The formula as we have used here is a generic pattern that can be used to solve a lot of different problems. Remove the filter context from Power BI using the **ALL** function. Then use the **FILTER** function to specify yourself with rows you want to perform the aggregation over.

You may by now wonder why a simple, and often-used, calculation like a year to day is so complex in DAX. It is not. Year to date calculations can be done a lot simpler. However, the example has two goals. One goal is to understand DAX better. The example explains more about automatic context and changing the context. The second goal of the used example is to provide a generic pattern that can be used in a lot of scenarios, also when there is no easier DAX function that comes to the rescue.

Perform the following steps to create an easier formula for year to date:

1. Create a new measure in the table **_Time Intelligence** using the below DAX:
```
YTD NetSalesAmount = TOTALYTD([NetSalesAmount], 'Date'[Date])
```

2. Add this measure to the table visual.

It does the same! Microsoft created a lot of easy-to-use functions for often performed calculations. There is **TOTALYTD**, **TOTALQTD**, and **TOTALMTD** function. Year to date, quarter to date, and month to date. Whenever you need to calculate a semester or week to date, there is no easy function available. The generic pattern will help.

Note the use of **'Date'[Date]** as the second parameter. A **Date** table is needed for the **TOTALYTD** function.

Also note the value of € 440.623,866 in the total row of the table visual. Microsoft uses the same function **MAX** in their implementation of **TOTALYTD** as we did in our formula. When calculating the total row, there is no context on the date anymore, meaning the **Date** table is not filtered. **MAX ('Date'[Year])** is then equal to 2023 and **MAX ('Date'[Date])** is then equal to December 31st of 2023. So, the total row displays to total of the last year. Since year to date really does not have any meaning without a date filter, we want the total row to show a blank cell:

1. In the measure **YTD Sales** change **MAX ('Date'[Year])** into **SELECTEDVALUE ('Date'[Year])**.

2. Change the formula for **YTD NetSalesAmount** into the following code:
    ```
    YTD NetSalesAmount =
    IF (
        ISFILTERED ( 'Date' ),
        TOTALYTD ( [NetSalesAmount], 'Date'[Date] ),
        BLANK ()
    )
    ```

Using **SELECTEDVALUE** instead of **MAX** is enough for our own year to date formula. Since there is no selected value for the column year for the total row, a blank value is returned automatically. Since we cannot change Microsoft's definition of **TOTALYTD**, we need another trick. The function **ISFILTERED** tells you whether Power BI filters a column or table using the automatic filter context, and together with **IF** you can react to the outcome.

Let us look at one more time intelligence function: **SAMEPERIODLASTYEAR**.

Calculating growth

A lot of companies report on growth, which means that we need to be able to calculate growth. Since growth is mostly over years, Microsoft created the DAX function **SAMEPERIODLASTYEAR** to help calculate growth. Let us do that in a couple of steps:

1. Create a new measure in the table **_Time Intelligence** using the following DAX:
    ```
    NetSalesAmount Previous year = CALCULATE([NetSalesAmount],
    SAMEPERIODLASTYEAR ( 'Date'[Date]) )
    ```

2. Add this measure to the table visual and check what it does.

3. Change the formula into:
    ```
    year over year growth =
    DIVIDE (
    ```

```
[NetSalesAmount]
    - CALCULATE ( [NetSalesAmount], SAMEPERIODLASTYEAR (
'Date'[Date] ) ),
    CALCULATE ( [NetSalesAmount], SAMEPERIODLASTYEAR ( 'Date'[Date] ) ),
    BLANK ()
)
```

4. Also, add a **monthly growth** measure using below DAX:

```
monthly growth =
DIVIDE (
    [NetSalesAmount]
        - CALCULATE ( [NetSalesAmount], DATEADD ( 'Date'[Date]  , -1 ,
MONTH) ) ,
    CALCULATE ( [NetSalesAmount], DATEADD ( 'Date'[Date]  , -1 , MONTH)
),
    BLANK ()
)
```

5. Use an **IF** function to create blanks in the total row.

Using specialized functions, like **SAMEPERIODLASTYEAR**, makes a lot of DAX pretty straightforward. It can be even simpler by using quick measures.

Quick measures

Quick measures is a wizard to create measures for you. Let us try one out through the following steps:

1. Right-click on the table **_Time Intelligence** in the **Data** pane and select **New quick measure**:

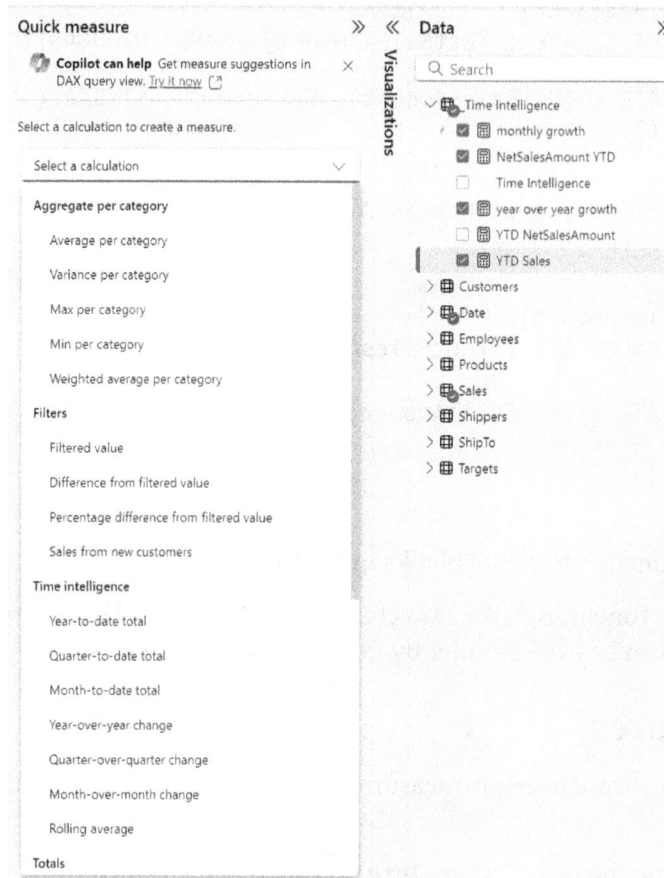

Figure 8.9: Quick measures

2. Select **Year-to-date total** in the **Quick measure** pane.

3. Drag the column **Date** from the table **Date** in the **Data** pane onto the **Date** field well reading **+Add data**.

4. Drag the measure **NetSalesAmount** from the table **Sales** in the **Data** pane onto the **Base value** field well reading **+Add data**.

5. Click on **Add** in the bottom of the **Quick measures** pane.

6. Add the measure **YTD NetSalesAmount** to the table visual on the report to test the result. Note that you can see the DAX code generated by the quick measure in the formula bar.

Conclusion

DAX is simple, but not easy. From here, it is getting to know more and more DAX functions. For a lot of common scenarios, Microsoft created simple DAX functions to use. However, sooner or later, those simple functions are not good enough anymore. That is when you start playing with context. Know that you can do basically any calculation. Just be aware of context and adjust the filter context with your filters where needed to create the proper query context.

In a lot of simple cases, Power BI's implicit measures work just fine. However, in most scenarios, it is considered a best practice to always use explicit measures.

We will go into DAX in a little more detail in the next chapter.

Multiple choice questions

1. **What is a parent-child hierarchy?**
    a. A hierarchy where a table contains a foreign key to itself
    b. A hierarchy with a fixed number of levels
    c. A hierarchy with a dynamic number of levels
    d. A hierarchy with one to many relationships between the parent and the children

2. **When using time intelligence functions you need...**
    a. To use the CALCULATE function
    b. A dummy table to place the measure in
    c. A date hierarchy
    d. A date table

3. **What are the differences between calculated measures and calculated columns?**
    a. Calculated columns are calculated during data refresh and calculated measures when used in a visual.
    b. Calculated columns are calculated when used in a visual and calculated measures during data refresh.
    c. Calculated columns are static in nature and measure are dynamic in nature.
    d. Calculated measures may slow down report rendering, calculated columns do not.

Answers

1	a, c, d
2	d
3	a, c, d

Join our Discord space

Join our Discord workspace for latest updates, offers, tech happenings around the world, new releases, and sessions with the authors:

https://discord.bpbonline.com

CHAPTER 9
Advanced DAX Concepts

Introduction

The previous chapter introduced the language, DAX, that is behind the Power BI semantic model. We use it to enrich our semantic model. In this chapter, we will introduce a couple of slightly more advanced DAX concepts. This book, as it focuses on the exam and on Power BI in general, is not a complete guide to DAX. We refer to *The Definitive Guide to DAX* from *Marco Russo* and *Alberto Ferrari* for that.

You will require Power BI Desktop to be installed on your workstation to understand the examples given in this chapter. You can continue in the Power BI Desktop file you created in the previous chapter. If you did not, you can use the file **Solution chapter 8.pbix** from the downloads of this book.

Structure

This chapter covers the following topics:

- Variables
- Calculation groups
- Calculate and context switch
- DAX queries and the valuate function

Objectives

In this chapter, you learn how to apply the same calculation to multiple facts. That can save a lot of development time. You also go one step further and write DAX queries instead of writing just DAX expressions, and you learn to use the function **CALCULATE** to apply context switches.

Variables

In the previous chapter, all calculated columns and measures existed out of a single DAX expression. This has three disadvantages when the expressions become more complex with more functions nested inside other functions. One disadvantage is that expressions can quickly become very complex to read. With all the explanations, we tried to work our way from the inside out. However, where exactly inside the expression should you start? It would be much clearer if the expression defined some steps that you can follow.

A second disadvantage is that the performance of evaluating the expressions by Power BI may drop because the same (sub) expression must be calculated multiple times. The overall total stays the same when dividing multiple values by the overall total. Recalculating the overall total each time is not efficient.

The last disadvantage is that inside the expression, the context will be different for each value calculated. What if part of the expression relies on this context and another part does not. Do you have to overrule the context for each iteration?

This is a long (and may be abstract) introduction to the use of variables. Let us improve some of the calculations from the previous chapter by using variables, through the following steps:

1. Open your own Power BI solution from the previous chapter or open the files **Solution chapter 8.pbix** from the downloads.

2. Create a new measure in the table **Sales** using the following DAX:

```
% of parent 2 =
-- Calculate totals first
VAR OverAllTotal =
    CALCULATE (
        [NetSalesAmount],
        REMOVEFILTERS ( Products[Category] ),
        REMOVEFILTERS ( Products[ProductName] )
    )

VAR CategoryTotal =
    CALCULATE ( [NetSalesAmount], REMOVEFILTERS ( Products[ProductName]
) )

-- Return Sales divided by appropriate total
RETURN
```

```
IF (
    ISINSCOPE ( Products[ProductName] ),
    DIVIDE ( [NetSalesAmount], CategoryTotal, BLANK () ),
    DIVIDE ( [NetSalesAmount], OverAllTotal, BLANK () )
)
```

3. Add the newly created measure to the table's visual on the **Simple DAX** report page. Verify that this measure is the same as the one created in the previous chapter, only this time created with the use of variables.

There are a couple of things to note in the preceding code.

The first new thing in this code is the use of **- -** (two minus signs). Everything coming after the two minus signs is a comment and, as such, is ignored by Power BI. This allows you to add some descriptive text to the code, making it easier to understand when you (or someone else) look back at the code at some later time. Instead of using the minus signs, you may also use slashes (**//**) to add comments. Adding comments is always a good idea.

The second thing new in the preceding code is the keyword **VAR**. This keyword lets you define a variable. A variable is a little piece of memory that allows you to temporarily store an intermediate result. A variable declaration is always the keyword **VAR** followed by a name that you choose yourself. The variable name is followed by an equal sign (**=**) and a DAX expression.

Choose your variable names carefully. Well-chosen names can clarify a lot about what you are about to calculate and hold in the variable. Some people like to start a variable name with an underscore as a means of making it clear it is a variable name. Our variable would then have looked like **_OverAllTotal**.

> Note: **You can use as many variables as you want. This allows you to break your code into as many steps as you like. This can help to improve the readability of the code.**

The preceding example uses two variables, one to calculate the overall sales and the other to calculate a category total. Note for the last one, that context applies like before. Without specifying it explicitly, DAX calculated the total of the category in scope.

Whenever you use **VAR** to declare and use a variable, you must use the keyword **RETURN** as well. By using **RETURN**, Power BI knows what it should return as the result of the calculated measure or column. In the preceding example, the **IF** function defines the result returned. The **IF** function is now easier to read than it was in the code of *Chapter 8, DAX*.

4. Create a new measure in the table **_Time Intelligence** using the following DAX:

```
year over year growth 2 =
```

```
-- Calculate overall sales of relevant periods first
VAR SalesCurrentPeriod = [NetSalesAmount]
VAR SalesPreviousPeriod =
    CALCULATE ( [NetSalesAmount], SAMEPERIODLASTYEAR ( 'Date'[Date] ) )

-- Divide difference in sales by sales of previous period
-- to calculate growth as a percentage
RETURN
    IF (
        ISFILTERED ( 'Date' ),
        DIVIDE (
            SalesCurrentPeriod - SalesPreviousPeriod,
            SalesPreviousPeriod,
            BLANK ()
        ),
        BLANK ()
    )
```

5. Add the new measure to the matrix visual on the **Time Intelligence** page of the report, and check the results are the same as the measure year over year growth from the previous chapter.

This code does not need any explanation anymore. It improves the measure created in the previous chapter in the same way as the first example.

The simple formula bar at the top of your report becomes very limited when you start writing more complex DAX expressions. There are numerous tools you can use to ease the DAX authoring experience. One free downloadable, often-used tool, is DAX Studio.

When you open **DAX Studio**, a dialog will show that allows you to connect DAX Studio to your Power BI solution. That means that you want to open Power BI first and then DAX Studio. With a connection to Power BI, DAX Studio shows the metadata (tables and columns) of your Power BI semantic model. You can drag-and-drop tables and columns onto the query canvas, allowing for easier DAX creation.

The **% of parent** measure written in DAX Studio looks like *Figure 9.1*:

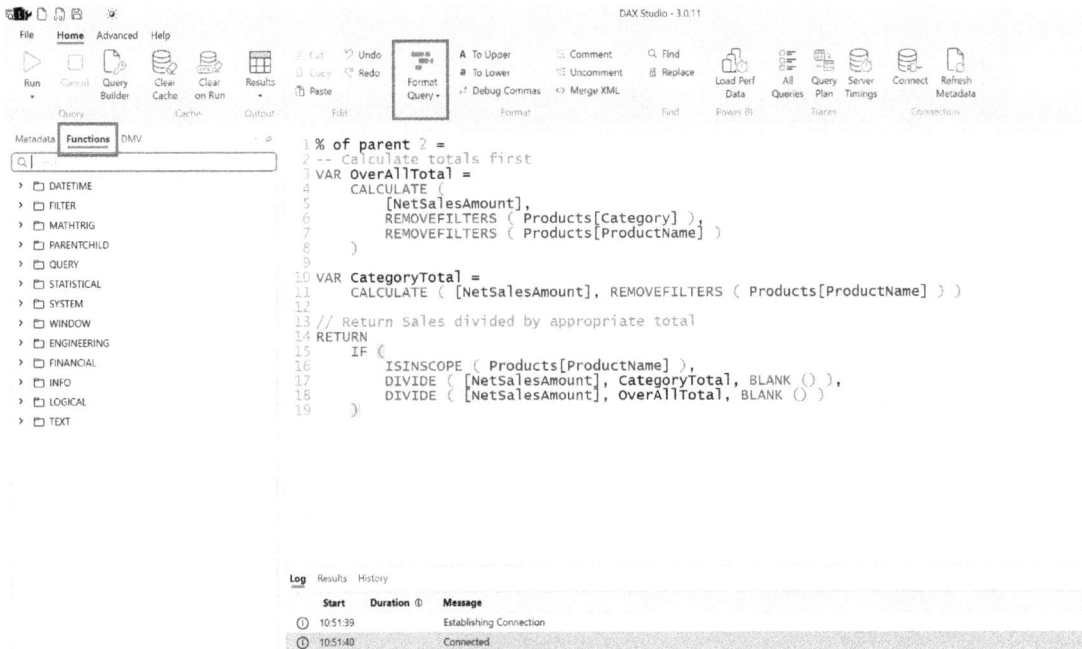

Figure 9.1: DAX Studio

There are a couple of interesting things to note about DAX Studio. A handy tool is the **Format Query** button in the **Home** ribbon. As the name of the button suggests, it formats the DAX expression. It creates a multi-line expression with consistent indentation for improved reading.

In the left-hand side of DAX Studio, you find three tabs. The first, **Metadata**, shows a list of all your tables and columns, allowing for easy drag-and-drop of both tables and columns into your expressions. The second tab, **Functions**, is a list of all DAX functions. This can be helpful in finding functions you need to use.

Creating a date dimension

A date dimension is, in most cases, a must in Power BI. The ideal way to create one is to import a **Date** dimension from a Data Warehouse. In this book, we created one using Power Query in *Chapter 5, Advanced Techniques of Power Query*. Often, people use DAX to create one. A table created using DAX is called a calculated table.

When using DAX to create a Date dimension, you can do so column by column. Using an entire script is easier. The following steps show you how to accomplish this:

1. Make sure you are on the **Report view** page of Power BI Desktop. Click on the button **New table** on the **Modeling** ribbon.

2. Enter the following DAX script (the script can be found in the downloads for this

book):

```
Date (DAX) =
-- GENERATE create a row as defines in line 29 to 39
-- for each row created by the CALENDAR function
GENERATE (
    -- Create a table with a single column [Date]
    -- with one row for each date
    -- starting at the 1st of January 2 years ago
    -- ending at 31st of December of the current year
    CALENDAR (
        DATE ( YEAR ( TODAY () ) - 2, 1, 1 ),
        DATE ( YEAR ( TODAY () ), 12, 31 )
    ),

    -- Use variables to create periods from the [Date]
    VAR CurrentDay = [Date]
    VAR Years =
        YEAR ( CurrentDay )
    VAR MonthNo =
        MONTH ( CurrentDay )
    VAR MonthName =
        FORMAT ( [Date], "MMMM" )
    VAR Quarters =
        QUARTER ( currentDay )

    -- Use the ROW function to create columns for the table
    -- based on the periods defined in the variables
    RETURN
        ROW (
            "Year", Years,
            "MonthNo", MonthNo,
            "Month Name", MonthName,
            "Quarter", Quarters,
            "MonthYear", MonthName & ", " & FORMAT ( CurrentDay, "YYYY"
),
            "MonthKey", Years * 100 + MonthNo,
            "QuarterYear", "Q" & Quarters
        )
)
```

The result should look like *Figure 9.2* DAX **Date** dimension:

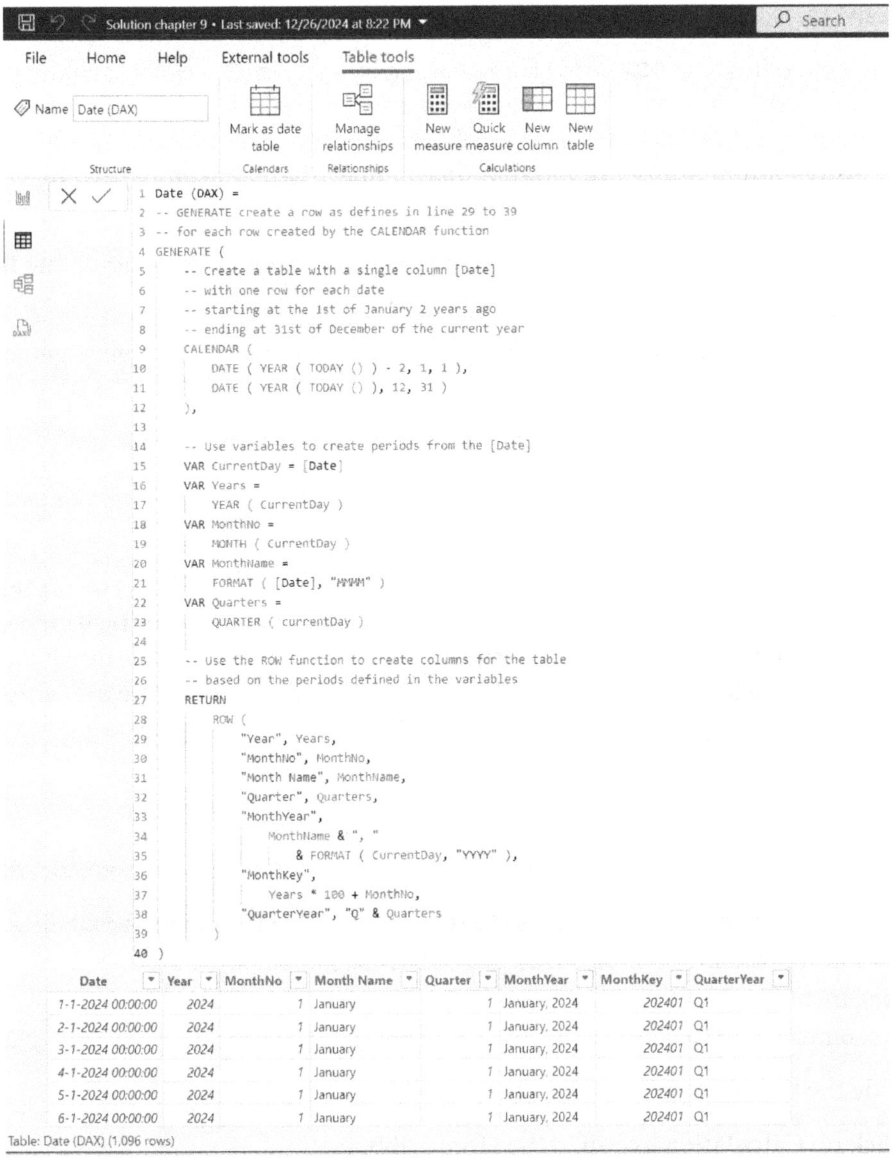

Figure 9.2: DAX Date dimension

Most of the explanation of this code is done in the comments within the code itself. The code results in the same **Date** table that we already created using Power Query, but with one exception. The one created in Power Query starts on January 1st, 2021, and ends on 31st of December 2023. The DAX version always ends at the last day of the of the current year (**YEAR (TODAY ())**) and always has three complete consecutives years in it.

Note: We could make the Power Query Date dimension dynamic as well if we want to.

May be the function **ROW** needs some more explanation. It accepts as many parameters as you need. However, the parameters always come in pairs. The first parameter of the pair defines the name of a column, for instance, **"Year"**. The second is then an expression or simply a variable that defines the value stored in the column, for instance, the variable **Years**.

There is not a lot of difference between using DAX or M to generate the **Date** table. Compression and performance are the same for both options.

3. Delete the **Date (DAX)** table because we already use the Power Query-generated **Date** table.

Now that we have seen and used variables in DAX, it is time to move on.

Calculation groups

In all calculated measures so far created in this book, we used the base fact **NetSales** from the **Sales** table. We completely ignored the other facts, like **GrossSales**, **Margin**, **DiscountAmount**, and so on. It would not be strange to want the same calculations to be done for all facts and not just for **NetSales**. Luckily, we do not have to copy-paste the code to create the same measures for all facts. Calculation groups are made just for that. The following steps show you how to create calculation groups:

1. Go to the Model view page of Power BI Desktop.

2. Rename the column **DiscountAmount** of the table **Sales** to **DiscountAmount_fact**.

3. Create explicit measures for **GrossSales**, **Margin**, and **DiscountAmount** like so:
    ```
    GrossSalesAmount = SUM(Sales[GrossSales])
    MarginInEuros = SUM(Sales[Margin])
    DiscountAmount = SUM(Sales[DiscountAmount_fact])
    ```

4. Hide the base facts (columns) in the table **Sales**.

5. Click on **Calculation group** in the **Home** ribbon.

6. Read the message displayed. That is why you created explicit measures in the previous steps. Click on **Yes**.

Note that the **Model** tab of the **Data** pane on the right-hand side of the screen is now selected. This is where you will find the calculation groups. Also note that in the formula bar between the Model view and the ribbon, you see the following code:
```
Calculation item = SELECTEDMEASURE()
```

Let us worry about the group in the **Data** pane first. A Power BI semantic model can contain multiple calculation groups. Each calculation group has a calculation column and multiple calculation items.

7. Rename the **Calculation groups** to **Time Intelligence** and the **Calculation groups column** to **Time calculation** by double-clicking on them in the **Data** pane and typing the new name.

8. When necessary, open the **Calculation items (1)** in the **Data** pane and rename **Calculation item** to **Current**.

On the **Model** tab, your calculation group should now look as in *Figure 9.3*:

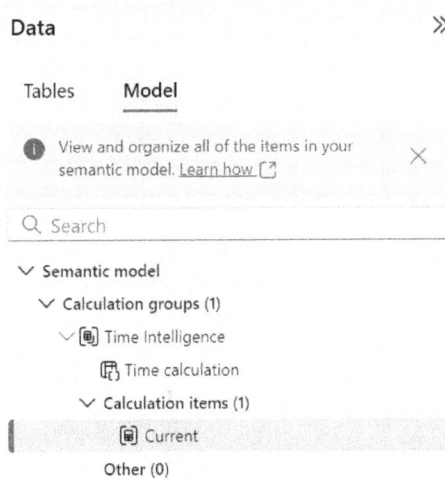

Data   »

    Tables   **Model**

    ⓘ View and organize all of the items in your   ✕
           semantic model. Learn how ⌐

    Q Search

    ∨ Semantic model
       ∨ Calculation groups (1)
          ∨ 🔲 Time Intelligence
              🔲 Time calculation
          ∨ Calculation items (1)
              🔲 Current
          Other (0)

Figure 9.3: Calculation groups

The formula for the first calculation item, **Current**, is now the expression **Current = SELECTEDMEASURE()**. This function is a place holder for the actual measure that we will use later in the report. Remember what we are trying to do: create calculations once and re-use for several facts instead of creating the same calculations multiple times because we have multiple facts to analyze.

9. Click on **Calculation items (1)** on the **Model** tab of the **Data** pane. You should now see the **Properties** pane to the left of the **Data** pane.

10. Click on + **New calculation** item in the **Property** pane. Look at the formula displayed in the formula bar.

11. Change the formula **Calculation item = SELECTEDMEASURE()** into the following DAX expression:

```
YTD =
IF (
    ISFILTERED ( 'Date' ),
```

```
    TOTALYTD ( SELECTEDMEASURE (), 'Date'[Date] ),
    BLANK ()
)
```

You should now have a calculation item called **YTD** in a section, **Calculation items (2)**, on the **Model** tab of the **Data** pane.

Note: The DAX expression we used is almost the same as the one created in the previous chapter for calculating year to date for NetSalesAmount.

We chose another name (just **YTD**) and replaced **[NetSalesAMount]** by **SELECTEDMEASURE()**.

12. Create another new calculation item using the following DAX:

```
YoY growth =

-- Calculate overall sales of relevant periods first
VAR SalesCurrentPeriod = SELECTEDMEASURE()
VAR SalesPreviousPeriod =
    CALCULATE ( SELECTEDMEASURE(), SAMEPERIODLASTYEAR ( 'Date'[Date] ) )

-- Divide difference in sales by sales of previous period
-- to calculate growth as a percentage
RETURN
    IF (
        ISFILTERED ( 'Date' ),
        DIVIDE (
            SalesCurrentPeriod - SalesPreviousPeriod,
            SalesPreviousPeriod,
            BLANK ()
        ),
        BLANK ()
    )
```

We have used the DAX for year over year growth from the previous chapter and changed just two things. We came up with a new name for the calculation and replaced the measure **[NetSalesAMount]** by **SELECTEDMEASURE()**.

You can add as many calculation items as you wish.

With three items in the calculation group, it is time to see how calculation groups work on the report.

13. Create a new report page with the name **Calculation groups**.

14. Place an empty **Matrix** visual on the report.

15. Drag the column **MonthYear** to the rows of the matrix.

16. Drag the column **Time Calculations** from the table **Time Intelligence** (without underscore) to the columns of the matrix visual. Ignore the error in the visual.

17. Drag the measure **NetSalesAmount** to the values of the matrix visual.

    You should now have a matrix visual with three columns. The first shows **NetSalesAmount**. The second and third show the **YoY growth** and the **YTD** of **NetSalesAmount**.

18. Replace **NetSalesAmount** by **GrossSalesAmount**. All three columns work just fine, but now for another measure.

    Although we said the calculation items work fine, the formatting might not be.

19. Select the calculation item **YoY growth** and toggle **Dynamic format string** in the **Properties** pane on.

20. Add a dynamic format string like "**#,##0.00%**".

    Your report should now look like *Figure 9.4*:

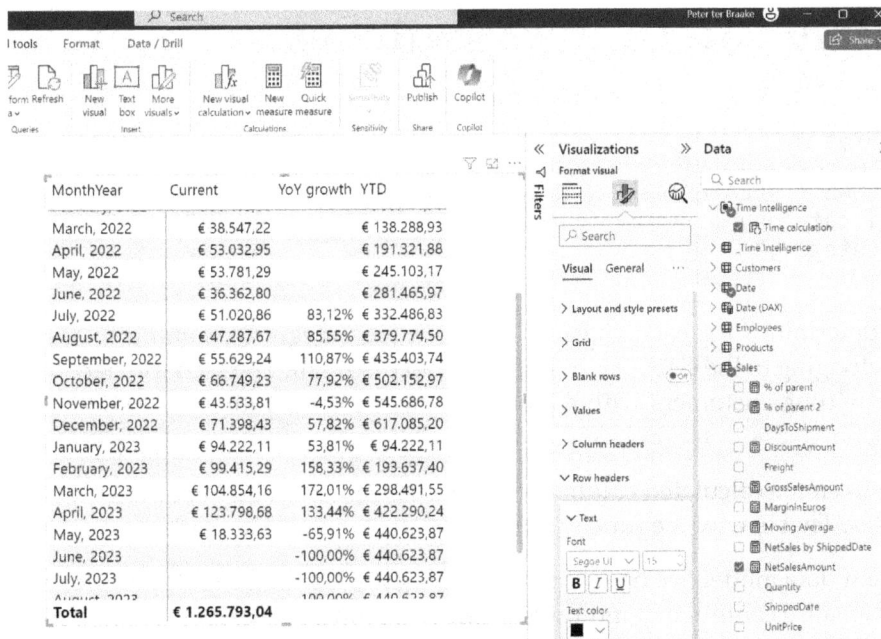

Figure 9.4: Calculation groups result

A disadvantage of calculation groups is that it is difficult (impossible) to use the items individually.

21. Add a table visual to the report using the column **MonthYear** and the measure **GrossSalesAmount**.

22. Drag the **Time Calculation** from the **Time Intelligence** calculation group to the table visual. Note the error.

23. Remove the **Time Calculation** from the table visual.

24. Create a new measure inside the **_Time Intelligence** table using the following DAX code:

```
GrossSalesAmount YOY% =
CALCULATE (
    [GrossSalesAmount],
    'Time Intelligence'[Time Calculation] = "YoY growth"
)
```

25. Add this measure to the table visual.

As already said, you cannot use calculation items individually. You can, however, create *normal* measures based on calculation items.

This concludes the calculation items. Time to move to more serious DAX and context switches.

Calculate and context switches

At the start of *Chapter 8, DAX,* we created a calculated column using the following DAX:

```
# of products =
IF (
    COUNTROWS ( RELATEDTABLE ( Products ) ) < 10,
    "Small category",
    "Big category"
)
```

This code determines for each category if it is a big category, meaning it has ten or more products belonging to the category, or if the category is small. The scenario here was to analyze whether providing customers with a lot of options within a category to choose from, affects customer behavior.

It was easy to create calculated columns because **Categories** and **Products** were separate but related tables. That is why the function **RELATEDTABLE** did all the work.

In our current data model, we have a column **Category** inside the table **Products**. Let us see if we can still create a column that indicates whether a product belongs to a big or small category.

The basis of the query is the same; we need to count the number of rows that have the same value in the column **Category**. Let us start simply by trying **COUNTROWS ('Products')**:

1. Go to the Report view of Power BI Desktop and create a new report page called **ProductCount**.

2. Create a new calculated column in the table **Products** using the preceding DAX expression. Name the column **ProductCount**.

3. Create a table visual with the **Categories** hierarchy in it, plus the column **ProductCount**.

Using **COUNTROWS** inside a calculated column is different than inside a calculated measure. A calculated column uses row context, keeping expressions inside rows. That is strange for an aggregation that combines multiple rows into a single value. Ignoring this context leads to our formula showing 77 for all rows.

Previously, we used **RELATEDTABLE** together with **COUNTROWS**. **RELATEDTABLE** returns a table from the row context of the other (related) table and **COUNTROWS** calculates the overall row count of that returned table.

We must somehow filter the table **Products** before we use **COUNTROWS**. Luckily, we know the function **FILTER**.

4. Change the DAX of the calculated column **ProductCount** into the following DAX:

```
ProductCount =
COUNTROWS (
    FILTER (
        'Products',
        'Products'[Category] = SELECTEDVALUE ( 'Products'[Category] )
    )
)
```

Here, we use the **FILTER** function to filter the table **Products** to only contain rows for which the value in the column **Category** is the same as the **Category** of the context. However, the function **SELECTEDVALUE** suffers from the same problem as the function **COUNTROWS** did. We do not really have a selected value because within the row context of the calculated column, there is always just a single value. Due to this, **SELECTEDVALUE** returns a blank value, resulting in a blank result in the table visual.

5. Change the DAX of the calculated column **ProductCount** into the following DAX:

```
ProductCount =
CALCULATE (
    COUNTROWS (
        FILTER (
            ALL ( 'Products' ),
            'Products'[Category] = SELECTEDVALUE ( 'Products'[Category]
)
        )
    )
)
```

This last attempt finally gives the desired result. The function **CALCULATE** is an iterator. It forces Power BI to go over each row in the visual individually and determine context over the tables each time. A crucial part of the preceding DAX expression is the addition of the function **ALL**. For each iteration (for each row in the table visual), we force Power BI to start with the entire table **Products**. We then force it to look at the context to get the category of the row using **SELECTEDVALUE**. Finally, we can count the rows in the filtered table. The function **CALCULATE** forces Power BI to switch the context from row to row, and that makes our expression work.

6. Check the column in the Table view page.

7. To finish the column, change the DAX into the following:

```
Category type =
IF (
    CALCULATE (
        COUNTROWS (
            FILTER (
                ALL ( Products ),
                Products[Category] = SELECTEDVALUE ( Products[Category]
    )
            )
        )
    ) < 10,
    "Small category",
    "Big category"
)
```

This example shows the use of **CALCULATE** as an iterator. Let us also look at an example for a calculated measure.

Moving average

We already mentioned that comparing values to some reference value adds perspective to the values, making them more informative. Let us, as another example, compare monthly sales with the average sales. However, with a changing world, an average calculated over a long period may not be that informative. Therefore, we want a moving average. We want to compare the sales of each month with the average sales of that month, including the previous two months. The moving average is the average calculated over three consecutive months ending with the month we compare it to.

On analyzing the requirement, you can see that we have a double aggregation. We do not have monthly sales in our data model. The grain we chose way back in *Chapter 2, Dimensional Modeling,* was to get data at the order detail (order line) level. We need to sum all the sales amounts from within the same month to get a monthly total. We then need to calculate an average over the summed amounts.

We start by creating an in-memory table representing sales by month. **SUMMARIZECOLUMNS** can do that. Look at the following code:

```
SUMMARIZECOLUMNS (
    'Date'[MonthKey],
    'Sales',
    "SummedNetSales", SUM ( 'Sales'[NetSales] )
)
```

The function **SUMMARIZECOLUMNS** in this code example will take the table **'Sales'** and reduce it to one row for each value in the column **'Date'[MonthKey]**. It will create a column named **"SummedNetSales"**, while doing so. The value for this column is calculated using the expression **SUM ('Sales'[NetSales])**. The result is a table consisting of two columns, **MonthKey** and **SummedNetSales,** with a single row for each month of data we have in our data model.

With this table, we can start calculating averages. DAX has at least two different functions for each aggregation you can do. There is a **SUM** and a **SUMX** function. There is a **COUNT** and a **COUNTX**, an **AVERAGE** and an **AVERAGEX**, and so on. The function without the **X** takes a simple single column as its sole parameter. The functions with the **X** take two parameters. The first parameter is the table that you want to use the aggregation on. That can be a table directly from the data model or a calculated table like the one we just created using **SUMMARIZECOLUMNS**. The second parameter is the column to aggregate. This can be an expression creating a column or a column referenced by its name.

Knowing what we just learned and applying that on the partial code we already have, we can now extend the code to look like:

```
AVERAGEX (
    SUMMARIZECOLUMNS (
        'Date'[MonthKey],
        'Sales',
        "SummedNetSales", SUM ( 'Sales'[NetSales] )
    ),
    [SummedNetSales]
)
```

Let us go ahead and actually create this calculated measure:

1. Create a new calculated measure using the preceding code.

2. Create a new report page and test the measure in a table visual with the columns **MonthYear** and **NetSalesAmount**.

3. Try to explain what happens.

   Since we are creating a measure using an aggregation, the query context is applied. We are basically taking the average of a single value. We need an iterator to add another context to the calculation for each row in the table visual.

4. Change the DAX code into the following code:

```
Moving Average =
CALCULATE (
    AVERAGEX (
        SUMMARIZECOLUMNS (
            'Date'[MonthKey],
            'Sales',
            "SummedNetSales", SUM ( 'Sales'[NetSales] )
        ),
        [SummedNetSales]
```

```
    ),
        DATESINPERIOD ( 'Date'[Date], LASTDATE ( 'Date'[Date] ), -3, MONTH )
)
```

In the preceding code, the function **LASTDATE ('Date'[Date])** takes the last date (or maximum date) from the current query context. The function **DATESINPERIOD** creates a table. The first argument must be a reference to your date table. The second argument, **LASTDATE ('Date'[Date])** in our case, forms the starting point of the table that will be created. The **-3** and **MONTH** mean that we go three months back in time, starting from the start date.

CALCULATE calculates this table based on the context for each row in the table visual. These dates will then be used to calculate the wanted average.

Creating this last example would have been much easier when you can see the results of some of the in between steps. With a lot of examples in this book, we tried to start simple and then, in steps, reach the desired result. In this example, a lot of steps are involved in creating tables. With **EVALUATE**, you can visualize those as well.

DAX queries and the valuate function

Up until this point in the book, we used the Report view page, the Table view page, and the Model view page. We ignored the DAX query view page. It is time to start using this last page as well, through the following steps:

1. Go to the DAX query view page in Power BI Desktop.

    The semantic model we have created can be seen as a database. A *real* database can be queried to view the results. We can do that using our model as well. There are two use cases for this. One is that you might need to get to know the data inside the model. In most cases, you would create visualizations (and maybe the Table view page) to get to know the data you are working with. However, sometimes querying the database might prove to be better.

    A second use case is to test the partial code you use when creating calculated columns and measures.

    Let us go through the previous example again, but now with the use and help of the DAX query view page.

    The first step was to create a table that aggregates **Sales** to the month level.

2. Enter the following code in the DAX query view page and click on **Run**.
    ```
    EVALUATE
    SUMMARIZECOLUMNS (
        'Date'[MonthKey],
        'Sales',
        "SummedNetSales", SUM ( 'Sales'[NetSales] )
    )
    ```

You should get the result as shown in *Figure 9.5*:

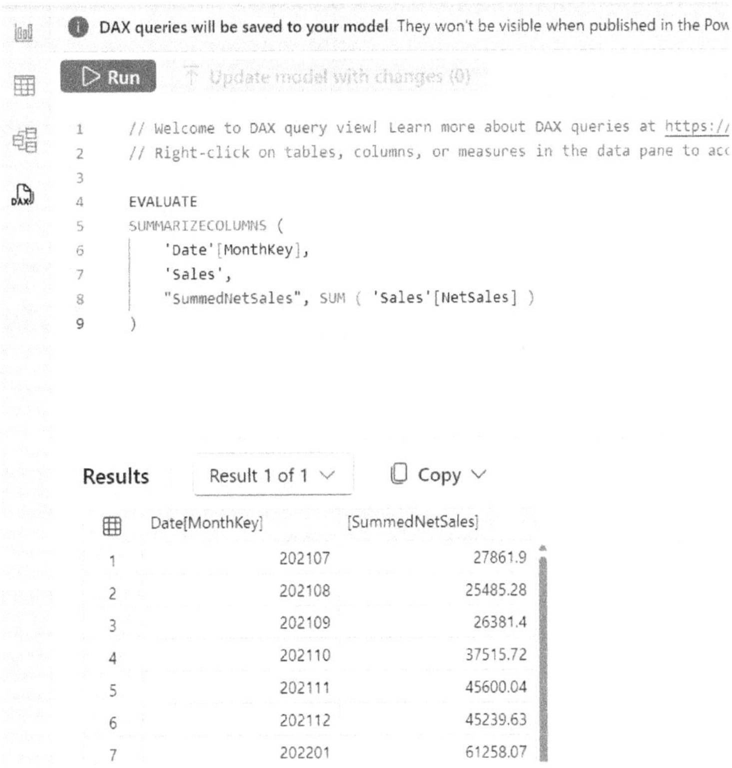

Figure 9.5: *DAX query view*

Seeing this result before continuing with the DAX measure would have been easier. A lot of DAX functions create tables. Most of the time when you use **CALCUATE**, the second parameter is a table. Often, these tables take values from the context, which means they cannot easily be displayed as a query because that context is lacking here. When the lack of context coming from a report is not an issue, you can use the function **EVALUATE** to query the semantic model, retrieving a table from it.

The function **DATESINPERIOD** was also said to return a table.

3. Type **EVALUATE** in the DAX query view page, followed by the **DATESINPERIOD** from the earlier example.

Note: Queries can be saved. Note also that there are tabs at the bottom of the DAX query view page, meaning you can create and save multiple queries. They have no real meaning for the reports you create and will not be published to the cloud when the entire Power BI Desktop is published.

You can use DAX Studio as an alternative to the DAX Query view in Power BI Desktop. DAX Studio is a more advanced tool that provides more data. Especially, performance-related data in DAX Studio can help you optimize DAX expressions or queries. A further discussion of DAX Studio is outside the scope of this book.

Although there is (always) more to say about DAX, this concludes this chapter. Start using DAX, and it will get easier with experience.

Conclusion

In this chapter, you learned about variables. Variables make DAX expressions easier to read because the expressions are divided into easy-to-read, small steps. They can also make DAX expressions run faster. The combination makes it the best practice to use variables once DAX expressions start to become more complex.

Calculation groups were introduced in this chapter. Calculation groups should shorten development time when doing the same calculations for a lot of different base facts. However, their use on the report visual is limited, which is a serious drawback.

An important takeaway from this chapter is to remember to always think in terms of context. Calculated columns and measures behave differently. Although the DAX functions you use are the same, columns and measures are inherently different artifacts. CALCULATE is the function that allows you to manipulate the context for each row dynamically, making it one of the most powerful functions of DAX.

Now, that we know DAX, it is time to think about solutions that use large datasets. How do you make Power BI work smoothly even when you have millions or more of rows? The next chapter teaches you how to handle large datasets.

Multiple choice questions

1. **What is true about SUM and SUMX?**
   a. They both SUM the values in a column
   b. They can both sum an expression like [Quantity] * [Price]
   c. They both accept two parameters
   d. They both take query context into consideration

2. **A calculation group is what?**
   a. Multiple different calculations for the same base fact
   b. A single calculation that can be used on multiple base facts
   c. Multiple different calculations that can be used on multiple base facts
   d. A formatting option in a matrix visual

3. **A variable in DAX is declared using which of the following keyword?**

    a. let

    b. declare

    c. type

    d. VAR

Answers

1	a, d
2	c
3	d

Join our Discord space

Join our Discord workspace for latest updates, offers, tech happenings around the world, new releases, and sessions with the authors:

https://discord.bpbonline.com

CHAPTER 10

Scalable Power BI Solutions

Introduction

Power BI Desktop is designed for easy and quick report development. When you open the Power BI Desktop, you are immediately on the Report view page. This invites you to get some data and start creating visualizations. In theory, you should carefully plan where to get the data from and how to connect to it. The second step is to transform the raw data into proper facts and dimensions. Then you consider other data preparations that need to be done. With all data transformations done, you create a semantic model and finally start building visuals.

Real life is way more iterative. Create a visual and run into an issue. Solve the issue and continue with the visuals. This can be great for productivity, but it can also lead to solutions that are not scalable. Will everything work well with new data and larger datasets? That is precisely what we will talk about in this chapter.

You will require Power BI Desktop to be installed on your workstation to understand the examples given in this chapter. You will also require access to a SQL Server with the AdventureWorksDW2022 database on it.

Structure

This chapter covers the following topics:

- Connectivity mode
- Table aggregations
- Incremental refresh and real-time data
- Fabric
- Best practices

Objectives

Some Power BI reports use small datasets that fit easily into memory and do not lead to performance issues. However, the larger the dataset becomes that you need to work with, the more you need to take the size into account to avoid issues. This chapter teaches readers best practices and settings that allow us to work with large datasets. By the end of this chapter, readers will know the different connectivity modes available in Power BI. You will also be aware of the best practices, properties, and features allowing for the scalability of Power BI solutions. After this chapter, you will be able to create well-functioning Power BI reports on large datasets.

Connectivity mode

There are four ways that you can use in Power BI to connect to and work with data. These four ways are called **connectivity modes** or **storage modes**. Some people say that there are more than four because you can combine the different connectivity modes in a single Power BI solution. The connectivity modes are:

- Import
- DirectQuery
- Live connection
- Direct Lake

It is important to understand these connectivity modes and especially the consequences each mode has. You can even combine these modes. A so-called composite model uses data from different sources, where each source may be configured independently. A hybrid solution allows for the combination of storage models within a single table.

Import

So far in this book, we have imported all the data we used into Power BI. This is called **Import mode**, or more formally, the **Data Connectivity mode** is set to **Import**. Import is possible for all the data sources that Power BI supports. Whether data comes from a file, an **application programming interface (API)**, or a database, you can import data into Power BI. In Power BI Desktop, that means that a copy of the data is stored in the `.pbix` file you create. It also means that everyone you share that `.pbix` file with can see the data. Once published to the Power BI service, a copy of the data is stored in the cloud.

All connectivity modes have advantages and disadvantages. The main advantages of **Import** are:

- **Good performance**: The data is part of the report. It does not need to be fetched from somewhere else when it is needed. This means that a report reacts quickly to users changing a slicer setting, a filter, or a selection inside a visual on the report. Quick responses in the report to user actions are important for user acceptance of reports. Users get irritated when they need to wait for a report to refresh every time they click on something.

- **Power Query and DAX functionality**: With data being an internal part of the Power BI solution, you get full functionality of both Power Query and DAX. All functionality of both languages is available. This also means that with the other connectivity modes, limitations to both Power Query functionality and to the use of DAX functions exist.

- **Offline access**: A local copy of the data is stored with the report, which is why the actual source does not have to be available to use the report. What you see in the report comes from the local copy. It is no problem when the source of the data is unavailable for some reason.

The disadvantages of Import are also a direct result of working from a copy of the data. The disadvantages are:

- **Need for data refresh**: The copy of the data slowly becomes old data. The report always shows old data. It shows the data as it was at the time of the last data refresh, which can be a few seconds ago, a few hours ago, or worse. The data must be refreshed frequently to keep it up-to-date. In data warehousing, it is still common to see the data of yesterday. Data is refreshed in nightly batches, providing users today with the data up to yesterday. That means that what you look at is data that is a day old. Data refresh can be scheduled in the Power BI service up to a maximum of eight times per 24 hours when you have a Pro license. You decide how you want to schedule those eight times over the day. You can refresh every hour during office hours. Report users now have data that is, at most, one hour old. You can refresh up to a maximum of 48 times every 24 hours, depending on your license with fabric capacity licensing. That is, when you configure refresh through the portal. Using the API, you can refresh even more often.

- **Compliancy**: Data security should always by in your mind, playing a role in every decision you make when working with data. With **Import** mode, your data is on the laptop of everyone having the `.pbix` file. This can be mitigated by letting Power BI developers use data especially created for development, by, for instance, anonymizing it. Once in production in the Power BI service, the report connects to the real data. That data does reside somewhere in Microsoft's cloud data center. Depending on data compliance rules you need to adhere to, data being stored in the cloud may pose a problem.

- **Data volume**: There is a limit on how big an imported dataset can be is. The maximum size of the imported dataset depends on the license you have. However, consider a nationwide grocery company that stores data at the individual line-item grain and wants to visualize trends over the past three years. That is a lot of data, and it would never fit in with the allowed maximum size of imported data.

Import is the default **Data Connectivity mode** of Power BI. The report's performance is the main argument for preferring **Import** over alternatives. A lot of reporting scenarios do not need the data to be refreshed in real-time. Data volumes can be an issue. A lot of normal report requirements can be fulfilled within the limits of Power BI import with careful planning. Compliancy is another thing. When it poses a problem with your data, **Import** will be a no go. Generally speaking, **Import** is considered to be the best practice. Only use other options when you have specific arguments for these options or against the use of **Import**.

DirectQuery

We saw connectivity mode **DirectQuery** back in *Chapter 3, The Basics of Power Query*. Look at *Figure 10.1*, which we also saw in *Chapter 3, The Basics of Power Query*:

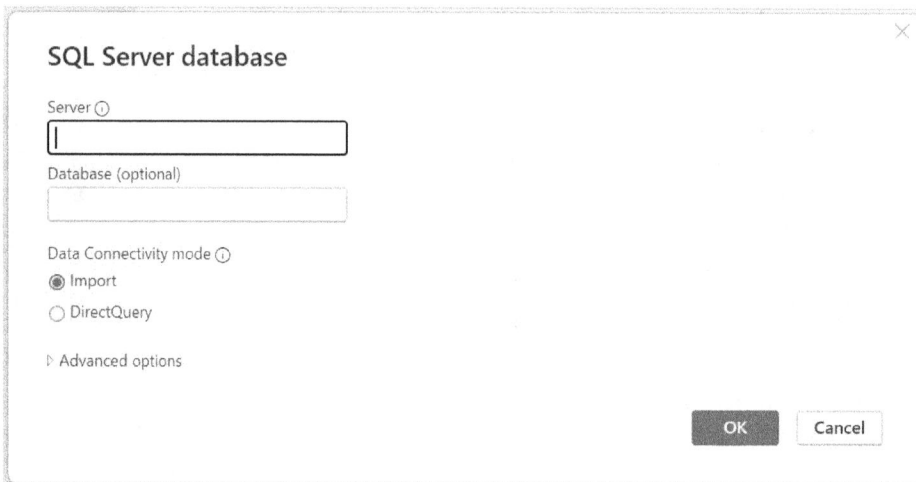

Figure 10.1: Import vs. DirectQuery

With the connectivity mode set to **DirectQuery,** data is not imported. There is no data in the `.pbix` file, and no copy is stored in the Power BI service. The nuance here is that limited aggregated data is in the report. When the report shows a bar chart with sales by month of a single year, the 12 months and 12 sales figures are in the report. The underlying detailed data that is needed to get to this bar chart is not.

DirectQuery, as the name suggests, queries the underlying data source directly and only when necessary. A query is issued to the source whenever data is needed to show or refresh a report. Only the aggregated values as needed for the visuals are retrieved, not the underlying detailed data.

Let us start discussing the disadvantages of the connectivity mode **DirectQuery**:

- **Type of source**: Although the list of sources that support **DirectQuery** today is long, not all data sources that Power BI supports also support **DirectQuery**. Power BI can query a database. It cannot query notepad to get a single row out of a **.csv** file.

- **Impact on the source**: Every time a report page is opened and every time something changes on a report because of user interaction, a query is issued to the underlying source to fetch data. Be aware that this is a single query per visual on the report. With 20 visuals on a report page, 20 single queries will be issued against the underlying database. This can add a considerable extra load on the source system, affecting the performance of the system and potentially the process the system supports. Power BI reports can then negatively impact the performance of primary processes. This should be avoided and often is refused by **database administrators** (**DBAs**) responsible for these systems. When the underlying source is a data warehouse, especially created for this type of workload, it may not be a disadvantage at all. However, the databases should be optimized for this workload by, for instance, having a proper indexing strategy implemented.

- **Report performance**: A performance overhead is introduced because queries are issued to the source every time data is needed. A new query is generated when a user makes, for instance, a selection in a slicer. The query is sent to the source, and Power BI waits for the response. Power BI then processes the response to create the visuals on the report. This is a lot of extra work to be done. Power BI now depends a lot on the performance of the source and on network latency, and as mentioned earlier, report performance is important for user acceptance.

- **Data manipulation limitations**: Between the raw data in a data source and the visuals on a report is Power Query and DAX. Power Query transforms the data and DAX, then calculates the aggregations shown in the visuals. All this has to be put in a query to the source. Query folding is applied, where Power Query lets the source do the work instead of performing transformations by itself. However, not everything we can do in DAX and Power Query can be used in generated queries to the source.

All disadvantages have one thing in common. They are serious drawbacks when it comes to connecting to **line of business** (**LOB**) applications. These sources can get busy without the extra Power BI workload. The systems are most likely not in the same network as Power BI. The systems probably do not store the data in a format we like for Power BI.

However, when you create a data warehouse, all disadvantages disappear or are at least not as serious anymore. When you use a data warehouse, you do not need a lot of transformations because the data is already prepared. The data warehouse can also be tuned to optimize the Power BI workload to minimize the performance overhead. Using connectivity mode in combination with a data warehouse is a good fit.

The advantages of DirectQuery are as follows:

- **Supports large datasets**: Raw data is not imported. Only aggregated values, as shown in reports, are in the report. That means that there is no limit imposed by Power BI on how big the source database is. You may need to worry about the performance of large databases, but size is no longer a technical limitation posed by Power BI.

- **Real-time data access**: Power BI gets the data from the source at the time it needs the data. It gets the data as it is at that point in time, not an old version of the data. The data you see is as up-to-date as the source is. Do note that queries are only issued in response to use the interaction. When a report is on screen and nobody has interacted with the report for an hour, the data is still an hour old. With Power BI streaming data sets, you can have up-to-date data with Power BI dashboards automatically refreshing when new data arrives.

- **Compliancy**: Only aggregated data goes into the Power BI service. The raw data stays behind in your organization's database. That database can be managed by your own DBA according to the rules and regulations you have to adhere to.

Figure 10.2 is a summary of importing data vs. using DirectQuery connectivity mode:

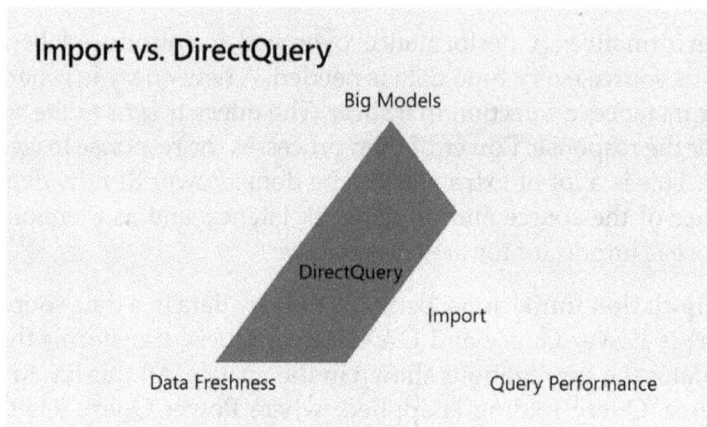

Figure 10.2: Import vs. DirectQuery

We should define what we mean by a big model. For Power BI Desktop, there is a 4 GB limit. However, with a Premium license and an (advanced) setting called **enable large semantic model**, imported data models can become as large as 400 GB. That should be enough for most use cases.

Live connection

This connectivity mode was used for SSAS and is now used when connecting to Power BI semantic models. Once you publish a Power BI Desktop solution to the Power BI service, your **.pbix** file is split into a semantic model and a report. What is one and the same within Power BI Desktop are two separate artifacts in the Power BI service. Whenever you start creating a new report, you can connect to an existing Power BI semantic model. This allows you to create multiple reports based on the same semantic model.

Live connections to Power BI semantic models allow you to create golden semantic models. This is a central semantic model created by a specialized BI team. They apply best practices when developing the semantic model. They implement well-accepted business rules. They make sure the semantic model is well-tested before using. Once ready, they publish the semantic model to the Power BI service.

With a golden semantic model in place, more business-oriented people can create Power BI reports on top of this semantic model. By doing so, they use the connectivity mode known as **live connection**. This means that the report visualizes the data, and the semantic model does all the rest, like calculating DAX expressions.

The main advantage is:

- **Single source of truth**: The main advantage here is that multiple reports use the same definitions as implemented in the semantic model. Overall reporting quality improves with well-tested and well-accepted central logic implemented in the semantic model.

The main disadvantage is:

- The semantic model must be generic to support a variety of reporting requirements. The semantic model is either a fit for a report or not. When it is not a fit, you cannot use it. You can add some local DAX, but that is it. Really generic semantic models are hard to create. They also often lose the important part of being intuitive because too much is added to the model to make it generic.

The semantic model you connect the report to is itself based on data sources. The semantic model uses the same connectivity modes we describe here. That means it benefits or suffers from the same advantages and disadvantages described previously.

Direct Lake

The connectivity mode, Direct Lake, is the newest addition. It was introduced with the introduction of Microsoft Fabric. With big data came the introduction of data lakes. OneLake is the data lake technology that is at the heart of Microsoft Fabric. A data lake can be seen as a huge storage environment where you store a lot of files and likely a lot of big files. The predominant file type for data lakes, including OneLake, is parquet files.

When you start adding parquet files to your OneLake environment using Fabric lakehouses or Fabric warehouses, a default semantic model is created automatically. You can also create your own semantic models inside Fabric. The Fabric semantic models use the connectivity mode Direct Lake. This is a new technology where the semantic model can work directly with parquet files stored on OneLake. It does not use a SQL query layer between the files and the semantic model, but works with the parquet files directly.

From Power BI Desktop, you can connect to Fabric semantic models. You can then edit the models using Power BI Desktop (although that is a preview feature at the time of writing this book).

You can compare Direct Lake with DirectQuery, although it is completely different from a technology perspective. However, the same pros and cons apply.

Composite models

There may be scenarios where your solution would greatly benefit from combining the pros of **Import** with the pros of **DirectQuery**. You can combine both connectivity modes in a single Power BI semantic model. Power BI allows composite models, where some data is imported while other data sources use DirectQuery. You can, for instance, use DirectQuery against a SQL Server database with too much data to import and combine it with target data imported from a **.csv** file.

The advantage is:

- **Scalability**: When a dataset is too large to import, you can connect using DirectQuery. However, with careful consideration, you may be able to import some aggregated data to make visuals on the report respond fast to user interaction. We will see an example of this in the next section.

The disadvantages are:

- **Resource utilization**: In some scenarios, you will see that Power BI uses more resources. This may impact the required licenses you need for Power BI.

- **Maintainability**: Composite models are more complex. This can lead to performance issues. You also need to take extra care with data refresh. You have to handle any possible consistency issues when some data is real-time and other data is refreshed periodically, and compliance becomes more complex to deal with as well.

Carefully choosing the connectivity mode for your Power BI solution is important.

Let us look at a composite model and table aggregations to create a scalable solution while using a large dataset.

Table aggregations

The OData feed we used so far in this book does not support DirectQuery. We will use SQL Server and the AdventureWorksDW example database in this section.

If you want to follow along with the steps in this section and you do not have a SQL Server, you can download SQL Server Express (the free edition) from here: **https://www.microsoft. com/en-us/sql-server/sql-server-downloads**. Once downloaded, you can install SQL Server 2022 by accepting all defaults from the installation wizard.

If you want to follow along, you also need the AdventureWorksDW2022 database. It can be downloaded from **https://learn.microsoft.com/en-us/sql/samples/adventureworks-install-configure?view=sql-server-ver16&tabs=ssms**. This site also has instructions on how to restore the database into your SQL Server.

Suppose a scenario with a fact table that is too large to import in Power BI. Pre-aggregating the fact table (deciding to use a higher grain) is not an option because some specific requirements state that detailed level data is needed. However, you expect that 80% or more of the visuals on the report will show aggregated data. Only every now and then is the detailed data needed. The last requirement is to make the visuals as responsive as possible. This last requirement makes you want to use import mode, but the first sentence stated that your table is too large to do so. Power BI aggregations can help, as shown in the following steps:

1. Open a new Power BI Desktop solution.

2. Click on the **Get data** button on the **Home** ribbon and select **SQL Server**.

3. Enter your **Server** name (`localhost\sqlexpress`, if you have a default SQL Server Express installation on your workstation, but it can be something else).

4. Enter `AdventureWorksDW2022` as **Database**.

5. Select **DirectQuery** as the **Data Connectivity mode**.

6. Click on **OK**.

7. Select the tables `DimDate`, `DimProduct`, `DimProductSubcategory`, `DimReseller` and `FactResellerSales`.

8. Click on **Transform Data** to close the **Navigator** and open Power Query Editor.

   The fact table is (almost) always the biggest table in the model. We want to reduce the overall size of this table by pre-aggregating it. We want to reduce it enough to be able to import the aggregated table. We want to keep enough detail available on the aggregated table for the table to be useful for about 80% (or more) of the visuals used in the report.

   The first step is to make a reference and perform the aggregation on the reference table, as shown in the following steps:

1. Select the table **FactResellerSales** in the **Queries** pane.

2. Click on **Choose Columns** on the **Home** ribbon.

3. Select the columns **ProductKey**, **OrderDateKey**, **ResellerKey**, **OrderQuantity**, **SalesAmount**, and **DimProduct**.

4. Expand the column **DimProduct** and select the column **ProductSubcategoryKey**.

5. Rename the query to **ResellerSales**.

6. Right-click on the query **ResellerSales** in the **Queries** pane in the left-hand side of Power Query Editor and select **Reference**.

7. Rename the new query **ResellerSales (2)** to **AggregatedTable**.

   All these steps were just preparation steps. To make it easier to follow, we dropped most of the columns of the original fact table. The important step is the creation of a reference. A reference shows up as a separate table, but the data is not copied. The changes made to the query **ResellerSales** are also applied to the reference query.

8. Select the table **AggregatedTable** in the **Queries** pane.

9. Select the **Transform** ribbon.

10. Click on the button **Group by** in the **Transform** ribbon.

11. Select the option **Advanced**.

12. Select the column **ProductSubcategoryKey** in the drop-down list.

13. Click on **Add grouping** and select the column **ResellerKey** in the second drop-down list that appears.

14. Repeat *Step 21* to add a grouping on the column **OrderDateKey**.

15. Click on **Add aggregation** and enter **Sales** as the **New column name**. Select **Sum** under **Operation** and select the column **SalesAmount** from the drop-down list under **Column**.

16. Repeat the previous step to create an aggregation named **Quantity** that is the **Sum** of the column **OrderQuantity**.

17. Check that your **Group by** dialog looks like *Figure 10.3* and click on **OK**:

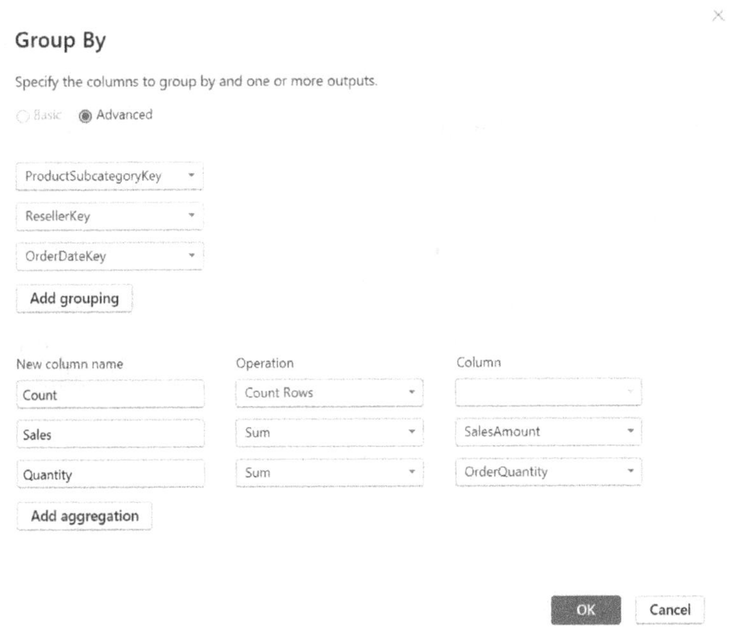

Group By

Specify the columns to group by and one or more outputs.

○ Basic ● Advanced

ProductSubcategoryKey ▾

ResellerKey ▾

OrderDateKey ▾

Add grouping

New column name	Operation	Column
Count	Count Rows ▾	▾
Sales	Sum ▾	SalesAmount ▾
Quantity	Sum ▾	OrderQuantity ▾

Add aggregation

OK   Cancel

Figure 10.3: Group By

The table **FactResellerSales** has more than 60.000 rows. The aggregated table has a little less than 20.000 rows. It only has one row per reseller, per subcategory, and per day. You can do less with the aggregated table in terms of possible data analysis options, but it is a lot smaller. We now have a small, aggregated table and a large table with all the details.

Before we close the Power Query Editor, we have to make sure that the aggregated columns **Sales** and **Quantity** have the same data types as the underlying columns by changing the data type of the original columns.

16. Select the table **FactResellerSales** in the **Queries** pane.

17. Change the data type of the column **SalesAmount** to **Decimal number**.

18. Click on **Close & Apply**.

19. Go to the Model view page of Power BI Editor.

20. Ensure you have the following active relationships (and create/change them if not):

   a. **DimDate.DateKey**: `ResellerSales.OrderDateKey`

   b. **DimReseller.ResellerKey**: `ResellerSales.ResellerKey`

   c. **DimProductSubcategory.ProductSubcategoryKey**:   `ResellerSales.ProductSubcategoryKey`

21. Create the following relationships:

    a. **DimDate.DateKey**: `AggregatedTable.OrderDateKey`

    b. **DimReseller.ResellerKey**: `AggregatedTable.ResellerKey`

    c. **DimProductSubcategory.ProductSubcategoryKey**: `AggregatedTable.ProductSubcategoryKey`

    Notice that all tables have a blue bar at the top. This indicates the table has the **Data Connectivity mode** set to **DirectQuery**. We had to do this for the table `ResellerSales` because (in our scenario) this table is too big to import. After performing the above steps we ended up with an aggregated table that is much smaller. So much so that it can be imported.

22. Select the table `AggregatedTable` on the Model view page.

23. Open the **Advanced section** of the **Property** pane and change the **Storage mode** to **Import**.

    You get a dialog with a lot of text. It basically tells you that the storage mode of all the shared dimension tables has to be set to **Dual**. If, for instance, the `ResellerSales` table with storage mode **DirectQuery** is used in combination with the dimension table `DimDate`, the dimension table should also be in connectivity mode **DirectQuery**. However, when the `AggregatedTable` table with storage mode **Import** is used in combination with the dimension table `DimDate`, the dimension table should also be in connectivity mode **Import**. The connectivity of the table `DimDate` should sometimes be **DirectQuery** and sometimes **Import**. That is exactly what storage mode **Dual** is. It is imported but can be used in **DirectQuery** mode when necessary.

24. Click on **OK**.

    The table `AggregatedTable` does not have a blue bar in the top anymore. The tables `DimReseller`, `DimDate`, and `DimProductSubcategory` have a dashed blue top indication, **Dual** storage mode. The tables `ResellerSales` and `DimProduct` are still configured to use **DirectQuery**.

    We are halfway to what we want to achieve. We now have an aggregated table and a detailed table. If you start creating visuals now, you have to choose when to use which table. However, Power BI can make that choice when we tell it what we did in Power Query when creating the aggregated table.

25. Select the column `Quantity` in the table `AggregatedTable` in the **Data** pane.

26. Change the **Data type** and **Format** of the column `Quantity` to **Whole number** in the **Properties** pane.

27. Right-click on the table `AggregatedTable` in the **Data** pane and select **Manage aggregations**.

28. Fill in the **Manage aggregations** dialog as in *Figure 10.4*:

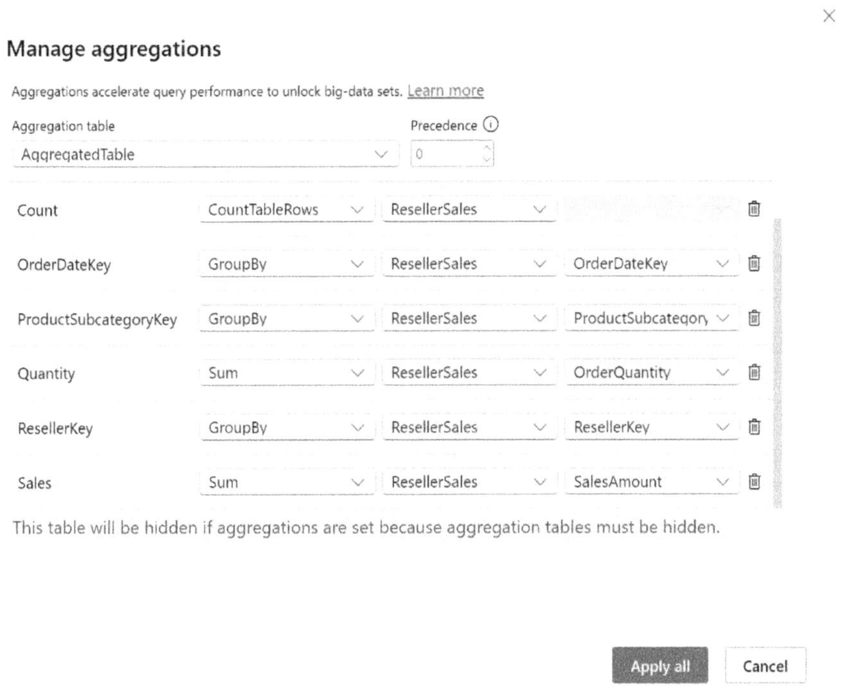

Manage aggregations

Aggregations accelerate query performance to unlock big-data sets. Learn more

Aggregation table			Precedence ⓘ			
AggregatedTable		∨	0			
Count	CountTableRows	∨	ResellerSales	∨		🗑
OrderDateKey	GroupBy	∨	ResellerSales	∨	OrderDateKey ∨	🗑
ProductSubcategoryKey	GroupBy	∨	ResellerSales	∨	ProductSubcategory ∨	🗑
Quantity	Sum	∨	ResellerSales	∨	OrderQuantity ∨	🗑
ResellerKey	GroupBy	∨	ResellerSales	∨	ResellerKey ∨	🗑
Sales	Sum	∨	ResellerSales	∨	SalesAmount ∨	🗑

This table will be hidden if aggregations are set because aggregation tables must be hidden.

Apply all   Cancel

Figure 10.4: Manage aggregations

Note the message displayed at the bottom of the dialog: **This table will be hidden if aggregations are set because aggregation tables must be hidden.** With **Manage aggregations**, you tell Power BI how this table is created from, and therefore how it is related to, the table **ResellerSales**.

29. Click on **Apply all** to close the dialog.

30. Go to the Report view page of Power BI Desktop.

31. Create two table visuals: one with **SalesAmount** by **EnglishProductName** (**DimProduct**) and the other with **Quantity** by **EnglishProductSubcategoryName** (**DimProductSubcategory**).

First, note that the table **AggregatedTable** is indeed hidden. Hence, you cannot use it. You always use the detailed **ResellerSales** table when creating visuals. Further note that the first table visual is too detailed to get its data from the aggregated table. The SQL Server database is queried to get and display this data. The second visual will use the aggregated table!

The real challenge here is to find an aggregation level that can be used for most visuals. This will keep the reports fast and responsive. At the same time, the table has to become small enough to import the data.

Do note that all **Dual** and **Import** tables need data refreshes. Data refresh itself can also be a time and resource-consuming process. Data refresh can be optimized by using incremental refresh.

Incremental refresh and real-time data

Consider a **point of sale** (**POS**) system for a very large chain of stores. You may have billions of rows, which makes data refresh of semantic models resource-intensive and time-consuming. Normally, Power BI data refresh will create a new semantic model, read in all the data, while users still work on the old semantic model. When the refresh is complete, the old and new semantic models are switched, and the old one is deleted. However, in most POS systems, data is immutable. A very large percentage of the time it takes to refresh that data, the same rows are read into Power BI that are already in.

Add to that a requirement for low latency. Report users need new data in Power BI as soon as possible. It is obvious that normal data refresh is not working for you anymore. Incremental refresh can help you out.

When you implement incremental refresh on a table, the data gets partitioned. Have a look at *Figure 10.5* from the Microsoft documentation:

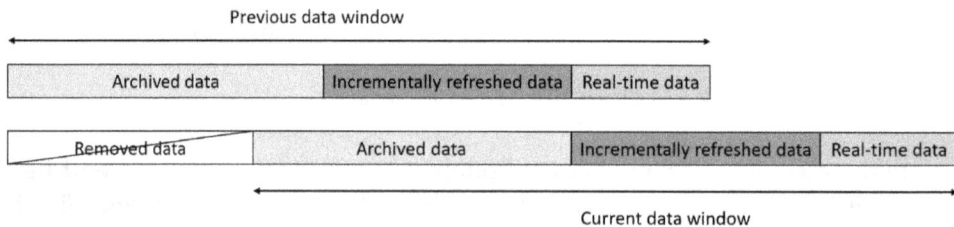

Figure 10.5: Table partitions

The partition called Archived data is immutable data and will not be refreshed during data refresh. This should be the biggest partition in your table. You configure it as a moving window. This means that on each refresh, the oldest data is deleted and a more recent part of the data, which used to be in the partition Incrementally refreshed data, becomes Archived data. The partition Incrementally refreshed data, is the part of the data that is loaded (again) on data refresh. Optionally, you can add a Real-time data partition to the table that uses DirectQuery to get the latest data every time a visual is refreshed. The boundaries between the partitions are based on date columns, and you need to configure these boundaries. Let us see how to do that. We will use the database AdventureWorksDW2022 again for this part:

1. Open the Power BI Desktop solution from the previous section, if necessary.

2. Click on the **Get data** button on the **Home** ribbon and select **SQL Server**.

3. Enter your server's name and enter **AdventureWorksDW2022** as **Database**.

4. Select **Import** as the **Data Connectivity mode** and click on **OK**.

5. Select the table **FactInternetSales** and click **Transform Data** to close the **Navigator**.

You need parameters to dynamically partition the table. Please follow these steps to create parameters:

1. Click on **Manage Parameters** on the **Home** ribbon.

2. Click on **New**.

3. Name the new parameter **RangeStart**, use **Date/Time** as the **Type**, and enter **1-1-2010** as the **Current Value**. (see *Figure 10.6*):

4. Create a second parameter **RangeEnd**, use **Date/Time** as the **Type**, and enter **1-1-2014** as the **Current Value**.

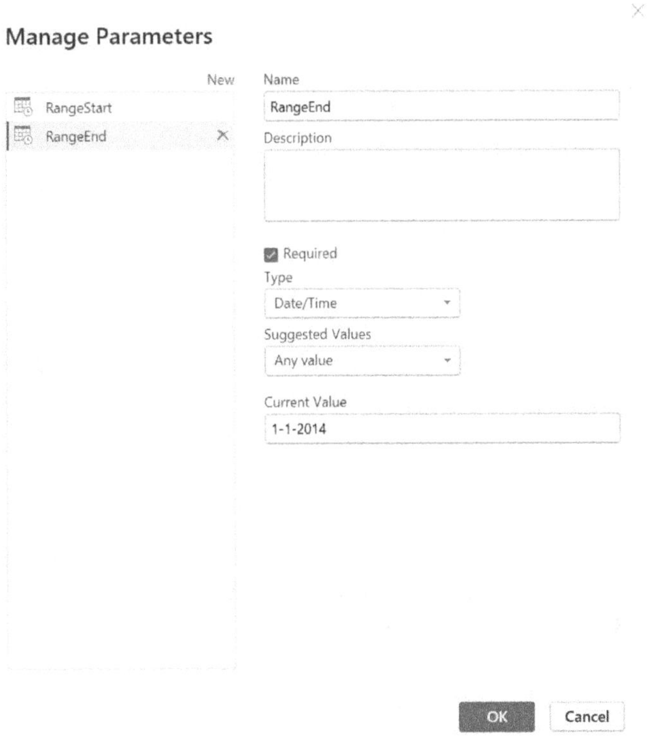

Manage Parameters

	New	Name
RangeStart		RangeEnd
RangeEnd	✕	Description

☑ Required

Type

Date/Time

Suggested Values

Any value

Current Value

1-1-2014

OK   Cancel

Figure 10.6: Range parameters

The **RangeStart** and **RangeEnd** dates define the **Archived data** partition. Data older than **RangeStart** is no longer imported. Data more recent than **RangeEnd** is refreshed upon every data refresh.

These parameters are used by Power Query to filter the data.

5. Select the query **FactInternetSales** and find the column **OrderDate**.

6. Click on the filter button in the column header of the column **OrderDate**. Select **Date/Time Filters**, followed by **Custom Filter ….**.

7. Configure the filter as in *Figure 10.7* to read data after or equal to the **RangeStart** parameter and before the **RangeEnd** parameter.

8. Click on **Close & Apply** to close the Power Query Editor.

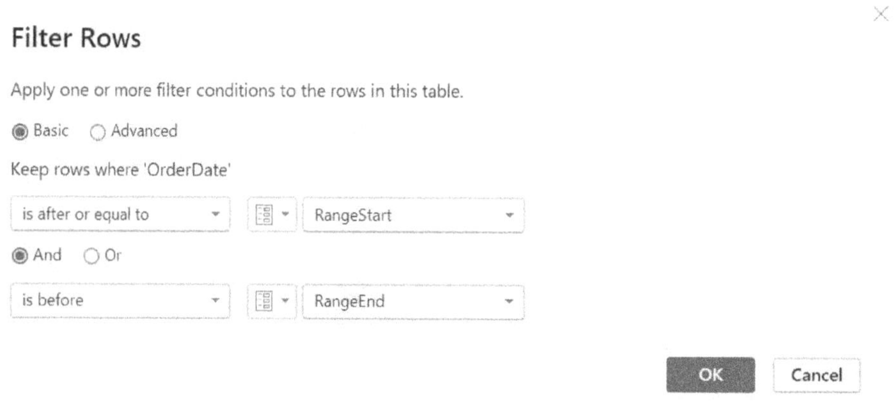

Filter Rows

Apply one or more filter conditions to the rows in this table.

◉ Basic   ○ Advanced

Keep rows where 'OrderDate'

| is after or equal to ▾ | ▤ ▾ | RangeStart ▾ |

◉ And   ○ Or

| is before ▾ | ▤ ▾ | RangeEnd ▾ |

[OK]   [Cancel]

Figure 10.7: Filter Rows

Now that we have setup the query, we must make sure the parameters are set to proper values on each data refresh. We define the refresh policy in Power BI Desktop:

1. Right-click on the table **FactInternetSales** in the **Data** pane on any page in Power BI Desktop and select **Incremental refresh**.

2. Toggle **Incrementally refresh this table** to on.

3. Enter values in the **Incremental refresh and real-time data** dialog in such a way that it reads (see *Figure 10.8*): **Archive data starting 3 Years before refresh date. Incrementally refresh data 3 Days before refresh date.**

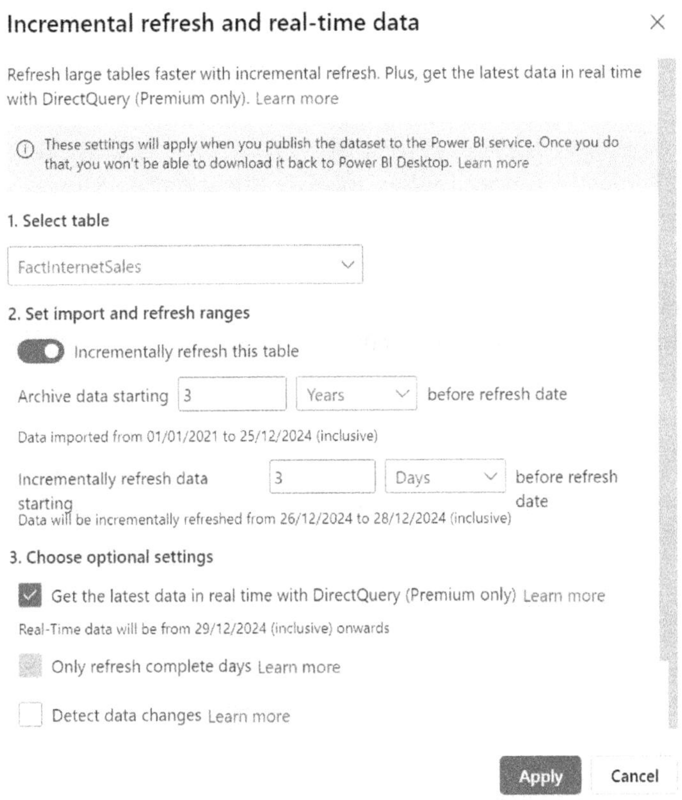

Figure 10.8: Incremental refresh and real-time data

4. Also, select the check mark **Get the latest data in real time with DirectQuery (Premium only)**.

5. Click on **Apply**.

These settings should speak for themselves. You always have three years of data available, counted from the moment of data refresh. Only the last three days are refreshed; the rest just stay in the dataset you already have. Every time a visual is rendered, a query gets data newer than the last refresh date using **DirectQuery**.

Note: You do not reference the parameters directly. The dialog checks for their existence and gives an error when they are not present. They always need to be named RangeStart and RangeEnd.

Incremental refresh is available for many sources of data. However, some sources support a feature called **query folding,** and some do not. Query folding means that the PowerQuery engine tries to make the source database do the work. So instead of reading in all data and then filter the data itself, it will *push* the filter to the source in order to read in only the needed data. This means the data source should be able to perform the filtering, which a database can, but a `.csv` file cannot. Only a source that supports query folding will benefit from incremental refresh.

There are two extra options to choose from. The first option is **Only refresh complete days**. This option is automatically checked when the **Get latest data** option is selected. The option does what it says: it refreshes complete days regardless of the time of day a refresh takes place on.

The option **Detect data changes** is an optimalization on the incremental refresh. Some databases have a column like **LastChangedDate** that keeps track of when a row was changed for the last time. You can specify this column, and only when this date is more recent than the last refresh date, is a row being read.

Note: **The option to get data in real-time requires a premium workspace.**

Fabric

In 2024, Power BI became part of Microsoft Fabric. Basically, Microsoft combined Azure Synapse Analytics with Power BI to get an even tighter integration between the backend (data warehouse and data lake) and the frontend (Power BI). Although Fabric is outside the scope of this book (and exam), we need to mention a couple of things when we talk about scalable solutions. Fabric becomes important when you are required to work with large datasets and complex data preparation is needed.

Let us discuss a few components of Fabric:

- **Dataflow Gen2**: This is Power Query in the cloud. It is Power Query, as you learned in *Chapter 3, The Basics of Power Query*, and *Chapter 5, Advanced Techniques of Power Query*. It is not a part of a Power BI Desktop solution file. It is separate, and is made, and stored in Fabric (in the cloud). This enables the re-use of data transformation logic. It also has an enhanced engine, optimizing Power Query performance.

- **ETL tools**: **Extract, transform, and load** (ETL) are an important part of BI. Microsoft Fabric includes **Spark, Transact-SQL (T-SQL)**, and **Data Factory pipelines** next to **Dataflow Gen2** to do ETL. These options allow for even more functionality and scalability than Dataflow Gen2 does.

- **Lakehouse and warehouse**: Both Fabric lakehouse and Fabric warehouse are built on OneLake, Fabric's limitless data lake implementation. Data sizes can grow (almost) limitless, and the ETL tools mentioned can still work with those volumes to prepare the data and make it available to Power BI using parquet files on OneLake or tables in either the lakehouse or warehouse.

- **Semantic model**: In Fabric, you can create a semantic model outside of Power BI Desktop. Like with the Dataflow Gen2, this allows for better re-use and more central solutions.

Best practices

Back to Power BI and back to building scalable solutions using Power BI Desktop. Adhering to best practices is the best option to create solutions that will keep functioning as expected with growing data sizes and increased workload. A lot of those best practices have been mentioned throughout the book. Some of them are as follows:

- **Load what you need**: When connecting to a source, remove all columns and all rows that you will not use in the report. Smaller datasets are better in all aspects. Data refreshes will be faster, and report rendering will be faster. Data growth might be at a slower rate. All this may enable you to use smaller Fabric licenses. When applying report level filters, consider using Power Query to filter the data instead.

   The exception here might be the scenario when you need to create a generic semantic model that should support a lot of different reports. Then, more data and more columns could improve the value of a semantic model. It does hurt the scalability.

- **Data types**: Always choose proper data types for your columns. Sometimes, all columns are read in as text, and sometimes you get away with text. However, text is inefficient in a lot of scenarios. Dimension attributes are mostly text by nature because they *describe* the data. Dates are also often-used as dimension attributes. Often, we get columns with the data type Date/Time from sources where we only need the date-part in the reports. In such a case, change the data type from Datetime to Date. When you do need both date and time, consider creating two separate columns, one with the date and the other with the time. Oftentimes, this increases the analytical value of the data while decreasing the overall size of your dataset.

   When using numerical data, favor the Fixed decimal number over the Decimal number. Use Decimal number when needing more than four digits of precision. Change the formatting to make the number appear on screen in the way you want. Avoid binary data type where possible.

- **Decrease cardinality of columns where possible**: Columns with low cardinality are stored a lot more efficiently than columns with high cardinality. The cardinality is the number of distinct values in a column.

   Suppose you have a thousand customers, and you store the date of birth of each. Maybe some are born on the same day. So, let us guess that there are roughly 990 different dates in your data set. When calculating the age from the birthdate, that number can be reduced to, let us say, 80 unique ages. When working with age groups like *child, adult,* and *elderly,* it is even reduced to only three different values. Age group is extremely more efficient than date of birth in this example. When you really need to use the date of birth, this may all be true, but it is still useless to you. However, grouping data will often increase the analytical power of the data as well as decreasing its size.

- **Use a limited amount of data points in visuals where possible**: Remember that all measures are dynamic and calculated on each refresh of the visual. Now, envision a visual (like, for instance, a scatterplot) with thousands of data points coming from complex DAX calculated measures. On each refresh, thousands of calculations have to be performed. It will make the report *refresh* slow. It takes a lot of Fabric capacity units. A line chart that shows a sales trend over the past ten years can be made at the day granularity. That is 3650 data points. With a legend that has five categories, you have to multiply that by five. When doing the same trend line on a weekly basis, you can divide the number of data points to be calculated by seven.

- **Favor columns over measures whenever possible**: Measures are dynamic, and that is what makes Power BI as powerful as it is. However, measures are calculated each time a visual is refreshed. In some scenarios, we just want the numbers without the ability to slice and dice. We do not always need dynamic behavior. Columns are static but only calculated during data refresh. That means less often than measures, and not in the time the users wait for the report to refresh. Sometimes, preparing static data during *refresh* caters to all requirements, making the report cheaper and faster. The draw-back is that your model will become bigger because you add a column. Also, be aware that when you create a DAX calculated column instead of a Power Query custom column, the column is not compressed well in the model.

- **Apply all slicers setting**: We learned about the Apply all slicers button in *Chapter 6, Create Interactive Reports.* This may drastically reduce the number of calculations that need to be done. With DirectQuery, it also reduces the number of round trips that have to be made to the database, reducing latency.

- **Use star schema**: Using a star schema should arguably be at the top of this list. With less tables, less joins have to be performed. With a star schema, a dimension filters a fact. Only one relationship is involved. When less relationships are involved, less filters must propagate from one table to the next. Evaluating DAX expressions becomes easier and easier often means quicker and cheaper.

- **Use a single source wherever possible**: The M of Power Query M-code stands for mashup language. It refers to the ability to easily combine different sources in one Power BI solution. The most efficient relationship, however, is what is called a **regular inter-source group relationship**. That is a one to many relationship between tables coming from the same source.

- **Use DAX only when no data model solution is available**: Almost every challenge you face when creating a report can be solved with DAX. Some of these challenges can also be solved in the data model. Using data modeling techniques can help in keeping

DAX simpler (and faster and cheaper). Let us say, for example, that you want to count the number of sales orders with an overall sales amount over $100.000. You can create a measure for this using **CALCULATE** and **FILTER**. You could also create a custom column in Power Query with a 1 in it for all orders with an amount over $100.000 and a 0 in all other cases. You can now simply **SUM** this custom column to get a filtered count.

- **Consider using the Tabular Editor**: It is a community tool to develop Power BI or Analysis Services semantic models. It is only for semantic models, not for reporting development. Tabular Editor offers some extra functionality that originates from Analysis Services. Two options that you should consider is enabling large storage mode and disabling attribute hierarchies for not attribute columns like key columns. There are other useful community tools available as well, like DAX Studio and Measure Killer.

Not all best practices mentioned here are always possible to adhere to. Know your report requirements and build the best possible solution that fits the requirements. Having best practices in mind when thinking of solutions is always a good idea. Doing it right the first time is often a lot easier than making changes later.

Conclusion

Power BI is a great visualization tool for many scenarios. When you have some Excel data that you want to analyze and visualize easily, Power BI is great. You probably do not have to worry too much about most of what is explained in this chapter. Import the data and start building visuals.

Power BI is also meant for big corporations with terabytes (or more) of data. Power BI can work with large datasets. It does, however, take some careful planning. Stick to best practices to avoid issues as much as possible. Think carefully about what you will use Power BI for and what can or should be done outside of Power BI. Power BI is part of the bigger ecosystem of Fabric. Preparing data in Fabric is almost unlimited, and with the use of DirectQuery and Direct Lake, that unlimited amount of data is easily reachable by Power BI. Combining that with aggregate tables and incremental refresh gives you a lot of options to make Power BI great for use with large datasets.

Now that you have created great reports, it is time to consider who to share the reports with. Security should be a priority whenever you work with data. The next chapter teaches you all about security in Power BI.

Multiple choice questions

1. **What connectivity options can you use when using SQL Server as a source for your data?**

   a. Import

   b. DirectQuery

   c. Direct Lake

   d. Dual

   e. Live connection

2. **Which parameters do you need when configuring incremental refresh?**

   a. StartTime

   b. RangeStart

   c. EndTime

   d. RangeEnd

3. **How do you tell Power BI you have a detail and an aggregated table?**

   a. Manage aggregations in Power BI Desktop

   b. Create reference table and use Group by in Power Query

   c. By setting dimensions to Dual storage mode

   d. All of the above

Answers

1	a, b, d
2	b, d
3	a

Join our Discord space

Join our Discord workspace for latest updates, offers, tech happenings around the world, new releases, and sessions with the authors:

https://discord.bpbonline.com

CHAPTER 11
Security

Introduction

Security is an important part of working with data. You may have already encountered it. You need data for a report, but you do not get access to the data. The other way around is important as well. When you create reports, you have to control who may use the report and read the data in your report. From the first idea of a report, security should be part of the design. Who gets to use the report, and what will they see when opening a report?

Security in general and data security specifically are broad topics that deserve a book by themselves. This book covers just the settings we have inside Power BI to control who can work with reports and what data people see.

You will require Power BI Desktop to be installed on your workstation to understand the examples given in this chapter better. You can continue in the Power BI Desktop file you created in the previous chapter. If you did not, you can use the file **Solution chapter 9.pbix** from the GitHub repository of this book.

You also need a Power BI account and the ability to create a workspace within the Power BI tenant you are using. If you cannot create workspaces, you need at least to be able to add reports to the workspace.

Structure

This chapter will cover the following topics:

- Row level security
- Publish a report to a workspace
- Object level security
- Sharing a report
- Manage report permissions
- Configure workspace access
- Sensitivity labels

Objectives

In this chapter, you will learn the difference between **row level security** (**RLS**) and object security. You will learn to implement RLS and how to publish a report to the Power BI service. Once inside the Power BI service, you will learn different ways to share a report with others. You will learn about the different permissions you can set that determine what users can and cannot do with the report and the data inside.

Row level security

RLS defines the data a user sees in a report he or she is using. Think about a multinational where salespeople may only see sales data for the country they work in. You could, of course, create a separate report for each country you do business in. However, that means that you basically create the same report multiple times. Any changes to the report at a later moment in time have to be applied to all copies. Multiple copies of the same report are not an ideal solution. Creating a single report that automatically filters the data depending on the user who is logged in is less work and easier to maintain.

Let us start with a simple static example. In Northwind, we sell different categories of products. Suppose we have employees responsible for a single category. Managers can see all categories, but we want the employees to see only the sales of the category they are responsible for:

1. Open your Power BI solution of *Chapter 9, Advanced DAX Concepts,* or open the file **Solution chapter 9.pbix** from the GitHub repo of this book.

2. Click on **Manage roles** on the **Modeling** ribbon of the Report view page. (It is also on the **Home** ribbon of both the Table view and Model view page.)

3. Click on + **New** in the **Manage security roles** dialog to create a new role.

4. Double click on the new role to change the default name of **Untitled** into **Beverages**.

5. Click on the table **Products** under **Select tables**.

6. Click on + **New** under **Filter data**. Select the column **Category** if needed and type **Beverages** under **Value**. Your dialog should now look like *Figure 11.1*:

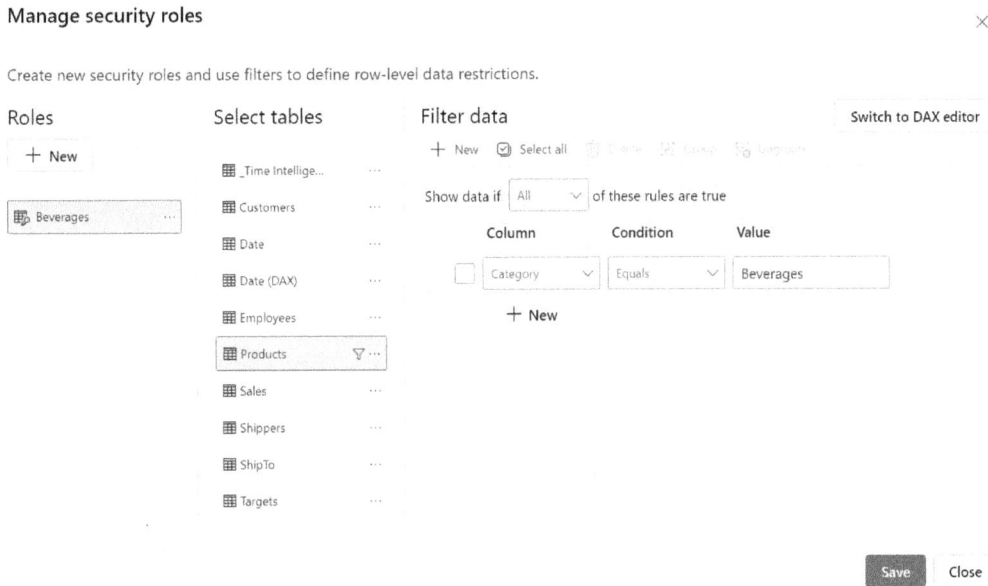

Figure 11.1: Manage security role

7. Repeat *Steps 3* to *6* to create another role named **Produce** that filters the column **Category** on the value **Produce**. You can create roles for all categories if you want.

8. Repeat *Steps 3* and *4* to create a role called **Managers** that does not have a filter.

9. Click on **Save** followed by **Close** to close the **Manage security roles** dialog.

    Setting up RLS is done in two phases. First, you define roles. You do that in Power BI Desktop. Roles are nothing more than extra DAX filters that will be applied to specific people. The second phase of configuring RLS is to add people to the defined roles. You can only do that after a semantic model is published to the service. You do it using the properties of the semantic model in the service, which will be covered later.

    Note that the role **Managers** does not have a filter defined. That is because managers are allowed to see all data of all categories.

    Even though we have to wait until the semantic model is published to finish what we started here, we can test the roles we created in Power BI Desktop.

10. Go to the Report view page if you are not already there.

11. Select the page **Sales report** of the report.

12. Click on **View as** on the **Modeling** ribbon.

13. Select **Beverages** and click on **OK**. The report now only shows data pertaining to **Beverages**.

14. Click on **View as** on the **Modeling** ribbon and select both **Beverages** and **Produce** followed by **OK**. Roles add up to show the data of either role.

15. Click on **View as** on the **Modeling** ribbon and select only **Managers**. You should see all categories.

16. Click on **Stop viewing** in the red bar that is now visible between the report and the ribbon.

The filters that are applied are DAX filters. We used simple, straightforward filters in this first example. The dialog did hide the DAX and allowed for simple editing. The advantage of the filters being DAX filters is that we can create scenarios that are a lot more complex than the above example.

We created an employee hierarchy in *Chapter 9, Advanced DAX Concepts*. Suppose a scenario where each employee can see his or her own sales data, but also that of sales persons in the hierarchy below them. We can implement that with RLS as well.

The first thing is that we need to know in DAX who is logged into Power BI when the report is being used by someone. The function `USERPRINCIPALNAME` can do that. It returns the email address of the currently logged in user. That means we need email addresses. Let us assume here that an email address is always the first name and last name with a dot in between and ending with `@Northwind.com`.

17. Open Power Query Editor (**Transform Data** on **Home** ribbon).

18. Select the query **Employees** in the **Queries** pane.

19. Click on **Custom Column** in the **Add Column** ribbon.

20. Create a column using the following M-expression and name the column `Email`:
`[FirstName] & "." & [LastName] & "@Northwind.com"`

21. Click on **Close & Apply** to close Power Query Editor.

This takes care of email addresses. Let us now create a role that filters the data.

22. Click on **Manage roles** on the **Modeling** ribbon of the **Report view** page.

23. Click on **+ New** in the **Manage security roles** dialog to create a new role.

24. Double click on the new role to change the default name of `Untitled` into `Employee hierarchy`.

25. Click on the table **Employees** under **Select tables**.

26. Click on + **New** under **Filter data**.

27. Click on **Switch to DAX editor** and enter the following DAX expression (overriding what is in by default):

```
PATHCONTAINS (
    Employees[Path],
    MAXX (
        FILTER ( Employees, Employees[Email] = USERPRINCIPALNAME () ),
        Employees[EmployeeID]
    )
)
```

Reading from inside out, as before, we first notice the function **USERPRINCIPALNAME**. As said, this function returns the email address of the currently logged in user. The function **FILTER** filters the entire **Employees** table back to only the row of the currently logged in user. This is why we needed an **Email** column in the **Employees** table. The **MAXX** function takes the filtered **Employees** table as its first argument to return the maximum value of the column **EmployeeID**. Since we have filtered the table down to a single employee, it just returns the **EmployeeID** of the logged user. This basically translates the email address into an **EmployeeID**. The real trick is in the function **PATHCONTAINS**. It checks the column **Path** created in *Chapter 9, Advanced DAX concepts*. It returns **TRUE** if the **EmployeeID** calculated with **MAXX** is within the **Path** column. Otherwise, it will return **FALSE**.

28. Click on **Save** followed by **Close** to close the **Manage security roles** dialog.

29. Click on **View as** on the **Modeling** ribbon and select both **Employee hierarchy** as well as the option **Other user**.

30. Type **Nancy.Davolio@Northwind.com** in the textbox that appears behind **Other user** and click on **OK**. The report shows data for *Nancy Davolio* only.

31. Try **Steven.Buchanan@Northwind.com**. The report shows data for four different users. *Steven* himself and his three subordinates.

32. Try **Andrew.Fuller@Northwind.com**. You should see all the data again because *Andrew* is the CEO of Northwind.

33. Click on **Stop viewing** in the red bar that is now visible between the report and the ribbon.

With RLS setup. It is time to add users to the roles. We need to publish the report first.

Publish a report to a workspace

We want our report in a separate workspace inside Power BI. A workspace can be seen as a top-level folder. You can create sub folders in it, and you place your Power BI artifacts in them. There are different artifacts in Power BI, but most notably your report and semantic models.

Workspaces are important in your overall security strategy. You can provide access to a workspace for users. This access is hierarchical, which means that if someone has read access to a workspace, that person can read all reports in the workspace, including reports in sub folders. When new reports get added to the workspace, these reports can immediately be seen by users with access to the workspace without setting any additional security settings.

Perform the following steps to create a workspace:

1. Open a browser and go to **https://app.powerbi.com/**

   A few things can happen:

   a. **One**: You need to sign in to Power BI using your email and password, and possibly MFA.

   b. **Two**: The login of your workstation is a Microsoft 365 identity. This means that you are always automatically logged in.

   c. **Three**: The last possibility is that your Windows workstation has a couple of accounts for you that are linked to different Microsoft 365 tenants. In this case, you get a dialog that lets you pick the account you want to use.

   A very important thing to note here is the mention of Microsoft 365. Power BI is part of Microsoft 365 with SharePoint, Teams, OneDrive, and other applications. The most important aspect of this is that Power BI does not keep track of users. It uses Microsoft's identity management of the cloud. Identity management is creating, deleting, and keeping track of users and user accounts. We do not create users in Power BI. We use the users created in Microsoft 365. This does mean we have to collaborate with Microsoft 365 admins.

2. Login to Power BI, if necessary.

   What you see on your screen once logged in depends on your situation. The Power BI portal can be customized by organizations. Also, the Power BI portal shows recently used and recommended items.

   Whatever you see on your screen, you should see a bunch of icons in the left-hand side of the screen. Again, which icons you see depend on what you were doing before and what you are doing currently. Due to all the options there are, Microsoft tries to keep it simple by showing what they think you need.

   No matter what, you should see an icon with the text **Workspaces**.

3. Click on the **Workspaces** icon on the left-hand side of the Power BI window.

4. Click on the button + **New workspace** all the way down in the list of workspaces that appears.

5. Enter `Power BI Book` in the **Create a workspace** dialog that appears in the right-hand side of the screen under **Name**.

6. Click on **Apply**. (For now, all the other settings you can configure when creating a workspace, are not important).

   The Power BI service has a lot of functionality. It is easy to get lost in all the options. We will focus on sharing and security options in this chapter. We will look at other options in *Chapter 12, Working with the Power BI Service*.

   Now that we have a workspace, we can get our report in the workspace in two different ways. We can upload the `.pbix` file from the cloud, or we can switch back to Power BI Desktop and publish the report from there.

7. Switch back to Power BI Desktop.

8. Click on **Publish** in the **Home** ribbon of the Report view page.

9. Save your Power BI file if asked, and sign in into Power BI if asked.

10. Select **Power BI Book** in the **Publish to Power BI** dialog and click on **Select**.

11. Switch back to the browser in which you opened Power BI.

    After publishing a single `.pbix` file to the Power BI service, you will have two new items (artifacts) in the workspace you published the report to. You get a semantic model and you get a report. Both have the name of the Power BI Desktop file that you created.

12. Click on the report.

    All report pages should be there, except the ones we made hidden. Everything should work as it did in Power BI Desktop. Buttons can now be clicked (without holding down the *Ctrl* key).

13. Click in the icon **Power BI Book** on the left-hand side of the Power BI window to go back to your workspace. (You can select workspaces first and then select the workspace if you do not see an icon for the workspace **Power BI Book**.)

14. Hover your mouse over the semantic model that is listed on the workspace page.

15. Click on the button with three dots (**...**) that appears when hovering your mouse over the semantic model and select **Security** in the list that appears.

Note that all the roles we created in the previous section are shown here. You can enter the email addresses of the persons belonging to a role here. Working with the email addresses of individual people is not recommended. You always want to work with groups.

Consider for instance the role **Employee hierarchy** that we created. Everyone should be a member of that role. There are two compelling reasons not to enter all email addresses of all employees here. First, that would be a lot of work in larger companies. However, even more importantly, people leave the company, and new people join. You do not want to go back here and delete or add email addresses every time something changes.

We need groups. In Microsoft 365, the admin can create groups. Groups are literally what the word suggests: a group of people. You can create a group for all sales persons, for all managers, for all employees in the *Netherlands*, and so on. There is a default group called **EveryOne**, and it only needs an email address configured for it to be used here. We need to work with the Microsoft 365 admin to create the groups that we need for securing Power BI.

The ideal and best practice is that you add the email address of a group as a member of an RLS security role. Changes in user accounts, people leaving or joining the company, or people switching to different functions in the company, are not your concern anymore. The Microsoft 365 admin adds and removes people from groups as is appropriate. You configure security once.

16. Add some groups (or emails of coworkers) to your roles, if possible, to test them.

We have now created roles and added users and groups to the roles. Let us look at **object level security (OLS)**.

Object level security

To implement OLS, we need to create roles as we did for RLS. Once we have roles and once we have published the semantic model to the Power BI service, we can add users and groups to the roles. These roles show up where the RLS roles also show in the Power BI portal.

The difference between OLS and RLS is that objects, aka tables and columns, are secured. Let us go back to our RLS example, where we needed the email addresses of our employees. Email addresses are **personal identifiable information (PII)**, and extra regulations like the *General Data Protection Regulation (GDPR)* may limit what we are allowed to do with the email addresses. Adding them to the table `dimEmployee` is probably not allowed. So, we may want to create a table, `dimEmployee`, with generic columns in it that cannot be traced back to an individual. We use this table for data analysis purposes.

We then create an extra `Employee` table with more critical columns that we need to implement RLS scenarios. This table should be completely hidden from report users, and even for people creating new reports based on our semantic model. We can implement OLS to make our table hidden.

OLS cannot be implemented using Power BI Desktop. There is a community tool called Tabular Editor. Version 2 is downloadable for free. Version 3 is a licensed version. You can use the following link if you want to know more:

https://learn.microsoft.com/en-us/fabric/security/service-admin-object-level-security?tabs=table

You need to know what OLS is and recognize scenarios where to use it for the *PL-300* exam. Working with Tabular Editor is outside the scope of the exam (and this book).

Note: **As of May 2025, you can enable the Tabular Model Definition Language (TMDL) view in Power BI Desktop. This is, at the time of writing, still in preview. This view allows you to script the data model. Through this view it is possible to implement OLS using TMDL scripts.**

Another thing to be aware of is the Power BI workspace security model. OLS is enforced for users who are in the Viewer role. Users in any other role can still see objects even if they are secured using OLS. The same is true for RLS. You will learn about these roles later in this chapter.

Sharing a report

Sometimes you create a report just for yourself. Everyone with a valid Power BI account has a workspace called **My workspace** for these kinds of reports. It is your personal playground. An important part of Power BI is collaborating with coworkers. Reports and other items, like semantic models, need to be shared with others. One way of doing that is to share an individual report with others.

1. Go to the **Power BI Book** workspace. Use the icon **Power BI Book** in the left-hand side of the Power BI window or select workspaces first. You can also click on the **Home** icon in the left-hand side of the Power BI window, hoping that the report or workspace will show in the list of recently used items.

2. Open the report you published earlier in this chapter.

3. Click on the button, **Share**, that is visible on top of the report.

   You will get the **Send link** dialog as shown in *Figure 11.2*:

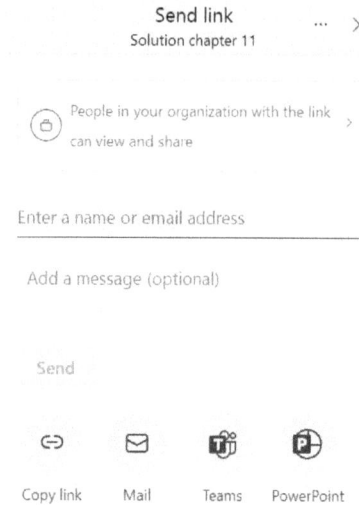

Figure 11.2: Send link

At the top of the dialog, you can see a button with the text **People in your organization with the link can view and share**. If this is ok for you, the bottom part gives a couple of alternatives for how to share the link to the report. The options are:

a. **PowerPoint**: This generates a link that opens PowerPoint with a direct link to the Power BI report. This combines the presentation capabilities of PowerPoint with the data visualization capabilities of Power BI without the need to create screenshots in Power BI to paste them into PowerPoint. You do need an add-in in PowerPoint for this to work.

b. **Teams**: This option sends a message in a team chat in Microsoft Teams with the link to the report in it.

c. **Mail**: This opens your default email application, creates a new mail, and adds the link to the report in the mail. You can finish the mail any way you like.

d. **Copy link**: This just opens a dialog allowing you to create a copy of the link to the report.

   Halfway through the **Send link** dialog is a textbox allowing you to enter an email address. When you enter an address, you can optionally add some text as well. Then, you click on **Send** to let Power BI send an email to the person you invite to use the report.

   Back to the top of the dialog.

4. Click on **People in your organization with the link can view and share**. The dialog shown in *Figure 11.3* opens:

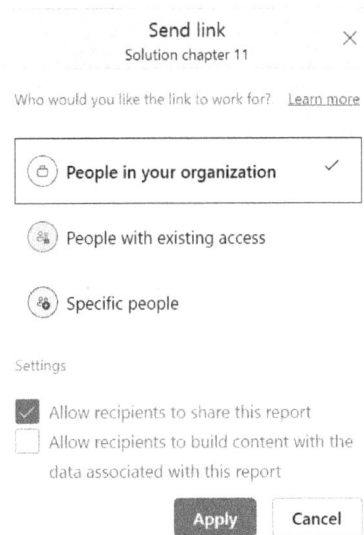

Figure 11.3: Send link

Let us go through the options:

- **People in your organization**: When you keep this default option selected, the link cannot be used by people outside your organization. It can be used by anyone in the organization, also people you do not share it with directly. Anyone with the link can now open the report. However, the link will not work for guest users or external users. In the case of our example report created in this book, anyone logging in with an email other than **@Northwind.com** will not be able to see the report. At the tenant level, an administrator can disable the functionality to share reports to people in your organization.

- **People with existing access**: This option generates a link, but does not give access. The main thing to learn here is that the other options do grant access to the report that you share. This option is mainly to remind people of the report.

- **Specific people**: This option allows you to specify a select group of users who you want to get access to the report. You specify either individual email addresses or Microsoft 365-defined groups. Guest users are allowed if there is a guest account created for the users in your organization's Entra ID.

When sharing a link in any way with someone, the link includes reading access to the report (excluding the **People with existing access** option).

There are two extra permissions that you may or may not want users to have:

  o **Allow recipients to share this report**: With this option, users you share the report with get the **Reshare** permission.

    o **Allow recipients to build content with the data associated with this report**: Users that you share this with can create their own reports based on the semantic model that forms the basis of the report you share. The reports they create do not have to be in the same workspace as the report you share. This might give access to a whole lot of extra people who can read data in that other workspace. This option gives users the **Build** permission.

Sharing a report the way we just discussed is mainly meant for people sharing reports with individual coworkers or a limited number of coworkers. When you want to share reports with many people, using workspace access or creating apps is a better option. You learn about workspace access later in this chapter.

Manage report permissions

Sending a link may not always be necessary. You can also configure access without sending a link. This is called **direct access**. You may also need to check who has access to a report from time to time. For both cases, Power BI has a **Manage permissions** option as shown in the following steps:

1. Click in the header of the **Send link** dialog on the three dots (**...**) and select **Manage permissions**. The three dots (**...**) are only available in the dialog where you define how to share the report.

   The **Manage permissions** pane opens on the right-hand side of the window. In the top half, it shows links that you created to share reports with specific people. It also shows the link used to share with people in your organization. The bottom half of the **Manage permissions** pane shows a list of people with permissions on this report.

2. Click on the three dots (**...**) behind the **Copy** button of a link to the report to manage the permissions given by the link.

   Clicking on **Manage permission** for a link allows you to change the **Reshare** permission and the **Build** permission discussed earlier.

3. Click on **Cancel**.

4. Click on the + icon (grant people access) behind **Direct access** in the second half of the **Manage permissions** pane.

   Clicking on + (grant people access) allows you to enter an email address (from a user or belonging to a group) or a list of email addresses. When you click on **Grant access**, people get **Read** permission on the report. With the top two checkboxes, you can enable or disable **Reshare** and **Build** permission as well. You can also choose for Power BI to send the user notification (email).

5. Click on **Advanced** all the way in the bottom of the **Manage permissions** pane.

The **Advanced** option brings you to the related content page of the report. When you hover over a report in the workspace view, you can select **Manage permissions** to get to this same page.

The **Links and Direct access** tabs show what we just discussed. Under **Pending,** you see people who asked for access. People who somehow got a link to a report but do not have access to that report can click on a link to request access. Those requests end up here.

The tab **Shared views** is interesting. When you make selections on a report and then share a link, you get the option **To include my changes**. When checked, a view of the report including these settings is created. When the link is used, it shows the view or, in other words, the report with the selections applied.

The last tab shows reports and dashboards that have a direct link to this report.

You can, of course, stop sharing a report as well.

6. Go to the **Power BI Book** workspace by clicking the workspace icon on the left-hand side of the screen.

7. Hover your mouse over the name of the report and click on the three dots (...) that appear, followed by **Manage permissions**.

8. On the tab **Links**, click on the three dots (...) behind the link and select **Delete**.

9. On the tab **Direct access**, click on the three dots (...) at the end of the line that shows a user and select **Remove access**.

To recap, when sharing reports, you have three permissions that you can give to people: **Read, Reshare, Build.**

When sharing a semantic model, there is a fourth permission: Write. This allows users to republish the semantic model. See for a full list of semantic model permissions and their descriptions: **https://learn.microsoft.com/en-us/power-bi/connect-data/service-datasets-permissions**

Configure workspace access

We explained a workspace as being like a folder. It is, however, called a workspace for a reason instead of simply being called a folder. It is a confined space within the Power BI tenant of the organization where colleagues collaborate. They work together in this area, hence the name workspace.

You can create workspaces in any way you want and give people access in any way you want. However, you should consider mapping groups of users to groups of reports or, even broader, on groups of data they may work with. Instead of sharing individual items, as discussed before, place all the data items that have similar security requirements in a single workspace. Then provide access to that workspace to the appropriate users.

Work together with the Microsoft 365 admin to map workspaces and groups to each other. This will greatly simplify Power BI's security:

1. Click on the icon **Workspaces** in the left-hand side of the Power BI window.

2. Hover your mouse over the name of the workspace **Power BI Book** and click on the three dots (...) that appear.

3. Select **Workspace access**.

   The **Manage access** pane appears on the right-hand side of the Power BI window. This is where you give access to the workspace to people or groups of people.

4. Click on + **Add people or groups**.

5. Enter the email address of the person or group you want to have access to this workspace.

6. Click on **Viewer** under the textbox where you entered the email address in.

   When giving access to a workspace, you choose from four roles that the person will be a member of. The role that you are a member of determines the permissions you have on all items in the workspace. The four roles are:

   a. **Viewer**:

      i.   A Viewer can use all items in the workspace. He or she can work with all reports. All reports are fully functional. Viewers can also use dashboards and Excel workbooks in the workspace. Viewers cannot work with (and do not see) semantic models.

   b. **Contributor**:

      i.   A Contributor can do anything a viewer can.

      ii. Additionally, a Contributor can publish new items to the workspace.

      iii. A Contributor can also edit existing reports, create new reports in the portal using the semantic model available within the workspace, and delete reports. The same goes for dashboards and Excel workbooks.

   c. **Member**:

      i.   A Member can do anything a Contributor can.

      ii. Additionally, a Member can share items with other users, and a Member can give other users the reshare permission.

      iii. A Member can add other users to the workspace in either the Viewer or Contributor role.

        iv.   Members can publish a workspace app.

    d. **Admin**:

        i.   An Admin can do anything a member can.

        ii.   Additionally, an Admin can add or remove others to or from the workspace in any role.

        iii.   Admins can delete the workspace.

The creator of the workspace is Admin by default.

You can change the role or remove someone from a workspace.

7. If necessary, open the **Manage access** pane again.

8. Click on the role of a user and either select the new role you want the user to be part of or select **Remove**.

Users that only need to read reports do not need access to the workspace. We will create an app for these users. You will learn about Power BI apps in *Chapter 13, Create App*.

Sensitivity labels

Purview is Microsoft's cloud data governance tool. Data governance can be seen as a set of rules and policies to make accurate data available to users in a secure way. The use of data may be limited by external laws like GDPR. Other data can be deemed highly sensitive by an organization itself. Purview allows you to classify data in whatever way you want.

In Purview, you can, for instance, create labels such as Personal, Public, General, Confidential, Highly Confidential, etc. You can then assign these labels to datasets. Apart from just labeling and categorizing the data, extra policies can be configured for these datasets. You can, for instance, automatically encrypt data. You need special permissions to be able to set sensitivity labels on data.

There are two ways data can get a sensitivity label in Power BI Desktop. The first way is to apply the sensitivity label manually. You can see the option to apply labels in *Figure 11.4*. If the option is grayed out, you are either not signed in or you do not have the proper permissions to set sensitivity labels. Refer to the following figure:

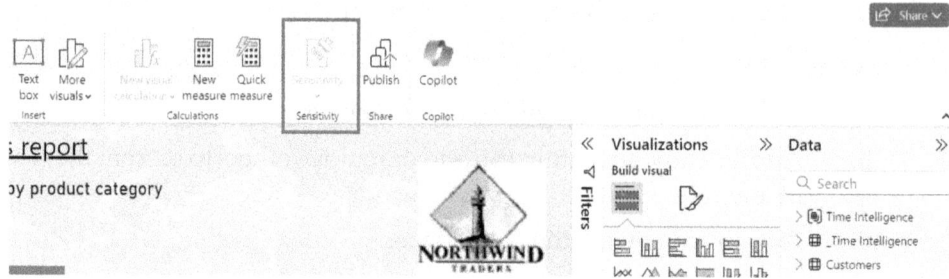

Figure 11.4: Sensitivity in Power BI Desktop

When you use data from Azure Synapse Analytics or Azure SQL Database, and that data is labeled in Purview, that label is automatically inherited. Downstream inheritance means that the label is also inherited by reports made on a semantic model with a sensitivity label defined for it.

Data sensitivity labels applied to your Power BI Desktop file are also applied to the semantic model and report in the Power BI service. When you do not apply the label already in Power BI Desktop, the label can be applied to the semantic model and/or the report in the cloud. You can see whether a sensitivity label is applied in the list of items of a workspace. The label will also show up in the report, both in the service as well as in Power BI Desktop. Since the label itself is just text, it tells the user what kind of data he or she is currently working with.

A great feature of sensitivity labels is the ability to apply encryption to sensitive data. When the label is already applied in Power BI Desktop, the data in the `.pbix` file is also encrypted. This means that when the `.pbix` file itself is shared with someone without sufficient permission, the file cannot be opened. When data is exported, the label is exported as well for Excel files, PDF files, PowerPoint, Analyze in Excel, PivotTable in Excel with a live connection to a Power BI semantic model, and downloaded `.pbix` files. The label is visible, but without sufficient permission, it does not work.

It is important to note that within Power BI, sensitivity labels are nothing more than labels that tell the user something about the sensitivity of the data. All access is controlled by Power BI security as discussed earlier in this chapter.

A default label policy can be created that will automatically apply a label to a Power BI artifact if the creator does not do so. Another possible policy is to make sensitivity labels mandatory.

Refer to the following link to read more about sensitivity labels: **https://learn.microsoft.com/en-us/power-bi/enterprise/service-security-sensitivity-label-overview**

Conclusion

There are three types of security to consider in Power BI. First, we can configure RLS so that report users see only specific rows. Different report users may see different content in the same report because they are assigned different roles.

Using external tools, we can also configure OLS. With OLS, we can hide entire tables and columns for users. Not all tables in a semantic model contain data to be used in our data analysis. Tables used for configuring dynamic RLS and containing PII can be better hidden.

Once published, people need to get access to reports. We learned three ways to give people access to reports. Share a link to a report with users, provide users with direct access to a report, or share the entire workspace a report is in with users. The best option depends on the scenario. When sharing a report, you use permissions that define what a user can do with a report. When giving access to a workspace, you place users in a role that defines what they can and cannot do.

This chapter taught you about the Power BI service from a security perspective. There is much more to learn about the Power BI service. The next chapter teaches you about other, need to know settings, in the service.

Multiple choice questions

1. **You want the easiest way to share reports, including future reports, that contain sales data with all users from the sales department. What should you do?**

    a. Create links for all reports and share the links on the sales SharePoint site.

    b. Create a workspace sales and provide access to it to all sales personnel.

    c. Create a workspace sales and provide access to it to a Microsoft 365 group sales.

    d. Share all reports and give all users the Reshare permission.

2. **You want your coworker to be able to use and change one of your reports. Which permission do you need to give him or her?**

    a. Build

    b. Read

    c. Reshare

    d. Write

3. **Nursing staff in a hospital can see patients' medication in a report. You want to make sure that they only see the patient they treat themselves. What should you do?**

   a. Implement dynamic OLS

   b. Implement dynamic RLS

   c. Implement static OLS

   d. Implement static RLS

Answers

1	c
2	a
3	b

Join our Discord space

Join our Discord workspace for latest updates, offers, tech happenings around the world, new releases, and sessions with the authors:

https://discord.bpbonline.com

CHAPTER 12

Working with the Power BI Service

Introduction

We published a report to the Power BI service in the previous chapter and saw how to share the report with others to collaborate with each other and the reports. Now, we need to configure access to the source data before we can work with the reports.

The Power BI service is a lot more than just a portal where we have all our reports. We will learn how to create dashboards. We will have a closer look at working with reports, and we will discuss some important Power BI settings.

If you want to follow along with the examples presented in this chapter, you need a Power BI account with admin rights.

Structure

This chapter will cover the following topics:

- Configure semantic model connectivity and data refresh
- Creating a dashboard
- Working with reports in the Power BI service

- Configure workspace settings
- Power BI settings

Objectives

Reports get published to the Power BI service after finishing creating them in Power BI Desktop. This chapter teaches how to configure the semantic model after publishing a report. You specifically learn how to keep data up to date once working in the service. The Power BI service is also where Power BI dashboards are created. This chapter shows you how to do that. Lastly, you will learn about tenant settings and how to change them.

Configure semantic model connectivity and data refresh

In *Chapter 10, Scalable Power BI Solutions*, we talked about the different connectivity modes of Power BI. However, now that our report and semantic model are in the Power BI service, we have to think about connectivity again. The main reason is that Power BI will not upload any needed credentials when publishing a report. So, if you connected through a user account and password in Power BI Desktop, the semantic model has lost connectivity after publishing the semantic model. A report using import works immediately because the data that was imported into Power BI Desktop is published to the cloud. However, you cannot refresh the data. The report will not work when DirectQuery is used. It will not be able to connect to the data source.

Let us first consider the different scenarios that exist. We will then enter credentials and refresh the data where needed. Have a look at *Figure 12.1*. It basically depicts three scenarios:

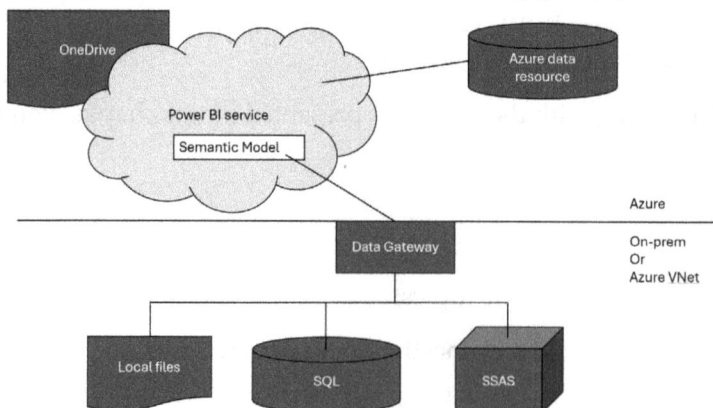

Figure 12.1: Power BI data gateway

Let us look at the scenarios in detail:

- **The data source are files on OneDrive or an online SharePoint list**: In this case, you do not have to refresh the data in the Power BI semantic model yourself. The overlap in *Figure 12.1* of the Power BI cloud and OneDrive is because they are both part of the same Microsoft 365 tenant. Power BI can see the metadata of the files, and whenever the last changed date of the files is more recent than the last refresh date of Power BI, an automatic refresh is triggered. This option relies on users working with the files stored on OneDrive or with lists in SharePoint. Users open, for example, Excel files stored on OneDrive, edit the files, and save them.

  There are two versions of OneDrive: OneDrive for business and OneDrive personal. The automatic refresh is only available for OneDrive for business. Usage of OneDrive personal can be allowed or disallowed by a Power BI tenant setting. Disallowed is the default.

- **Data sources are located on premise or they are in a secured Azure Virtual Network**: In this case, there is no direct connectivity from Power BI to your data sources. The Power BI data gateway needs to be installed somewhere in your local network or in the Azure **Virtual Network** (**VNet**). The data gateway (also called **on-premise data gateway**) can be downloaded from the Power BI portal (download icon in the upper right corner of the Power BI window). When installing the data gateway, you need to add an email address that the gateway uses to connect to Power BI.

  There is a standard data gateway and a personal gateway. The personal gateway is usually installed on the local machine of an individual user and works only for the user who installs it. The standard gateway is normally installed by IT on a server somewhere in the network. It is advised to use a server that is up and running 24/7. It does not have to be installed on a database server or on the server where the data lives. It is meant for use by multiple users and for accessing multiple data sources. A data source has to be registered whenever Power BI has to connect to the data source using a gateway. You link the data source to a specific gateway once. This only has to be done the very first time a new data source is used.

- **Data sources are in the cloud and configured to use shared Microsoft networking**: A security best practice in Azure is to configure your Azure resources to only communicate on your own configured VNet inside Azure. However, sometimes allowing communication on shared Azure networks is fine. In that case, Power BI is on the same network as your data source. You do not need a gateway or anything else.

- **Public data sources**: There are completely public data sources, like websites, that you can connect to without needing any extra infrastructure, like the gateway.

So, suppose we have a new report using an on-premise database that was not used before in Power BI reports. We will have to tell Power BI which gateway to use to connect to that database. The following steps show how to create a new connection:

1. Open Power BI in a browser, if necessary.

2. Click on the gear icon in the top right corner of the Power BI window. The **Settings** pane opens.

3. Click on **Manage connections and gateways ->**

4. Click on **+ New**. The **New connection** pane opens in the right-hand side of the window. See *Figure 12.2*.

5. You have to enter the name of the gateway to use. This name is given to the gateway upon installation. You can install two gateways for high availability. You then have what is called a **cluster**. That is why you have to provide the name of the **Gateway cluster name** even when you have just a single one.

6. Enter a **Connection name** you like.

7. Then, you have to enter the **Connection type**. The screenshot of *Figure 12.2* has a **SQL Server** connection as an example.

8. The rest of the information you need to provide depends on the **Connection type** you are configuring:

New connection

| On-premises | Virtual network | Cloud |

Gateway cluster name *

powerbi-docs

Connection name *

AdventureWorksProducts

Connection type *

SQL Server

Server *

LAPTOP-R5

Database *

AdventureWorksDW2017

Figure 12.2: New connection

When you select a connection in the list of connections, you can change the settings (**Settings** button at the top), remove the connection, or change the users allowed to use the connection. The last only determines who can publish reports using this source. Using a report is controlled by the security settings you learned in *Chapter 11, Security*.

With the data source registered, we can move on to configure our newly published report.

9. Click on the **Workspaces** icon on the left-hand side of the Power BI window.

10. Select your workspace (**Power BI Book**).

11. Find the semantic model published in the previous chapter in the list with items in the bottom half of the screen, hover your mouse over it, and click on the three dots (**...**) that appear.

12. Click on **Settings**.

Let us go through the settings in turn:

a. **Semantic model description**: A description has no functional meaning. You can add whatever you want. It can help, however, in self-service scenarios where users search for semantic models that they can use to build their own reports on.

b. **Gateway and cloud connections**: After publishing a report, you might need to go here to see if the correct gateway is used. On publishing a report, you may get a message that publishing was successful, but the report is not linked to a source. Here is where you select the gateway to use when that happens. You also see a list of cloud connections when used in the report. In our case, the OData URL is shown here. This is ok. For other URLs, you might want to create a generic connection to them. Do this by personal cloud connect and select create a connection. When you need standard settings applied every time a report uses the same URL, you want to create a connection.

c. **Data source credentials**: This is where we need to apply some settings. A yellow bar indicates that Power BI cannot connect to our data.

13. Click on **Edit credentials** in the line that is *not* the OData feed. This is the link to the target text files that we imported in *Chapter 5, Advanced Techniques of Power Query*.

14. Select **Private** in the **Privacy level settings for this data source**.

There are three privacy level settings to choose from: **Private**, **Organizational**, and **Public**. When Power Query uses query folding to optimize query processing, Power BI may send data from one source to another to optimize query performance. This can, however, be a potential data breach when sensitive data is sent to another source, and someone is monitoring network traffic to and from that source, or when they are monitoring the workload of that source. When the privacy level of your source is set to **Private**, this will not happen. Data coming from a course marked as **Private** will not be send to another source unless the other source is private as well. **Organizational** data can be sent to other **Organizational** data sources, and to **Private** data sources, but never to **Public** data sources. Data from **Public** data sources can be used in whatever way Power Query sees fit to optimize its queries. When in doubt, always use **Private**.

15. Check that the only **Authentication method** for local files is **Windows without impersonation**.

16. Click on **Sign in**. This will only work with a gateway installed because Power BI must read files from your local machine.

    The yellow warning is gone. Power BI can now connect to your data sources. You do not have to do anything for the OData source since it uses anonymous access. When your tables use **DirectQuery**, **Direct Lake**, or **Live connect**, you are all done when all sources are configured with the proper security credentials. The report should work. For **Import** mode, you still need to schedule data refresh.

    Let us continue the list of settings for the semantic model:

    a. **Parameters**: Here you find all the parameters you created in Power Query. In this case, you can see the URL to the Northwind OData feed. Whenever the data source's names or locations change (and you used parameters), you can apply that change here. Depending on what you change, you might have to edit the credentials again because you now connect to a different source.

    b. **Query caching**: This option only works when you have Power BI Premium or Embedded. You can turn it on or off, or use the default as configured for the entire workspace. When a user first opens a report, the data of that report page is cached in Power BI's local cache. This reduces the number of queries when that page has to be displayed again and speeds up the rendering of that page.

    c. **Refresh**: This is where you configure data refresh.

17. Select the **Time zone** you are in.

18. Toggle **Configure a refresh schedule** on.

19. Select **Daily** for the **Refresh frequency**.

    When you select **Weekly** for the **Refresh frequency**, you can uncheck certain days. May be the data does not have to be refreshed during the weekend, for instance.

20. Click on **Add another time**.

21. Select a time, for instance, 7:00 AM. Add more times if you want. You can add up to eight times on a Pro account.

22. Optionally, add users who get notified when failures occur.

23. Click on **Apply**.

You can see the refresh history of a semantic model when you navigate to the semantic model in the workspace.

There are some more settings to discuss:

- **Endorsement and discovery**: A workspace is where coworkers work together with data. Power BI, in general, is meant to work with data throughout the organization, independent of an organization's BI maturity level, as discussed in *Chapter 1, Introduction to Data and Power BI*. When an organization grows to higher maturity, higher standards are needed, and more people need to be aware of data and of the standard that data adheres to. A promoted semantic model tells other users that this might be an interesting semantic model. It is ready to be used as a shared dataset. A certified semantic model goes even a step further. By certifying a dataset, you tell other users that the data in the model is compliant with all sorts of criteria deemed important within an organization.

  Master data, still in preview at the time of writing this book, goes even further than certifying data. Master data is seen as the single source of truth within an organization. Master data is often-used for dimension data. For example, it can be the best and most trustworthy list of customers available to use for reporting. When you promote or certify a semantic model, it is automatically made discoverable for people in the organization, even if they do not have permission to use it (yet). This is the point of certifying and promoting datasets. People should be able to easily find data. Discovery of datasets can be turned off. Models that do get promoted or certified get a badge. When you are in a workspace and looking at the list of items, badges make it easier to detect special semantic models.

  Note, as a last remark, that this setting is not changing anything to the semantic model. There are also no validations applied. It is just you telling other people how good or trustworthy a semantic model is. A semantic model can be promoted or certified by someone in the admin role of the workspace or by Fabric admins.

- **Large semantic model storage format**: This can be toggled on when in a premium capacity workspace and increases the amount of data that can be imported. It also enhances the performance of the model.

- **Query scale-out**: In large organizations, a lot of users may access reports based on a semantic model at the same time. Data refresh operations may occur during this workload as well. With query scale-out enabled, multiple replicas of the model are created, and the workload is divided over those replicas. This enables Power BI to have good report performance even with lots of concurrent users.

Note: **There are some more settings. They either speak for themselves or fall outside the scope of this book. Feel free to have a look at them.**

Creating a dashboard

Once in the Power BI service, we can create dashboards. Let us start with a little bit of theory.

Theoretically, a dashboard shows highly aggregated data. A dashboard is usually interactive and a dashboard is highly graphical. A dashboard may, for instance, show a scorecard.

A scorecard is a list of **key performance indicators** (**KPIs**). A KPI shows the status of an important measure, usually with an icon like a traffic light. A report is, in theory, more detailed, more text-oriented, like tables and matrices, and less interactive.

A lot of Power BI reports are more dashboards than reports when you follow this description. A lot of Power BI reports are called **dashboards** by users in organizations. This is important to note here because we can call a report a dashboard, but technically, it is still a Power BI report. A Power BI dashboard is another item that we can create. You cannot create a dashboard in Power BI Desktop; they can only be created in the Power BI service.

One way of looking at a Power BI dashboard is as a start page. There can be many reports based on many semantic models in a workspace. Each report can have many report pages, and you can have multiple visuals on a single report page. That is a lot of information *hidden* away behind a lot of mouse-clicks. A Power BI dashboard brings the most important visuals of all reports together on a single page. That makes it an ideal page to start when looking for data in reports. Let us look at the steps for creating a dashboard:

1. Navigate to your workspace and open the report `Solution Chapter 11.pbix` by simply clicking on it.

2. Go to the page **Sales report** within the report if that is not the page showing when you opened the report.

3. Hover your mouse over the bar chart **Net Sales by product category**.

4. Click on the pin icon (the pushpin symbol) that appears in the top right corner of the bar chart.

5. Select **New dashboard** in the **Pin to dashboard** dialog that opens, and enter `Power BI book` as the name of the new dashboard.

6. Ignore the popup in your screen.

7. Go to the report page **Sales by Year by Sales person**. Hover your mouse over the bar chart **Variance from target**. Notice that you do not see the **Pin** icon. That is because the visual uses visual calculations.

8. Add the cards, **Sum of NetSales**, **Sum of GrossSales**, and **Sum of Margin**, from the report page **Bookmarks** to the dashboard.

9. Click on **Go to dashboard** in the popup that appears each time you add a visual to a dashboard. (You can also go to the dashboard using the left-hand side menu and select the dashboard from the list of items in the workspace.)

   Each time you add a visual to a dashboard, it is like a screenshot is made of the visual and added to the dashboard. The visual is shown on the dashboard in a **tile**. It is not literally a screenshot. The data you see will change after a data refresh. You see up-to-date data. It is, however, static in two other ways. Firstly, you cannot interact with the tile. Standard tooltips will show when they are defined, but tooltip pages are ignored. The tile is a button. Clicking anywhere in a tile brings you to the report page that the visual shown in the tile is on.

The second way in which tiles are static is applied filtering. The visual in the tile is shown with slicer and filter settings that were applied at the time the visual was pinned. You do not see this in the dashboard, but the tile stays filtered.

10. Go back to the report and pin the visual **Net Sales by product category**, but after you select a single sales person in the slicer.

11. Go back to the dashboard and see the difference between the two tiles showing the same visual.

    Tiles on a dashboard can be rearranged by simply dragging them to another position on the screen. Tiles can be resized by dragging the little resize handle that appears in the bottom right-hand side of the tile when you hover over it. The size is, however, a multiple of a fixed standard size.

12. Rearrange the tiles on the dashboard so that the three cards are on top and the bar charts are under each other and under the cards.

13. Try resizing a bar chart tile.

    You can customize a dashboard to make it look as you wish.

14. Click on **Edit** at the top of the dashboard and select + **Add a tile**.

    As you can see, there are different types of content you can add to your dashboard. A textbox lets you add your own hard-coded text. You can use this to create a title or add comments for users to better understand the dashboard. You can add an image to add your logo to the dashboard.

15. Select **Image** and click **Next**.

16. Use *Google* to find the Northwind logo. Right-click on the logo and select **Copy Image Address**.

17. Paste the link into the textbox **URL** under **Content**.

    Note the option **Set custom link**. When you check this option, you can enter an URL to any site, or you can select another dashboard. Whatever you choose, the image is now a button that links to the site or dashboard you configure.

18. Click on **Apply**.

    You can also add any web content or any video on the dashboard using the corresponding tiles.

19. Click on **Edit** at the top of the dashboard again and select **Dashboard theme**.

20. Choose a theme of your liking, noting the options available.

    Note the two ways to completely customize the look and feel of a dashboard. You can choose the option **Custom** from the drop-down list, allowing you to specify different colors and select a background picture. You can also create a JSON file that specifies the theme and upload that file.

    You can customize individual tiles as well.

21. Hover your mouse over the **Sum of NetSales** tile and click **More option** in the upper right corner of the tile, followed by **Edit details**.

22. Select the option **Display last refresh time**.

    > Note: **You can change the title and add a subtitle for tiles. You can change the default behavior of acting as a button to the report, and set a custom link as with the image before.**

    We will discuss the other options in the **More options** dialog when we discuss working with reports later in this chapter.

    One thing that we have ignored so far is the option to have a different layout when viewed on a mobile phone. Power BI has native apps for all phone types (Android and iPhone). This allows for easy access anywhere and anytime. A report or dashboard layout might, however, not be suitable when watched on a small screen of a phone.

23. Click on **Edit** at the top of the dashboard again and select **Mobile layout**.

24. Hover over one of the bar charts and click the unpin icon that appears.

25. Rearrange the remaining tiles by dragging them.

    Some visuals will not be informative on a small screen. You can completely omit them from the dashboard when viewed on a phone.

26. Click on **Web layout** in the top right corner of the window, above the list with unpinned tiles, to switch back to the normal view.

Users do not have to choose between the web and mobile layout. Power BI chooses one or the other based on the screen orientation of the phone you are using.

As a last remark, notice the **Share** option at the top of the **Dashboard**. It is like sharing a report.

Working with reports in the Power BI service

Working with reports in the Power BI service is not different from working with them in Power BI Desktop. There are, however, some extra options to use as shown in the following steps:

1. Open the Power BI service home page (**Home** icon on top of the menu on the left-hand side of the window.)

   The home page is personalized. Power BI shows items that it recommends to you. In the second part of the screen, you can switch between three lists: **Recent**, **Favorites**, and **My apps**.

2. Open the report **Solution Chapter 11.pbix**. If you followed along this far, it should be in the list **Recent**. (You can always search for it in the search box in the center top of the screen or navigate to the workspace using the left-hand side menu.)

3. Click on the star icon in the menu bar at the top of the report (see *Figure 12.3*). It is the furthest icon to the right. You can hover over items to see a tooltip. The tooltip that you want to see displays favorite.

Figure 12.3: Report view with menu bar

With this setting applied, your report will be in the favorite list on the Power BI home page next time you visit the home page.

4. Click on the second icon in the menu on top of the report. The tooltip displays comment.

   You can leave comments with this report. You can enter any text you like. You can mention specific people using the @ sign, like in social media applications. People you mention will automatically receive an email and get a notification in the Power BI mobile app if they have the app. They can react to the comment.

5. Click on the third icon in the menu on top of the report. The tooltip displays refresh visuals.

   After data refresh of a semantic model, it may take some time for visuals to refresh. Visuals will refresh automatically, but this button allows you to force refresh so that you do not have to wait for the automatic refresh.

6. Click on the fourth icon in the menu on top of the report. The tooltip displays view.

   As you can see, you can show the report full screen. With all the menus gone, it is easier to focus on the actual report. Pressing escape brings you back to the normal view. Another interesting option is to show visuals as tables, which is in preview at the time of writing. It does what it promises. Try it out!

7. Click on the fifth icon in the menu on top of the report. The tooltip displays bookmarks.

   You learned about bookmarks in *Chapter 6, Create Interactive Reports*. This is where you find all the bookmarks that were created in the report. They are available for all users of the report. The presentation mode is available here as well.

   You can also add your own personal bookmarks here. They work as any bookmark. The only difference is that other report users will not see the bookmarks you create here. They are personal.

   The next button is Copilot, Microsoft's AI assistant. Copilot can make summaries of your report and create narratives. It helps people understand the report and digest the information in it.

   Let us continue from the left-hand side in the menu, the **File** menu.

8. Click on **File** in the menu on top of the report and check the available options.

   The options you find here are:

   a. **Save a copy**: You can create a copy of the report. The copy is still a report in the Power BI service. It can be copied to another workspace.

   b. **Download this file**: You can download the report as a `.pbix` file. You can include the semantic model in the download or download the report only with a live connection to the semantic model that stays behind in the Power BI service. In some cases, downloading the `.pbix` file is not possible.

   c. **Manage permission**: This is a link to the page where you can see all links creates to the report and all users with direct access to this report. You learned about this in *Chapter 11, Security*.

   d. **Print this page**: The standard windows print dialog opens, allowing you to print a single report page.

   e. **Embed report**: You can create embed codes for SharePoint online, websites or portals or for the Developer Playground. Embedding your report in SharePoint or in portals is another way of sharing reports. It is the most customized option available because you create your own site/portal and make Power BI reports or visuals part of it.

   f. **Generate a QR code**: Generates a QR code representing the URL of the report.

   g. **Setting**: This opens the **Settings** pane with a lot of settings you can set. You can also find most of these settings in Power BI Desktop under **Report settings** in the **Options and settings**. For a list of all settings see **https://learn.microsoft.com/en-us/power-bi/create-reports/power-bi-report-settings?tabs=powerbi-service**

   Moving back to the menu at the top of the report.

9. Click on **Export** in the menu on top of the report and check the available options.

    You can open Excel online with a connection to the semantic model of the report and analyze the data further in Excel. There are some limitations with regard to data sources used in the semantic model. You can also export the report to PowerPoint either as screenshots or with a live connection to the data. The last option available is to create a PDF version of the report.

    We skip the **Share** and **Chat in Teams** menu item because it has been discussed in *Chapter 11, Security*.

10. Click on **Explore this data** in the menu on top of the report.

11. Click on **Got it** if the **Data exploration made easy** dialog shows.

    This feature (still in preview at the time of writing) allows users to create their own visuals of the data. The experience is very similar to creating visuals on a report. You need **Build** permission to access this functionality. You can start data exploration directly from a workspace as well.

12. Click on **Insights** in the menu on top of the report.

    This feature analyzes your data and tries to detect anomalies and trends and performs a KPI analysis.

13. Click on **Subscribe to report** in the menu at the top of the report.

    When you create a subscription, an email with a link to the report is sent on a schedule you set. You can create a subscription for yourself or for others, you can use personal email addresses, or Microsoft 365 groups (except security groups). You can create personalized views of the report with the option **Include my changes**. In this way, you can send people a view of the report with filters set in a way that is right for them. You can read all about creating subscriptions here: **https://learn.microsoft.com/en-us/power-bi/collaborate-share/end-user-subscribe?tabs=creator**

14. Click on **Set alert** in the menu on the top of the report.

    A subscription is based on predefined schedules. An alert is a notification sent by email or as a Teams message that is triggered when some threshold is passed. You can get notified when a measure changes or when it becomes bigger or smaller than the preset threshold.

15. Click on **Edit** in the menu on top of the report.

    With the proper permission, you can continue developing this report from the Power BI service. The experience is identical to creating visuals in Power BI Desktop. You only miss the semantic model settings, like the **Column tools** and **Measure tools**, for instance.

16. Click on **Reading view** in the menu on the top of the report to close the editing view.

We will discuss the options under the more (…) later.

You will also see buttons appearing when you hover your mouse over a visual. You will recognize most options already from either Power BI Desktop or from the list just discussed for the entire report. Two options are worth mentioning: under more (…) is the option **Spotlight**. It will make the rest of the report appear grayed out in the background. Directly in the visual is a button **Focus mode** (use the tooltips when necessary to find it) that makes the visual show over your entire screen.

There are a lot of possibilities to actively engage with the reports. Reports are meant to be far more than static lists of data.

Configure workspace settings

There are a lot of settings you can use to configure a workspace as you can see in *Figure 12.4*:

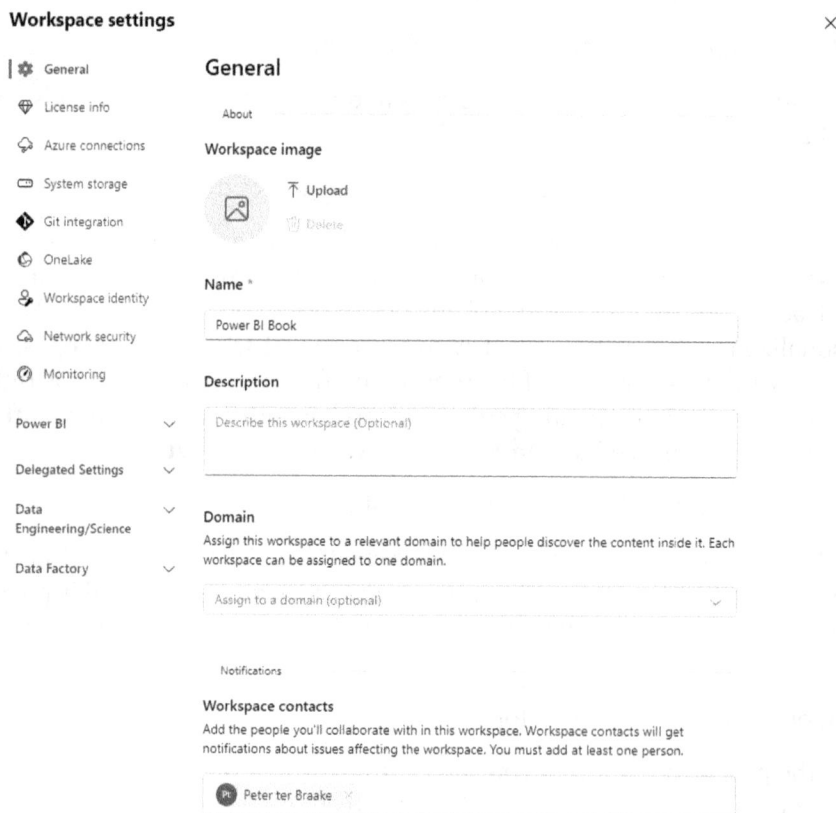

Figure 12.4: Workspace settings

You can open the workspace settings in a couple of ways:

1. Click on **Workspaces** in the left-hand side menu of Power BI. Hover the mouse over the workspace **Power BI Book**, and select **Workspace settings**. You can also open the workspace and click on the gear icon in the top right corner of the window.

   Most of the settings you do here are outside the scope of this book. However, a couple of them do deserve some attention:

   - **General tab | Workspace image, Name and Description**: The workspace needs to have a name. The other two settings are optional. All three should help users understand what this workspace is for.

   - **General tab | Domain**: A domain is a level up in a hierarchy compared to the workspace. Companies can create a domain for manufacturing, for instance, with multiple workspaces in it. Each workspace has a separate purpose and possibly a separate target audience. However, they are all in some way about manufacturing. A separate domain could be made for sales, human resources, etc. It is a way to better manage the total reporting environment in large organizations. Domains have their own security roles.

   - **General tab | OneDrive**: We discussed OneDrive for Business earlier in this chapter. You can create a Microsoft 365 group and get a OneDrive with it. Assign access to this group to a workspace and assign the OneDrive to the workspace as well. All data-related management is now in one place.

   - **General tab | Remove this workspace**: This option speaks for itself. This is the only place to remove a workspace. You need to be in the Owner role of the workspace or have a higher role (Fabric admin).

   - **License info**: Here you can see and edit the license this workspace operates under. This is where you can increase (or decrease) your capacity settings when needed.

   - **System storage**: Here, you see how much storage the semantic models are currently using and how much free space is still available.

As already said, this list is not exhaustive. Go to the documentation if you need to learn about other settings.

Power BI settings

Apart from all the report settings and workspace settings, there are also tenant settings. Refer to this URL to get an exhaustive list: **https://learn.microsoft.com/en-us/fabric/admin/tenant-settings-index**

You get to the Power BI tenant settings by clicking on the gear icon in the top right corner of the Power BI window from everywhere within Power BI and then selecting **Admin portal**. Refer to *Figure 12.5* to see the **Admin portal**. Note that there are some items marked as **New** and some marked as **(preview)**. By the time you read this, the settings may have changed.

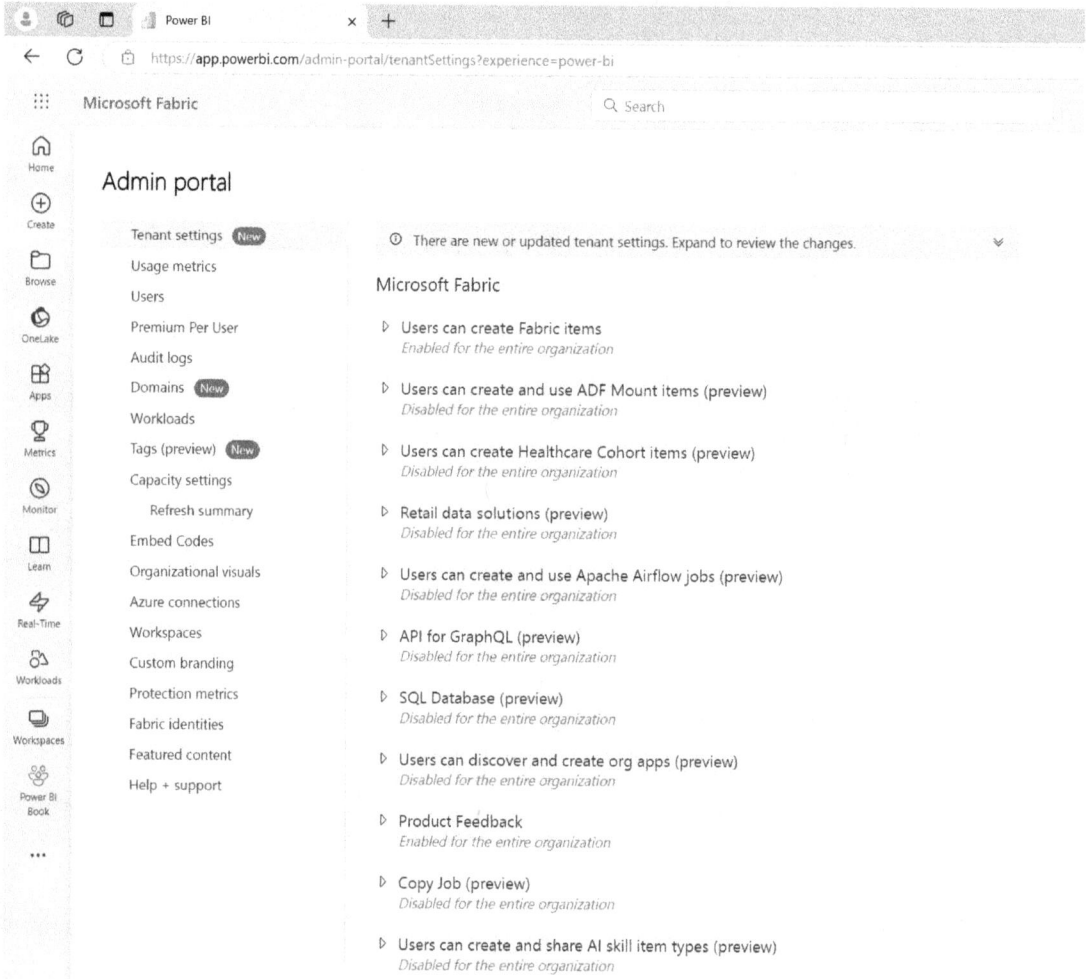

Figure 12.5: Admin portal

Let us mention just a couple of them here:

- **Use semantic models across workspaces**: This option allows or disallows a report in one workspace to use a semantic model from another workspace.

- **Define workspace retention period**: This option defines how long Microsoft keeps a workspace after it is deleted. Within this period, you can restore a deleted workspace. The default, when turned off, is seven days.

- **Export and sharing setting**: There are a lot of settings allowing or disallowing external users to use various resources. You can also allow or disallow your users to accept links to Power BI resources from outside your organization. There are also settings that control if and how data can be exported. You can for instance disallow exports to Excel or various other formats.

- **Integration settings**: There are a lot of settings in this category. Most notably to allow **single sign-on** (**SSO**) to some third-party data sources like Snowflake.

Conclusion

In the first part of this chapter, you learned to configure a semantic model for published reports to function. You connected to used data sources and scheduled refreshes of the data. You also learned how to create and use dashboards. Dashboards function as a sort of summary of all reports in the workspace and allow for easy access to those reports by simply clicking on dashboard tiles.

You then learned about a lot of options available to users when working with reports. There is more than the interactivity in the report itself. It is all about being actively involved as a user.

The last part of the chapter introduced the most important settings of Power BI. There are too many settings to list them all in this book. You can find all the settings and what they do on **https://learn.microsoft.com/**

Now that you understand the Power BI service, it is time to learn about the Power BI app. The service is meant to collaborate on reports, which includes creating content. The Power BI service can be a daunting environment for report users with all the options present in the interface. In the next chapter, you will learn to create an app. The app is the end user experience when working with reports.

Multiple choice questions

1. **What actions must you perform when you publish a report that uses DirectQuery to read data from an on-premise database that was never used before in Power BI reports?**

    a. Register the data source to a gateway

    b. Edit credentials to connect to the database

    c. Schedule data refresh

    d. Link the report to the semantic model

2. **How can you when a semantic model has been refreshed?**

    a. Add the last refresh data to tiles in a dashboard

    b. Click on Refresh visuals in a report

    c. Check the refresh history of a semantic model

    d. On the overview page of a semantic model

3. **You need to know when sick leave in your organization rises above 5%. What should you do? Choose one.**

    a. Place sick leave on a dashboard tile

    b. Open the sick leave report and check the KPI

    c. Subscribe to the report to get a mail daily

    d. Create an Alert to notify you when the measure is above 5%

Answers

1	a, b
2	a, c, d
3	d

Join our Discord space

Join our Discord workspace for latest updates, offers, tech happenings around the world, new releases, and sessions with the authors:

https://discord.bpbonline.com

CHAPTER 13

Create App

Introduction

Power BI apps are a great way to share reports. You learned multiple ways to share reports in *Chapter 11, Security*. There is another way to share reports: you can create an app. A Power BI app is the end result and arguably the best way to share reports with end users. The settings, buttons, and menu items of the Power BI service interface that you learned about in the previous chapter are too complex for end users, which is why Power BI offers a more user-friendly interface, the Power BI app.

You will require a Power BI account with admin rights to follow along with the steps in this chapter. You also need the workspace named **Power BI Book** created in *Chapter 11, Security*. It is assumed the report named **Solution Chapter 11.pbix** is published to that workspace.

Structure

This chapter covers the following topics:

- Deployment pipeline
- Power BI project
- Creating a Power BI app

- Working with apps

- Template apps

Objectives

In this chapter, you will learn what a deployment pipeline is first. Then, you will create an app from a workspace. You will learn how to share the app with users and how to use and find shared apps. You will also learn about template apps.

Deployment pipeline

Power BI Desktop focuses on quick report development. It opens the Report view page when you open a new Power BI Desktop file. You get some data, after which you can quickly move to creating visuals. Once they are ready, you can publish your report.

In some scenarios, this is fine. However, in other scenarios, we need some more control over the end product that we create. In software development, it is common to work with stages throughout the software development process. The stages are **Development, Test, Acceptance, and Production (DTAP)**:

- **Development**: As the name suggests, this is the stage where most of the development is done. During this stage, it may be impossible to work with the actual data due to security limitations. Developers are not always allowed to see the actual data, with, for instance, **personally identifiable information (PII)** in it. As a developer, you may not want to work with the full dataset when it is large. Developing using smaller datasets can make the development process more efficient.

- **Test**: Software needs to be tested. Reports are no exception to this rule. DAX measures must be tested, for instance. Interactivity must be tested. In large organizations, testing is done by a special team of testers. They can create their own datasets to test on. That allows them to test on special circumstances, like what happens when we have missing data.

- **Acceptance**: This is the stage where a select group of business users works with the reports to see if the reports deliver what was promised and what is needed in everyday life. To have minimal impact on actual business processes, this is often done on a copy of the real database that is used for the report.

- **Production**: In this stage, the people the report(s) is meant for work with the report in their actual day-to-day work.

Going through all these stages increases the quality of the delivered product. When Power BI is used by BI developers to create critical reports for business users, a DTAP approach is advised. Power BI deployment pipelines can help.

In Power BI, you can create a deployment pipeline to help you get content you develop through all stages. You need at least a **Premium Per User (PPU)** license. You create a deployment pipeline from the workspace overview page (see *Figure 13.1*):

Figure 13.1: Deployment pipeline

After creating and naming the pipeline, there are a couple of steps to take:

- In the first step, you define how many stages you want. The default for Power BI is three; DTAP is four. You name the pipeline as well as each stage.

- If you did not create the pipeline from a workspace, you have to assign a workspace to it. Each stage is implemented as a workspace.

Developers publish Power BI Desktop files to the development workspace. This workspace can be shared with all developers. Other developers can publish their work as well. They can also use the report authoring functionality of the Power BI service to change content or create new content. Developers can also create dashboards in the normal way.

Once the development is ready, the pipeline offers a simple **Deploy** button to copy content to the next stage. You can do a full deployment or specify individual items to be deployed. Before you deploy, you can check the differences between your current workspace and the one you deploy to.

It is possible to create deployment rules.Deployment rules allow you to automatically make configuration changes when deploying items to the next stage in your deployment process. Remember that we mentioned that each stage of the deployment may use a different database to connect to. If you used query parameters in PowerQuery to connect to data sources, you can setup a rule that automatically changes the value of a query parameter to the appropriate value for the stage.

You can make any stage public, although this is meant for the last stage. This stage appears as a normal workspace to people in your organization.

Note: **The stage implementation using workspaces allows for different users to be able to access different stages.**

You can share the development and test stage with developers, for instance, while the production stage is only for designated business users.

Power BI projects

In the previous section, you learned about four deployment stages. Let us zoom in on the first stage a little bit. You can create Power BI projects in Power BI Desktop. This feature is still in preview at the time of writing this book.

In development, source control and version control are important. Sometimes you make changes to a report in Power BI Desktop that break the report or make it worse. In such scenarios, you want an easy way to roll back to the previous version of the report. There are also scenarios when you are not the sole developer of a report. You must collaborate even when still working in Power BI Desktop.

In Power BI Desktop, you can save your work as a Power BI project, that is, a **.pbip** file, instead of the normal **.pbix** file. You get a **.pbip** file and two folders. One for the report and one for the semantic model. Refer to *Figure 13.2*:

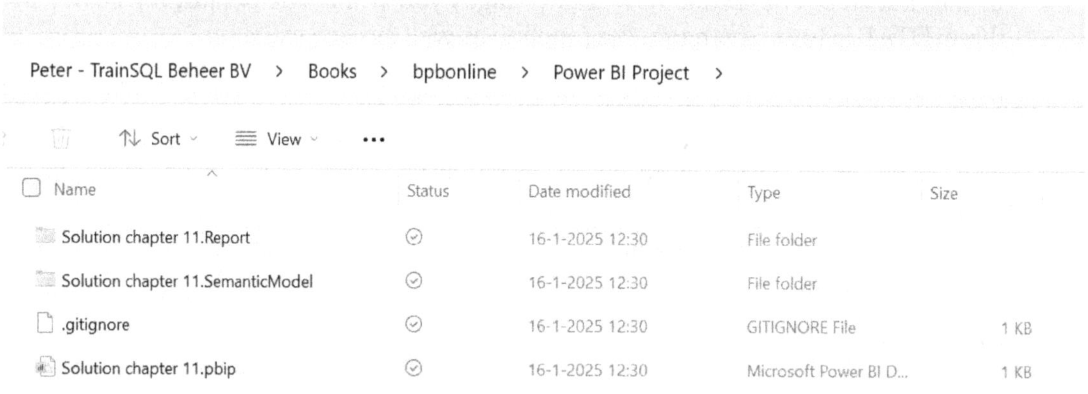

Name	Status	Date modified	Type	Size
Solution chapter 11.Report	⊘	16-1-2025 12:30	File folder	
Solution chapter 11.SemanticModel	⊘	16-1-2025 12:30	File folder	
.gitignore	⊘	16-1-2025 12:30	GITIGNORE File	1 KB
Solution chapter 11.pbip	⊘	16-1-2025 12:30	Microsoft Power BI D...	1 KB

Peter - TrainSQL Beheer BV > Books > bpbonline > Power BI Project >

Figure 13.2: Power BI project files

Everything you created is now stored in JSON files. The structure of the JSON files is published by Microsoft. This combination allows you to change the files outside of Power BI Desktop. You can change the files manually or programmatically, allowing for a lot of flexibility.

You can add the Power BI project files to a source control system like Git. It will create a new version every time you save the files to Git. This way, you can easily open an old version. Git can also show you the difference between versions, and it allows you to merge versions. This enables you, for instance, to add a report page to a report. A coworker can add another page to the same report. When you are both ready, you merge the two versions into a new version that has both new pages.

The easiest way to publish your report to Git is to install Visual Studio Code. You then open the Power BI project folder in Visual Studio Code and initialize a new Git repository from there. Once the repository is created, you commit your project and publish it to Git. You will see the same folder structure in Git as you have locally, as you can see in *Figure 13.3*:

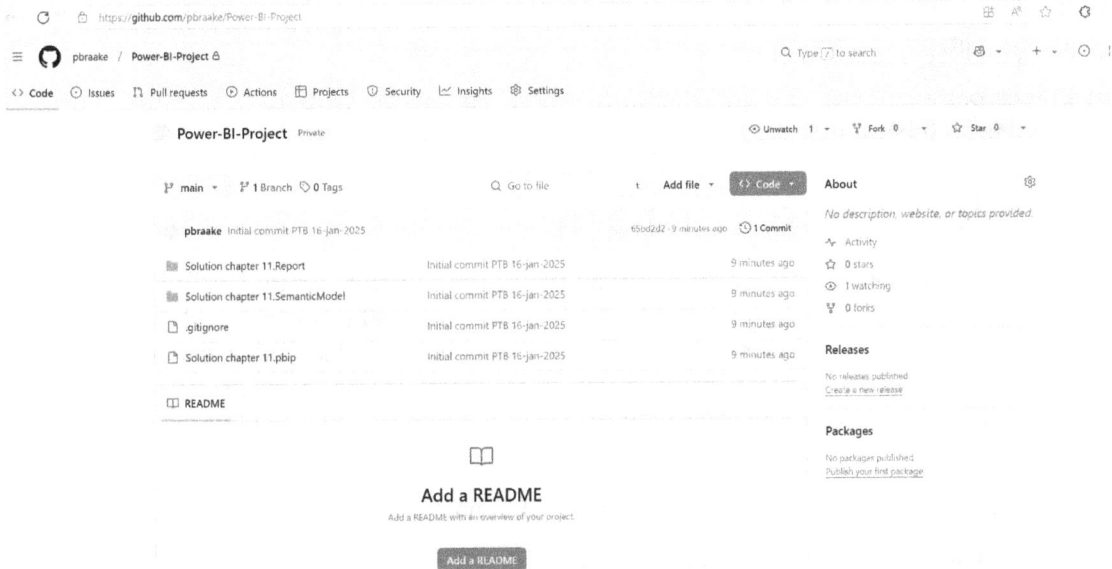

Figure 13.3: GitHub

Once you have a link setup between your project folder and Git, you can work in Power BI Desktop as usual. In Visual Studio Code, you can track the changes you have made, as you can see in *Figure 13.4*: on the left-hand side, you select a report, and in the middle, you will see the version of the report as it is in Git. In the right-hand side you will see highlighted parts (the green area in the figure). These highlighted parts show where there are differences between your current version in Power BI Desktop and the most recent version saved to Git:

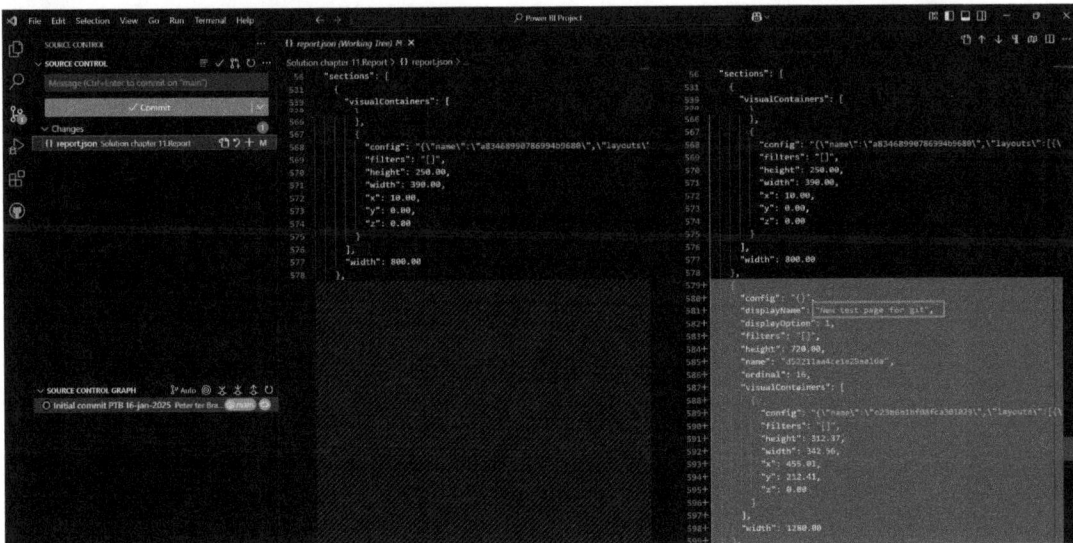

Figure 13.4: Track changes

You can now publish those changes, publish them as a new branch, or get the older version back from Git.

In bigger organizations and in situations where you work with two or more Power BI developers on the same projects, Git integration is very much advised.

Creating a Power BI app

Now that we understand the development stage to an extent, let us also zoom in on the production bit. Within the deployment pipeline, you can make stages (workspaces) public. Normal users with access can work with the workspace, as we learned in earlier chapters in the book. However, for many users, the Power BI portal can be overwhelming with all the options it offers. We need an easier way to bring our reports and dashboards to end users, which is where the app helps us. Refer to the following steps:

1. Open a browser and navigate to Power BI, if necessary.

2. Navigate to the **Power BI Book** workspace.

3. Click on **Create app** at the top of the page (refer to *Figure 13.1*).

   You should now have opened the create app pages that guide you through the creation process in three tabs. Refer to *Figure 13.5*:

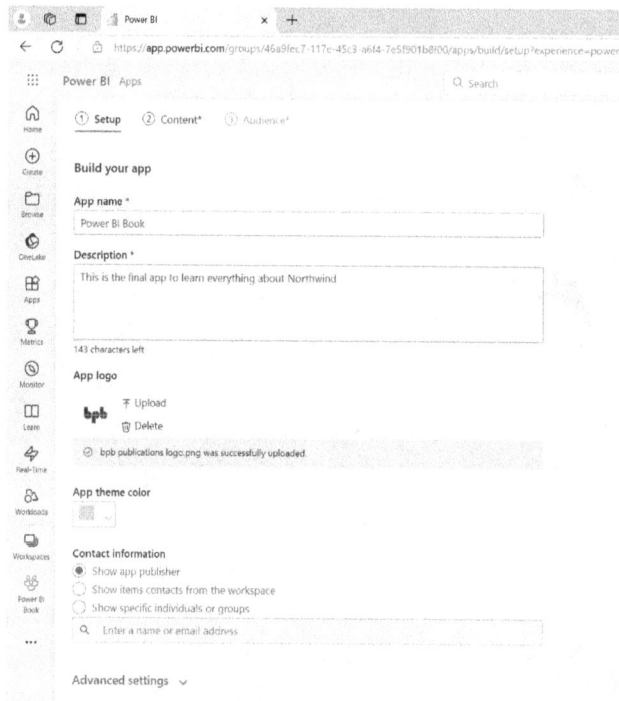

Figure 13.5: Create App

You are guided through the steps to make a real app from your workspace.

4. Add a descriptive name for the app. The default is the name of the workspace. That should be descriptive already.

5. Enter a **Description**. This is a mandatory field.

6. Upload the BPB publications logo from the downloads that come with the book.

7. Apply a light blue **App theme color**.

8. Check the **Advanced settings**.

9. Click on **Next: Add content**. The button is in the far-right bottom corner of the window.

A Power BI app is based on a workspace. It contains only reports and dashboards. You cannot see or use the semantic models or other items. You do not have to add all the content to the app. You select the reports and dashboards that you want the app to contain on the **Content** tab.

10. Click on + **Add content**.

11. Select the **Power BI book** dashboard and the report `Solution Chapter 11`. You can select more items if you wish when you have them available in your workspace.

When you add a lot of items, you may need some structure. This makes navigating the app easier.

12. Click on the down arrow behind + **Add content** and select **Add a new section**.

13. Click on the three dots (...) that appear when you hover over the new section and change the name to `Really interesting`.

14. Hover your mouse over the dashboard **Power BI Book**, click the three dots (...), and select **Move to** followed by **Really interesting**.

15. Create a second section with the name `Nice Read` and add the report to this section.

16. Move the section **Really interesting** to the top.

17. Click on the down arrow behind + **Add content** and select **Add a link**.

18. Copy a link to another report you have to **Link** in the **Add a link** tab.

19. Select another report in the **Add from workspace** tab.

20. Create a new section called `Extra links`, move the section all the way down, and add any links you created to it.

When you have selected and organized all you want to share, it is time to think about who to share it with.

21. Click on **Next: Add audience**. The button is in the far-right bottom corner of the window.

22. For now, select **Entire organization** on the right-hand side of the window.

23. Make sure all defined sections are visible.

24. Click on **Publish app**. The button is in the far-right bottom corner of the window.

25. Click on **Publish** in the dialog (if it shows).

   You should get the **Successfully published** dialog. You can copy the link to the app and use it to create shortcuts on the desktop of the people it is for. There is also a button to go directly to the app.

26. Click on **Go to app**. You should see something like *Figure 13.6*:

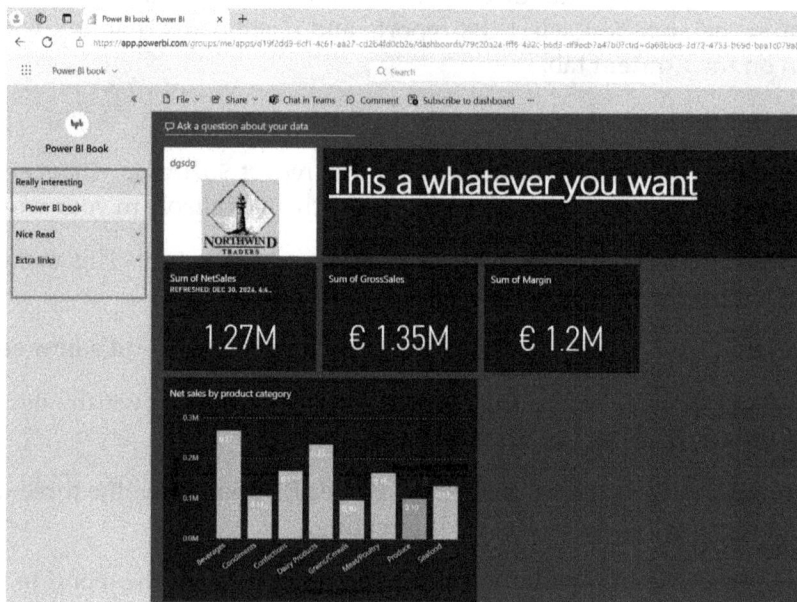

Figure 13.6: Finished app

Note: **The sections are on the left-hand side of the app.**

Notice how much simpler the screen looks compared to the Power BI interface itself with all of its options. The app focuses on content usage only.

The data in the app is refreshed on the same schedule as the semantic models that the reports and dashboards are based on. Changes made to the workspace do not affect the app. When you want changes to apply to the app as well, you have to update the app. You can do that by clicking **Update app**. The button is where the **Create app** button is for every workspace that does not have an app.

It may be that your app does not show the report and dashboard as expected. This is because row level security is applied to the report. Unless you configure it with users from your organization, Power BI cannot show the report. Try publishing some other reports and dashboards to your workspace and use them in the app.

In the app, we created a single audience, giving access to the app to the entire organization, meaning everyone within the organization. This means that everyone can use this app with all the reports and dashboards we added to the app.

It is also possible to create multiple audiences for an app. You may, for instance, create reports that all people working in the department sales may use, and other reports that are intended for sales managers only. You now create an audience for a Microsoft 365 group sales (assuming this group exists) and select only the reports intended for every person in this group. You then create a second audience for the group sales managers. For this second audience, you select all reports and dashboards in the workspace.

An app is always linked to a workspace. This means you can create a single app for a workspace. When all reports and dashboards within a workspace are meant to be used by the same people, a single audience suffices. Otherwise, you create multiple audiences.

Working with apps

The easiest way to share your app with intended users is to share the link. Creating a shortcut on the desktop of managers gives them easy access to the app. All they need to do is double-click the shortcut.

Apps can also be found in the Power BI service. Refer to the following steps to find your apps:

1. Click on the icon **Apps** in the left-hand side menu of Power BI.

   You will see a list of all the apps that are shared with you. Next to the apps that you or your coworkers created, there is an app store with all sorts of content that you can use.

2. Click on **Get apps** in the upper right corner of the window.

   You now see the Power BI apps screen as shown in *Figure 13.7*:

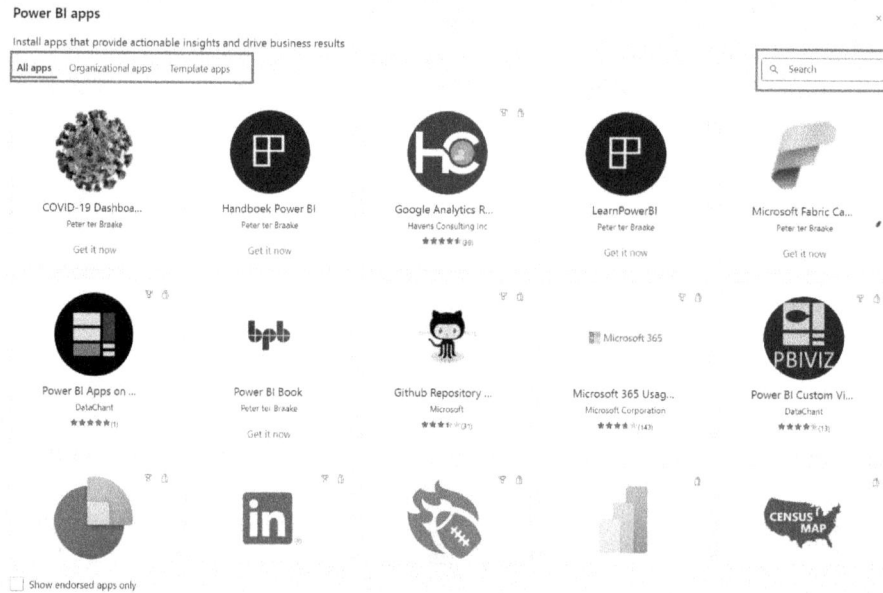

Figure 13.7: Power BI apps

There are three tabs: **All apps**, **Organizational apps**, and **Template apps**. You will find all apps created within your organization on the **Organizational apps** tab. We will discuss **Template apps** in the next section.

Template apps

Let us have a look at **Template apps** before we explain them. Continue with the following steps:

1. Continuing from the previous section, type **Covid** in the **Search** box in the top right corner of the **Power BI app** dialog.

2. Select the app made by **DataChant**.

   You will get a window with information on the app you selected. On the left-hand side, you see a button **Get it now**. Under the button is the pricing for this app. This one is for free.

3. Click on **Get it now** (twice).

   If you already have the app, you will get a message asking you how to update it. After a while, the app shows up in your list of apps.

4. Select the **Covid app** and see what it has to offer. You may have to enter your email address before it works.

Once you have an app installed, it works just like the app you created in your own workspace.

Microsoft invites people and companies to create apps and share them with the world. You can create an app as well and share it with the world.

Conclusion

Using the Power BI portal may be a good fit for developers and other people who are used to working in more complex environments. However, it can also be overwhelming, especially for business users who do not spend their entire day behind a computer. Power BI apps simplify the use of Power BI reports. You simply open the app without the hassle of navigating the portal to find a workspace and the reports in it. The reports in it are well-structured into sections, so everyone should find it easy to look for the information they need.

With apps created, we are fully setup to use Power BI to its full potential. All apps used in an organization need to be monitored. Power BI is no exception. You will learn about Power BI monitoring in the next chapter.

Multiple choice questions

1. **What do you do when you need source control on Power BI Desktop files?**

    a. Create a template app

    b. Create a deployment pipeline

    c. Save a Power BI file as a .pbip file

    d. Create a copy of a file before making any changes to it

2. **What can you add to a Power BI app?**

    a. A link to external site

    b. A link a report in another workspace

    c. A link a report in the same workspace

    d. A link a sematic model in the same workspace

3. **What should you do when you are an ISV and you want to offer customers access to their data using Power BI in a controlled way.**

    a. Create a template app

    b. Create a deployment pipeline

    c. Save a Power BI file .pbix file and send it to the customer

    d. Create a workspace and share it with customers using Entra guest accounts to allow external access

Answers

1	c
2	a, b, c
3	a

Join our Discord space

Join our Discord workspace for latest updates, offers, tech happenings around the world, new releases, and sessions with the authors:

https://discord.bpbonline.com

CHAPTER 14

Monitor Power BI and Fabric

Introduction

In each reporting system, monitoring is an important part of working with the systems. In *Chapter 4, The Basics of Visualizations*, we said that having too many reports can be a pitfall. This means there is a need to know which reports are out there and which reports are no longer used. You also want to know who is using a particular report and if the report is used by a limited number of people when the report was intended to be used by many people.

With Fabric licenses, the number of **capacity units** (**CUs**) spent the need to be monitored. Are you paying too much money because the CUs are not used? Also interesting to know is whether there is an upward trend in usage. More report usage may mean you reach the limits of your current license, and that license might have to be upgraded.

Let us not forget that monitoring is part of security. Anomalies in the usage of a system can be an indication of a security breach.

In short, monitoring Power BI is important.

If you want to follow along with the examples presented in this chapter, you need a Power BI account with admin rights.

Structure

This chapter covers the following topics:

- Monitor report usage metrics
- View item or workspace lineage
- Admin monitoring workspace
- Microsoft Fabric Capacity Metrics app
- Power BI Desktop tools
- Power BI activity log
- Application programming interface

Objectives

In this chapter, you will learn different ways to get insight into the Power BI environment and know about different reports to use. You will also become aware of different metrics that are important, and you learn about tools that can be used.

The purpose of this chapter is to provide an overview. Links are provided to websites providing more details.

Monitoring report usage metrics

Knowing how reports are used and by whom is important to understand your reporting environment. Power BI has built-in reports to show usage metrics of reports and dashboards. Let us start by looking at them. Refer to the following steps:

1. Open Power BI in a browser, if necessary.

2. Open the workspace, **Power BI Book**.

3. Hover over the report and click on the three dots (...) that appear and select **View usage metric report**. (You can also open the report from the more options menu item in the menu bar of an opened report).

   It can take a little while for the report to open. A popup in the upper-right corner of the screen tells you Microsoft is gathering the needed information. Microsoft created a Power BI report itself. The underlying semantic model might need to be refreshed when you open the usage metrics report.

4. Click on **View usage metrics** when the report is ready in the upper right corner of the screen. You may get a prompt asking you to try the new usage metrics report.

5. Toggle the **New usage metrics report on**. You can find the toggle in the upper-right corner of the usage metrics report.

The new report is still in preview at the time of writing of this book. It is, however, the more interesting of the two. *Figure 14.1* shows a screenshot of the old version of the report (thanks to **https://help.zebrabi.com/kb/power-bi/how-to-monitor-usage-with-usage-metrics-report-in-power-bi/**).

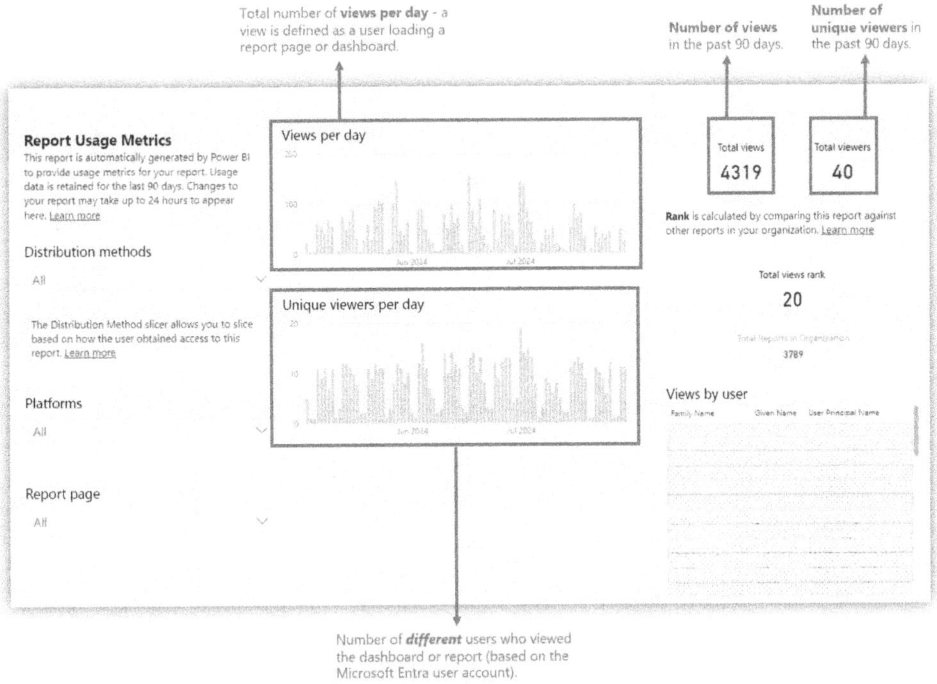

Figure 14.1: Old usage metrics report

Figure 14.2 shows a screenshots of the new version of the usage metric report. It is more informative than the old version:

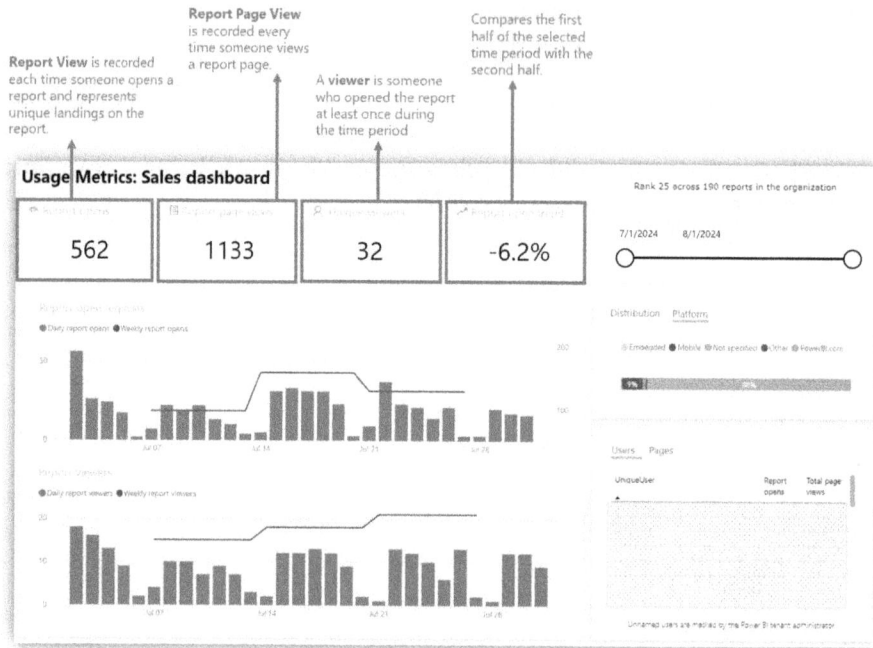

Figure 14.2: New usage metrics report

The report shows usage metrics for the specific report (or dashboard) you opened it for. By default, the old report shows data for the last 90 days, the new one for the last 30 days. Usage metrics for all users is captured regardless of the license the user has. The following prerequisites exist for viewing the usage metrics report:

- You need a Power BI Pro or **Premium Per User** (**PPU**). However, the usage metrics feature captures usage information from all users, regardless of the license they are assigned.

- You must have edit access to the report you are viewing metrics of.

- The **Enable usage metrics for content creators** tenant settings must be turned on. The **Collecting per-user data in usage metrics** tenant setting determines what you see exactly.

The new **Report Usage Metrics** report consists of four pages:

- **Report usage**: Here, you can see how often a report is being used and by how many users. The table in the bottom right-hand side corner of the report has two tabs. One shows a list of the users who viewed the report. The **Pages** tab shows the views per report page.

- **Report performance**: A line chart shows the time it takes to open the report. It shows three lines. The lowest one shows the time that 25% of views showed the report within this time or quicker. The middle line shows the time for which 50% of the views were this time or quicker. The last line shows to 3rd quartile (75%). You can analyze the influence of the browser or the environment used by interacting with the bar chart in the bottom right-hand side corner of the report.

- **Report list**: As the name suggests, you get a list of all reports and some usage statistics for the entire workspace.

- **FAQ**: The last report page is basically helping to better understand the metrics shown in the report.

To see a full explanation of each metric on the report, browse to:

https://learn.microsoft.com/en-us/power-bi/collaborate-share/service-modern-usage-metrics

The usage metrics report is read-only. However, you can save a copy of the report. The copy can be edited. When you open the copy in edit mode, you can see the entire semantic model behind it. One of the first things you might want to do is remove the filter that makes the usage metrics report only show stats of the one report you used to open it for. You do not want to go to each report in your workspace and open the usage metrics report separately for each of them.

View item or workspace lineage

Once you know which reports are being used by whom, you might be interested in the actual data they are viewing. Lineage information can tell you that:

1. Open the **Power BI Book** workspace.
2. Click on the **Lineage view** button in the top right corner of the screen (see *Figure 14.3*):

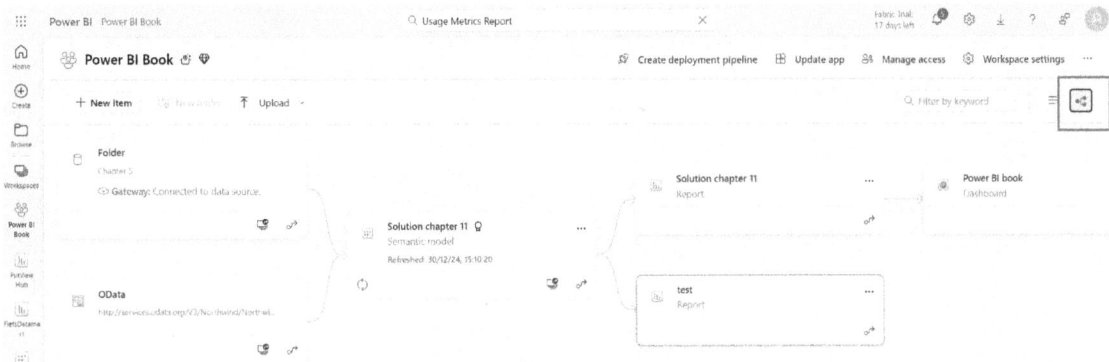

Figure 14.3: Workspace lineage view

The lineage view lets you track down where data is coming from. All the way on the right, you see the **Power BI Book** dashboard. The dashboard gets its tiles from the report **Solution chapter 11**, which is based on the semantic model **Solution chapter 11**. There is also a report called **test**, based on the same semantic model. The semantic model uses two sources. The first source of type **Folder** is called **Chapter 5**. It uses a gateway for connections. The second source is the OData feed to Northwind.

Clicking a tile shows a pane on the right-hand side of the window.

Tiles can have little icons in the bottom right corner. The icon with the circle and arrow highlights the lineage path. This is useful when it gets complex with multiple sources being used by multiple semantic models that have multiple reports based on them. The other icon opens a pane showing dependencies. You might want to change or delete a semantic model. In that case, you want to figure out beforehand what reports and dashboards will be affected by your intended change.

3. Return to the List view of the workspace. Click the button next to the lineage view icon in the top right corner of the screen.

4. Hover your mouse over a report and click on the three dots (...) and select **View lineage**.

Notice that you get the lineage of just the report you clicked on. This is sometimes easier to read than the lineage view of the entire workspace.

Admin monitoring workspace

There is a special workspace, called the admin monitoring workspace, that is designed for Fabric administrators to monitor workloads and usage within their tenant. At the time of writing, it is still in preview. When you click on workspaces on the left-hand side menu of Power BI, it will show if you are the Fabric administrator. It is automatically created the first time you open it.

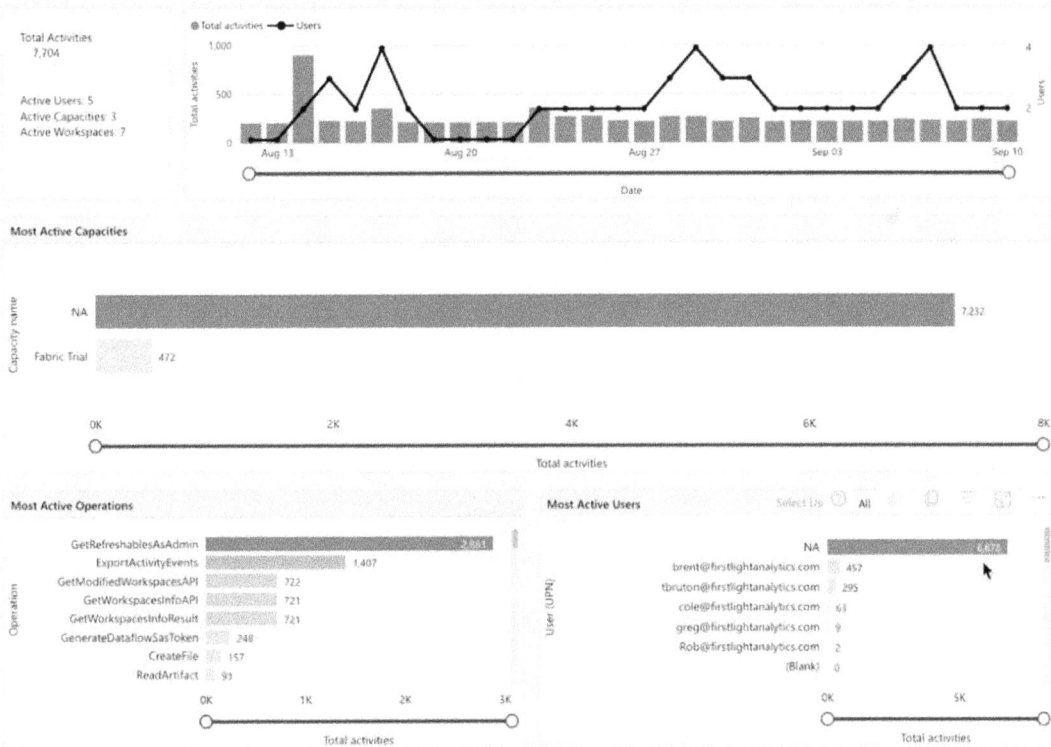

Figure 14.4: *Feature usage and adoption report*

Figure 14.4 shows a screenshot of the **Feature Usage and Adoption** report. It provides an overall sense of what is being done within the tenant. The admin monitoring workspace also contains the **Purview Hub** report. It provides insight into the usage of sensitivity labels, domains, and endorsed items. It also includes a list of all items in the tenant.

An exhaustive discussion on the admin monitoring workspace is outside the scope of this book. Please refer to **https://learn.microsoft.com/en-us/fabric/admin/monitoring-workspace** for more detailed information.

Microsoft Fabric Capacity Metrics app

Until now, we have been looking at how items are used. We looked at the more functional side of things. However, throughout the book, we have talked about best practices that can save CUs needed in Fabric. Having learned those best practices makes it interesting to see the CUs used. You use this knowledge to tune your workloads, scale down your capacity license, or, if necessary, scale up your license.

Microsoft created the Microsoft **Fabric Capacity Metrics** app to monitor the capacity consumption in your tenant. The app must be installed before you can use it. You must be a capacity admin in order to install and view the Microsoft **Fabric Capacity Metrics** app. *Figure 14.5* shows a screenshot of the **Fabric Capacity Metrics** app:

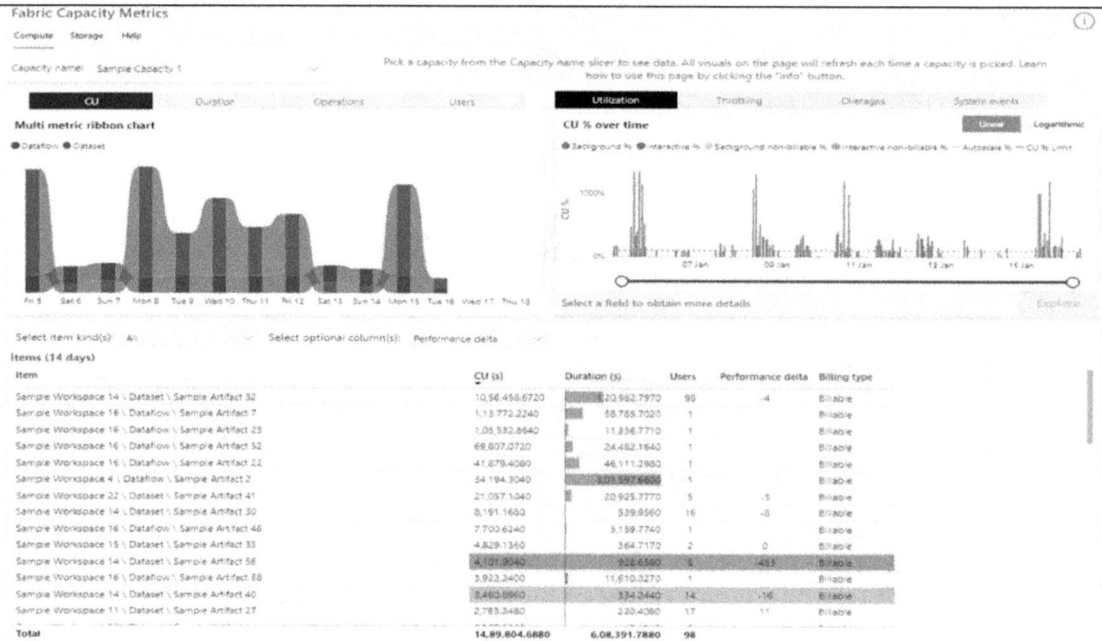

Figure 14.5: Microsoft Fabric Capacity Metrics app

The Microsoft **Fabric Capacity Metrics** app is a Power BI template app, as discussed in *Chapter 13, Create App*. For installation instructions, please follow this link: **https://learn.microsoft.com/en-us/fabric/enterprise/metrics-app-install?tabs=1st**

The Microsoft **Fabric Capacity Metrics** app has a couple of pages:

- **Compute page**: Most importantly, you can see here the utilization of your CUs. It is shown both as an absolute number as well as a percentage of the overall available CUs for your capacity. CU consumption is split out over different types of workloads.

  You can also get insight into throttling. This occurs when you need more CUs than what you pay for. It results in decreased performance and possibly time out errors. You can get this information for your overall tenant or by item and operation using the CUs.

- **Storage page**: The name speaks for itself. It shows billed storage and used storage in your tenant.

- **Timepoint page**: When analyzing your capacity, it is vital to know where your CUs are used the most. CUs are needed for both background operations and interactive operations. This page gives you easy insights into the most expensive operations in your tenant.

Power BI Desktop tools

When you see which reports are used often in combination with which reports take a lot of resources, you might want to optimize those reports. There are some features that can help with optimizing Power Query. Here are some easy steps to follow:

1. Open the Power BI Desktop file you created throughout this book (or **Solution chapter 11.pbix** from the downloads).

2. Open the Power Query Editor.

3. Select the query **Targets** and then select the step **Expanded Target** in the list with **APPLIED STEPS**.

4. Click on **Diagnose Step** in the **Tools** ribbon.

    Note that a new group is created in the **Queries** pane called **Diagnostics**. Three queries are added to the group. The aggregated is most of the time enough to get insight into the impact the selected step has.

    Reading the result of the recorded query **Diagnostics** is not easy. Here is a link that shows you how to create some visualizations on top of the **Diagnostics** data to make interpreting it more easy: **https://learn.microsoft.com/en-us/power-query/read-query-diagnostics**

5. Delete the **Diagnostic** group in the **Queries** pane.

6. Select the query **Targets**.

7. Click on **Start Diagnostics** in the **Tools** ribbon.

8. Refresh the preview of the query **Targets**.

9. Click on **Stop Diagnostics** in the **Tools** ribbon.

    Note that the group **Diagnostics** was created again. It has similar queries in it this time. The queries now have data of all steps that make up the entire query. Visualizing the data may give you some insight in expensive steps in your query.

10. Click on **Close & Apply** to close the Power Query Editor.

    The efficiency of Power Query influences the sematic model refresh time and cost. Another thing you may want to optimize is report rendering. The rendering of visuals on reports impacts performance and CU usage. The following steps show features in Power BI Desktop to get insight into the rendering of visuals.

11. Create a new empty report page.

12. Save and close Power BI Desktop with this new empty page selected.

13. Open the Power BI solution again.

    Note that the empty report page is shown. Power BI Desktop always opens with the page selected that was selected when closing Power BI Desktop. Opening Power BI with an empty page means that no data has been retrieved from the semantic model on opening the report. It also means no data is cached yet. This is the best way to figure out which visuals are expensive and why.

14. Click on **Performance analyzer** in the **View** ribbon.

15. Click on **Start recording** in the **Performance analyzer** pane that opened.

16. Open the **Sales report** page.

17. Click on **Stop** in the **Performance analyzer** pane.

    You should now see something like *Figure 14.6*:

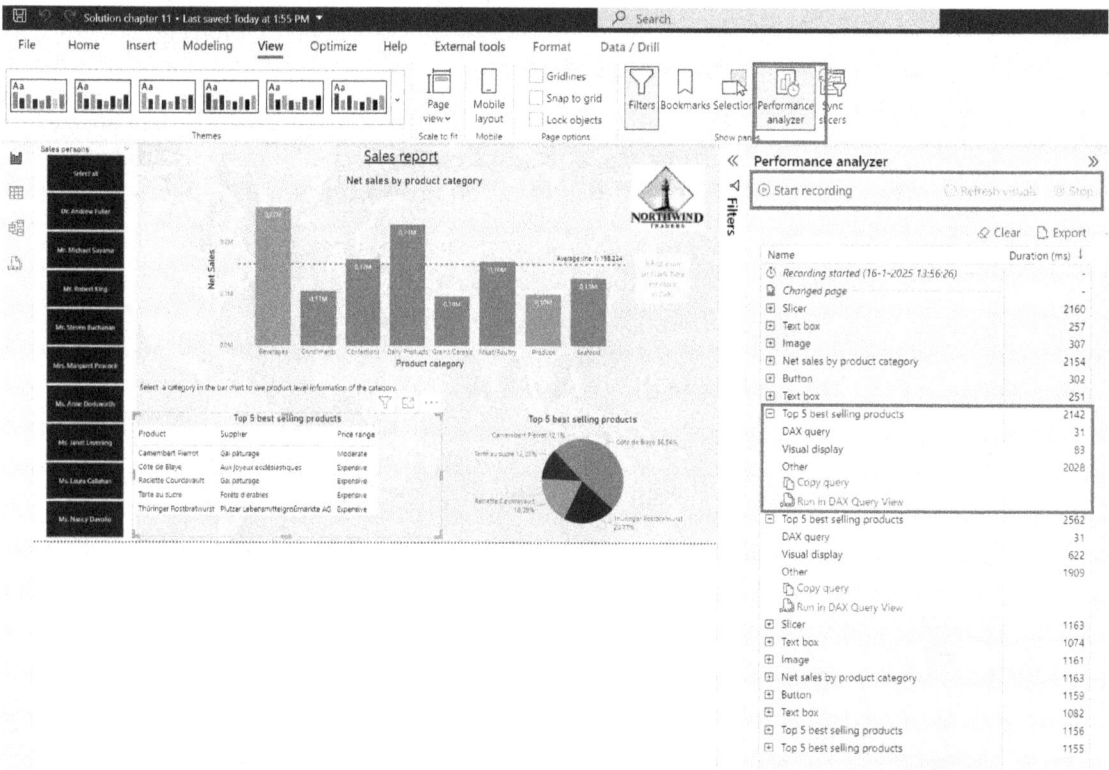

Figure 14.6: Performance analyzer

In the **Performance analyzer** pane, there is now a list of all visuals on your report. You can see how long it took for each visual to render. When you click on the plus icon in front of the name of a visual, you can see how long it took the DAX query to fetch the data from the model. You can also see how long it took Power BI to create the visual once the data was fetched. The option **Other** can usually be ignored. There is not much you can do about it anyway. Most of the time, it means rendering the visual had to wait for some other operation to finish first.

When using **DirectQuery** mode, you will see a wait time on the server query as well. The option **Visual display** may show up twice depending on bookmarks that are created in the report, overlapping filters, and some other reasons.

18. Click on the plus icon in front of the **Top 5 best selling products** visual.

19. Click on the link **Run in DAX Query View**.

You can copy the DAX query to a tool like DAX Studio that has all sorts of DAX optimization tools to help you figure out what is happening.

When using **DirectQuery**, the source of bad performance can be the underlying database. Most databases have their own toolset to troubleshoot queries. For SQL Server, you could use SQL Server Profiler or extended events.

Power BI activity log

Almost all applications have some sort of log that keeps track of activities that took place in or with the application. Power BI is no different. The Power BI activity log records all sorts of activities within a tenant. Activities can be the creation or deletion of a workspace or the failure of a semantic model refresh. Basically, anything you do in the Power BI portal is logged.

The Power BI activity log is based on the unified audit log of Microsoft 365. The unified audit log is filtered to only include Power BI-related auditing events. Refer to *Figure 14.7*:

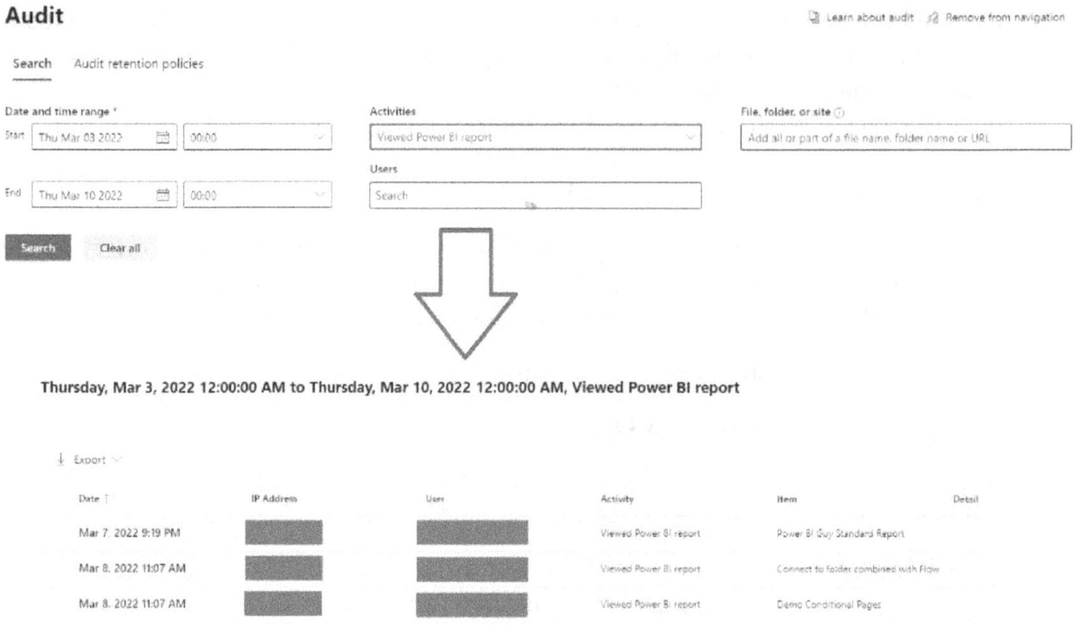

Figure 14.7: Audit log

Unfortunately, there is no user interface to access and query the Power BI activity log. Microsoft made an **application programming interface (API)** available to read this data. You can find guidance in how to access this API here: **https://learn.microsoft.com/en-us/power-bi/guidance/admin-activity-log**

Application programming interface

An API gives access to an application from code. Most APIs use standards. That means that the programming language used to access the API is not relevant. Maybe you have used APIs already. A lot of companies nowadays work with **software as a service (SaaS)** solutions. That means that you most likely need to use the API of that SaaS application to get to your data. Power Query uses the **From Web** data connector for that.

A lot of administrators working in the Microsoft ecosystem use PowerShell as the language to automate as much of their work as they can. Power BI administrators can use PowerShell in combination with the Power BI API to automate a lot of their tasks. How do you, for instance, get a list of all domains, workspaces, and reports in your tenant, inclusive of the permissions set on the reports? When you try to get this sort of information by clicking around on the portal, you need to be patient. Using the API can really help here.

Programming against the API is out of the scope of this book.

Conclusion

As you can see, there are a lot of ways to get information about how your Power BI environment is used. You can see which reports are being used. You can see how the reports are used. The other way around might be just as interesting: which reports are not used, and who is not using reports that they should use?

Except for usage metrics, we need capacity metrics as well. You want to make sure your license gives you neither too much nor too little CUs to perform your workload efficiently. You need to be able to track resources that consume a lot of CUs. Ideally, you then monitor this resource to see where it can be optimized.

This chapter provided you with the necessary links to get more detailed information than is provided in this book. Administering a Power BI environment deserves a book by itself. For the exam, you need to know the tools available to you to monitor and troubleshoot Power BI. Based on the scenario, you will get asked which tool to use. The exact details of how to use each tool are outside the scope of the exam. What is written in this chapter should be enough to get you through the exam.

You cannot have missed the rise of **artificial intelligence (AI)**. AI is everywhere, also in Power BI. You learn about AI capabilities in the next chapter.

Multiple choice questions

1. **You have a gateway that you need to remove, and you need to make sure that no item in the workspace Sales uses this gateway. What is the solution to get this data?**
   a. Find the gateway in the Admin portal and view the data sources associated with the gateway.
   b. Go the workspace sales and switch the view to lineage view. Check all sources shown in this view.
   c. Open the usage metrics report and check the list of data sources.
   d. Use PowerShell to get all data gateway dependencies from the API.

2. **You need to know the last time a specific user logged in into Power BI. What do you need to do?**
   a. Create an admin monitoring workspace and use the feature usage and adoption report.
   b. Go to the Power BI Admin portal and select the section Users. Find the user there.
   c. Open the usage metrics report and search for the user.
   d. Query the Power BI activity log.

3. **You need to find semantic models without sensitivity labels plied to them. What can you do?**

   a. Use the Fabric Capacity Metrics app.

   b. Use the Lineage view of the workspace and inspect the sources.

   c. Use the Purview Hub report of the admin monitoring workspace.

   d. Use the usage metrics report for the tenant.

Answers

1	a, b, d
2	d
3	c

Join our Discord space

Join our Discord workspace for latest updates, offers, tech happenings around the world, new releases, and sessions with the authors:

https://discord.bpbonline.com

CHAPTER 15
Copilot in Power BI

Introduction

Copilot is Microsoft's generative **artificial intelligence (AI)** tool. Copilot is a generic generative AI tool that Microsoft uses throughout its stack of products. Copilot is also tightly integrated with Power BI and can help in numerous ways. It can help both report authors and business users working with reports and semantic models. It can also be used both in the Power BI service and on the Power BI Desktop. Copilot is largely dependent on the semantic model. Building a clear semantic model is crucial for every aspect of Power BI. Everything starts with a good semantic model. Copilot can even help to improve your Power BI semantic model.

Before you can start using Copilot in Power BI, there are a couple of prerequisites: Copilot needs to be enabled by an administrator in your Power BI (Fabric) tenant. Also, the tenant setting *Data sent to Azure OpenAI can be processed outside your tenant's geographic region, compliance boundary, or national cloud instance tenant* should be enabled for tenants outside France or the US.

Structure

This chapter will cover the following topics:

- Generative AI prompts
- Copilot for business users

- Copilot for developers
- Prep data for AI

Objectives

After reading this chapter, you will know Copilot's functions within Power BI. This chapter outlines how Copilot can help with authoring and understanding **Data Analysis Expressions (DAX)**. It describes how to use Copilot to enhance the Power BI semantic model. It also describes how Copilot assists in using the model and the data contained in the model.

Generative AI prompts

The first thing to know about using generative AI is how to write prompts. Prompts are the questions or commands you give to Copilot. There are a few points to remember when using Copilot:

- **It is a chat**: This means that you can ask follow-up questions. You can, for example, ask to provide more details on something it has already done for you. When Copilot does not do what you want, clarifying your prompt might work better than rewriting the prompt.

- **Be specific**: You can, for example, ask for a summary of the report. That is a generic question that might not give the desired result. You can make your prompt more specific by asking a summary, especially for junior sales representatives, in a bullet way based on *page 4* of the report. You can include specific data values you want in the summary, like summarizing *bike sales in the Netherlands*. People tend to be sloppy in how they ask questions. Often, another human understands this and interprets the question accordingly or asks a question in return, which AI does not. So, try to be as specific as you can. Remember that this does not mean your prompt has to be perfect to start with. Use the conversational abilities to get to the right prompt in steps.

- **Be positive**: `Do not include sales data` is a more difficult command to process than `include only marketing data`. Positive formulations are easier to interpret for humans than negations. So, we use more positive commands. That means that AI is better trained in it because it has more examples.

The good thing about prompt writing is that you cannot do it wrong. Type whatever, just about anything, and see what the response is. You can then always say something like: *that is not what I meant, what I need is ….*

Copilot for business users

The main thing Copilot can contribute to business users is that Copilot can generate a summary of a report. Both in Power BI Desktop and in Power BI service, you will find a **Copilot** button in the upper-right corner of a report. When you click this button, the **Copilot** pane opens on the right-hand side of the report, as you can see in *Figure 15.1* from Microsoft learn:

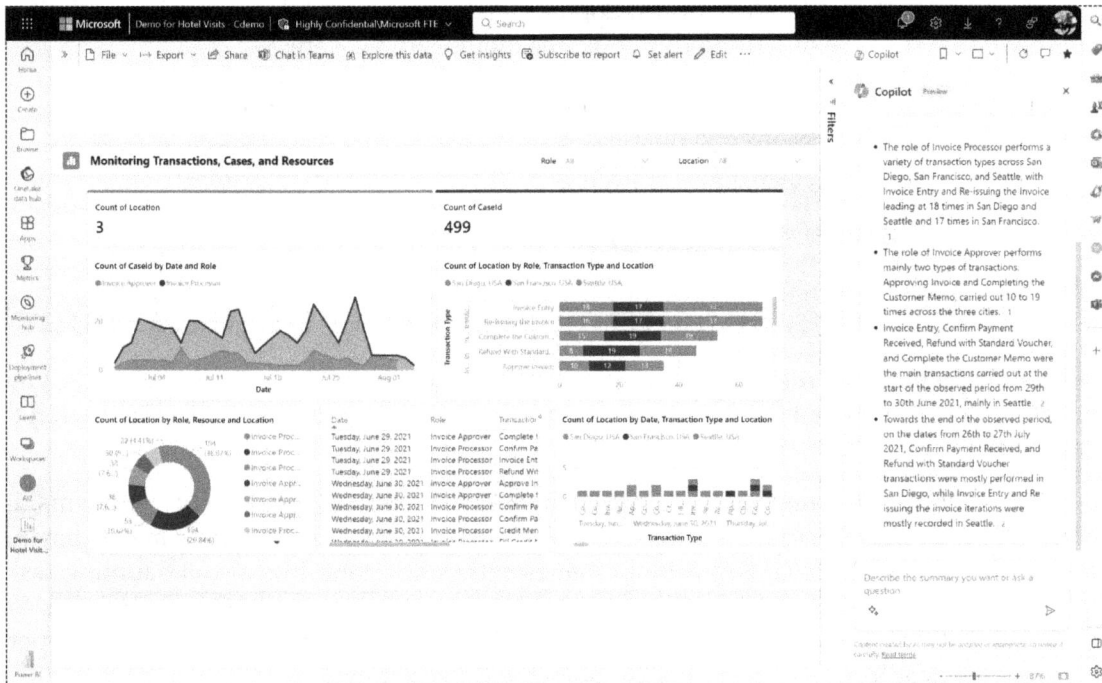

Figure 15.1: Copilot report summary

When you open the **Copilot** pane, it has some suggestions for prompts you can use. You can also write your own prompts to ask more specific questions. There is even a user prompt guide that can help you create your prompts. You can specifically ask the summary to be about a visual, the report page, or even the entire report. Copilot will generate a summary in text. It will only use data as currently visible on the report, ignoring data that is not on the report due to applied filters.

Even though this feature is called **summarize**, you can ask additional questions about the data. Copilot can engage in a chat where you ask questions based on what you learned from Copilot's previous answers.

Be aware of what it means when you need AI to summarize and explain a report to you. A well-designed report is clear and intuitive and answers well-defined questions for a well-defined audience. It starts with aggregated data and allows users with interactivity to get to more detailed data for a clearer understanding. This should make Copilot summarizing a report unnecessary.

Having said that, the ideal report does not exist. Often, follow-up questions will arise when you learn something from your data, and Copilot can certainly be an addition in this scenario.

Copilot for developers

Copilot can do even more for developers. Copilot can do a number of things and its capabilities are growing. At the time of writing this book, the main features were:

- Help you understand the data model, enhance the model, and use it.
- Write DAX expressions and queries.
- Create a narrative visual on your report.

Let us go through all of them in a little more detail.

Understanding, enhancing and using the data model

The first help you can get is to let Copilot summarize a Power BI semantic model for you. Just navigate to the semantic model in your workspace that has Copilot enabled and ask it to summarize the model.

You learned about the **question and answer (Q&A)** feature, and specifically, synonyms, in *Chapter 7, The Basics of Semantic Model*. Q&A itself does not rely on AI, which makes having synonyms available for table and column names extra important. It is also a daunting task, especially in larger models and multilingual companies. Copilot can generate synonyms for you, making it an easy, straightforward task. Simply use Q&A to create a visual on a report and select the gear icon (see *Figure 15.2*) to open the Q&A settings:

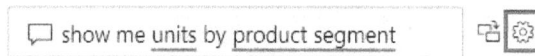

Figure 15.2: Q&A settings

Once in the settings, navigate to the **Synonyms** page and click **Add synonyms** in the **Copilot** pane. At the time of writing this book, this feature is still in preview.

Another preview feature is to let Copilot add descriptions for measures. See *Figure 15.3*:

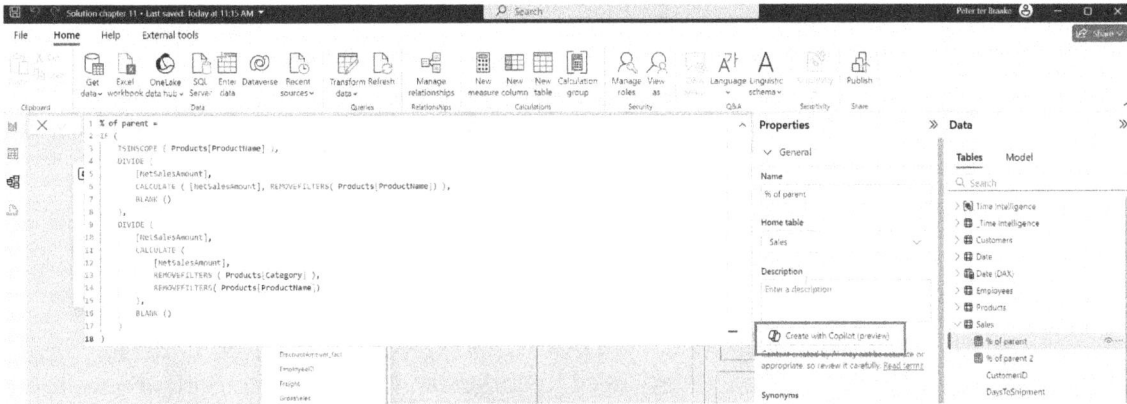

Figure 15.3: Copilot measure descriptions

When other people create reports based on a semantic model you create, it is crucial for those people to understand the model. Especially for measures, it is important to know how they were created and what they actually mean. The report authors will be able to see measure descriptions when using the semantic model. Descriptions are then a vital part of semantic model documentation.

We just described two features that enhance the meta data of the model to increase its usability. Copilot can also be used to understand the data inside the model better. This feature is also still in preview at the time of writing and is only available in the service. Q&A must be enabled for the data model since this feature uses the Q&A engine for its suggestions. Refer to *Figure 15.4*:

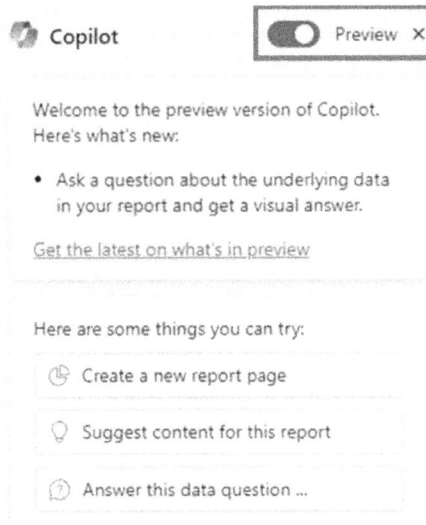

Figure 15.4: Ask Copilot about the data model

As you can see, there are three options to get you started working with this model. The middle option, **Suggest content for this report**, might be a good place to start. When you get a better understanding of what the data is about and what you need from the data, it can generate report pages for you. You can customize these pages any way you want afterwards or by engaging in a chat until Copilot generates the report page or visual you want.

The Power BI service and Power BI Desktop both support similar authoring experiences.

Write DAX expressions and queries

Generative AI is capable of writing code. DAX is no exception. However, understand that generative AI is not flawless. You always need to understand and, more importantly, validate the code it suggests and the results it generates.

When you want to create a new measure using Copilot, perform the following steps:

- Select the table you want to add your new measure to in the **Data** pane in Power BI Desktop.

- Either right-click on the table and select **New quick measure** or click on the **Copilot** button in the ribbon.

- Enter a prompt asking for a measure and click on **Generate**. See *Figure 15.5*:

Quick measures » ✕

Select a calculation to create a measure or describe the measure you need and we'll generate suggestions in DAX, which you can customize later.

Calculations   Suggestions

Sales amount for California in 2020

Generate

Suggested measures

Total sales amount where state-province is California ⌃ and year of date is 2020

Preview value

$1,785,099.77

DAX ⑦

```
Measure =
CALCULATE(
    SUM('Sales'[Sales Amount]),
    KEEPFILTERS(
```

Show more ⌄

Add

Total sales amount where state-province is California ⌄ and order quantity is 2020

Total sales amount where state-province is California ⌄ and extended amount is 2020

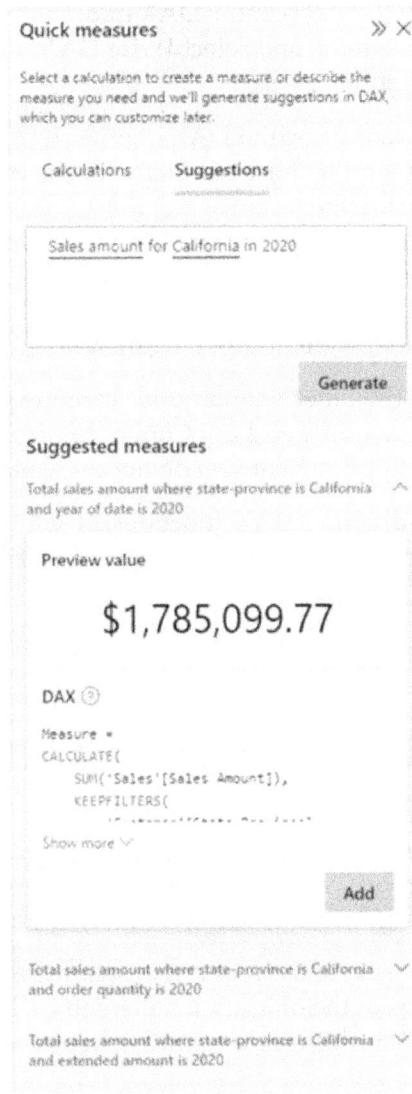

Figure 15.5: DAX suggested measure by Copilot
Source: Microsoft learn

- Scroll through the suggestions and click on **Add** to add a suggestion to your model.

Like always, it is about how you formulate the prompt. So, vary in the way you ask your question to get the result you are after.

In *Chapter 9, Advanced DAX Concepts,* we learned about DAX queries and the function **EVALUATE**. Copilot can help here as well.

Copilot is available on Power BI Desktop in the **DAX query view** pane. Alternatively, you can browse to a published semantic model and select **Write DAX queries** from the context menu. Either way, Copilot can help in three ways:

- It can translate natural language into DAX queries. It is up to you again to write good prompts. You can start simple, for example, with the prompt: Write a DAX query to show sales by product category. Since Copilot is conversational, you can then ask for changes in a conversational way. Just say something like `Add units sold and only show data from the US` to change the original DAX query. When you change the query with the query selected, it can even show you the original query and the changed one side-by-side, highlighting the differences.

- Copilot can also work the other way around. It can explain a DAX query in natural language. Simply select a query and ask Copilot to explain it. If the explanation is not to your liking, just tell Copilot what you do not understand.

- Copilot can explain individual DAX functions. If you write DAX yourself and you are not sure how to use a specific DAX function, or you do not know exactly what the function does, just ask Copilot.

Now that we know what Copilot has to offer in terms of DAX, let us look at creating summaries on report pages.

Creating narrative visuals on your report

You can let Copilot create narratives on your report both in the service and in Power BI Desktop. In the desktop, you create a report first and let Copilot create the narrative on the visuals on the report. In the service, you can create a narrative directly on a semantic model. In that case, you start by creating a report based on the semantic model.

In both cases, add a narrative visual to the report and select Copilot as the narrative type. *Figure 15.6* shows an example from the official documentation: **https://learn.microsoft.com/en-us/power-bi/create-reports/copilot-create-narrative?tabs=powerbi-service**

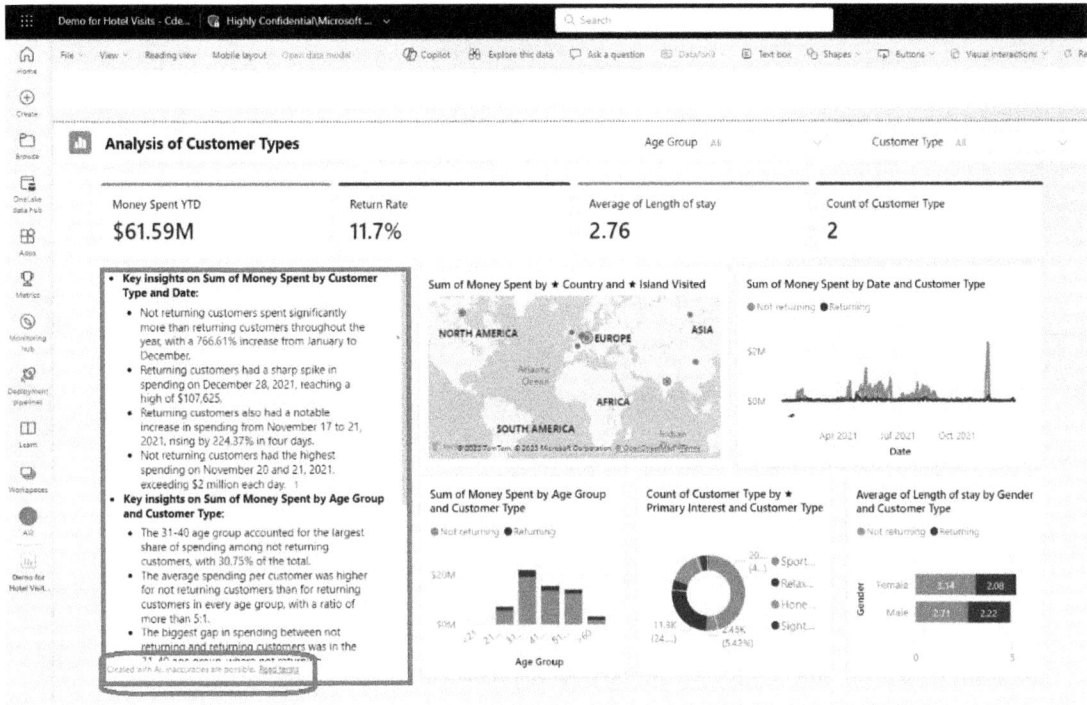

Figure 15.6: *Report with narrative visual*

A narrative can clarify a report. However, as stated before, consider creating a better report when a narrative is needed to understand the report. A great use case for a narrative is when you prepare a presentation that you need to do using the report, but chances are people will not read all the text on the report, as in *Figure 15.6*.

Prep data for AI

Within Power BI Desktop, you will now find a button called **Prep data for AI**. You need to connect to a workspace that allows the use of Copilot to use this feature. Using this feature, you can select the more important columns of the dataset. This simplifies the dataset, making it easier for Copilot to generate meaningful answers and content.

Conclusion

Copilot is important in Microsoft's strategy. As you have learned, a lot of the capabilities are in preview at the time of writing this book. Copilot is too important not to mention in the book. Preview features, however, are not part of any exam. However, stay tuned. As features come out of preview, questions about these features will be added to the exam. You can be certain to get some questions about Copilot and its capabilities.

With Copilot, you reached the end of the book. All that remains are some practice exam questions in the last chapter.

Multiple choice questions

1. **What can Copilot do for you? Select all that apply.**

   a. Create a measure

   b. Create a column

   c. Create a measure group

   d. Create aggregations

2. **How do Copilot and Q&A work together? Select all that apply.**

   a. Q&A is built on top of Copilot

   b. Copilot uses Q&A when you ask questions about the data

   c. Copilot can make Q&A better by generating synonyms

   d. Copilot will replace Q&A

3. **Which license types do you need to work with Copilot?**

   a. None, if you work in Power BI Desktop

   b. Pro

   c. F2 or higher

   d. P1 or higher

Answers

1	a, b
2	b, c
3	c, d

Join our Discord space

Join our Discord workspace for latest updates, offers, tech happenings around the world, new releases, and sessions with the authors:

https://discord.bpbonline.com

CHAPTER 16
Practice Exam

Introduction

This book is meant to help you pass the official Microsoft exam, the *PL-300 Microsoft Certified: Power BI Data Analyst Associate*. Apart from reading the book, we strongly advise getting real-world experience using Power BI. As you probably realize by now, there is a lot to know about Power BI. The exam may contain questions about every Power Query transformation and data connector, and every DAX function. Every visual and every setting available in the Power BI service. You cannot know all that by heart. Reading this book and realizing what Power BI is in general, and what it is meant for, will give you a big start to passing the exam.

The official exam consists of approximately 45 questions. You need a score of 700 out of 1000 to pass the exam. All questions are multiple-choice questions of some sort. There are questions for which you need to select all possible answers, where each answer can either be a solution by itself or just a part of the solution. Sometimes it is stated explicitly how many answers you should select, sometimes it is not.

The questions at the end of each chapter are in no way representative of the exam questions. This chapter contains 15 questions that closely resemble real exam questions.

Question 1

You are importing data into Power BI from an Excel file using Power Query. The Excel file has multiple sheets where the name of each sheet is a year, like 2025. All sheets have the exact same structure. In the future, sheets will be added to the Excel workbook when new data for new years becomes available. You need to import all sheets. What are the solutions for this scenario? Select two answers:

a. Create a query for each sheet and use Power Query's append transformation to combine all queries into one.

b. Create a query for each sheet and use DAX expressions to combine data from all tables into a single measure value.

c. Create a query for each sheet and use Power Query's merge transformation to combine all queries into one.

d. Import a single sheet and change the query into a function. In a separate query, create a list of years and create a custom column using the function.

Question 2

Look at the following code:

```
    #"Inserted Merged Column" = Table.AddColumn(#"Split Column by Position",
"Date", each Text.Combine({"1-", [Month], "-", [Name.1.2]})),


    #"Removed Other Columns1" = Table.SelectColumns( . . .  )
```

The second line should select the columns **Date**, **TargetAmount**, and **EmployeeID** from the table created in the first line of code. What code do you need to enter inside the **Table. SelectColumns** to complete this code?

a. **#"Inserted Merged Column", {"Date", "TargetAmount", "EmployeeID"}**

b. **Table, {"Date", "TargetAmount", "EmployeeID"}**

c. **#"Inserted Merged Column", (Date, TargetAmount, EmployeeID)**

d. **Table, (Date, TargetAmount, EmployeeID)**

Question 3

You have a slicer that can be used to filter a bar chart showing sick leave by month. On the same report, there are two tables. One containing the top five employees, the other with the least sick leave, and one with the top five employees with the maximum number of sick leaves. The tables should always show the top five lists over the last two years, independent of the slicer selection.

What should you do?

    a. **Create a top five filter and apply it to the report page**: Add a relative data slicer to the report and filter on the last two years.

    b. **Disable visual interaction**: Disable visual interaction between the relative filter and bar chart.

    c. **Create a tooltip page**: Place both tables on the tooltip page and add a top five filter to the tooltip. Link the tooltip to the bar chart.

    d. **Create a top five filter and apply it to both tables**: Create a filter to select only the last two years and apply it to both filters. Change the visual interaction of both tables to no interaction with the slicer.

    e. **Create the top five filters for both tables**: Create filters to select only the last two years for both filters. Change the visual interaction of both tables to no interaction with the slicer.

Question 4

You write a DAX measure. You need the table **Date** to be filtered by the fact table just for this measure. What should you do?

    a. Change the cross-filter direction of the relationship between the **Date** table and the fact table to both.

    b. Change the cross-filter direction of the relationship between the **Date** table and the fact table to single.

    c. Use the DAX function **CROSSFILTER**.

    d. Use the DAX function **USERELATIONSHIP**.

Question 5

You have a semantic model that is using DirectQuery. The model contains two tables. The tables are related by a composite key based on two columns named **Col1** and **Col2**. What must you do to create a relationship between the tables?

    a. Create a calculated column in DAX that is the concatenation of **Col1** and **Col2**, and use the custom column to create the relationship.

    b. Create a custom column in Power Query that is the concatenation of **Col1** and **Col2**, and use the custom column to create the relationship.

    c. Open Power Query and merge both tables.

    d. Open the **Manage relationships** window and create a relationship by first selecting **Col1** and then selecting **Col2** while holding down the *Ctrl* key on your keyboard.

Question 6

You have users complaining that a report in a Fabric capacity workspace is slow. Upon further investigation, users report that the query is sometimes slow but not always. You want to know if throttling can cause this issue. Where can you investigate further?

    a. Power BI activity log.

    b. SQL Server profiler connected to your semantic model.

    c. The report usage metrics report.

    d. The Fabric Capacity Metrics app.

Question 7

You created a report that uses a locally installed SQL Server as its source with data that should stay on premise. You publish the report to the Power BI service, where you work with the report for a while without problems. When a coworker likes what you are doing, you decide to share the report with her. She informs you that she gets the error: *We could not load the data for this report. Please try again later*. When she tries to open the report, what should you do?

    a. Create an Azure SQL database in a VNet and migrate your database to the new cloud database. Connect the report to the new database.

    b. Install a data gateway instead of a personal gateway, and register the data source to use the data gateway.

    c. Make your coworker part of the Member role of the workspace the report is in.

    d. Refresh the report and share it again.

Question 8

Have a look at the following DAX expression. The expression should return the sum of **[Quantity]** * **[Price]**. Which DAX function completes the expression?

```
. . . ( FILTER ( 'Order' , Date[Year] = 2025 ) , [Quantity] * [Price] )
```

    a. **COUNT**

    b. **COUNTX**

    c. **SUM**

    d. **SUMX**

Question 9

You have a large table, **TableX**, that is too big to fit into Power BI memory. The table is related to **Table1** and **Table2**, with **TableX** being on the many sides of both relationships. You define an aggregated version of **TableX** called **TableY** that you import into the semantic model. You can create the same relationships for **TableY** as exist for **TableX**. How should you configure **Table1**, **Table2**, and **TableX**?

a. DirectQuery for **TableX**, Dual for **Table1** and **Table2**

b. DirectQuery for **TableX**, Import for **Table1** and **Table2**

c. DirectQuery for **TableX**, **Table1**, and **Table2**

d. Dual for **TableX**, **Table1**, and **Table2**

Question 10

You see that sales in your company is down. You need to figure out why to stop the downward trend. Which visualization should you use?

a. Key influencers

b. Line chart

c. Matrix

d. Narrative

Question 11

You have two queries in Power Query. One query has product information. The column **ProductKey** is unique in this table. The other table holds sales information and has the same column **ProductKey**. You need only those products in your report that have never been sold. You start the Power Query merge transformation from the products table. Which type of join should you use?

a. Left anti

b. Left outer

c. Right anti

d. Right outer

Question 12

You start a new project and you invite coworkers from different departments in the organization to be members of your project team. You plan to keep track of project progress through several Power BI reports. All project members should be able to see all reports, as well as edit them.

People not working on the project should not be able to use the reports. There is a workspace called Projects that has reports from other projects in it.

You need to achieve these requirements with the least amount of effort and the least possible permissions. What should you do?

a. Create a folder with the name of your project in the existing Projects workspace. Create a group for the project in Microsoft 365 and add the group to the Contributor role of the folder.

b. Create a group for the project in Microsoft 365. Create a new domain and add the group to the Users role of the domain. Add a workspace to the domain.

c. Create a group for the project in Microsoft 365. Create a workspace and add the group to the Contributor role of the workspace.

d. Create a new workspace for the project and add each member of the project to the Member role of the workspace.

Question 13

You create a Power BI report based on Excel data. The Excel workbook is stored on OneDrive. You need to be able to refresh the data after publishing the Power BI service. How should you connect to the Excel workbook?

a. Use the Excel connector

b. Use the Folder connector

c. Use the Text/CSV connector

d. Use the Web connector

Question 14

You are using an SQL Server database to import data. To optimize refresh performance, you want to take advantage of query folding as much as possible. What should you do?

a. Start each query by selecting a table in the Navigator.

b. Switch the connectivity model of the tables to Dual.

c. Use the optimized engine of Dataflow Gen2.

d. Write your own SQL statements to import data.

Question 15

You have a Power BI report based on an Azure SQL Database. Your DBA decides to create a VNET and place all resources that need access to the database into that VNet. What should you do for your report to keep functioning correctly?

    a. Change the connector used to connect to SQL Server to an Azure SQL Server connector.

    b. Have the DBA add the Power BI IP Address to the firewall of the VNet.

    c. Have the DBA install the on-premise data gateway on a VM inside the VNet.

    d. Nothing, if the database stays in Azure, Power BI can connect to it.

Answers

1	a, d
2	a
3	d
4	c
5	a
6	d
7	b
8	d
9	a
10	a
11	a
12	c
13	d
14	a
15	c

Join our Discord space

Join our Discord workspace for latest updates, offers, tech happenings around the world, new releases, and sessions with the authors:

https://discord.bpbonline.com

Index

R

www.ingramcontent.com/pod-product-compliance
Lightning Source LLC
Chambersburg PA
CBHW061759210326
41599CB00034B/6818